The Ten-Minute Guide to Psychiatric Diagnosis and Treatment

Theodore A. Stern, MD, Editor-in-Chief
Chief, Psychiatric Consultation Service,
Massachusetts General Hospital
Professor of Psychiatry,
Harvard Medical School

A complimentary copy of this book has been provided to you through
financial support from McNeil Consumer & Specialty Pharmaceuticals

Medicine is an ever-changing field. Standard safety precautions must be followed, but as new research and clinical experience broaden our knowledge, changes in treatment and drug therapy may become necessary or appropriate. Readers are advised to check the most current product information provided by the manufacturer of each drug to be administered to verify the recommended dose, the method and duration of administration, and contraindications. It is the responsibility of the treating physician, relying on experience and knowledge of the patient, to determine dosages and the best treatment for each individual patient. Neither the publisher nor the authors assume any liability for any injury and/or damage to persons or property arising from this publication.

Every effort has been made to ensure that the drug dosage schedules within this text are accurate and conform to standards accepted at the time of publication. However, as treatment recommendations vary in the light of continuing research and clinical experience, the reader is advised to verify drug dosage schedules herein with information found on product information sheets. This is especially true in cases of new or infrequently used drugs.

Front cover illustration: Alfred Pasieka/Photo Researchers, Inc.

© 2005 Professional Publishing Group, Ltd.
17 Battery Place, Suite 643
New York, NY 10004

ISBN 0-9713017-6-X

Dedication

To my friends and colleagues, young and old,
and to their spirit of collaboration and teamwork.

Preface

Busy practitioners always need something to help them get through the day (and to cope with their seemingly endless clinical responsibilities). This book was designed to help those clinicians care for patients who manifest a variety of psychiatric symptoms and problems. Our intent was to focus on rapid recognition of problems and on timely and effective treatments.

This book would not have been possible without the vision and stewardship of Michael Wolf (at Professional Publishing Group, Ltd.) and the keen editorial assistance of Mike Shelton and Wendy Turner. In addition, Sara Nadelman and Judy Byford helped shepherd us through hundreds of emails, voice mails, faxes, photocopies, and express mail packages associated with 34 chapters and 40 authors.

On behalf of those who suffer from psychiatric problems, we hope this edition improves the recognition and management of psychiatric problems and brings much needed relief.

T.A.S.

Contents

JACOB HOLZER, MD
Staff Psychiatrist, Spaulding Rehabilitation Hospital
Instructor in Psychiatry, Harvard Medical School

NICOLE DANFORTH, MD
Consultant, Massachusetts General Hospital Pediatric Epilepsy
and Tuberous Sclerosis Programs
Clinical Assistant in Psychiatry, Massachusetts General Hospital
Instructor in Psychiatry, Harvard Medical School

ANNAH N. ABRAMS, MD
Clinical Assistant in Psychiatry, Massachusetts General Hospital
Instructor in Psychiatry, Harvard Medical School

B.J. BECK, MSN, MD
Clinical Assistant in Psychiatry, Massachusetts General Hospital
Medical Director, Mental Health and
Social Services, East Boston Neighborhood Health Center
Clinical Instructor in Psychiatry, Harvard Medical School

AMY M. TAYLOR, MD
Fourth-Year Resident in Psychiatry,
Massachusetts General Hospital and McLean Hospital
Chief Resident, Inpatient Psychiatry Service, Massachusetts General Hospital
Clinical Fellow in Psychiatry, Harvard Medical School

JOHN QUERQUES, MD
Associate Director, Psychiatry Consultation Service,
Beth Israel Deaconess Medical Center
Instructor in Psychiatry, Harvard Medical School

ANTHONY P. WEISS, MD
Assistant Psychiatrist, Massachusetts General Hospital
Instructor in Psychiatry, Harvard Medical School

STEPHAN HECKERS, MD
Director, Schizophrenia and Bipolar Disorder Program,
McLean Hospital
Assistant Professor of Psychiatry, Harvard Medical School

DAN V. IOSIFESCU, MD
Director of Neurophysiology Studies,
Depression Clinical and Research Program, Massachusetts General Hospital
Assistant Professor of Psychiatry, Harvard Medical School

MARK H. POLLACK, MD
Director, Center for Anxiety and Traumatic Stress Disorders,
Massachusetts General Hospital
Associate Professor of Psychiatry, Harvard Medical School

TERRY RABINOWITZ, MD, DDS
Associate Professor of Psychiatry and Family Practice,
University of Vermont College of Medicine
Director, Psychiatric Consultation Service,
Director of Telepsychiatry,
Associate Clinical Director of Telemedicine,
University of Vermont College of Medicine

JOSEPH LASEK, MD
Instructor in Psychiatry and Chief Resident of Psychiatry,
University of Vermont College of Medicine

JENNIFER L. DERENNE, MD
Fellow in Child and Adolescent Psychiatry,
Massachusetts General Hospital and McLean Hospital
Clinical Fellow in Psychiatry, Harvard Medical School

KATHY SANDERS, MD
Director, Massachusetts General Hospital and
McLean Adult Psychiatry Residency Training Program
Psychiatrist, Department of Psychiatry, Massachusetts General Hospital
Associate Psychiatrist, McLean Hospital
Assistant Professor of Psychiatry, Harvard Medical School

WILLIAM C. WOOD, MD
Fellow in Child and Adolescent Psychiatry,
Massachusetts General Hospital and McLean Hospital
Clinical Fellow in Psychiatry, Harvard Medical School

ROBERT M. STERN, MD
Director, Behavioral Health Services,
Emerson Hospital, Department of Psychiatry
Concord, Massachusetts

ANNA C. MURIEL, MD, MPH
Clinical Assistant in Psychiatry, Massachusetts General Hospital
Instructor in Psychiatry, Harvard Medical School

EDWARD MESSNER, MD
Psychiatrist, Massachusetts General Hospital
Associate Clinical Professor of Psychiatry, Harvard Medical School

BRIAN P. BRENNAN, MD
Attending Psychiatrist, Schizophrenia and Bipolar Disorder Program,
McLean Hospital
Instructor in Psychiatry, Harvard Medical School

Chapter 1

Professionalism and the Doctor-Patient Relationship in Psychiatry

REBECCA W. BRENDEL MD, JD
DAVID H. BRENDEL MD, PHD

I.   Introduction

A.   The Doctor-Patient Relationship
The doctor-patient relationship is **the foundation on which all psychiatric treatment occurs.** It is a **fiduciary relationship** that is **rooted in mutual respect and trust;** the physician must act in the best interest of the patient, and the patient's needs must be put before those of the physician.

B.   Evolution of the Doctor-Patient Relationship
1.   **The relationship is grounded in custom and ethics,** but today it has also become legally regulated by federal and state law.
2.   As early as 430 BC, many of the cornerstones of the doctor-patient relationship were present in the Hippocratic Writings and the **Hippocratic Oath.** These elements included using medical science to **help the ill,** to **abstain from doing harm,** to **maintain boundaries** (including strict prohibitions on sexual relationships with patients), and to **preserve confidentiality.**
3.   In more recent times, professional organizations, such as the American Medical Association and the American Psychiatric Association, have adopted principles of ethics to guide practice and to preserve the integrity of the doctor-patient relationship in an ever more complex society.
4.   In addition, state licensing boards and the federal government have developed laws to govern certain aspects of the doctor-patient relationship.

C.   Scope of this Chapter
This chapter addresses key aspects of the doctor-patient relationship from the standpoint of ethical and professional standards. Legal parameters of the relationship are discussed in Chapter 27.

Address for correspondence: Dr. Rebecca W. Brendel, Department of Psychiatry, Massachusetts General Hospital, 55 Fruit St., Psychiatry/WRN605, Boston, MA 02114, email: rbrendel@partners.org.

II.   Fundamental Principles

A.   **Basic Principles**

Many principles of the doctor-patient relationship are **derived from common sense and basic humanity.** For example, respect for boundaries and patient dignity, basic decency and compassion, and competent care are crucial guideposts to the establishment of a strong doctor-patient relationship and sound clinical practice.

B.   **Ethical Approaches**

Many ethical approaches are relevant to psychiatric and medical practice. Some of these approaches are:

1. **Common morality** is the idea that morally seriously people in all societies share certain universal ethical precepts and norms. The limitation of this theory is the obvious problem of defining what constitutes the common morality.

2. **Utilitarianism** focuses on minimizing harms and maximizing benefits in the treatment of individual patients. Because it focuses primarily on treatment outcomes, it is sometimes referred to as **consequentialism.** This approach may make sense regarding individuals, but taken as an overall philosophy on a societal level it may lead to a stark "ends-justifies-the-means" implementation of medical policy, such that individual rights could be sacrificed for the good of the medical system or public health.

3. **Deontological** theory views acts as morally good only if they are motivated by a compelling moral duty. In comparison to utilitarian theory, this view treats every person as an end in himself or herself and never merely as a means to an end. It requires action based on good and dutiful motives.

C.   **The Four Principles Approach**

This approach to the doctor-patient relationship is useful in guiding sound clinical practice and considering the impact of treatment interventions. The principles are autonomy, non-maleficence, beneficence, and justice.

1. **Autonomy** is defined as **the patient's right to determine his or her own treatment and decisions regarding treatment.** Competent, adult patients are entitled to make treatment decisions for themselves, even if these decisions are contrary to medical advice. A treatment forced on a patient by a well-intentioned psychiatrist, acting in what the psychiatrist believes is the patient's "best interest," may be an impermissible intrusion on the patient's right to be free from unwanted interventions, even when such interventions are potentially beneficial.

2. **Nonmaleficence** is the principle derived from the well-known phrase of the Hippocratic Oath **"primum non nocere" or "first, do no harm."** Nonmaleficence refers to the principle that psychiatrists and other physicians should not act in a way that could cause negative consequences for the patient. It is a proscription against actions harmful to the patient.

3. Conversely, **beneficence** refers to **an affirmative obligation to act for the sake of the patient's well-being.** Although this principle initially appears straightforward, adhering to beneficence can be difficult for many psychiatrists. For example, how should a psychiatrist act when a competent patient refuses a treatment the psychiatrist knows is in the patient's best interest from a medical standpoint? Although physicians tend to judge best interest according to medical standards, **beneficence is a broader principle referring to overall patient interest, not just medical concerns.**

4. The **justice** principle represents **the idea that medical care and medical decisions must be impartially rendered to each individual patient.** Distributive justice represents the idea that all patients must be treated fairly, regardless of diagnosis, background, race, socioeconomic circumstance, or other factors.

D.   Alternative Theories
The above "classical" theories of ethics that relate to the doctor-patient relationship may be criticized for their overly analytical, logical, and deductive methods. They fail to address emotional components of ethical action. Other theories have emerged to encompass affective dimensions of ethics and to emphasize the importance of other factors, such as compassion and social bonding. Psychiatrists, as experts in assessment of affect, have a unique role in appreciating and understanding the affective contribution to decision-making in the doctor-patient relationship. Some of these approaches include:

1. **Virtue Ethics** rejects the utilitarian principle that good results make an action moral and the deontological principle that following rules is sufficient for true morality. Instead, this Aristotelian view **emphasizes the importance of conscientiousness and emotional commitment for moral decision-making.**

2. **Ethics of Care** similarly avoids utilitarian and rule-based approaches to morality. Instead, it **focuses on a close doctor-patient relationship and emotions underlying morality.** These emotions include empathy, compassion, and kindness.

3. **Casuistry** is a form of practical, situational ethics in which **overarching ethical principles are rejected in favor of a case-based approach to medical decision-making.** Casuistry at-

tends to the patient's lived experience and makes use of case studies and clinical narratives.

III.   Codes of Ethics

Codes of ethics exist in psychiatry to guide practice and to prevent abuse and harm to patients. These codes serve multiple functions, including sensitizing psychiatrists to moral dimensions of psychiatry, protecting and promoting professional status, and providing education about appropriate practices.

A.   **The Hippocratic Oath**
While the **Hippocratic Oath** is the predecessor of many current aspects of the doctor-patient relationship (such as confidentiality, maintenance of boundaries, beneficence, and nonmaleficence), other elements are considered problematic and outdated. Some controversial aspects of the Oath include proscriptions on assisting patients with abortions and assisting patients in ending their lives.

B.   **Other Commonly Cited Ethical Codes**
Other widely adopted and cited ethical codes include the **Declaration of Geneva** (a modern version of the Hippocratic Oath), the **Nuremberg Code** and the **Declaration of Helsinki** (that provide recommendations for ethical conduct of biomedical research on human subjects), and the **Declaration of Madrid** (which was formulated by the World Psychiatric Association and highlights a wide range of ethical principles that ground psychiatric care).

C.   **The American Medical Association**
Principles of Medical Ethics
This is the most important professionally derived code for psychiatrists. These principles have **annotations for psychiatry** and are regularly reviewed by the Ethics Committee of the American Psychiatric Association. This code is divided into seven overarching principles:
1. Competent and compassionate treatment
2. Honesty and exposure of unsound practices
3. Respect for the law and advocacy for changes in laws that adversely affect patients
4. Respect for rights of patients and colleagues and maintenance of confidentiality
5. Continuing medical education and use of consultation
6. Obligation to provide emergency care, but otherwise freedom to choose nature of clinical practice
7. Responsibility to the community

IV. Professionalism and the Doctor-Patient Relationship

A. **Professional Competence**

Professional competence incorporates multiple domains that extend beyond cognitive knowledge to include integrative and interpersonal skills as well. One recent definition of professional competence, according to Epstein and Hundert, is **"the habitual and judicious use of communication, knowledge, technical skills, clinical reasoning, emotions, values, and reflection in daily practice for the benefit of the individual and community being served."** Seven core areas of professional competence exist:

1. **Cognitive areas** encompass knowledge and appreciation of the limits of one's knowledge, management of information, application of knowledge, ability to use resources, experiential learning, abstract problem-solving, and basic communication skills.

2. **Technical competence** refers to physical examination (including mental status examination) and surgical/procedural skills.

3. **Integrative skills** require the use of scientific, clinical, and humanistic judgment in the management of patients. This area of competence also requires the use of clinical reasoning, the ability to link basic and clinical knowledge across disciplines, and strategies for managing clinical uncertainty. Integrative ability entails thinking, feeling, and acting like a physician.

4. **Competent physicians must also adapt well to the context** in which care is delivered. Physicians must be able to incorporate the external realities of the health care system, such as insurance and systems of delivery into their practice to effect comprehensive and competent clinical care. Time constraints and clinical settings must be managed.

5. Psychiatrists, and physicians in general, interact in multiple **relationships** in the course of clinical practice. In addition to using communication skills, handling conflict, and teaching patients, **doctors also must communicate with other professionals and staff to promote teamwork** in the interest of providing competent clinical care to patients.

6. **Affective and moral dimensions of practice** are involved in clinical judgment and decision-making. The affective/moral dimension of such decision-making is currently the subject of neurobiological study. Patients and peers are often accurate judges of these qualities in physicians. Physicians must tolerate ambiguity and anxiety, possess emotional intelligence, respect patients, be responsive to patients and society, and demonstrate caring.

7. **Habits of mind** are qualities in physicians allowing them to be self-reflective. This area of professional **competence refers to qualities of attentiveness, critical curiosity (including willingness to recognize and correct errors), and self-awareness of biases.**

B. **Professionalism**
    Professionalism serves an important role in the current climate of medical practice. Medical professionalism may be seen as a stabilizing and moral force in a society characterized by market competition and government regulation. In a practice climate impacted by economic and political pressures, professionalism can serve to focus physicians' obligations to all patients, especially vulnerable individuals. According to one model, professionalism has three core values:

    1. **Devotion to medical service** refers to an expansion of the physician's fiduciary duty to the patient. As a core value of professionalism, this principle means that **doctors should put the goals of individual patient health and public health ahead of other concerns.** The primary concern for providing health care trumps potential and actual social, economic, and political costs to physicians.

    2. **Professionalism also requires that physicians publicly profess their values.** Thus, by simply delivering health care, individual doctors cannot do all that is needed for the field to develop a shared sense of public values and an expectation of standards by patients.

    3. This modern concept of medical professionalism also requires physicians to **negotiate publicly about medical values and other social values.** Physicians have a critical role in making sure that social priorities take medical concerns and public health into account.

C. **Respect for the Doctor-Patient Relationship**
    Professionalism and respect for the doctor-patient relationship requires an understanding that psychiatry (and medicine in general) is a pragmatic enterprise that requires collaboration between doctor and patient. The psychiatrists' most important guiding principle may be seen as a **commitment to clinical pragmatism** and to the needs of patients in their care. Principles of pragmatic care include **professionalism** (described above) as well as:

    1. **Practicality** is the idea that medical care occurs with actual patients rather than in a scientific vacuum; it must take practical, real concerns and limitations into account.

    2. **Pluralism** is the concept that multiple explanatory models must

be included in case formulation to include biological, psychological, interpersonal, and social elements (see Chapter 2).

3. **Psychiatric care, and all medical care, must be participatory.** In order to respect patient autonomy and the role of the patient as a co-equal partner in care, diagnostic and treatment processes must be collaborative (see Chapter 2).

4. **Psychiatric diagnoses must be considered provisional.** Without a mind-frame allowing for uncertainty or the possibility of error, the psychiatrist risks losing a comprehensive yet flexible understanding of the patient.

V.   Conclusion

The doctor-patient relationship forms the central scaffold of effective psychiatric treatment. This unique relationship derives from multiple sources from basic humanism and principles of ethics, to legal and professional codes and professionalism. At its core, the relationship ensures that any patient seeking treatment receives that treatment in a setting grounded on trust, autonomy, confidentiality, and moral and competent care.

Suggested Readings

American Psychiatric Association: *Opinions of the Ethics Committee on the Principles of Medical Ethics with Annotations Especially Applicable to Psychiatry,* 2001 edition. Washington, DC: American Psychiatric Association, 2001.

American Psychiatric Association: *The Principles of Medical Ethics with Annotations Especially Applicable to Psychiatry,* 1993 edition. Washington, DC: American Psychiatric Association, 1998.

Beauchamp TL, Childress JF: *Principles of Biomedical Ethics,* 4th edition. New York: Oxford Press, 1994.

Beauchamp TL: The philosophical basis of psychiatric ethics. In Bloch S, Chodoff P, Green SA (eds): *Psychiatric Ethics,* 3rd edition. New York: Oxford University Press, 1999:25–48.

Bloch S, Pargiter R: Codes of ethics in psychiatry. In Bloch S, Chodoff P, Green SA (eds): *Psychiatric Ethics,* 3rd edition. New York: Oxford University Press, 1999:81–103.

Brendel DH: Reductionism, eclecticism, and pragmatism in psychiatry: the dialectic of clinical explanation. *J Med Philos* 2003;28:563–580.

Epstein RM, Hundert EM: Defining and assessing professional competence. *JAMA* 2002;287:226–235.

Lloyd GER (ed): *Hippocratic Writings.* London: Penguin Books, 1978.

Schouten R, Brendel RW: Legal aspects of consultation. In Stern TA, Fricchione GL, Cassem NH, Jellinek MS, Rosenbaum JF (eds): *The Massachusetts General Hospital Handbook of General Hospital Psychiatry,* 5th edition. St. Louis: Mosby, 2004:349–364.

Wynia MK, Latham SR, Kao AC, Berg JW, Emanuel LL: Medical professionalism in society (Sounding Board). *N Engl J Med* 1999;341:1612–1616.

Chapter 2

A Negotiated Treatment Approach to Care: Assessment and Negotiation

Rebecca W. Brendel MD, JD

I.   Introduction

A.   **The Biopsychosocial Approach**
Psychiatric diagnosis and care rely on the biopsychosocial model as a framework. Therefore, attunement to biologic, psychological, and social/interpersonal factors are critical as one approaches every psychiatric patient.

B.   **Relationships and Trust**
Establishment of a trusting relationship between the psychiatrist and the patient is essential to **gather adequate information,** to **establish a diagnosis,** to **implement a treatment plan,** and to **maximize patient adherence** (compliance). Establishing rapport with a patient also requires **careful attention to interviewing technique.**

C.   **Collaboration and Respect**
A collaborative approach to treatment facilitates respect for patient autonomy and allows a patient to participate fully in their care.

II.   The Biopsychosocial Approach

A.   **A comprehensive approach to psychiatric diagnosis requires attention to biologic, psychological, and social/interpersonal aspects of each patient's presentation.** These perspectives are **not mutually exclusive;** they often combine to create the patient's current presenting condition.
  1. **Biologic factors** include both **primary psychiatric disorders** and psychiatric manifestations of **general medical conditions.** These factors are generally treated with psychopharmacological or other somatic interventions, sometimes used in combination with psychotherapy.
      a. Factors helpful in characterizing primary psychiatric disorders include: clusters of signs and symptoms, prior episodes

Address for correspondence: Dr. Rebecca W. Brendel, Department of Psychiatry, Massachusetts General Hospital, 55 Fruit St., Psychiatry/WRN605, Boston, MA 02114, email: rbrendel@partners.org.

with a similar course, family history, and other elements of
the history.

b. Because general medical conditions often have psychiatric
manifestations, a careful medical history and screening tests
may reveal an underlying cause of a psychiatric presentation (e.g., hypothyroidism that is manifest as depression).

2. **Psychological factors** may be more difficult to ascertain; they
refer to recurrent patterns of response and behavior that impair
a person's maximum level of functioning.

a. Psychological factors occur along a continuum from mild to
severe; they affect every individual's function and lead to a
variety of symptoms, such as anxiety, and struggles with authority.

b. In severe cases, these factors may be associated with a character (or personality) disorder.

c. In motivated patients, these problems may be approached
with psychotherapy. Identification of patterns with negative
outcomes for the patient and a strong desire for change are
predictors of a positive outcome in psychotherapy.

3. **Social problems** occur as the result of interpersonal issues or
current social events. Attention to such problems, expression of
feelings, and catharsis often is sufficient to address social contributions to psychiatric presentations (although psychotherapy
and other interventions to improve social situations may be
required).

B. **Elements of the History**
With a careful ear to the biologic, psychological, and social components of the presenting problem, it is critical to collect a full psychiatric and medical history; this facilitates formulation of a differential
diagnosis of the patient's presenting problem. Psychiatrists may use
the relationship-building and interviewing techniques outlined
below (see section III) to facilitate and improve data collection.

1. **The history of the present illness** should be elicited by allowing the patient to tell the course of events in his or her own
words and by asking open-ended questions. This approach allows for a broad view of the patient's presenting problem and
the contribution of biologic, psychological, and social factors.
Symptom checklists should not be used early in the interview as
they can lead to premature narrowing of the differential diagnosis. Ascertaining the last time the patient felt well is an important way of exploring what factors may have contributed to the
problem since its inception.

2. **The past psychiatric history** should include assessment of

both similar and dissimilar episodes of psychiatric illness and treatment response and/or nonresponse. In addition, inquiring about periods of emotional stress that have occurred independent of psychiatric illness may offer clues into social and psychological aspects of the presenting problem.

3. **The past medical history and review of systems** should cover routine medical and surgical information, but also establish the presence of any other organic symptoms the patient has not yet reported in the interview. This approach may lead to detection of an underlying organic cause of a psychiatric presentation.

4. **The family, social, and developmental history** can lead to information about treatment response, family models of coping, past emotional stressors, presence of abuse, the patient's current level of function in work and relationships, and the patient's highest level of function (to serve as a comparison).

5. The **mental status examination** (MSE) is a critical part of every psychiatric assessment. Some of the information that comprises the MSE may be inferred or obtained from other parts of the interview; certain elements must always be included. A **current assessment of safety** (including the risk to oneself [by suicide or inability to attend to basic self-care] or others) **should always be performed and carefully documented.** In addition, impaired reality testing and psychotic symptoms should always be ruled out.

III. The Diagnostic Interview

Establishing a relationship with a patient can contribute to patient participation in data gathering and effective interviewing. Without cooperation between the psychiatrist and the patient, the patient may be dissuaded from engaging in a discussion of private and sensitive material.

A. **An Approach to the Patient**
   Patients often experience or see their difficulties differently than do clinicians. Approaches the psychiatrist can take that promote the patient's sharing of personal data include:
   1. **Avoiding assumptions** about how the patient views the problem;
   2. **Sharing information** he or she has with the patient and allowing the patient to modify or correct the information;
   3. **Using nonclinical language to express an understanding** of the patient's problem or feelings;
   4. **Obtaining permission** from the patient to discuss a problem before asking questions;

5. **Paying attention to nonverbal signs** of acceptance, agreement, confusion or disagreement; and,
6. **Summarizing and reflecting** on the information and the patient's situation as the interview progresses.

B. Appreciation of the Patient's Perspective
Appreciation of the patient's perspective requires that the psychiatrist understand the problem and how the patient experiences it. Understanding the patient's strengths in dealing with past difficulties can inform both the psychiatrist and the patient about how the current problem can be understood and managed.

C. Facilitation of Connection
Successful interviewing often depends in large part on simple human kindness and connection. Humanity, warmth, and friendliness can contribute to demystifying medicine and psychiatry, to putting patients at ease, and to establishing rapport.

D. Common Pitfalls
Errors in interviewing can inhibit a patient from sharing information and lead to alienation, an incorrect diagnosis, and suboptimal treatment recommendations. Examples of common pitfalls in interviewing include accidental or inadvertent humiliation of the patient, jumping to premature conclusions about the problem, and offering solutions or advice too quickly.

E. Problematic Areas
Difficult situations may arise while interviewing a patient. Some challenges include dealing with sensitive material, denial, and psychiatric emergencies.
1. **Handling Sensitive Material**
    Sensitive material often arises in psychiatric interviews; a patient may be ashamed or sensitive when discussing these topics or may avoid discussion of them. A number of techniques may be used to help the patient discuss difficult material.
    a. **Planning for the problem, approaching potentially sensitive information indirectly, asking for permission to discuss and/or explore the topic, and using open-ended questions to elicit further information may facilitate a patient's ability to share sensitive material.**
2. **Dealing with Denial**
    A patient may exhibit **denial** (conscious and/or unconscious) in dealing with a serious psychiatric problem. When the existence

of the problem is denied, it is difficult for the psychiatrist to ally with the patient and address the problem. Techniques that may facilitate interactions with the denying patient include:

    a. **Acknowledging the disagreement** about the existence of the problem, considering the presence of **third-party participation** in the discussion (with the patient's permission), **informing patients of potential bad outcomes** without threatening, and **attempting to sustain the relationship,** even in the setting of disagreement.

  3. **Emergencies**

    Emergencies may arise, for example, when **patients pose a risk to themselves or to others and when the psychiatrist has an obligation to protect the patient or a third party and/or to report a situation to authorities.** Psychiatrists should be clear about their **obligations and responsibilities** in the jurisdictions in which they practice, in order to facilitate rapid and safe responses to emergency situations. Psychiatrists should know **the options for back-up** in all practice settings and call upon back-up when necessary to ensure the safety of all involved individuals.

IV. Treatment Planning

Development of a treatment plan should be a collaborative effort between the psychiatrist and the patient. It begins with agreement about the problem and a mutual appreciation of the contributing elements.

    1. However, even after a careful assessment with attention to the patient's attitudes and perspectives, disagreement may persist. In these situations, **the psychiatrist should address the areas of disagreement explicitly** and also return to the data to assess whether the disagreement is the result of misinformation or misunderstanding.

    2. Approaching the assessment from a **psychoeducational perspective** may help the patient understand the contribution of biologic, psychological, and social factors, and set the groundwork for consideration of treatment options. **Patients who do not have enough information about their condition or the proposed treatments may be reluctant to follow through with any treatment.**

    3. The psychiatrist should attempt to present **treatment options** instead of a single proposed treatment or solution; this allows the patient to participate in shaping the treatment plan. The psychiatrist should also elicit the patient's thoughts and opinions regarding proposed treatments. For example, a patient who does

not believe a condition is biological is unlikely to adhere to a proposed biological treatment, such as medication. In addition, many patients experience shame around mental illness, and as a result may be hesitant to accept medication or another treatment. Exploration of the patient's attitude towards the problem and proposed treatments facilitates effective treatment.

V.   Adherence to Treatment Regimens

Since nearly 80% of patients deviate from medical treatment regimes in some way, **patient compliance with treatment recommendations** should be an area of concern for all physicians. Only two-thirds of depressed patients complete the recommended course of treatment, and only half of chronically ill patients use medications as they are prescribed. Noncompliance has negative consequences for patients; they may experience worsening or persistence of illness as a result of nontreatment or improper treatment.

A.   **Assessment of Compliance**
       Assessment of noncompliance begins when a patient is asked about treatment. Open-ended questions about treatment, such as, "How is it going with X?" or "What medications are you taking and how often?" are often useful. Some patients will attempt to conceal noncompliance out of shame; however, direct communication about treatment and assessment of the form of noncompliance in an open and nonjudgmental manner can improve both the doctor-patient relationship and compliance. Other methods of monitoring medication compliance include use of daily diaries, review of medication refill records, pill counting, and monitoring of drug and drug metabolite levels.

B.   **Reasons for Noncompliance**
       Many reasons exist for noncompliance, including patient attitudes and beliefs regarding their illnesses, cultural and religious factors, poor coping or emotional immaturity, cognitive limitations, negative past experiences with the health care system, and the nature of the underlying illnesses. For example, depressed patients may fail to comply due to poor self-care as a result of the depression, while hypomanic and manic patients may not comply because they are euphoric (a component of their mood disorder) and do not wish to be slowed down. Other psychiatric and medical illnesses may also impact compliance.

C. Methods of Improving Compliance

Methods to improve compliance revolve around the doctor-patient relationship, which is the strongest factor affecting compliance. As discussed above, a strong relationship requires appreciation of the patient's view of the problem, establishment of a mutual understanding of the problem and the treatment goals, and support of the patient's beliefs and culture. Other methods of improving compliance may include shaping the treatment to the patient's schedule (e.g., taking medications with meals), enlisting the support of family members, checking in with the patient between appointments, scheduling frequent follow-up appointments, and communicating instructions clearly. An emphasis on the collaboration between the psychiatrist and the patient is also crucial.

VI. Summary

A collaborative, negotiated approach to the psychiatric patient is critical from the beginning of the initial assessment to ongoing treatment and compliance. A thoughtful, nonjudgmental, and respectful interview style combined with an approach to the problem from the patient's perspective can enhance the history, the ability to formulate the problem, and the creation of rapport. When approaching treatment, a good working relationship between the psychiatrist and the patient is central to ongoing compliance and to treatment outcome.

Suggested Readings

Galardy C, Herman JB: Enhancing patient compliance with treatment recommendations. In Stern TA, Herman JB, Slavin PL (eds): *Massachusetts General Hospital Guide to Primary Care Psychiatry,* 2nd edition. New York: McGraw-Hill, 2004:725–733.

Galardy C, Maxwell DJ, Herman JB: Patient compliance. In Stern TA, Herman JB (eds): *Massachusetts General Hospital Psychiatry Update and Board Preparation,* 2nd edition. New York: McGraw-Hill, 2004:423–424.

Gordon C, Goroll, A: Effective psychiatric interviewing in primary care medicine. In Stern TA, Herman JB, Slavin PL (eds): *Massachusetts General Hospital Guide to Primary Care Psychiatry,* 2nd edition. New York: McGraw-Hill, 2004:19–26.

Chapter 3

The Psychiatric Interview

EUGENE V. BERESIN, MD

I.   Overview

The purpose of the psychiatric interview is to gather and organize data about an individual's or a family's thoughts, feelings, and behavior. The examiner should integrate this information in order to develop a clinical formulation that seamlessly connects important aspects of a patient's life in its biological, psychological, and social/interpersonal dimensions. **A complete interview should allow the physician to construct a differential diagnosis and recommendations for treatment planning.** The interview requires that the examiner create a safe space where the patient feels comfortable revealing some of the most private aspects of his or her life, including experiences that are deeply frightening and shameful. The relationship that develops should provide a foundation for collaborative problem-solving and treatment negotiation. **The goals of the psychiatric interview are:**
  A. Establishment of a relationship and an alliance that promotes self-revelation
  B. Collection of data through observing the patient, being aware of the examiner's reactions to the patient, taking a medical/psychiatric history, and performing a mental status examination
  C. Integration of data to establish a formulation of the patient's strengths and weaknesses, a differential diagnosis, and a treatment plan
  D. Education about the nature of psychological and interpersonal problems and psychiatric illness
  E. Preparation for psychiatric treatment, if indicated, and creation of arrangements for follow-up
  F. Documentation of findings for the medical record

II.   The Context of the Interview

When conducting a psychiatric interview, the examiner must be cognizant of the context of the interview. **There are four elements of the context that influence the interview's form and content: The setting, the situation, the subject, and the significance.**

Address for correspondence: Dr. Eugene V. Beresin, Massachusetts General Hospital, Fruit Street, Bulfinch 449, Boston, MA 02114, email: eberesin @partners.org.

A.   **The Setting**
A patient who undergoes a psychiatric evaluation is often sensitive
to the location of the interview. An interview may occur in an outpatient office setting; in a community health center; on a psychiatric
inpatient or partial hospital unit; on a medical or surgical ward (or
an intensive care unit); in a school, a court, or another public facility; or in an emergency room. Each location has its assets and liabil-
ities, and these should be taken into account by the evaluator. For
example, an emergency room or medical floor has limited space for
privacy, and exposure to numerous other professionals, patients, and
support staff. The frantic pace of such units, along with their public
nature may make it uncomfortable for patients to discuss highly confidential and personal issues. In community centers or schools, a
patient may be concerned about being recognized by neighbors or
friends during a psychiatric examination. This, of course, would be
a major factor in inhibiting their responsiveness. The examiner
should try to find a place that is quiet, private, and protected as much
as possible from interruption.

B.   **The Situation**
Some patients come voluntarily for evaluation. Others come at the
behest of a family member, a friend, or an employer, who is deeply
worried about them and who convinces them to seek assistance. At
times, a physician is asked to consult on a patient who is exhibiting
psychiatric symptoms in the context of medical or surgical treatment. Psychiatric evaluation may be requested for family members
of a sick relative, or following a medical emergency or the death of
a loved one. An individual may also be brought by police or ambu-
lance against their will, because they are judged to be dangerous to
self or others. In each case, the evaluating psychiatrist must take into
account the nature of the situation, and tailor the approach accordingly. It is often useful to get as much information as possible before
the interview. Talking with relatives or friends, discussing the situation with health professionals working with the patient, or reading
the medical record may do this. For example, if one knows that a
patient has recently suffered a myocardial infarction and is fright-
ened, agitated, and possibly hallucinating, one could begin an interview by addressing the bizarre experience: "Good morning, Mr.
Jones, I heard about your heart attack from your doctor and understand you have been very scared by some strange experiences. This
is not unusual in your condition, and I would like to help determine
what is causing the problem." Or in the case of a patient brought to
the emergency department in restraints having just been picked up
by police on the edge of a local bridge: "Hello, Ms. Smith, my name

is Dr. Beresin. I am so sorry that you are strapped down, but the police were very concerned about your safety. I would like to talk with you about what is going on, and see what we can do together to help you sort things out."

C. The Subject
The interview technique will naturally be different depending on the age of the patient. Young children, for example, may be best helped to express what they are experiencing by asking them to draw or by using figures in a doll house. Techniques will also vary if the examination involves a family, a couple, or a child with a parent. An adolescent unwillingly brought for an evaluation by a parent may best be approached by acknowledging how difficult it is to be "hauled" into the office, and how angry he or she is at this insult.

D. The Significance
Psychiatric symptoms are often compounded by fear, uncertainty, and shame. The public is poorly educated about psychological problems, or is at worst grossly misinformed by myth. **There are vast differences in the way mental illness is viewed by different cultures.** An individual may have a relative or friend with a psychiatric disorder, and may be concerned that his or her symptoms are indicative of that condition. Finally, **a particular symptom may have idiosyncratic significance to the patient.** Any one of these factors may make revealing the symptom threatening or humiliating. **It is of critical importance to understand the meaning of symptoms for each patient.** Obsessions or compulsions, for example, could be viewed as evidence of being possessed and controlled by demons, evidence of a brain tumor, or the heralding of Aunt Mary's chronic psychosis. Most patients, even well-educated individuals, have no clear idea about what is involved in a psychiatric evaluation or treatment, other than the many distortions portrayed in the media. The examiner should not minimize the prevailing stigma of mental illness and its treatment.

III. Facilitating a Collaborative Self-Reflective Dialogue

In traditional medical education, the student learns to "take a history." This model implies that the patient is the recipient of questions, often delivered in a checklist style. A one-sided interviewing method, which puts the patient into a passive role, is antithetical to gaining the kind of self-revelation needed in a psychiatric interview. Think of the psychiatric interview as a collaborative dialogue in which the patient's self-revelation is encouraged and reinforced by active feedback from the physician. Several techniques foster a relationship in which the patient feels comfortable discussing his or her life.

A.   Establishing Rapport and an Alliance

1. **Introduce yourself and set the frame for a dialogue.** It is advisable not to use medical or psychiatric jargon: e.g., "Hi, Mr. Smith, my name is Dr. Beresin, and I would like to talk with you about some problems that you have been dealing with. In order to do this, I hope we can discuss many important parts of your background and life. I will try my best to understand, and I will frequently ask you if I 'get it.' Would you let me know if I do or if I am incorrect?" This framework establishes the mutual nature of the interview, allows for misinterpretations on your part, and invites the patient to correct you. Many times you will look for affirmation, and the patient will be reluctant to say that you, the authority figure, did not get it right. Allowing the patient to disagree, correct, and modify your understanding from the outset is quite important. Invite the patient to be an active participant, to ask you questions, or to make comments. These strategies set the tone, frame, and style of the interview from its inception.

2. **Establish safety.** Demonstrate warmth, empathy, and respect, as well as authentic interest and curiosity while exploring the patient's problem. Remember that this is a very difficult task for a patient. The psychiatric interview may be quite confusing if not disarming to a patient. It is professional, yet deeply personal and intimate. You are asking a patient to reveal parts of their life that they may not have exposed to anyone else. Hence, they may need encouragement, friendliness, kindness, and appreciation for how difficult this task may be. Be explicit in your thankfulness for sharing their personal story, and acknowledging how hard it is to discuss certain issues.

3. **Be aware of the patient's perspective.** The patient may have a very different understanding of his or her problems than you do. If you do not appreciate what the patient believes, any chance of negotiating a treatment plan is doomed to failure. Remember that a patient's cultural background, ethnicity, gender, age, sexual orientation, life experience, previous experience with psychiatric clinicians, and cognitive processes (including cognitive distortions) may all influence an understanding about the origin, meaning, and treatment of symptoms. For example, a deeply religious elderly man with a psychotic depression may shamefully experience his angry, hateful auditory hallucinations as evidence of his moral transgressions and be plunged into deep despair. While you may see this as a symptom of a biological

psychotic mood disorder, his personal experience speaks differently. Your verbal appreciation of his perspective—seeing the problem through his eyes, and his knowing you "get it"—will go a long way in solidifying an alliance and a future collaboration. It may be wisest after hearing parts of a patient's history to ask, "What do you think is going on and why did this happen?" Later it is helpful to ask, "What do you think would be helpful to you?" Remember that a patient's framework for understanding symptoms and their treatment, both medical and behavioral, usually dictate their choice of actions. If you are to become a participant in your patient's life, you need to know what principles and beliefs guide them.

B. **Using Self-Reflection**
   1. **Model self-reflection, clarification, and summaries for your patients.** A primary goal of the psychiatric interview is the process of self-reflection. Self-reflection has two different, but interrelated, meanings. Personal self-reflection implies looking inward to become aware of our past as well as our present thoughts and feelings. Interpersonal self-reflection refers to a mirroring process—i.e., letting another person in a dialogue know that you understand their perspective. Both doctor and patient should aim at these forms of reflection. A patient may quickly assimilate this mode of communication, if the doctor demonstrates it. For the physician, it is best to give frequent summaries of what you have heard, and to invite acknowledgement. "So, Mr. Jones, let's see if I get it: You have been afraid to leave your house for work, because on three occasions, you had events on the subway involving a rapid heart beat, shortness of breath, dizziness, nausea, trembling, and the feeling that you were dying. These were dreadful, terrifying experiences. And you are concerned that if you take the subway again, this horrible thing will happen again. Is that right?" Be sure to look for affirmation in both verbal and nonverbal ways, such as nodding and facial expressions. If you notice that you do not get this feedback, consider that you have misinterpreted the patient's description, or have said something offensive, critical, or judgmental. Note that a common misconception about the psychiatric interview is that a patient will be told what they are doing "wrong" and given "counseling" for doing the right thing. In this case, it may be useful to say, "Mr. Jones, your tendency to avoid such a horrible experience in the subway is quite natural. The feelings you had were really unbearable. While a safe and protective response, you were caught in a real jam—avoid that

awful situation, but miss work. Later we can think through other ways of coping with this situation, and I can make some helpful suggestions that have proven very useful to others with this problem." In this way, you "normalize" his problem, destigmatize his panic disorder without labeling it just yet, reflect on his personal experience, and provide supportive affirming feedback. Later in the interview, you will come back to his description, re-frame it as a part of a panic disorder, explain in lay terms what a panic attack is, and provide an alternative means of dealing with the problem.

2. **Reflect on your own emotional reaction to a patient.** Many patients will evoke strong reactions—e.g., anger, hate, aversion, sympathy, impulses to rescue, boredom, or sexual arousal. It is imperative to be aware of your own emotional reactions, as they may present important clues about the internal world of our patients. Your response may be indicative of projection, splitting, denial, or other defenses wielded by patients; or they may be the result of overt manipulation. Attending to your responses can prevent you from reacting in a negative way that could harm the patient. While it is not useful to comment on your personal reactions, be aware of them as you create your formulation of a patient's strengths and weaknesses, personal style, and defensive structure. It will also provide data for what form of treatment may be helpful, given that these responses may be evoked in the treatment setting and may need to be dealt with as a focus of therapy, especially if the patient's problem is interpersonal.

IV. Data Collection: Observation, the History, and the Mental Status Examination

A. **Observation**
Carefully observe the patient prior to and during the interview. Note how that patient interacts with family and staff. In the interview, observe the patient's clothes, grooming, posture, gait, and remarkable physical features. Be aware of the use of language, including vocabulary and sentence structure. Watch for eye contact, facial expressions, and affective range. All these observations are important in developing a clear picture of your patient.

B. **The History**
1. An outline of the psychiatric history is presented in Table 3-1.
2. **Begin by concentrating on the history of present illness.** In each component of the history, explain to the patient what you

Table 3-1. The Psychiatric History

I.   Identifying information
    A. Name, address, phone number, and email address
    B. Age, gender, marital status, occupation, children, ethnicity, and religion
    C. Primary care physician
    D. Referral source
    E. Sources of information
    F. Reliability

II. Chief complaint

III. History of present illness
    A. Onset and precipitants
    B. Signs and symptoms
    C. Course, duration, and treatment
    D. Effects on personal, social, and occupational functioning
    E. Comorbid psychiatric or medical disorders

IV. Past psychiatric history
    A. Previous episodes of the problem(s)
       1. Symptoms, course, duration, and treatment (inpatient or outpatient)
    B. Psychiatric disorders
       1. Symptoms, course, duration, and treatment (inpatient or outpatient)

V. Past medical history
    A. Medical problems: Past and current
    B. Surgical problems: Past and current
    C. Allergies
    D. Immunizations
    E. Current medications: Prescribed and over-the-counter
    F. Other treatments: Acupuncture, chiropractic, homeopathic, yoga, or meditation
    G. Tobacco
    H. Substance use: Past and present
    I. Pregnancy history: Births, miscarriages, and abortions
    J. Sexual history: Birth control, safe sex practices, history of sexually transmitted diseases
    K. Review of systems

(continued)

Table 3-1. The Psychiatric History (continued)

VI. Family history
    A. Family psychiatric history
    B. Family medical history

VII. Personal history: Developmental and social history
    A. Early childhood
        1. Developmental milestones
        2. Family relationships
    B. Middle childhood
        1. School performance
        2. Friends
    C. Adolescence
        1. School performance
        2. Friends
        3. Psychosexual history
        4. Dating and peer relationships
        5. Substance use
        6. Problems with parents, peers, and courts
    D. Early adulthood
        1. Education
        2. Friends
        3. Hobbies and interests
        4. Marital and other partners
        5. Military and prison experiences
        6. Work
    E. Midlife and older adulthood
        1. Career development
        2. Changes in family
        3. Losses
        4. Aging process

are about to discuss and the rationale. The following are valuable guides to the present illness:

    a. **Begin with open-ended questions,** and let the patient tell her or his own story. Avoid interruptions. This helps foster a sense that the patient is the "real expert" in his own narrative, and you are an empathic listener.

    b. **Ask for clarifying comments.** "Nervous," for example does not mean the same thing to everyone. Ask what a patient means by "I was really nervous." You may find it really means sad, irritated, agitated, or confused and not anxious. Your assumptions about what a patient experiences may be far from the truth. By asking clarifying statements, a patient gets the message that you really care about his or her personal experience. This fosters collaboration and mutual understanding. Getting on the same page as the patient is critical. Use the words of the patient throughout the interview to help him or her know that you are listening.

c. **Realize that the patient's primary concerns may not be the same as yours.** While the patient may be suffering from an agitated depression and you are most concerned with treating the disorder, he may really be worried about his son's academic problems or his job situation. If this was the reason for the office visit, be attentive and sympathetic to the patient's perspective. **Ask about what the patient wants to see changed, and what he or she thinks would help.**

d. **Determine the nature of the problem (its duration, frequency, and intensity) and what has been done about it prior to your interview.** What is being done about it currently, personally, and professionally? Are their other problems that compound the primary one, such as co-morbid disorders, psychosocial stressors, medical illnesses, or family problems? Ask about symptoms of mood, anxiety, other behavioral disorders, and the impact of the problem on relationships and work. It is useful to ask why the patient came for help now, and to get a sense about the motivation for getting help.

e. **Be sure to get important identifying data** including: age, marital status, living situation, occupation, culture, ethnicity, religion, and sexual orientation. This may not be your first order of business, since much of this is obtained in a checklist fashion. It is most important to start with "where the patient is" and ask about what is most troubling at the moment. This helps emphasize your interest in the patient as a person, and not as an object to be studied. It is easy to get identifying information throughout the interview; avoid impersonal checklist interviewing, at least at the beginning. Checklists may be helpful for specific parts of the mental status examination, and that may come later, once an alliance is formed.

C.   **Past Psychiatric History**
1.   **Ask about DSM-IV Axis I and II disorders, partial syn-dromes, and treatment history.** Be sure to consider any impact of personal, social, and occupational functioning.
2.   **Ask about the success or failures in past treatment and the patient's commentary about the course and experience of past treatment.** If there was never treatment, ask about the patient's attitude and opinions about psychiatric treatment. This may give you data that would influence your current treatment recommendations.
3.   **Try to understand the patient's coping and problem-solving style in relationship to stress.** Some patients, for example, thrive on emotional support, ventilation, and sharing of feelings with others. Others shun emotions and rely on rational and cognitive styles of problem-solving. Learning about the patient's typical way of handling problems may be valuable in treatment planning.

D.   **Past Medical History and Review of Systems**
1.   Many psychiatric and behavioral disorders are secondary to primary medical and surgical conditions, adverse effects of medications, or drug-drug interactions. **The medical history should include a thorough review of past and current illnesses; surgery; hospitalizations; medications used in past and present,** including over-the-counter medications and herbal or nontraditional therapies; allergies; and the use of tobacco, alcohol, and other substances.
2.   Given the formal, checklist style of questioning used to perform this part of the interview, this may be a good time to go through a current review of symptoms.
3.   Document the sexual history, including sexual activity, use of safe sexual practices, and forms of birth control. The history of sexually transmitted diseases (including HIV testing, pregnancies, and history of abortions and miscarriages) could also be elicited at this time.

E.   **Family History**
1.   The family history of medical, surgical, and psychiatric illness should also include the types of treatment obtained and the responses to intervention.

F.   **Personal History: Social and Developmental History**
1.   **The developmental history is outlined in Table 3-1. It should include developmental milestones, family structure and re-**

lationships (past and present), school history (including grade level reached and academic performance), friends, hobbies, activities, and interests. The interviewer should have some sense of what it was like for the patient at different stages of life.

2. **The social history should include current educational level, occupation, employment, interests, religious affiliation, friendships, and current family relationships. There should also be questions about problems with the legal or social system.**

3. The patient should be encouraged to discuss his or her marital relationship or connection with a significant other. If there are children (biological, adopted, or stepchildren), it is important to inquire about their development and the quality of the relationships with the patient.

4. The patient should be asked about his or her cultural heritage and the influence it has had on past and present life.

5. This is a good time to ask about current or past physical or sexual abuse. It is also useful to inquire about community safety and violence.

6. The social history is an excellent place to develop a sense of the personal life of the patient and the nature and quality of supports in his or her world. It is a good idea to ask about what others think about the patient's problems. Sometimes it is useful to ask for a spouse, partner, parent, or child to come in to participate in the interview. This may reveal important attitudes and/or conflicts. For example, if in your estimation the patient has a depression complicated by alcohol dependence that is denied by the patient, but family members appear to consider this a real problem, then a gentle request to include others at home may be helpful both in resolving conflicts and in facilitating a supportive home environment for future intervention. This may be very important in considering treatment options.

G.   Mental Status Examination

1. An outline of the mental status examination is seen in Table 3-2. Most of the mental status examination is an outgrowth of the entire psychiatric interview. When asking questions about the history of present illness, much of the patient's current functioning, including signs and symptoms of major psychiatric disorders, are asked about.

2. If not asked in the history of present illness or in the past psychiatric history, the examiner should be sure to ask about discrete symptoms of mood, anxiety, psychotic, medically-in-

Table 3-2. The Mental Status Examination
I.   General appearance and behavior
II.   Speech
III. Affect
IV.   Mood
V.   Perception
VI.   Thought
A. Form
B. Content
VII. Cognition
A. Level of consciousness
B. Orientation
C. Attention and concentration
D. Memory: registration, recent, and remote
E. Calculation
F. Abstraction
G. Judgment
H. Insight

duced, substance-related, learning, and other psychiatric disorders.

3. If in the course of an interview a thought disorder or impairment in reality testing is suspected, then specific questions related to thinking and cognition must be asked. Tests for thought disorders and cognitive impairment must always be done if one suspects dementia or delirium.

4. Thought disorders may involve the form of thought, the content of thought, and perception. The form of thought does not require specific questioning, since the important qualities of formal thought disorder can be inferred from the patient's discourse. A formal thought disorder refers to the way ideas are connected, and not the thoughts themselves. One needs to consider the logic and coherence of the thinking process. Manifestations of formal thought disorders include:

    a. Circumstantiality
    b. Tangentiality
    c. Loose associations
    d. Clang associations
    e. Flight of ideas

     f.   Thought blocking
     g. Perseveration
     h. Neologisms
     i.   Derailment

5. The content of thought refers to the specific ideas themselves. If one suspects serious problems with the content of thought, ask about:
   a. Ideas of reference
   b. Delusions
   c. Obsessions
   d. Suicidal thoughts
   e. Homicidal thoughts

6. Perceptual abnormalities include hallucinations and illusions. Illusions are sensory stimuli that a person misperceives. An example of this is seeing the wrinkles in one's sheets as snakes, or seeing objects larger or smaller than they actually are (macropsia and micropsia). Hallucinations are misperceptions that are generated entirely by the individual him- or herself. They include one or more modalities, and each should be asked about:
   a. Auditory
   b. Visual
   c. Olfactory
   d. Gustatory
   e. Kinesthetic

7. **The cognitive examination should include assessment of orientation, attention, memory (immediate, recent, and remote), calculations, fund of knowledge, judgment, and insight.** A formal mental status examination useful for distinguishing between dementia and depression complicated by organicity, **the Mini-Mental State Examination, may be used (see Figure 3-1).** It is a brief, efficient, and reliable cognitive examination that takes about 5 minutes to perform.

8. In every psychiatric interview you must ask about suicidal and homicidal ideation.

V.   Education and Preparation for Treatment

A. Education

1. **A patient should be prepared for the kinds of sensitive questions asked in the psychiatric interview;** this interview often explores areas left out of many general medical evaluations. It is useful to explain that these personal subjects need inquiry to understand the patient as a whole person.

Mean Scores

Dementia 9.7
Depression with impaired cognition 19.0
Uncomplicated depression 25.1
Normals 27.6

Maximum Score	Score	
		Orientation
5	( )	What is the (year) (date) (day) (month)?
5	( )	Where are we (state) (county) (town) (hospital)(floor)?
		Registration
3	( )	Name 3 objects: 1 second to say each. Then

ask

the patient all 3 after you have said them. Give 1 point for each correct answer. Then repeat them until he/she learns all 3. Count trials and record. Trials _____

		Attention and Calculation
5	( )	Serial 7s: 1 point for each correct. Stop after 5 answers. Alternatively spell "world" backward.
3	( )	*Recall* Ask for 3 objects repeated above. Give 1 point for each correct answer.
		Language
2	( )	Name a pencil and watch (2 points)
1	( )	Repeat the following: "no ifs ands or buts." (1 point)
3	( )	Follow a 3-stage command: "Take a pencil in your right hand, fold it in half, and put if on the floor." (3 points)
1	( )	Read and obey the following: "Close your eyes." (1 point)
1	( )	Write a sentence. Must contain a subject and a verb and be sensible (1 point)
1	( )	*Visual-Motor Integrity* Copy design (2 intersecting pentagons. All 10 angles must be present and 2 must intersect). (1 point).

Total Score _____

Assess level of consciousness along a continuum:

_____

Alert   Drowsy   Stupor   Coma

Figure 3-1. Mini-Mental State Examination

Reproduced with permission from Folstein MF, Folstein SE, McHugh PE: The Mini-Mental State Exam: A practical method for grading the cognitive state of patients for the clinician. *J Psychiatr Res* 1975;12:189–198.

2. **Psychiatric symptoms, as well as psychological and inter-personal problems, are typically a mystery to most patients.** It is best to provide detailed explanations of symptoms, diagnoses, and treatment methods during the course of the interview. Sometimes recommending books or useful websites may be suggested.

B. **Preparation for Treatment**
 1. **Once you have explained the meaning of symptoms and problems in preparation for treatment recommendations, it is crucial to establish an agreement with the patient about the symptoms.** If the patient does not agree with you about your summary of the findings, then it is most useful to revisit the parts of the examination that covered those areas of disagreement. Once you agree on the problem, discussion about treatment may begin.
 2. **All treatment involves a negotiation as to the methods and a collaborative effort in carrying out the plan.** The examiner should review the nature of the problem, including its biological and psychological social/environmental components. Few psychiatric disorders can be treated with medications alone, and often require some additional form of therapeutics. A detailed discussion of the pros and cons of various options should be provided to the patient. This is perhaps the most delicate and difficult part of the interview, as many people may have a hard time acknowledging the psychological or interpersonal part of the treatment. Others have problems accepting the need for "mind-altering drugs" and may balk at the thought of pharmacotherapy. In these instances it is highly useful to "medicalize" the psychiatric disorder and demonstrate how common medical conditions often involve attention to biopsychosocial treatment. For example, most patients will appreciate that asthma, migraines, and gastric ulcers are medical conditions and require pharmacotherapy. Few people would say they would rather not take a medication if it means they cannot breathe. At the same time, most would agree that various stressful situations exacerbate asthma, migraines, and ulcers, as do many foods and environmental conditions. It simply makes sense to attend to the psychological stressors and environmental contributors to these problems. You may then point out that depression, panic attacks, and other so-called psychiatric disorders are no different.

VI.   Problems in Psychiatric Interviews

A.   **Avoiding Sensitive Subjects**

1. Many patients feel extremely uncomfortable discussing certain topics (such as domestic violence, sexual dysfunction, substance abuse, legal problems, psychotic symptoms, or any symptom that is incongruent with cultural expectations for behavior). In these cases it is wise to prepare the patient with a gentle expression that conveys that you know how difficult it is to discuss the issue. If the patient is appropriately prepared, and you use nonthreatening open-ended questions, you may be successful.

2. If an area is not discussed, you may skip it, but note in your documentation that the patient was not ready to discuss it. On the other hand, there are times when direct questioning is crucial, and you cannot leave anything out. These include possible life-threatening situations (such as symptoms or situations that are potentially dangerous to self or others).

B.   **Disagreements About Treatment**

1. There may be times when you make a diagnosis, describe the nature of the problem, and make treatment recommendations, but the patient disagrees with your assessment. **In these instances you must first listen to the patient's point of view, since you may have not attended to the discussion carefully,** or you have come to premature closure on an issue that needed further elaboration. Be aware of your tendency to dig in your heels and to get into power struggles.

2. At other times, the patient denies the existence of a problem or minimizes it. If you are certain of your conclusion, then it is wise to review your findings, and carefully go over them again with the patient. Sometimes it is useful to ask a close relative or friend to come in to discuss the issue. The process of negotiating a treatment plan may take more than one interview. On the other hand, there are patients that simply refuse to acknowledge a problem, especially if they did not come in voluntarily. In these cases it is crucial to know your ethical and professional obligations. In cases in which there is threat to self or others, you must do whatever it takes to protect the patient. In less severe cases, you have to respect the right of a patient to make his or her own treatment decisions.

Suggested Readings

Beresin EV: The psychiatric interview examination. In Stern TA, Herman JB (editors): *Massachusetts General Hospital Psychiatry Update and Board Preparation,* 2nd Edition. New York: McGraw-Hill, 2004:13–19.

Folstein MF, Folstein SE, McHugh PE: The Mini-Mental State Exam: A practical method for grading the cognitive state of patients for the clinician. *J Psychiatr Res* 1975;12:189–198.

Gordon C, Goroll A: Effective psychiatric interviewing in primary care medicine. In Stern TA, Herman JB, Slavin PL (editors): *Massachusetts General Hospital Guide to Primary Care Psychiatry,* 2nd Edition. New York: McGraw-Hill, 2004:19–26.

Manley MRRS: Psychiatric interview, history and mental status examination. In Sadock BJ, Sadock VA (editors): *Comprehensive Textbook of Psychiatry,* 7th Edition. Philadelphia: Lippincott Williams & Williams, 2002:652–665.

Silberman SE: Psychiatric interview: settings and techniques. In Tasman A, Kay J, Lieberman JA (editors): *Psychiatry.* Philadelphia: WB Saunders, 1997:19–34.

Chapter 4

Multiaxial Assessment According to the DSM-IV-TR

TERRY RABINOWITZ, MD, DDS
JOSHUA CW JONES, MD

I.   Introduction

A.   Overview

In order to treat a disease or disorder it makes sense to classify that condition and to distinguish it from other conditions for which different therapies may be more appropriate. This is the approach taken by the multiaxial system used for the diagnosis of psychiatric disorders. The five axes that comprise the system attempt to create a "snapshot" of a person that is accurate (i.e., valid) and that conveys to others the essential characteristics of a person. It can be thought of as "shorthand" by which clinicians communicate the essential characteristics of a patient to one another. **Application of this so-called "DSM classification" is often one of the first steps taken by most clinicians when developing and communicating a comprehensive treatment plan to their patient.**

B.   Case Example

Consider Mr. A, a young man admitted to an inpatient psychiatric service after an acetaminophen overdose in response to being fired from his seventh job in the last 12 months. The work-up reveals that he has had a depressed mood for the past year, that was accompanied by loss of interest, poor concentration, decreased appetite, insomnia, and thoughts of suicide. This was Mr. A's first suicide attempt, a suicide note addressed to his parents was left, but nobody was called for help following the overdose, and he took measures so as not to be discovered.

Mr. A has been diagnosed as having a borderline personality disorder and type II diabetes. Current stressors include difficulty with employers, a recent significant increase in his rent, and an arrest for driving while intoxicated. No social supports are apparent and he had been neglecting his personal hygiene.

Address for correspondence: Dr. Terry Rabinowitz, Fletcher Allen Health Care, 111 Colchester Ave., Burlington, VT 05401-1473, email: Terry.Rabinowitz @vtmednet.org.

In describing Mr. A, your multiaxial approach to diagnosis might look something like this:

Axis I:	296.23	Major Depressive Disorder, Single Episode, Severe Without Psychotic Features
Axis II:	301.83	Borderline Personality Disorder
Axis III:		Diabetes Mellitus, type II
Axis IV:		Fired from job
		Conflicts with employer
		Unaffordable rent
		Recent arrest
Axis V:	GAF = 9 (current)	

Of course, these five axes are in no way a comprehensive profile of this patient, but their utility in helping the clinician describe their overall impression of the patient to others has been well established. A history of the multiaxial system follows.

C.　Development of the Multiaxial System

The multiaxial system is a direct consequence of the effort to transform the classification of mental disorders from theoretical groupings to a descriptive, syndrome-based system in which biological influences and pharmacological responses influence the classification of a specific disorder. The classification of mental disorders in the United States has its origins in 1840 when a single category, "idiocy (insanity)" was used in that year's census (Williams, 1999).

The *Diagnostic and Statistical Manual of Mental Disorders* (DSM) was first published in 1952 by the American Psychiatric Association. It contained descriptions of various mental disorders; DSM-II, which differed little from its predecessor, followed in 1968.

DSM-III (1980) introduced a new system that was based on diagnostic categories and used a true multiaxial approach to classification. The DSM-III developed as an alternative to the World Health Organization (WHO) classification system, ICD-9 (International Classification of Diseases, 9th revision). DSM-III came about after concern was raised by the American Psychiatric Association (APA) that the ICD-9 classification system contained insufficient detail for clinical and research applications. The Task Force on Nomenclature and Statistics of the APA thus created over 150 diagnostic categories for DSM-III. An extensive field trial of the included diagnostic criteria was performed on more than 12,000 patients before the manual was made available (Spitzer et al, 1979; Spitzer and Forman, 1979).

DSM-III had a major impact on psychiatry in the United States. Soon after, its impact was felt worldwide. **Diagnostic criteria con-**

tained within each iteration of the DSM have become the standard by which psychiatric diagnoses are made, shared, and reported (Williams, 1999). Although other classification systems are available, virtually every scientific journal or other academic publication requires that "DSM criteria" be met for a particular disorder. In addition, third-party payers generally require that DSM criteria be met when a particular psychiatric diagnosis is proffered.

The most recent edition of the DSM is the DSM-IV-TR ("TR" stands for "Text Revision"), published in 2000. Diagnostic criteria are not intended to imply causality for disorders (except for Post-traumatic Stress Disorder [PTSD], Mental Disorders due to a General Medical Condition, and Substance-Induced Mental Disorders); moreover, the DSM-IV-TR does not attempt to provide a comprehensive guide for the management and treatment of any psychiatric disorder.

Where relevant, the DSM-IV-TR provides a description of the associated features of each disorder and includes epidemiological factors, predisposing factors, clinical course, and differential diagnosis. Preserved in the DSM-IV-TR is the five-axis diagnostic system that first appeared in the DSM-III, and which is described below.

II.   The Multiaxial System of DSM-IV-TR Described

The multiaxial system of DSM-IV-TR "facilitates comprehensive and systematic evaluation with attention to the various mental disorders and general medical conditions, psychosocial and environmental problems, and level of functioning that might be overlooked if the focus was more on assessing a single presenting problem" (APA, 2000). Table 4-1 describes the essential items of the multiaxial system per DSM-IV-TR.

Table 4-1. Multiaxial System per DSM-IV-TR

Axis	Item
Axis I	Clinical disorders
	Other conditions that may be a focus of clinical attention
Axis II	Personality disorders
	Mental retardation
Axis III	General medical conditions
Axis IV	Psychosocial and environmental problems
Axis V	Global assessment of functioning

A.   **Axis I**

Axis I items comprise all psychiatric disorders contained within the DSM-IV-TR *except* personality disorders and mental retardation. In addition, Axis I includes other conditions that may be a focus of clinical attention. **Each diagnosis listed in Axis I has a corresponding number and (sometimes) letter.** For instance, the diagnostic code for alcohol withdrawal is 291.81; for schizotypal personality disorder it is 301.22; and for major depressive disorder, recurrent, moderate it is 296.32. Other conditions that may be a focus of clinical attention include mathematics disorder (315.1), phonological disorder (315.39), and religious or spiritual problems (V62.89). To determine the precise code for a specific Axis I disorder, one should refer to the DSM-IV-TR criteria.

   DSM-IV-TR rates certain disorders with respect to severity. Thus, the specifiers *mild, moderate,* and *severe,* which correspond to the numbers 1, 2, and 3, respectively, should be included for certain conditions (such as major depressive disorder). Therefore, as in the example provided at the beginning of this chapter, the disorder is coded as 296.23, which translates as 296 (major depressive disorder), 2 (single episode), 3 (severe). Another set of specifiers allowed by DSM-IV-TR include *in partial remission, in full remission,* and *prior history.* These specifiers are added for certain conditions (such as major depressive disorder and bipolar disorder). So-called "V-codes" suggest a disorder that should be identified on either Axis I or II, but which is not considered a strict psychiatric disorder according to DSM-IV-TR.

   The designation "Not Otherwise Specified" (NOS) is used to describe an Axis I or II condition that has features consistent with a *bona fide* mental disorder per DSM-IV-TR but *does not* meet full criteria for the disorder or for which required etiology is uncertain. Such classification might be used to describe an anxiety disorder that has elements of generalized anxiety disorder (thus, Anxiety Disorder NOS, 300.00). Each diagnostic class has at *least* one NOS category. Table 4-2 presents the Axis I diagnostic classes that appear in the DSM-IV-TR.

   Although the DSM-IV-TR classification is not intended to imply causation for mental illness, the system does allow for the establishment of an etiology for a mental disorder if there is clinical evidence that the disorder is the direct consequence of a general medical condition. For instance, Ms. B, a 45-year-old woman with hallucinations in the context of ovarian cancer metastatic to the brain would be appropriately diagnosed with psychotic disorder due to metastatic carcinoma with hallucinations. It should be noted that the term "general medical condition" is used for convenience in distin-

Table 4-2. Axis I Diagnostic Classes Included in the DSM-IV-TR

- Disorders usually first diagnosed in infancy, childhood, or adolescence
- Delirium, dementia, and amnestic and other cognitive disorders
- Mental disorders due to a general medical condition
- Substance-related disorders
- Schizophrenia and other psychotic disorders
- Mood disorders
- Anxiety disorders
- Somatoform disorders
- Factitious disorders
- Dissociative disorders
- Sexual and gender identity disorders
- Eating disorders
- Sleep disorders
- Impulse-control disorders not elsewhere classified
- Adjustment disorders
- Other conditions that may be a focus of clinical attention

guishing between psychiatric and nonpsychiatric causes of mental disorders, but this should not be interpreted to mean that there is no physical connection to the causes of psychiatric illness.

Comorbid and co-occurring conditions have been recognized as common and clinically relevant in psychiatry. To that end, multiple diagnoses in all axes except Axis V are allowed, with the condition whose symptoms are most prominent occupying the first position in each axis and other conditions arranged in descending order of focus of attention and treatment. In many instances, a patient referred for a psychiatric evaluation may not have an Axis I diagnosis. "No diagnosis on Axis I" (V71.09) is an appropriate code in these cases; likewise there may not be an Axis II condition present, and coding would be thus, V71.09.

B.   Axis II
       The Axis II diagnoses include personality disorders and mental retardation. The designation of personality disorders as a separate classification from major psychiatric diagnoses is a somewhat controversial aspect to the multiaxial system. Some clinicians believe that personality disorders are not true psychiatric disorders, but are severe manifestations of major psychiatric (i.e., Axis I) illnesses,

such as major depression or bipolar disorder. Others feel that personality disorders are appropriate holdovers from a more psychologically theoretical period in psychiatry and therefore warrant their own classification. Still others feel that the diagnosis of personality disorders is unhelpful in the treatment of a patient's symptoms and that the diagnosis implies a stigma of treatment resistance and "difficultness," both for the clinician and the patient.

All personality disorders are chronic, pervasive conditions; symptoms of them may vary in intensity. Therefore it is prudent to defer a diagnosis of a personality disorder at an initial visit unless a patient meets the diagnostic criteria. In addition, because personality disorders are maladaptive amplifications of traits that all humans possess and that acute psychiatric illnesses may aggravate, it is often prudent to defer a diagnosis of a personality disorder until an acute psychiatric illness (i.e., Axis I disorder) is brought under control.

All clinicians should use caution when diagnosing a personality disorder. Many patients diagnosed with a personality disorder are stigmatized and find the classification pejorative. On occasion, it may appear that a patient has a personality disorder but after a longer period of observation, an Axis I disorder (whose presentation mimicked that of a personality disorder) was present. **Once the diagnosis of a personality disorder is entered into the medical record, it is nearly impossible to expunge it; the diagnosis, whether correct or incorrect, will turn up in all subsequent records.**

C.   Axis III
      Axis III conditions comprise general medical conditions of clinical significance. This does not imply that psychiatric disorders do not have medical causes, nor does it imply that psychiatric conditions or social stressors do not affect medical conditions. Nonpsychiatric medical conditions are listed here "to encourage thoroughness in evaluation and to enhance communication among health care providers" (APA, 2000). Medical conditions that might be of clinical significance include but are not limited to hypothyroidism, diabetes mellitus, chronic obstructive pulmonary disease (COPD), and anemia. **No severity specifiers are used for conditions on Axis III.**

D.   Axis IV
      Axis IV comprises psychosocial and environmental problems that may affect the diagnosis, treatment, and prognosis of the disorder(s) identified on Axes I and II. No severity specifiers are used in Axis IV. Table 4-3 lists the nine problems included in DSM-IV-TR.

Table 4-3. Psychosocial and Environmental Problems in DSM-IV-TR

- Problems with primary support group
- Problems related to the social environment
- Educational problems
- Occupational problems
- Housing problems
- Economic problems
- Problems with access to health care services
- Problems related to interaction with the legal system/crime
- Other psychosocial and environmental problems

E.   **Axis V**

Global Assessment of Functioning (GAF) occupies Axis V. Again, no severity specifier is used, as the absolute number entered is an indicator of severity. Thus, the GAF is a number that may range between zero and 100 in one-unit increments; it may be applied in a variety of situations, e.g., present level, level on admission and discharge, and level in past year. A level of zero indicates no information is available and a score of 100 indicates superior functioning in a wide range of activities.

Many inpatient psychiatry units, insurers, crisis clinicians, and others, rely on the GAF score to help identify people who are in need of inpatient psychiatric treatment or a less restrictive environment. Therefore it is easy to see how this score might be intentionally "deflated" to increase the chance that a hospital admission is approved. Many facilities, insurers, and others have known or unpublished "cut-off" GAF scores below which a hospital admission is assured. In addition, patients who have had psychiatric admissions may be aware that they need a particular GAF to get into or to stay out of a hospital. We urge all clinicians to take the GAF score seriously and to glean corroborative information from as many reliable sources as possible before assigning a score.

III.   Conclusion

The multiaxial system used in DSM-IV-TR is useful for the diagnosis, care planning, treatment, and outcomes measurement of patients with psychiatric illnesses. DSM-IV-TR represents the latest iteration of a series of diagnostic and statistical manuals of mental disorders begun more than five decades ago. The diagnostic categories, individual psychiatric diagnoses, and associated symptoms have been subjected to some of the most rigorous tests of validity and reliability. Thousands of peer-reviewed scientific papers have been published using the diagnostic criteria contained therein. The multiaxial system in DSM-IV-TR is sound but by no means foolproof; it will no doubt continue to improve with each successive edition of the DSM.

References

American Psychiatric Association: Task Force on DSM-IV. *Diagnostic and Statistical Manual of Mental Disorders:* DSM-IV-TR, 4th ed. Washington, DC: American Psychiatric Association, 2000.

Hales RE, Yudofsky SC, (eds): *The American Psychiatric Publishing Textbook of Clinical Psychiatry,* 4th ed. Washington, DC: American Psychiatric Press, 2003.

Spitzer RL, Forman JB: DSM-III field trials: II. Initial experience with the multiaxial system. *Am J Psychiatry* 1979;136:818–820.

Spitzer RL, Forman JB, Nee J: DSM-III field trials: I. Initial inter-rater diagnostic reliability. *Am J Psychiatry* 1979;136:815–817.

Williams JBW: Psychiatric classification. In Hales RE, Yudofsky SC (eds): *The American Psychiatric Press Textbook of Psychiatry,* 3rd ed. Washington, DC: American Psychiatric Press, 1999:227–252.

Chapter 5

Decision Trees and Clinical Algorithms

JACOB HOLZER, MD

I.   Overview

Making a diagnosis involves a process that is based primarily on taking a history and performing a mental status examination; however, the process can be supplemented by the results of additional examinations and tests. Diagnostic decision trees or algorithms, based on the classification system of the *Diagnostic and Statistical Manual of Mental Disorders*, 4th Edition (DSM-IV), can facilitate this process by guiding the clinician's thinking during decision-making and helping to create a differential diagnosis. Clinical decision trees (as presented in Figures 5-1, 5-2, 5-3, and 5-4) tend to rely on common psychiatric symptoms and conditions. The following decision trees are adapted from the DSM-IV text. The reader is referred to the texts listed in the suggested readings at the end of this chapter for a more comprehensive listing of decision trees.

Address for correspondence: Dr. Jacob Holzer, Spaudling Hospital, 125 Nashua St., Boston, MA 02114, email: jholzer@partners.org.

II.   Figure 5-1. Cognitive Disorders

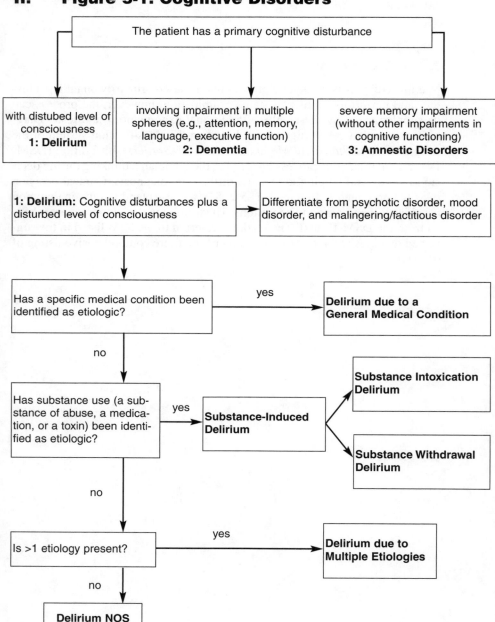

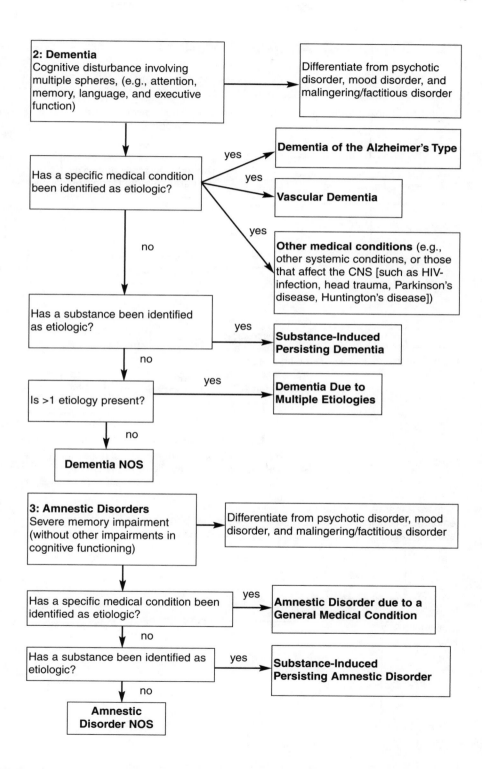

III.   Figure 5-2. Anxiety Disorders

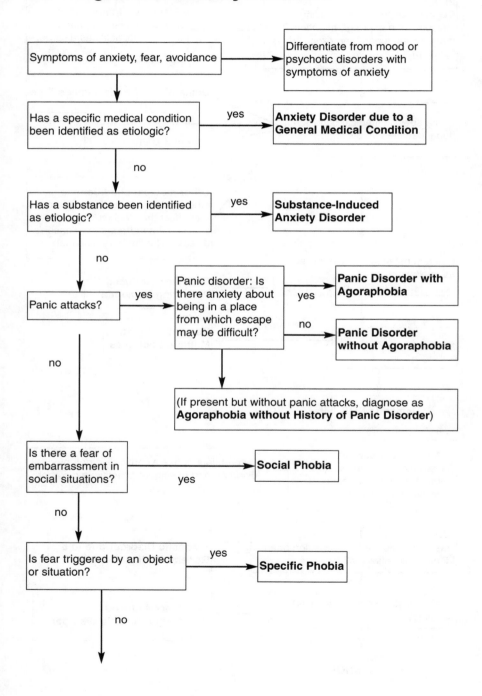

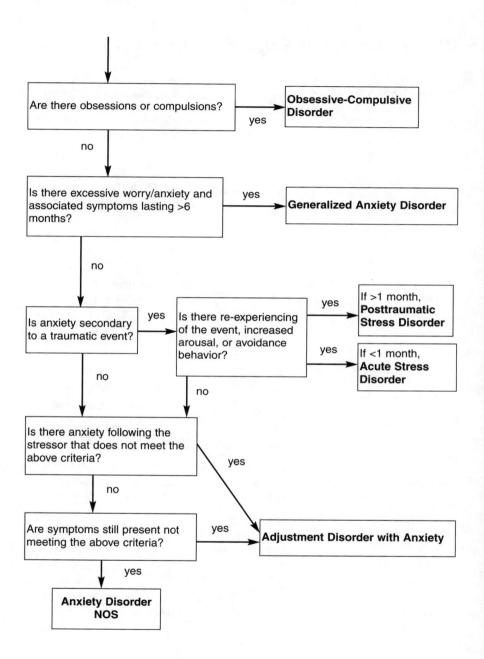

IV.   Figure 5-3. Psychotic Disorders

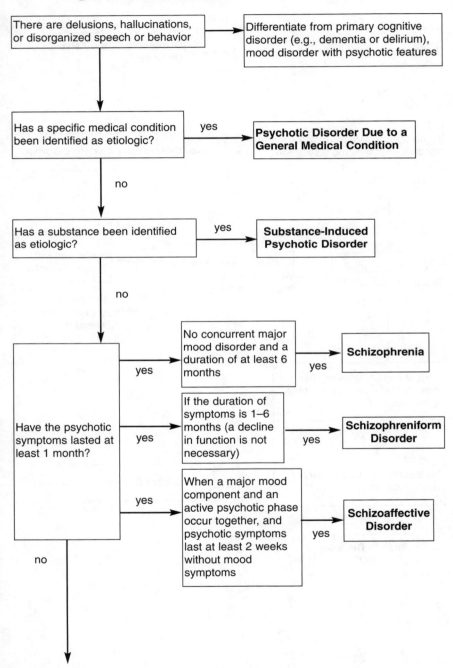

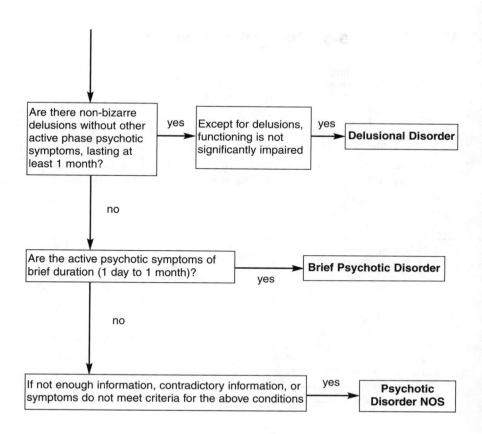

V.   Figure 5-4. Mood Disorders

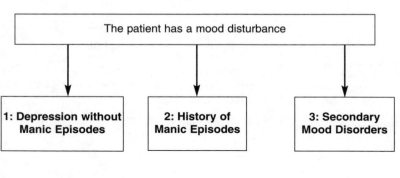

The patient has a mood disturbance

1: Depression without Manic Episodes

2: History of Manic Episodes

3: Secondary Mood Disorders

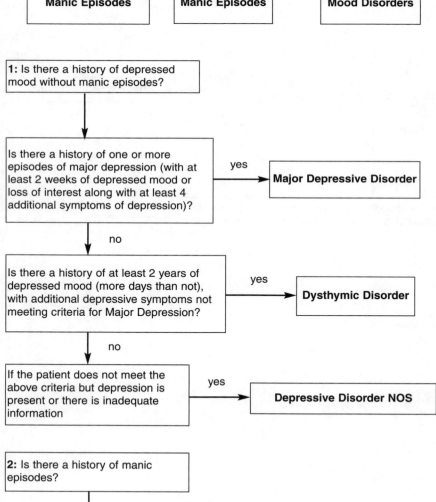

1: Is there a history of depressed mood without manic episodes?

Is there a history of one or more episodes of major depression (with at least 2 weeks of depressed mood or loss of interest along with at least 4 additional symptoms of depression)?

yes → **Major Depressive Disorder**

no

Is there a history of at least 2 years of depressed mood (more days than not), with additional depressive symptoms not meeting criteria for Major Depression?

yes → **Dysthymic Disorder**

no

If the patient does not meet the above criteria but depression is present or there is inadequate information

yes → **Depressive Disorder NOS**

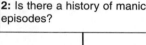

2: Is there a history of manic episodes?

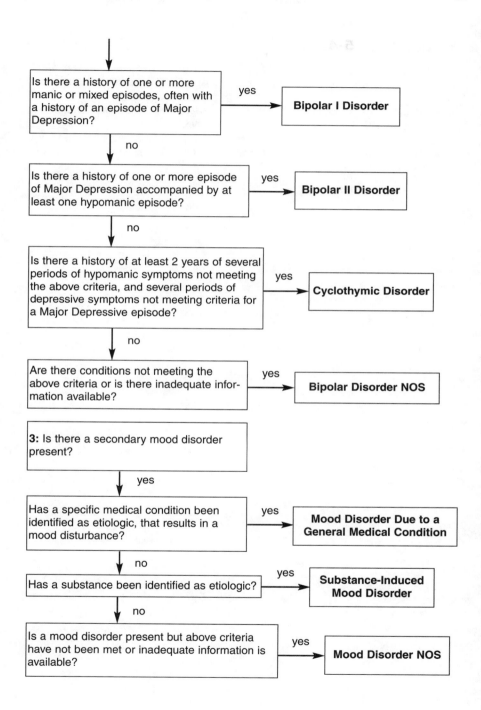

Suggested Readings

American Psychiatric Association (APA): *Diagnostic and Statistical Manual of Mental Disorders*, 4th Edition. Washington, DC: American Psychiatric Association, 1994.

First MG, Frances A, Pincus HA: *DSM-IV Handbook of Differential Diagnosis*. Washington, DC: American Psychiatric Press, 1995.

Kearns ME: The DSM-IV: A multi-axial system for psychiatric diagnosis. In Stern TA, Herman JB (eds): *Psychiatry Update and Board Preparation*, 2nd Edition. New York: McGraw-Hill, 2004:23–26.

Chapter 6

DSM-IV Diagnoses

Jacob Holzer, MD

I.   Overview

The *Diagnostic and Statistical Manual of Mental Disorders*, 4th Edition (DSM-IV), the official classification system of psychiatric conditions currently in use in the United States, describes the clinical features that must be present for the diagnosis of a disorder. It does not address etiology or treatment. The criteria presented in the DSM-IV facilitate communication among health care professionals, provide a common standard for research, and aid in communication with third-party payors. It is meant to assist in, and not replace, clinical diagnostic decision-making. The DSM-IV lists 16 major diagnostic classes, plus an additional section for 'other conditions,' such as psychological factors affecting medical conditions, medication-induced movement disorders, and relational problems. The DSM-IV allows several diagnoses to be given to a patient who presents with symptoms that meet criteria for more than one diagnosis, and provides exclusion criteria in certain situations that help in the process of creating a differential diagnosis. The DSM system is compatible with the International Classification of Disease (ICD) series used by the World Health Organization.

This chapter provides an overview of common clinical diagnoses seen in a general psychiatric setting. It is not meant to be all-encompassing. For a complete listing of DSM-IV diagnoses, their diagnostic criteria, and associated information on a condition (e.g., culture, age, impact of gender, prevalence, course of illness, differential diagnosis), the reader is referred to the DSM-IV text.

II.   The Multiaxial Diagnostic System

Using the DSM-IV, five axes are addressed for a patient at any given time. Axis I, II, and III can contain multiple diagnoses. For an individual patient, the information contained on the axes can change over time, with certain exceptions. The five axes are:

A.   **Axis I and II**
       Axis I includes categories of clinical disorders except for personality disorders and mental retardation, which are listed on Axis II (Table 6-1). Table 6-1 lists some of the more common Axis

Address for correspondence: Dr. Jacob Holzer, Spaudling Hospital, 125 Nashua St., Boston, MA 02114, email: jholzer@partners.org.

I and II diagnoses along with their corresponding numerical codes; some categories include subgroupings within a diagnosis. An 'x' indicates that a specific code number is needed. Specifiers indicate the severity of the condition, or if a condition is in full or partial remission. A *principal* diagnosis indicates which category is considered as the primary reason for evaluation or treatment, whereas a *provisional* diagnosis is given when the diagnosis is being considered, but has not yet been confirmed. A *not otherwise specified* (NOS) category may be used when atypical presentations are manifest or when there is uncertainty about the etiology of the presentation.

B.   **Axis III**

Axis III presents general medical conditions, as listed in the ICD, which may have bearing on a patient's psychiatric condition (Table 6-2).

C.   **Axis IV**

Axis IV describes psychosocial and environmental problems experienced by the patient that may have a bearing on the psychiatric condition. Several problems may be listed (Table 6-3).

D.   **Axis V**

Axis V, the Global Assessment of Functioning (GAF) Scale, assigns a numerical rank of functioning, which takes into account psychological, social, and occupational performance, but does not include dysfunction due to physical or environmental limitations. It is based on a 100-point scale, and it assesses the level of functioning at different times, such as at the present time or in the past year (Table 6-4).

Table 6-1. DSM-IV Axis I and II Disorders

DISORDERS DIAGNOSED IN INFANCY, CHILDHOOD, OR ADOLESCENCE

Mental Retardation (*coded on Axis II*)

317	Mild mental retardation
318.0	Moderate mental retardation
318.1	Severe mental retardation

Learning Disorders

315.00	Reading disorder
315.1	Mathematics disorder
315.2	Disorder of written expression
315.9	Learning disorder NOS

Communication Disorders

315.31	Expressive language disorder
315.32	Mixed receptive-expressive language disorder

Pervasive Developmental Disorders

299.00	Autistic disorder
299.80	Asperger's disorder
299.80	Pervasive developmental disorder NOS

Attention-Deficit and Disruptive Behavior Disorders

314.xx	Attention-deficit/hyperactivity disorder
.01	Combined type
.00	Predominantly inattentive type
.01	Predominantly hyperactive-impulsive type
312.xx	Conduct disorder
.81	Childhood-onset type
.82	Adolescent-onset type
313.81	Oppositional defiant disorder

Feeding and Eating Disorders of Infancy or Early Childhood

307.52	Pica

Tic Disorders

307.23	Tourette's disorder
307.22	Chronic motor or vocal tic disorder
307.20	Tic disorder NOS

Elimination Disorders

787.6	Encopresis with constipation/overflow incontinence
307.7	Encopresis without constipation/overflow incontinence
307.6	Enuresis (not due to a general medical condition)

(continued)

Table 6-1. DSM-IV Axis I and II Disorders (continued)

Other Disorders of Infancy, Childhood, or Adolescence

313.23   Selective mutism
307.3   Stereotypic movement disorder
313.9   Disorder of infancy, childhood, or adolescence NOS

DELIRIUM, DEMENTIA, AND AMNESTIC AND OTHER COGNITIVE DISORDERS

Delirium (*may need to code on Axis III*)

293.0   Delirium due to .....[Indicate the medical condition]
780.09   Delirium NOS

Dementia (*may need to code on Axis III*)

290.xx   Dementia of the Alzheimer's type, early onset
.10   Uncomplicated
.11   With delirium
.12   With delusions
.13   With depression
290.xx   Dementia of the Alzheimer's type, late onset
.0   Uncomplicated
.3   With delirium
.20   With delusions
.21   With depression
290.xx   Vascular Dementia
.40   Uncomplicated
.41   With delirium
.42   With delusions
.43   With depression
         Dementia due to:
294.1   HIV disease
294.1   Head trauma
294.1   Parkinson's disease
294.1   Huntington's disease
294.10   Pick's disease
294.1   Dementia due to… [*indicate the medical condition*]
294.8   Dementia NOS

Amnestic Disorders

294.0   Amnestic disorder due to…[*indicate the medical condition*]
294.8   Amnestic disorder NOS

Other Cognitive Disorders

294.9   Cognitive disorder NOS

Table 6-1. DSM-IV Axis I and II Disorders (continued)

MENTAL DISORDERS DUE TO A GENERAL MEDICAL CONDITION NOT ELSEWHERE CLASSIFIED

293.89	Catatonic disorder due to…[*indicate the medical condition*]
310.1	Personality change due to…[*indicate the medical condition*]
293.9	Mental disorder NOS due to…[*indicate the medical condition*]

SUBSTANCE-RELATED DISORDERS (*The reader is referred to the DSM-IV for specifiers regarding intoxication, withdrawal, and dependence*)

Alcohol-Related Disorders

303.90	Alcohol dependence
305.00	Alcohol abuse
303.00	Alcohol intoxication
291.81	Alcohol withdrawal
291.0	Alcohol intoxication delirium
291.0	Alcohol withdrawal delirium
291.2	Alcohol-induced persisting dementia
291.1	Alcohol-induced persisting amnestic disorder
291.x	Alcohol-induced psychotic disorder
.5	With delusions
.3	With hallucinations
291.9	Alcohol-related disorder NOS

Amphetamine-Related Disorders

304.40	Amphetamine dependence
305.70	Amphetamine abuse
282.89	Amphetamine intoxication
292.81	Amphetamine intoxication delirium
292.xx	Amphetamine-induced psychotic disorder
.11	With delusions
.12	With hallucinations
292.9	Amphetamine-related disorder NOS

Caffeine-Related Disorders

305.90	Caffeine intoxication
	Caffeine-induced:
292.89	Anxiety disorder
292.89	Sleep disorder

(continued)

Table 6-1. DSM-IV Axis I and II Disorders (continued)

Cannabis-Related Disorders

    304.30 Cannabis dependence

    305.20 Cannabis abuse

    292.89 Cannabis intoxication

    292.81 Cannabis intoxication delirium

Cocaine-Related Disorders

    304.20 Cocaine dependence

    305.60 Cocaine abuse

    292.89 Cocaine intoxication

    292.81 Cocaine intoxication delirium

    292.xx Cocaine-induced psychotic disorder

    .11   With delusions

    .12   With hallucinations

    292.84 Cocaine-induced mood disorder

Hallucinogen-Related Disorders

    304.50 Hallucinogen dependence

    305.30 Hallucinogen abuse

    292.89 Hallucinogen intoxication

    292.89 Hallucinogen persisting perception disorder (flashbacks)

Inhalant-Related Disorders

    304.60 Inhalant dependence

    305.90 Inhalant abuse

    292. 89 Inhalant intoxication

Nicotine-Related Disorders

    305.10 Nicotine dependence

    292.0   Nicotine withdrawal

Opioid-Related Disorders

    304.00 Opioid dependence

    305.50 Opioid abuse

    292.89 Opioid intoxication

    292.0   Opioid withdrawal

Phencyclidine-Related Disorders

    304.60 Phencyclidine dependence

    305.90 Phencyclidine abuse

    292.81 Phencyclidine intoxication delirium

    292.xx Phencyclidine-induced psychotic disorder

    .11   With delusions

    .12   With hallucinations

Table 6-1. DSM-IV Axis I and II Disorders (continued)

Sedative-, Hypnotic-, or Anxiolytic-Related Disorders

304.10	Sedative, hypnotic, or anxiolytic dependence
305.40	Sedative, hypnotic, or anxiolytic abuse
292.0	Sedative, hypnotic, or anxiolytic withdrawal
292.81	Sedative, hypnotic, or anxiolytic withdrawal delirium

Polysubstance-Related Disorder

304.80	Polysubstance dependence

SCHIZOPHRENIA/OTHER PSYCHOTIC DISORDERS

295.xx	Schizophrenia type:
.30	Paranoid
.10	Disorganized
.20	Catatonic
.90	Undifferentiated
295.70	Schizoaffective disorder
297.1	Delusional disorder
293.xx	Psychotic disorder due to…[*indicate medical condition*]
.81	With delusions
.82	With hallucinations
298.9	Psychotic disorder NOS

MOOD DISORDERS

(A fifth digit is used for codes of major depression and bipolar I episodes: 1 = mild, 2 = moderate, 3 = severe without psychosis, 4 = severe with psychosis, 5 = partial remission, 6 = full remission, 0 = unspecified)

Depressive Disorders

296.2x	Major depression, single episode
296.3x	Major depression, recurrent
300.4	Dysthymic disorder
311	Depressive disorder NOS

Bipolar Disorders

296.0x	Bipolar I, single manic episode
296.4x	Bipolar I, most recent episode manic
296.6x	Bipolar I, most recent episode mixed
296.5x	Bipolar I, most recent episode depressed
296.89	Bipolar II disorder
301.13	Cyclothymic disorder
296.80	Bipolar disorder NOS
293.83	Mood disorder due to…[indicate medical condition]

(continued)

Table 6-1. DSM-IV Axis I and II Disorders (continued)

ANXIETY DISORDERS

300.01	Panic disorder without agoraphobia
300.21	Panic disorder with agoraphobia
300.29	Specific phobia (specify type)
300.23	Social phobia
300.3	Obsessive-compulsive disorder
309.81	Post-traumatic stress disorder
300.02	Generalized anxiety disorder
293.84	Anxiety disorder due to…[*indicate medical condition*]
300.00	Anxiety disorder NOS

SOMATOFORM DISORDERS

300.81	Somatization disorder
300.82	Undifferentiated somatoform disorder
300.11	Conversion disorder
307.xx	Pain disorder
.80	With psychological factors
.89	With psychological factors and a medical condition
300.7	Body dysmorphic disorder

DISSOCIATIVE DISORDERS

300.14	Dissociative identity disorder
300.6	Depersonalization disorder

SEXUAL/GENDER IDENTITY DISORDERS

Sexual Dysfunctions

302.71	Hypoactive sexual desire disorder
302.75	Premature ejaculation
302.76	Dyspareunia
306.51	Vaginismus
607.84	Male erectile dysfunction due to…[*indicate medical condition*]
625.0	Female dyspareunia due to…[*indicate medical condition*]
608.89	Male dyspareunia due to…[*indicate medical condition*]

Paraphilias

302.4	Exhibitionism
302.81	Fetishism
302.2	Pedophilia
302.83	Sexual masochism
302.84	Sexual sadism

Table 6-1. DSM-IV Axis I and II Disorders (continued)

302.9   Paraphilia NOS

Gender Identity Disorders

Gender identity disorder:

302.6   In children

302.85   In adolescents or adults

302.9   Sexual disorder NOS

EATING DISORDERS

307.1   Anorexia nervosa

307.51   Bulimia nervosa

307.50   Eating disorder NOS

SLEEP DISORDERS

Primary Sleep Disorders

307.42   Primary insomnia

347   Narcolepsy

307.47   Dyssomnia NOS

307.46   Sleepwalking disorder

307.47   Parasomnia NOS

Sleep Disorders Related to Another Mental Disorder

307.42   Insomnia related to...[*indicate disorder*]

307.44   Hypersomnia related to...[*indicate disorder*]

Other Sleep Disorders

Sleep disorders due to...[*indicate medial condition*]

780.52   Insomnia type

780.54   Hypersomnia type

780.59   Parasomnia type

IMPULSE-CONTROL DISORDERS

312.34   Intermittent explosive disorder

312.31   Pathological gambling

312.39   Trichotillomania

312.30   Impulse-control disorder NOS

ADJUSTMENT DISORDERS

309.0   Adjustment disorder with depressed mood

309.24   Adjustment disorder with anxiety

309.28   Adjustment disorder with mixed anxiety and mood disorder

309.4   Adjustment disorder with mixed disturbance of emotions and conduct

(continued)

Table 6-1. DSM-IV Axis I and II Disorders (continued)

PERSONALITY DISORDERS (*coded on Axis II*)

Cluster A Disorders

301.0	Paranoid personality disorder
301.20	Schizoid personality disorder
301.22	Schizotypal personality disorder

Cluster B Disorders

301.7	Antisocial personality disorder
301.83	Borderline personality disorder
301.50	Histrionic personality disorder
301.81	Narcissistic personality disorder

Cluster C Disorders

301.82	Avoidant personality disorder
301.6	Dependent personality disorder
301.4	Obsessive-compulsive personality disorder

OTHER CONDITIONS THAT MAY BE A FOCUS OF CLINICAL ATTENTION

Psychological Factors Affecting Medical Condition

316	[*specify psychological factor*] affecting [*specify medical condition*]

Medication-Induced Movement Disorders

Neuroleptic-induced:

332.1	Parkinsonism
333.7	Acute dystonia
333.99	Acute akathisia
333.82	Tardive dyskinesia
333.92	Neuroleptic malignant syndrome

Relational Problems

V61.20	Parent-child relational problem
V62.81	Relational problem NOS

Problems Related to Abuse or Neglect

V61.21	Physical abuse of child
V61.21	Sexual abuse of child
V61.21	Neglect of child

Additional Codes That May Be a Focus of Clinical Attention

V15.81	Noncompliance with treatment
V65.2	Malingering
V62.89	Borderline intellectual functioning [*code on Axis II*]
780.9	Age-related cognitive decline
V62.82	Bereavement

Table 6-2. DSM-IV Codes on Axis III: General Medical Conditions (with ICD-9-CM Codes)

- Infectious and Parasitic Diseases (001-139)
- Neoplasms (140-239)
- Endocrine, Nutritional, and Metabolic Diseases and Immunity Disorders (240-279)
- Diseases of Blood and Blood-Forming Organs (280-289)
- Diseases of the Nervous System and Sense Organs (320-389)
- Diseases of the Circulatory System (390-459)
- Disease of the Respiratory System (460-519)
- Diseases of the Digestive System (520-579)
- Diseases of the Genitourinary System (580-629)
- Complications of Pregnancy, Childbirth, and the Puerperium (630-676)
- Diseases of the Skin and Subcutaneous Tissue (680-709)
- Diseases of the Musculoskeletal System and Connective Tissue (710-739)
- Congenital Abnormalities (740-759)
- Certain Conditions Originating in the Perinatal Period (760-779)
- Symptoms, Signs, and Ill-Defined Conditions (780-799)
- Injury and Poisoning (800-999)

Table 6-3. DSM-IV Categories on Axis IV: Psychosocial and Environmental Problems

- Problems with primary support group
- Problems related to the social environment
- Educational problems
- Occupational problems
- Housing problems
- Economic problems
- Problems with access to health care services
- Problems related to interaction with the legal system/crime
- Other psychosocial and environmental problems

Table 6-4. DSM-IV Axis V Categories: Global Assessment of Functioning (GAF)

Score	Description
91-100	Superior functioning in wide range of activities, no symptoms
81-90	Absent/minimal symptoms, good functioning in all areas, no more than everyday problems
71-80	If symptoms are present, they are transient/expectable reactions, no more than slight impairment in functioning (social, occupational, or school)
61-70	Mild symptoms or some difficulty in functioning, has meaningful relationships
51-60	Moderate symptoms or moderate difficulty in functioning
41-50	Serious symptoms or serious impairment in functioning
31-40	Some impaired reality testing/communication, or major impairment in several areas including work, school, judgment, or thinking
21-30	Behavior influenced by delusions/hallucinations; serious impairment in communication/judgment; inability to function in almost all areas
11-20	Some danger of hurting self/others; occasionally unable to maintain minimum personal hygiene; gross impaired communication
1-10	Persistent danger of severely hurting self/others; or persistently unable to maintain minimum personal hygiene; or serious suicidality with clear expectations of death
0	Inadequate information

Suggested Readings

American Psychiatric Association (APA): *Diagnostic and Statistical Manual of Mental Disorders*, 4th Edition. Washington, DC: American Psyciatric Association, 1994.

First MG, Frances A, Pincus HA: *DSM-IV Handbook of Differential Diagnosis*. Washington, DC: American Psyciatric Press, 1995.

Kearns ME: The DSM-IV: A multiaxial system for psychiatric diagnosis. In Stern TA, Herman JB (eds): *Psychiatry Update and Board Preparation*, 2nd Edition. New York: McGraw-Hill, 2004:23–26.

Chapter 7

An Approach to Child and Adolescent Disorders: Disorders of Affect, Behavior, and Cognition

NICOLE DANFORTH, MD
ANNAH N. ABRAMS, MD

I.   Pervasive Developmental Disorders

Pervasive developmental disorders (PDD) is a category of neuropsychological disorders that includes autistic disorder, Asperger's disorder, Rett's disorder, childhood disintegrative disorder, and PDD-not otherwise specified (a category of atypical or less severe developmental disorders). These disorders are characterized by severe and pervasive delays and by impairment across several domains (e.g., communication, socialization, and cognition).

A.   **Autistic Disorder**
  1.   **Definition. Children with autism have abnormal development in social interactions, communication skills, and patterns of behavior** (with restrictive, repetitive, and stereotyped behavior and interests). **Common symptoms include abnormal gaze and expression in social situations, a relative lack of peer relationships and emotional reciprocity, and impaired communication** (as seen with their verbal and social play).
  2.   **Prevalence.** The estimated prevalence is **2–6 per 1000** in the general population. Approximately **75%** of children with autism have mental retardation. The male:female ratio is 4 to 5:1.
  3.   **Etiology.** Autism is considered to be **a genetic condition.** Biological factors play a role as well, although there is no specific marker associated with autism. If a sibling is affected with autism, there is a 4.5% chance that another child in the same family will also be affected. There is no evidence that psychosocial factors or parenting styles cause autistic disorder.

B.   **Asperger's Disorder**
  1.   **Definition.** This disorder is **characterized by restricted, repetitive, and stereotyped behavior, interests, and activities, and**

Address for correspondence: Dr. Nicole Danforth, Massachusetts General Hospital, Fruit Street, WACC 725, Boston, MA 02114, email: NDanforth @Partners.org.

by abnormalities in social interactions. In contrast to autism, however, children with Asperger's disorder have no significant delay in language or cognitive development and do not suffer from mental retardation.

2. **Prevalence.** The male:female ratio is 5:1. The prevalence is not known.

C. **Rett's Disorder**

1. **Definition.** Children with Rett's disorder experience normal pre- and perinatal development and normal psychomotor development through their first six months of life. **Beginning between the ages of 5 and 48 months, several deficits (including decelerated head growth, losses of previously acquired purposeful hand movements and social interactions, onset of poor coordination and gait, and impaired language skills) develop.**

   a. These children often develop **characteristic hand wringing or hand washing-like movements.**

   b. Rett's disorder is associated with **profound to severe mental retardation.**

   c. **Seizures and breathing difficulties** are also common, and there is an increased risk of sudden death.

2. **Prevalence.** The prevalence of Rett's disorder is thought to be **1 in 10,000 to 15,000,** and it has been reported exclusively in females.

3. **Etiology.** Rett's disorder is an **X-linked dominant disorder,** and one-third of patients have a **mutation of a specific gene (MeCP2).**

D. **Childhood Disintegrative Disorder**

1. **Definition.** Children develop normally until age two and thereafter have progressive loss of skills across a wide range of areas (including language, behavior, bowel and bladder control, motor skills, and play). This disorder is usually associated with severe mental retardation.

2. **The prevalence** is relatively rare.

3. **Etiology.** The etiology is unknown. The majority of children with this disorder eventually stabilize, and occasionally they may recover some previously attained skills.

E. **Pervasive Developmental Disorder-Not Otherwise Specified (PDD-NOS)**

1. **Definition.** This diagnostic category includes a wide range of developmental patterns. Children with PDD-NOS demonstrate **sig-**

nificant impairment in reciprocal social interactions. These deficits are associated with poor verbal or nonverbal communication skills, and/or stereotyped interests or behaviors that interfere with normal development, but these children do not meet criteria of the other disorders in this category.

2. **Evaluation**
   a. **The diagnostic evaluation** of a child with a suspected developmental disorder includes a developmental and medical history as well as a physical examination (including testing of vision and hearing) and a psychiatric evaluation. In addition, speech, language, and sensory integration must be evaluated, the child should be assessed by occupational therapy, and neuropsychological testing should be performed.
   b. **Laboratory testing** may reveal conditions other than PDD. An EEG may be advised to rule out a seizure disorder; neuroimaging may be appropriate to rule out an underlying disorder.
   c. **The differential diagnosis** of a PDD includes:
      i. **Other developmental disorders,** such as a learning or communication disorder (these children have preserved social skills and do not have stereotypic or repetitive movements);
      ii. **Deafness** (these children often adapt to communicate effectively);
      iii. **Mental retardation** not associated with PDD (which is not marked by a lack of interest in communication);
      iv. **Schizophrenia** (children who exhibit psychotic and bizarre symptoms); and
      v. **Social anxiety disorder** (these children experience less pervasive and less severe communication difficulties); and
      vi. **Seizures or degenerative neurological disorders.**

3. **Treatment**
   a. The treatment of the pervasive developmental disorders is collaborative and multimodal. Treatment should include **behavioral, occupational, and speech and language therapy.** These children require individualized school programs to ensure appropriate placement and expectations. Early identification and intervention result in improved outcomes for most children with PDDs.
   b. Recognition and treatment of comorbid psychiatric disorders is important.
   c. Presently, no medications effectively treat PDD; rather, medications are used to treat associated symptoms (such as aggression, anxiety, ritualized behaviors, and inattention).

II.   Disruptive Behavior Disorders

A.   **Attention-Deficit/Hyperactivity Disorder**

1.   **Definition.** Attention-deficit/hyperactivity disorder (ADHD) **often presents as a classic triad of inattention, hyperactivity, and impulsivity.** However, some children may be primarily hyperactive and others primarily inattentive. The diagnosis is specified as combined type, predominantly inattentive type, or predominantly hyperactive-impulsive type. Symptoms must be present for 6 months prior to the age of 7 and include:

a.   At least six signs of inattention (failure to pay close attention to details, difficulty sustaining attention in tasks or activities, failure to listen when spoken to directly, difficulty organizing tasks, avoidance of activities that require mental effort, losing things necessary for tasks or activities, distractibility, and forgetfulness in daily activities); and

b.   Six signs of hyperactivity-impulsivity (fidgeting with the hands or feet, inability to sit still, running around when it is not appropriate, difficulty engaging in leisure activities quietly, feeling "on the go" or "driven by a motor," talking excessively [blurting out answers before questions are completed and having trouble waiting one's turn], and interrupting others).

c.   The behavior must be more frequent and severe than that observed in other children of the same developmental level.

d.   Impairment must cross situations and must be noted in at least two settings (e.g., school and home).

e.   The symptoms are not exclusively present when another disorder, such as depression, is present.

2.   **Prevalence.** The prevalence of ADHD is between 3 and 5% in school-aged children; it is the most common psychiatric disorder in children.

3.   **Etiology.** Evidence suggests that there is a significant genetic contribution. Siblings of children with ADHD have 2–3 times the risk of having the disorder as siblings of children without ADHD.

4.   **Treatment.** Medication is the first-line treatment of ADHD.

a.   There is a 70–80% response rate to psychostimulants. The most widely used stimulants include **methylphenidate** (including long-acting preparations), **dextroamphetamine,** and **amphetamine sulfate.**

b.   **Atomoxetine** is a nonstimulant medication that is FDA-approved to treat ADHD.

c.   **Alpha-adrenergic medications** (such as clonidine and guanfacine) may be used to treat the hyperactive-impulsive symptoms of ADHD, especially if stimulants are only partially effective, or if aggression or a tic disorder is present.

d. **Antidepressants,** including tricyclic antidepressants (TCAs) and buproprion, may also be used for the treatment of ADHD. Other treatment modalities such as behavior modification may be helpful in improving academic performance or with problematic behaviors not responsive to medications.

e. **Cognitive-behavioral therapy** is generally not effective in reducing ADHD symptoms.

B. **Conduct Disorder**
1. **Definition. A child with conduct disorder (CD) repeatedly violates the personal rights of others and/or societal norms and rules.** There are two subtypes of CD: childhood-onset (having one symptom present prior to the age of 10) and adolescent-onset. Behaviors, which must be present for at least 1 year, include:
   a. Aggression toward people and animals (including threats, bullying, or physical cruelty)
   b. Destruction of property (including deliberate fire-setting)
   c. Deceitfulness or theft
   d. Serious violations of rules (e.g., school truancy or disregard of parental prohibitions)
2. **Prevalence**
   a. The prevalence of CD is estimated to be **between 1.5 and 3.4%.** It is more commonly diagnosed in boys by a ratio of 3 to 5:1. Boys have an earlier age of onset: the age of onset is 10–12 for boys and 16 for girls.
   b. Disorders commonly associated with CD include ADHD (ADHD may be present in up to 60% of children with CD); mood disorders (rates of depressive disorders, suicidal ideation, suicide attempts, and completed suicide are higher in children and adolescents with CD); and substance use disorders.
3. **Etiology.** There is no known cause of CD.
4. **Differential diagnosis.** CD is a descriptive diagnosis. The differential diagnosis for CD includes learning disorders, ADHD, mild mental retardation, mood disorders (including depression and mania), schizophrenia, substance use disorders, and posttraumatic stress disorder (PTSD). Medical illnesses, e.g., head trauma or seizure disorder, must also be ruled out.
5. **Treatment**
   a. The most effective treatments for CD are **parent management training and cognitive problem-solving skills**

training. There are no specific medications for the treatment of this disorder.

b. For treatment of severe aggression, agents (such as alpha-agonists, propranolol, mood stabilizers, or antipsychotics) may be used.

III. Specific Developmental Disorders

A. **Disorders of Learning**

Listed under Axis II disorders, learning disorders (LD) are **associated with below expected abilities in academic achievement in a particular domain of functioning,** such as reading, mathematics, and/or writing. **A child with a suspected learning disorder usually comes to the attention of teachers during grade school, when a discrepancy appears between a child's skill level and intelligence.** A diagnosis of a LD is based on the child's chronological age, measured intelligence, and age-appropriate education. The difference between achievement and IQ must be at least two standard deviations below the mean. **Specific disorders include reading disorder (previously known as dyslexia), mathematics disorder, and disorder of written expression.** These disorders are often comorbid.

1. **Prevalence.** The prevalence of LD ranges from 2 to 10%; approximately 5% of students in public schools in the U.S. have a diagnosis of a LD.

    a. The prevalence of reading disorder is 4% of school-aged children, with a **male:female ratio of 4:1.**

    b. The prevalence of mathematics disorder is 1% and has no gender differences.

    c. The prevalence of disorder of written expression is not known.

2. **Etiology.** The etiology of LD is not clearly known, but there is **likely a genetic component.** Children of parents with reading disabilities are eight times more likely than the general public to have a reading problem. Studies of children with reading disorders have shown cortical anomalies in the left hemisphere, presumed to be deficits of neuronal migration, which occur in early gestation. The role of environmental toxins is not known.

3. **Evaluation.** Neurocognitive testing is necessary to make the diagnosis of an LD. A psychiatric evaluation is also helpful, as there is a high rate of comorbidity with other disorders (including ADHD, anxiety disorders, intermittent explosive disorder, OCD, and tic disorders).

4. **Treatment.** Treatment for LD **includes appropriate school accommodation and tutoring,** ongoing assessments, and management of social skills and possible emotional difficulties that

may be manifest as a mood disorder or as externalized behavioral problems.

B.   **Disorders of Speech and Language (Communication Disorders)**
Communication disorders are **defined as delays in specific speech or language abilities that compromise a child's academic or adaptive level of functioning.** A range of degree of impairment exists, from difficulties in expressive language (**expressive language disorder**), to a disorder of mixed receptive-expressive language, to difficulties with producing speech (**phonological disorder**) and **stuttering.** These disorders often present during or after first grade.

Assessment of communication disorders includes a developmental history, an audiological examination, and a referral to a speech and language specialist. A child's ability to sustain auditory attention, discriminate, and recall should be evaluated. Use of nonverbal measures of intelligence may be helpful.

The differential diagnosis of a communication disorder includes PDD, selective mutism, mental retardation, and aphasia.

Speech therapy for these disorders is the mainstay of treatment. If anxiety is contributing to a child's difficulty, the use of behavioral modification may be helpful.

1. **Expressive language disorder.** A child with expressive language disorder will perform below expectations on standardized tests of expressive language, given the child's intellectual capacity and development. The disorder may include a limited amount of speech or limited vocabulary, errors in tense, and immature sentence construction. A child may have a developmental type or acquired type (which occurs as a consequence of another illness after a period of normal development). Normal speech and language development requires a synthesis of motor, sensory, and cognitive skills, and any deficit along this continuum may contribute to the development of a communication problem. The etiology of such deficits is often unknown.
    a. **Prevalence.** The prevalence of the developmental type is 3–5%; the acquired type is less common. Communication problems are more common in males and in children with mental retardation (MR), hearing impairment, and psychiatric disorders.

2. **Mixed receptive-expressive language disorder.** This disorder involves deficits in understanding or comprehension and expressing or articulating. It has a prevalence of 3% in school-aged children.
    a. **Phonological disorder.** This is marked by difficulties or failure to use age-appropriate sounds in speech production.

The prevalence of phonological disorder is not known, but it is more common in boys than girls.

3. **Stuttering.** Stuttering is an impairment of normal speech fluency. Sound repetitions, involuntary pauses, prolongations, word repetitions, and word blocking characterize it.

   a. Stress and anxiety may worsen symptoms.

   b. Stuttering often does not occur when a child is singing, reading aloud, talking in groups, or talking to a pet.

   c. The disorder has its onset between the ages of 2 and 7 years, and almost all cases present by the age of 10.

   d. The prevalence of stuttering is approximately 2–4% of children and 1% of adolescents, with males more affected by 3 to 4:1.

   e. **There is a familial pattern of stuttering,** with 20–40% of first-degree relatives of people who stutter developing the disorder. There is a higher concordance in monozygotic than in dizygotic twins, suggesting genetic factors.

C. **Disorders of Motor Skills**

1. **Developmental coordination disorder.** A child with this disorder has **coordination difficulties that result in functional impairment** that is not caused by a medical condition. The child may have poor gross and fine motor skills, resulting in clumsiness, poor penmanship, or difficulty running or throwing a ball. The prevalence is 6% of school-aged children.

   a. **Evaluation.** Specific screening tests, such as the Test of Motor Impairment, are available. The child should have a thorough physical examination to rule out other possible causes of poor coordination, such as cerebral palsy or muscular dystrophy.

   b. **Treatment.** Children with this disorder will benefit from occupational therapy and from any relevant school accommodations.

IV. Mental Retardation

Mental retardation (MR) is diagnosed when a child has low general intelligence (IQ of 70 or below) as well as concurrent impairment in adaptive functioning. These deficits vary and occur in at least two of the following areas: communication, self-care, home living, and social/interpersonal skills.

A. **Categories**
Four categories of MR are described:
1. **Mild MR (IQ ranges from 50–70)** accounts for 85% of the MR population; these children are capable of communication skills and they achieve about a 6th grade academic level by adulthood.
2. **Moderate MR (IQ range of 35–40 to 50–55)** comprises 10% of the MR population; these children have limited social skills and can be trained to perform self-care. They generally will achieve a 2nd grade academic level and moderate supervision is likely to be required (such as a group home.)
3. **Severe MR (IQ range of 20–25 to 35–40)** accounts for 4% of the MR population; these children have impaired motor development and little or no speech. Close supervision is required.
4. **Profound MR (IQ below 20–25)** represents 1% of the MR population. Children with this degree of MR have poor cognitive and social abilities, and speech is often absent. Constant supervision is needed.

B. **Prevalence**
The prevalence of MR in the U.S. is 2–3%, depending on whether IQ or adaptive functioning criteria are used. MR is more commonly diagnosed in males at a ratio of 1.5:1.

C. **Etiology**
Mental retardation is the result of a combination of biological and psychosocial factors. The cause is idiopathic in up to 40% of cases. The most common causes of MR include Down's syndrome (the most common genetic cause), Fragile X syndrome (the most common inherited form), and fetal alcohol syndrome. The more severe forms of MR are more likely to be caused by a biological syndrome (e.g., a genetic disorder, prenatal illnesses [including exposure to toxins or infection, or due to perinatal trauma], or childhood diseases [such as a brain tumor or meningitis]). Psychiatric disorders are present in 30–70% of children with mental retardation.

D. **Evaluation**
1. For a child with suspected mental retardation, a standardized test for intelligence is indicated.
2. In addition, there should be an objective measure of the child's level of adaptive functioning.
3. A medical evaluation, including a physical examination, developmental history, and chromosomal and metabolic studies, will help define any possible treatable causes of MR.

    4.   If there are symptoms of a comorbid psychiatric condition (such as aggression, psychosis, irritability, or sadness) a full psychiatric evaluation is warranted.

    5.   The differential diagnosis of MR includes PDDs, learning disorders, communication disorders, and impairment of auditory or visual function.

E.   **Treatment**

The treatment of mental retardation occurs across several domains.

    1.   **Coordinated psychiatric and medical care, appropriate educational supports, and behavioral therapy** all may be indicated.

    2.   Families need **support** such as parental guidance and advocacy training.

    3.   A child with mild MR may benefit from supportive psychotherapy to help facilitate self-esteem and identify strengths.

    4.   **Medications** may be indicated for the treatment of a co-existing psychiatric illness.

        a.   Children with MR tend to be highly sensitive to psychoactive medications, and lower doses often produce effective results.

Suggested Readings

American Psychiatric Association: *Diagnostic and Statistical Manual of Mental Disorders,* 4th edition, text revision. Washington, DC: American Psychiatric Association, 2000.

Burke JD, Loeber R, Birnaher B: Oppositional defiant disorder and conduct disorder: a review of the past 10 years, part II. *J Am Acad Child Adolesc Psychiatry* 2002;41: 1275–1293.

Frazier JA: The person with mental retardation. In Nicoli AM (ed): *The New Harvard Guide to Psychiatry.* Cambridge, MA: Harvard University Press, 1999:660–671.

Jellinek M, Patel BP, Froehle MC (eds): *Bright Futures in Practice: Mental Health,* Volume 1. Arlington, VA: National Center for Education in Maternal and Child Health, 2001.

Johnston MV, Mullaney B, Blue ME: Neurobiology of Rett syndrome. *J Child Neurol* 2003;18:688–692.

Tuchman R: Autism. *Neurologic Clinics* 2003;21:915–932.

Wilens T, Spencer T: The stimulants revisited. In Stubbe C (ed): *Child and Adolescent Psychiatric Clinics of North America.* Philadelphia: Saunders, 2000:573–603.

Chapter 8

An Approach to the Diagnosis and Treatment of Mental Disorders in the Context of a General Medical Condition

B.J. BECK, MSN, MD
AMY M. TAYLOR, MD

I.   Introduction

A.   **DSM-IV Definition**
Mental Disorders Due to a General Medical Condition (DTGMC) involve psychiatric symptoms thought to be the direct, physiologic consequence of a nonpsychiatric medical condition. The psychiatric symptoms themselves are severe enough to **warrant recognition and treatment.**

B.   **General Qualifiers**
The mental disorder must:
1. **Be the direct pathophysiologic consequence of the medical condition**
2. **Not be better accounted for by another primary mental disorder**
3. **Not occur solely during the course of delirium** (i.e., a disturbance of consciousness in association with cognitive deficits)
4. **Not meet criteria for dementia** (i.e., a syndrome with memory impairment and aphasia, apraxia, agnosia, or disturbances of executive function)
5. **Not be substance-induced**

II.   Psychiatric Differential Diagnosis

A.   Primary Mental Disorders
It may be difficult to ascertain whether the mental disorder in question is the direct physiologic consequence of the medical condition, or whether the two merely coexist.
1. **Correlation between the onset or severity of the medical and mental conditions is helpful but inadequate to establish a causal link.**

Address for correspondence: Dr. B.J. Beck, Massachusetts General Hospital, WACC 812, Boston, MA 02114, email: bbeck@partners.org.

    a.   **Psychiatric symptoms may be the first symptoms of a medical condition** (e.g., depression as the first manifestation of pancreatic carcinoma). Alternatively, psychiatric symptoms **may occur late in the course of the medical condition** (e.g., psychosis years after the onset of epilepsy), or **may not resolve simultaneously** with the medical condition (e.g., depression that continues after hypothyroidism is corrected).

    b.   **Psychiatric symptoms may be out of proportion to the severity of the medical condition** (e.g., depression or irritability in patients with early or minimal sensorimotor symptoms of multiple sclerosis).

2.   **Typical features of the primary mental disorder** suggest that conditions may coexist:

    a.   **Recurrent episodes** (in the absence of the medical condition)

    b.   **A positive family history** of the primary mental disorder

3.   **Atypical features of the primary mental disorder support an etiologic relationship to the medical condition:**

    a.   **Age of onset:** e.g., the first onset of panic attacks in a 65-year-old man

    b.   **Course:** e.g., the sudden onset of depression in a patient without a history of depression

    c.   **Associated features:** e.g., cognitive deficits that are out of proportion to a mildly depressed mood

4.   **The scientific literature supports the causal relationship between some medical conditions and the occurrence of certain psychiatric symptoms.** That is, there is a **greater than base-rate occurrence** for a mental syndrome in patients with a particular medical condition, compared with an appropriate control group. Or, a mental syndrome may correlate with expected **deficits or symptoms and be based on the location of brain pathology** or pathophysiology (e.g., disinhibition or decreased executive function with frontal lobe damage).

5.   **When treatment of the general medical condition dissipates the psychiatric symptoms, an etiologic relationship is supported.** However, some mental disorders DTGMC are amenable to, and require, treatment in their own right (e.g., interictal depression); this does not imply that the diagnosis is a primary mental disorder.

B.   **Substance-Induced Disorders**
Prescription and over-the-counter medications, illicit drugs, or alcohol may be used, misused, or abused during the course of a general

medical condition. **A careful history, and possibly the use of urine or blood tests, should alert the clinician to drug use or abuse and be part of every evaluation.** Use, intoxication, or withdrawal can cause mental symptoms that may continue for up to a month after discontinuation of a substance. The therapeutic use of some medications causes psychiatric symptoms (e.g., steroids in a patient with systemic lupus erythematosus) that may mimic the symptoms (e.g., mood lability) of the disease itself.

III. Differential Diagnosis of Mental Disorders Due to a General Medical Condition

The mnemonic **GEN**eral **MED**ical **CONDIT**ions (Figure 8-1) should help the evaluating clinician recall the broad categories of medical conditions that can cause psychiatric syndromes.

A.   **Infectious Diseases**
Infection of the central nervous system (CNS), especially chronic meningitis, is increasingly prevalent as immune suppression is on the rise, either from acquired immunodeficiency syndrome (AIDS) or as a result of immune suppressant therapy for malignancy or for organ transplantation.
1.   **Herpes simplex virus (HSV) has a propensity for the temporal and inferomedial frontal lobes; it is the most commonly encountered focal encephalopathy.** Widely recognized as a

---

GENeral **MED**ical **CONDIT**ions

Germs (infectious diseases)
Epilepsy
Nutritional deficit

Metabolic disorders
Endocrine disorders
Demyelinating disorders

Cerebrovascular disease
Offensive toxins
Neoplasms
Degenerative disorders
Immune disorders
Trauma

Figure 8-1. Categories of General Medical Conditions

cause of loss of smell (anosmia), as well as olfactory or gustatory hallucinations, the limbic distribution of HSV may also result in psychosis, bizarre behavior, or personality change. These
personality changes, along with affective lability and decreased
cognitive function, may persist. Simple or complex partial seizures may also develop.

2. **Human immunodeficiency virus (HIV) infection** is associated with neuropsychiatric symptoms of multiple etiologies,
including direct CNS infection, HIV-related metabolic derangements, endocrinopathies, medication side effects, tumors, and
opportunistic infections. The **presence, severity, and location
of HIV-related CNS pathology does not correlate well with
symptoms.**

    a. Patients may experience depressed mood, dementia, anxi-
ety, and less commonly, mania or psychosis. Psychiatric
symptoms are more likely to be secondary in patients with
low CD4 counts (e.g., <600).

    b. **AIDS dementia complex (ADC) is the most common
CNS complication of HIV infection.** Early cognitive
deficits include impairments in attention, concentration, visuospatial performance, and coordination. Early affective
changes involve apathy, depression, social withdrawal, anxiety, mild disinhibition, and a lack of energy and motivation. In late ADC, patients may experience dementia, psychosis, seizures, agitation, severe disinhibition, and mutism.

3. **Lyme disease is a tick-borne spirochetal infection** most common in parts of Europe and the United States (especially the
Northeast, upper Midwest, and Pacific Coastal states). The
organism (*Borrelia burgdorferi*) may lie dormant for months to
years. **Because of the nonspecific nature of the symptoms
and the unreliable results of serologic tests, the clinician
must have a high level of suspicion for the neuropsychiatric
sequelae of Lyme disease.** Diagnostic delay is associated with
a chronic course, but symptoms may persist even with aggressive antibiotic treatment. **Lyme encephalitis may present with
fatigue, mood lability, irritability, confusion, and sleep disturbance.** A more chronic encephalopathy may develop with a
wide range of disturbances in personality, cognition (e.g., problems with short-term memory, memory retrieval, verbal fluency,
concentration, attention, orientation, and processing speed), behavior (e.g., disorganization, distractibility, catatonia, mutism,
and violence), mood (e.g., depression, mania, lability), thought
processes (e.g., paranoia), and perception (e.g., hallucinations,
depersonalization, hyperacusis, and photophobia).

4. **Neurosyphilis results from CNS invasion by *Treponema pallidum*; it can occur at any stage of infection, although it occurs most commonly in the tertiary stage. General paresis, a form of neurosyphilis that develops in less than 10% of untreated syphilitics, is on the rise among individuals with AIDS.** Features of general paresis can mimic nearly every psychiatric or neurological disorder. With diffuse (but particularly frontal lobe) involvement, early symptoms include personality change, irritability, poor judgment and insight, difficulty with calculations and recent memory, apathy, and decreased personal grooming. **If left untreated, mood lability, delusions of grandeur, hallucinations, disorientation, and dementia may follow, along with the classical neurological signs of tremor, dysarthria, hyperreflexia, hypotonia, ataxia, and Argyll Robertson pupils (i.e., small, irregular, unequal pupils that accommodate, but do not react to light).** Cerebrospinal fluid with elevated protein and lymphocyte count, and a positive Veneral Disease Research Laboratory (VDRL) test, confirms the diagnosis.

5. **Chronic meningitis is a potentially treatable condition that presents with minimal and subtle physical signs and symptoms (e.g., low-grade fever, headache) which, especially in the immunocompromised patient, may be overlooked or attributed to an underlying condition (e.g., AIDS).** Likewise, the common psychiatric concomitants (e.g., confusion, cognitive dysfunction, memory impairment, and behavioral problems) are nonspecific. The most common cause of chronic meningitis is *Mycobacterium tuberculosis*; common fungal agents are *Cryptococcus* and *Coccidioides.*

B. **Epilepsy**
Epilepsy is a common (1% lifetime prevalence) neurologic disorder characterized by episodic, disorganized firing of electrical impulses in the cortex of the brain. The location of these impulses dictates the seizure phenomena, which may include altered consciousness, as well as motor, cognitive, behavioral, affective, perceptual, and/or memory disturbances. **The diagnosis of seizures remains a clinical diagnosis that may be supported, but not ruled out, by EEG.**

1. **Complex partial seizures,** often of temporal lobe or other limbic origin, are of particular interest to the psychiatrist. It is estimated that **60% of the roughly 2 million epileptics in the United States have nonconvulsive seizures,** which are most commonly partial seizures. It is essential for the psychiatrist to

maintain a high level of suspicion for epilepsy since **40% of partial seizures do not exhibit focal findings on the EEG.**

a. **Depression occurs in slightly more than half of patients with epilepsy** compared to 30% of matched (medical and neurologic outpatient) controls. The incidence is thought to be even higher in patients with partial complex seizures and left hemispheric foci, which suggests that depression may be caused by seizure-induced limbic dysfunction. The **suicide rate in patients with epilepsy is five times that of the general population; in patients with temporal lobe epilepsy, the risk may be 25 times that of the general population.** Interictal mood symptoms should be treated, even when they are most likely caused by the seizure disorder. Since it may be difficult to confirm a diagnosis of partial seizures, a trial of an appropriate antiepileptic medication should be initiated in the setting of psychiatric symptoms resistant to treatment.

b. **Anxiety** symptoms are also more closely associated with partial seizures than other types of seizures. **It may be particularly difficult to differentiate partial seizures from panic attacks.** They are similar in that both may occur without warning with hyperarousal, intense fear, perceptual distortion, and dissociative symptoms. Both may be responsive to benzodiazepines. However, they are different in that loss of consciousness, olfactory or gustatory hallucinations, and automatic behavior (e.g., chewing or lip-smacking), are common with complex partial seizures but not panic attacks. Postevent phenomena also help to differentiate seizures from panic attacks: decreased awareness frequently follows a seizure, while there is usually no confusion following a panic attack; there is often incomplete memory of a seizure, while memory of panic experience leads to the "fear-of-fear" and to avoidance associated with panic disorder.

c. **Psychosis** is also more prevalent in patients with complex partial seizures. **The risk of psychosis in patients with epilepsy may be as much as 6–12 times that of the general public.** Besides the psychotic symptoms experienced as auras or as postictal delirium, **there are also brief, episodic, as well as chronic, psychoses that are thought to result from subictal temporal lobe dysrhythmias.** The most common symptoms are hallucinations, paranoia, and thought disorders. A notable difference in the psychosis of seizures is that the affect of the person with epilepsy is generally intact, and the affect of the person with schizophrenia is comparatively flat.

d. **Violence is rarely associated with an ictal event.**

C. **Nutritional Deficits**
   1. **Niacin (nicotinic acid) deficiency, and deficiency of its precursor, tryptophan, lead to pellagra,** which when left untreated leads to a chronic wasting, diarrheal, neurologic (with encephalopathy and peripheral neuropathy) and dermatologic (with sun-exposed skin rash, angular stomatitis, and glossitis) syndrome. **The early symptoms (insomnia, fatigue, irritability, anxiety, and depressed mood) are nonspecific and may easily be mistaken for depression.** Though rare in developed nations, pellagra still occurs in alcoholics.
   2. **Thiamine (vitamin B$_1$) deficiency occurs in two forms: beriberi, in areas of poverty or famine, and Wernicke-Korsakoff syndrome in alcoholism.** There are cardiovascular, neuropathic, and cerebral signs and symptoms that generally occur in combination; however, they can present as isolated forms. The syndrome **may be precipitated by the administration of glucose to an asymptomatic, thiamine-deficient patient. Early symptoms may include impaired concentration, apathy, mild agitation, and depressed mood. Confusion, amnesia, and confabulation are late signs** of severe, prolonged deficit.
   3. **Cobalamin (vitamin B$_{12}$) deficiency,** from lack of absorption (e.g., from absence of intrinsic factor in pernicious anemia or after gastric surgery) or a vegetarian diet, **leads to megaloblastic macrocytic anemia and neurodegenerative changes in the peripheral and central nervous systems. Neuropsychiatric symptoms, including apathy, irritability, depression, and mood lability, may precede hematologic findings.** Less common, and indicative of more severe disease, is **megaloblastic madness, a delirium with prominent hallucinations, paranoia, and intellectual decline.**

D. **Metabolic Encephalopathy**
   Metabolic encephalopathy should be considered whenever sudden or abrupt changes in mentation, orientation, behavior, or level of consciousness occur. Although the waxing and waning presentation of delirium may eventually become evident, early memory impairment, passivity, withdrawal, or anxiety and agitation may be wrongly attributed to a primary psychiatric disorder.
   1. **Hepatic encephalopathy** may result from acute, subacute, or chronic hepatocellular failure, with a **range of neuropsychi-**

atric symptoms (from mild personality change to coma), and many of the symptoms may precede the more classical neurological or physical findings (e.g., asterixis or icterus, respectively). **The earliest signs are mild intellectual difficulties, depressed or labile mood, irritability, sleep-wake reversal, and a decrease in personal grooming.** Later stages include inappropriate behavior, outbursts of rage, and progressive deterioration in consciousness and speech. The final stage is coma.

2. **Renal insufficiency, acute or chronic, is associated with neuropsychiatric symptoms.** Acute renal failure is most notable for delirium, often with bizarre visual hallucinations. **Chronic renal insufficiency is associated with a wide range of symptoms, from mild difficulties in concentration, problem-solving, or calculation, to more severe cognitive impairment and lethargy. Depression,** common both in patients with renal insufficiency and in patients undergoing dialysis, is thought to be associated with endocrine dysfunction (e.g., hyperparathyroidism). Finally, uremia may cause seizures.

3. **Hypoglycemic encephalopathy, whether from excess endogenous or exogenous insulin, can present with confusion, disorientation, hallucinations, or bizarre behavior.** Often, but not always, these symptoms are preceded by restlessness or by apprehension. **Physical signs and symptoms of hypoglycemia include nausea, hunger, diaphoresis, and tachycardia.** Left untreated, stupor and coma follow. **Repeated hypoglycemic episodes may cause permanent amnesia from hippocampal involvement.**

4. **Diabetic ketoacidosis can also present with nonspecific symptoms of fatigue and lethargy, before the "three Ps" (polyphagia, polydipsia, and polyuria), headache, nausea, and vomiting appear.** In a poorly controlled elderly diabetic patient, osmotic fluid shifts can cause a slowly resolving delirium that primarily affects cognitive function.

5. **Acute intermittent porphyria (AIP) is a rare autosomal dominant enzyme deficiency** that interferes with heme biosynthesis and causes the accumulation of porphyrins. It presents with **a classic triad of acute, colicky abdominal pain, motor polyneuropathy, and psychosis.** However, **AIP may present with only psychiatric symptoms** (e.g., insomnia, anxiety, mood lability, depression, and psychosis).

E. **Endocrine Disorders**
Endocrine disorders are associated with psychiatric symptoms, **most commonly depression and anxiety.** In years past, when endo-

crinopathies were diagnosed later in their course, delirium and dementia were more common.

1. **Thyroid dysfunction**
    a. **Hypothyroidism, which is at least four times more prevalent in women than in men, has an insidious onset of nonspecific symptoms (e.g., fatigue, lethargy, weight gain, decreased appetite, depressed mood, cold intolerance, and slowed mental and motor activity).** Later in the course, physical signs include dry skin, thin and dry hair, constipation, stiffness, a coarse voice, facial puffiness, carpal tunnel symptoms, loss of the outer third of the eyebrows, loss of hearing, and a delayed relaxation phase of deep tendon reflexes. Early symptoms may be attributed to aging, depression, dementia, or Parkinson's disease. **Hallucinations and paranoia,** the manifestations of the so-called **"myxedema madness," are late findings.** Roughly **10% of hypothyroid patients have residual psychiatric symptoms after hormone replacement.**
    b. **Hyperthyroid patients appear restless, anxious, fidgety, or labile.** Symptoms may overlap with those of anxiety or panic, with palpitations, tachycardia, sweating, irritability, tremulousness, decreased sleep, weakness, and fatigue. Weight loss occurs despite an increased appetite. **Elderly patients may manifest apathy, psychomotor retardation, and depression rather than hyperactive symptoms.**
2. **Parathyroid** dysfunction is closely linked to perturbations in calcium, phosphate, and bone metabolism. However, attempts to correlate symptoms with absolute serum calcium levels have been inconclusive.
    a. **Hyperparathyroidism, and its resultant hypercalcemia, may be asymptomatic** in as many as half of afflicted patients, **or present with nonspecific signs of mental slowness, lethargy, apathy, decreased attention and memory, and depressed mood. Delirium, disorientation,** and psychosis have also been reported.
    b. In **hypoparathyroidism,** a gradual onset of hypocalcemia may cause **personality change or delirium,** without the characteristic tetany of a more precipitous drop in serum calcium.
3. **Adrenal dysfunction**
    a. **Adrenal insufficiency,** whether from **autoimmune Addison's disease (primary hypocortisolism)** or the **sudden withdrawal of prolonged glucocorticoid therapy (secondary hypocortisolism),** presents with **initially mild psy-**

chiatric symptoms (e.g., apathy, negativism, social withdrawal, poverty of thought, fatigue, depressed mood, and irritability, as well as loss of appetite, interest, and enjoyment) that may be attributable to depression. Other signs and symptoms include nausea, vomiting, weakness, hypotension, and hypoglycemia. **Psychosis, delirium, and eventually coma** may develop. Psychiatric symptoms may not fully resolve with glucocorticoid treatment. Care should be taken to choose psychotropic medications that do not exacerbate hypotension.

b. **Hypercortisolism** may result from **chronic hypersecretion of adrenocorticotropic hormone (ACTH; ACTH-dependent hypercortisolism)** from **a pituitary adenoma (Cushing's disease)** or a **nonpituitary neoplasm (e.g., Cushing's syndrome). Less frequently,** it may result from the direct adrenal oversecretion of cortisol from a tumor or hyperplasia (ACTH-independent Cushing's syndrome). The vast majority of affected patients will experience psychiatric symptoms that include **anxiety, depression, irritability, and insomnia, as well as decreased interest, energy, concentration, and memory. Suicidal ideation may be prevalent.** Psychosis is rare.

c. Administration of **exogenous corticosteroids may precipitate mania.** When exogenous steroids are planned, **the prophylactic use of a mood stabilizer** is indicated when a patient has a history of steroid-induced mania.

4. **Pituitary dysfunction can cause a wide range of psychiatric symptoms.** The postpartum hemorrhagic destruction of the pituitary (**Sheehan's syndrome**), for example, may cause depression, mental slowness, and mood lability. An overactive pituitary can lead to adrenal hyperplasia and all of the symptoms of Cushing's syndrome described above.

F. **Demyelinating Disorders**
Demyelinating disorders are associated with neuropsychiatric symptoms as well as motor and sensory changes. These disorders are relatively rare in the general public and may present initially with **mild alterations in mood, behavior, cognition, or personality.** Early symptoms may be attributed to **depression, anxiety, somatization, or even malingering. Multiple sclerosis (MS) is by far the most prevalent of these disorders (50–60 cases per 100,000 population),** with amyotrophic lateral sclerosis (ALS) a distant second (3–5 cases per 100,000 population). Others include metachromatic leu-

kodystrophy, adrenoleukodystrophy, gangliosidoses, and subacute sclerosing panencephalitis (SSPE).

1. **Multiple sclerosis (MS),** an episodic, inflammatory, multifocal, demyelinating disease of unknown etiology, affects the cerebral hemispheres, optic nerves, brain stem, cerebellum, and spinal cord. **MS is more common in cold and temperate climates, has a predilection for women, and has an onset between the ages of 20 and 40 years.** Studies suggest that **psychiatric symptoms are prevalent throughout the course** of MS, do not clear during remission of physical symptoms, and **correlate poorly with** magnetic resonance imaging **(MRI) findings, severity of physical symptoms, or length of illness. Depression occurs in two-thirds** of patients with MS and is associated with an **increased risk of suicide.** Some patients might experience a mildly elevated mood that may seem incongruent with the severity of their illness. Other psychiatric symptoms include **agitation, anxiety, disinhibition, hallucinations, delusions, and cognitive impairment.** Irritability is the most common early symptom.

G. **Cerebrovascular Disease**
Cerebrovascular disease is the third most common cause of death in the United States, behind heart disease and cancer. **The vast majority (85%) of strokes are ischemic,** and about one-third of all strokes are the result of atherosclerotic thrombosis and cerebral embolism. Essential hypertension is the most common cause of hemorrhagic stroke; spontaneous aneurysmal rupture and arteriovenous malformation are much less frequent causes of parenchymal bleeding.

1. **Depression,** either major depression or dysthymia, is the **most common poststroke psychiatric syndrome;** it occurs in over half of patients following stroke. Roughly two-thirds of these patients experience depressive symptoms in the immediate poststroke period, while the rest become depressed after about 6 months. The natural course of untreated poststroke depression is about a year, while the course of dysthymia may be more protracted and variable. While the severity of deficits does not correlate with the onset of depression, **depression is correlated with poor recovery and decreased ability to participate in rehabilitative therapies.** Standard antidepressant therapies have been shown to shorten the course of poststroke depression, underscoring the importance of timely recognition and initiation of treatment. There is suggestive, but questioned, evidence that stroke location (left hemisphere frontal, prefrontal, or basal

ganglia) predisposes to depression; previous stroke, subcortical atrophy, and personal or family history of mood disorder may also increase the risk of poststroke depression.

2. **Aprosodia,** the inability to affectively modulate speech and gestures (motor aprosodia), or the inability to interpret the emotional components of another's speech or gestures (sensory aprosodia), may follow right (nondominant) hemisphere insults. **The aprosodic patient often appears affectively blunted, or "flat," but this is a disorder of** *expression,* **not mood, and it should be carefully differentiated from depression.**

3. **Anxiety,** as **an isolated syndrome, is relatively rare** in the poststroke period. However, **almost half of patients with poststroke depression have concomitant anxiety** symptoms.

4. **Mania,** although rare, correlates with **right-sided** lesions of the **orbitofrontal, basotemporal, basal ganglia, and thalamic areas.** This secondary mania may be more common in those with pre-existing subcortical atrophy, or a personal or family history of mood disorder.

5. **Affective incontinence** may be seen, with **multiple lacunar infarcts** affecting the **descending corticobulbar and fronto-pontine pathways.** This release of cortical inhibition over lower brain stem centers results in **uncontrollable outbursts of laughing or crying** and loss of more moderate emotional expression, such as smiling. This affective dyscontrol occurs along with **dysarthria, dysphagia, and bifacial weakness,** which together comprise the syndrome of **"pseudobulbar palsy."**

H. **Toxins**

Toxins of various types in miniscule amounts are gaining notoriety as the putative cause of myriad nonspecific symptoms in certain sensitive individuals. While there are few data to support the existence of **multiple chemical sensitivity or environmental illness,** there are syndromes from common environmental toxins, such as carbon monoxide or low-level lead exposure, that may be overlooked because of their similarity to common medical or primary mental disorders.

1. **Carbon monoxide** (CO) poisoning from faulty heating or exhaust systems may cause a flu-like illness with cough, nausea, and general malaise. More **chronic, low-level exposure can cause cognitive deterioration and depression.** Severe but sublethal poisoning can lead to memory dysfunction, visual problems, Parkinsonism, confabulation, psychosis, and delirium.

2. **Lead,** a known toxin in young children, also poses a risk to adults who are exposed in a variety of occupational, recreation-

al, and environmental settings. Potentially hazardous activities include home renovation, drinking from leaded crystal, and jogging in areas of heavy traffic. Stained glass, ceramic, and lead-figure artisans, as well as artists who use lead-based oil paints, and even art conservators, are at risk. Firearm enthusiasts should also monitor their lead levels. The psychiatric symptoms (e.g., **after-work fatigue, sleepiness, depressed mood, and apathy**) of **low-level lead exposure** are nondescript, and are easily dismissed as depression. **At higher levels, cognition and memory may be impaired, along with sensorimotor symptoms, restlessness, and gastrointestinal complaints.** Organic lead exposure from gasoline, solvents, and cleaning fluids can cause psychosis, restlessness, nightmares, and at very high levels, seizures and coma.

3. **Mercury exposure** from organic mercury, as from contaminated fish, results in a primarily **neurological syndrome,** while exposure to **inorganic mercury presents initially with psychiatric symptoms, known historically as the** *Mad Hatter syndrome.* The syndrome presents initially as depression, irritability, and psychosis, with less prominent headache, tremor, and weakness. In the past, inorganic mercury exposure was occupational or from broken thermometers; present-day sources may be less obvious. **Mercury is found in readily purchased botanical preparations and folk medicines.** It is also sold in easily broken capsules with instructions to sprinkle it in the home or car, a practice of certain cultural or religious sects.

4. **Drugs: overdose, herbal, nonprescription, prescribed, or recreational.** All should be considered potential toxins when evaluating changes in cognition, behavior, consciousness, or personality.

I. **Neoplasm**
    Neoplasm, either with unregulated focal or diffuse growth **within the cranial confines,** can produce any of the symptomatic presentations to which the CNS is prone. The clinical presentation may suggest the type, location, and primary versus metastatic nature of the lesion. In addition, **paraneoplastic syndromes** also cause psychiatric symptoms.

    1. **Brain tumors,** such as **gliomas,** which account for 50–60% of primary brain tumors, **tend to produce diffuse symptoms** (e.g., cognitive decline) as they grow slowly and diffusely throughout the cortex. Multiple metastases or lymphoma can also present with this nonfocal pattern. **Meningiomas** (which account for 25% of primary brain tumors) grow extrinsically to the brain

and **compress a limited area of the cortex, often causing focal symptoms and seizures. Psychiatric symptoms occur in half of patients with brain tumors; of those, over 80% have tumors in the frontal or limbic areas.** Besides **depression and personality changes,** frontal tumors are associated with bowel and bladder incontinence. Temporal lobe tumors are especially likely to cause seizures, often with ictal or interictal psychosis. **Poor memory, or Korsakoff syndrome, aphasia, depression, and personality changes are also seen with temporal lobe tumors. Akinetic mutism,** an alert but immobile state, **occurs with upper brain stem tumors.** Delirium may be a sign of rapidly growing, large, or metastatic tumors.

2. **Paraneoplastic syndromes,** most often associated with **small cell carcinoma** of the lung, produce **neuropsychiatric symptoms that may precede** by many months the detection of the causative non-CNS tumor. **Tumors of the breast, stomach, uterus, kidney, testicle, thyroid, and colon may also cause paraneoplastic syndromes.** These syndromes may arise from tumor production of hormones, and result in a syndrome of inappropriate antidiuretic hormone secretion (SIADH), hypercortisolism, hypercalcemia, or hyperparathyroidism.

3. **Pancreatic cancer,** among all types of cancer, is associated with a higher-than-expected incidence of **depression;** in fact, it **may be the initial presentation of pancreatic cancer.**

J.   Degenerative Disorders
Degenerative disorders, especially of the **basal ganglia,** produce not only motor and sensory dysfunction, but a spectrum of neuropsychiatric **symptoms that include depression, psychosis, and cognitive impairment.** In fact, the severity of the movement symptoms may vary with the level of emotional stress.

1. **Parkinson's disease,** which affects 1% of the population over the age of 65 years, is known for its classical features of bradykinesia, rigidity, and tremor, as well as its characteristic disturbances of gait and posture. The major degenerative loss is in the pars compacta of the substantia nigra, although other structures are also involved. Dopamine, and to some extent norepinephrine and possibly other neurotransmitters, are depleted, which may contribute to the **depression experienced by over half** of afflicted patients. **Dementia is also more common** than in age-matched controls. **Psychosis** can develop, and it is **complicated by the dopaminergic and anticholinergic medications** used to treat the disease.

2. **Huntington's chorea** is an autosomal dominant disorder of

primarily striatal destruction and gamma-aminobutyric acid (GABA) depletion. Besides atrophy of the caudate and putamen, there is mild frontal and temporal wasting. Most common in the age range of 30–40 years, its onset is extremely variable, and juvenile-onset disease has a more rapidly progressive course (the average duration is 8 years, as opposed to 15 years). The prevalence is 10 per 100,000 population. The classic choreiform movement disorder may present with, before, or after prominent psychiatric symptoms. Early on, memory may be intact, but **serious defects in attention, judgment, and executive function** become evident. This may be followed by **depression, apathy, social withdrawal, and a lack of attention to personal grooming. Irritability and impulsivity** are common. The initial presentation may also **mimic obsessive-compulsive disorder or schizophrenia.** The depression is responsive to antidepressants and it should be treated. The cognitive decline, like the movement disorder, is progressive and leads to dementia.

3. **Wilson's disease** is an autosomal recessive **defect in copper excretion** that causes deposition of copper in the liver, brain, cornea **(as indicated by Kayser-Fleischer rings),** and kidney. This genetic deficiency of ceruloplasmin has a prevalence of 3.3 cases per 100,000 population. Copper toxicity in the brain affects the lenticular nuclei, and to a lesser degree the pons, medulla, thalamus, cerebellum, and cerebral cortex. Neurologic features include bradykinesia, ataxia, tremor, dyskinesia, and dysarthria. Approximately 10–25% of affected patients **present with psychiatric problems** that range from **subtle personality changes** to **cognitive impairment, depression, and psychosis.** Psychiatric symptoms that fail to resolve after copper chelation therapy require more specific treatment and psychopharmacotherapy.

K.   Autoimmune Diseases
Systemic lupus erythematosus (SLE) is an autoimmune inflammatory disease of unknown etiology that affects women more often than men in a distribution of 9:1, usually in the third to fifth decades. Tissue damage occurs in multiple systems, which gives the disorder an extremely variable presentation and course. Laboratory tests may be confirmatory, but are not totally specific or reliable. When patients present with **depression, sleep disturbance, mood lability, mild cognitive dysfunction, or psychosis,** as up to one-half of patients do, the nonspecific nature of their complaints may lead to the erroneous diagnosis of a primary mental disorder, such as major

depression or somatization disorder. Correct diagnosis may lead to steroid therapy, which can worsen psychiatric symptoms.

L. **Trauma**

Trauma to the head is extremely common in the United States; roughly a million severe traumatic brain injuries occur each year. Young males are at highest risk. Motor vehicle accidents are responsible for about half of all closed-head injuries, with falls, violence, and sports causing most of the rest.

1. **Penetrating head injury,** such as that received from a gunshot wound, is often dramatic; it tends to cause focal symptoms related to the size and location of directly involved brain tissue.

2. **Closed head injury** is far **more common and complicated,** causing **diffuse symptoms and prolonged sequelae** that do not correlate with the severity of the injury. **Limbic areas of the brain, the anterior temporal lobes and the inferior surface of the frontal lobes, are the major sites of damage.** The neurobehavioral **dysfunction may persist** for years after the injury. **Cognitive slowing** may occur with **poor attention, memory difficulties, perseveration, and poor planning. Personality changes, irritability, impulsivity, depression, anxiety, and mood lability** are also common. Among the many somatic symptoms are headache, dizziness, fatigue, and sleep disturbance, which may be attributed to depression. Photophobia, noise sensitivity, tinnitus, and blurred vision also occur. Patients with head injuries **are often very sensitive to psychotropic medications,** and may require geriatric doses.

IV. Evaluation of the Problem

Mental Disorder DTGMC should be part of the differential diagnosis for any psychiatric syndrome. Alterations in cognition, behavior, or perception look much the same whether they derive from primary mental disorders, toxins, trauma, tumors, or seizures. As such, the evaluation is the same as for any careful psychiatric evaluation. A high level of **medical suspicion** is required to gather the necessary information to make the diagnosis.

A. **History**

The history should be obtained from records, the patient, other caregivers, and when possible, from family members or others close to the patient.

1. **Medical**

a. A careful review of past and present illnesses, treatments, procedures, all medications, exposures, travel, head injury, seizure, habits (e.g., use of caffeine and tobacco), and recreational drug use

    b.   Correlation in time between medical events and psychiatric symptoms

  2. **Psychiatric:** Pay close attention to the onset, course, treatment response, and past episodes, for typical and atypical features of primary mental disorders.

  3. **Family:** Note the presence of similar symptoms, other psychiatric disorders, and medical illnesses that run in the family, as well as early or unexplained deaths.

  4. **Social:** Inquire about education, occupation, living situation, interpersonal relationships (fights and violence), and recreational activities.

B.   **Examination of the Patient**

  1. **Interview:** A mental status exam (MSE) is not specific for general medical conditions, but it is comparable to the MSE in similar primary mental disorders. The **"draw a clock"** test and **Luria maneuvers** may help elicit subtle frontal lobe dysfunction that is otherwise difficult to detect.

  2. **Physical examination:** A thorough examination with careful attention to neurological function and to vital signs is essential.

  3. **Laboratory assessment:** Each planned laboratory test should aim to support or to rule out a suspected diagnosis (Table 8-1). Common tests include electrolytes, calcium, complete blood cell count, and thyroid-stimulating hormone. More specific tests (e.g., liver function, vitamin B_{12}, folic acid, and rapid plasmin reagin) should be employed as appropriate to the patient's overall presentation, including the context, history, physical signs, and symptoms.

  4. **Imaging:** Brain (or other) imaging should **target suspected diagnoses.** Sudden onset, focal signs, rapid progression, infectious disease, or trauma are indications for appropriate brain imaging.

  4. **Other tests** may be specific to a given medical condition (e.g., a sleep-deprived EEG in a patient with suspected complex partial seizures).

V. Treatment Considerations and Strategies

A.   **Underlying Medical Conditions**

Whenever possible, **underlying medical conditions** should be treated, controlled, and/or stabilized. For example, infections should be treated with appropriate agents, and metabolic perturbations should

Table 8-1. Medical Disorders Due to a General Medical Condition

Differential	Syndrome[1]	Associated Work-Up
Germs (infectious disease)		
HIV	D, P, M	ELISA/Western blot
Neurosyphilis	D, P, M,	RPR, VDRL, FTA-ABS
Lyme disease	D, M	Lyme titer
Rabies	P	dFA from animal
Herpes simplex virus	P	MRI/CT brain LP, EEG, HSV DNA
Meningitis	M	LP, EEG, MRI brain
Hepatitis	M	Hepatitis panel A, B, C,
Epilepsy		
Partial complex seizures	D, A, P, M	EEG
Nutritional deficit		
Vitamin B_{12}	D, P, M	Vitamin B_{12} level
Niacin	D, A	Niacin level
Folate	D	Folate level
Metabolic disorders		
Hypercalcemia	D, P, M	Serum calcium
Hypocalcemia	D, P	Serum calcium
Endocrine disorders		
Hypothyroidism	D, A, P	TSH
Hyperthyroidism	A, M	TSH
Hypocortisolism	D, P	Serum coritsol
Hypercortisolism	D, P, A	Serum cortisol
Hyperparathyroidism	D, P	PTH
Hypoglycemia	A	Serum glucose
Demyelinating disorders		
Multiple sclerosis	D, A, P, M	MRI brain, LP
Cerebrovascular disease		
Poststroke	D, A	MRI/CT scan
Offensive toxins		
Lead	D	Heavy metal screen
Mercury	D, P	Heavy metal screen
Carbon monoxide	P	Serum carboxyhemoglobin

Table 8-1. Medical Disorders Due to a General Medical Condition (continued)

Differential	Syndrome[1]	Associated Work-Up
Neoplasms		
Pancreatic	D	CT abdomen
Paraneoplastic syndrome (especially small cell)	D, A	Serum chemistry panel, anti-Hu/Ri/Yo antibodies
Brain tumors	D, P, M	MRI/CT brain
Degenerative disorders		
Parkinson's disease	D, P	MRI brain
Huntington's chorea	P	Genetic testing
Wilson disease	D, P	Serum ceruloplasmin
Immune disorders		
Systemic lupus erythematosus	D, P, M	ANA
Rheumatoid arthirtis	D	Rheumatoid factor, x-rays, ESR
Trauma		
Head injury	A, P, M	MRI/CT brain

[1]D, depression, A, anxiety; M, mania; P, psychosis.
ANA, antineoplastic antibody test; dFA, direct fluorescent antibody test; EEG, electroencephalogram; ELISA, enzyme-linked immunosorbent assay test; ESR, erythrocyte sedimentation rate; FTA-ABS, fluorescent treponemal antibody (absorbed) test; HSV DNA, herpes simplex virus DNA test; LP, lumbar puncture; PTH, parathyroid hormone level; RPR, rapid plasmin reagin test; TSH, thyroid-stimulating hormone level; VDRL, Veneral Disease Research Laboratory test.

be normalized, while diabetic control and renal function are optimized.

1. **Some mental disorders will clear** when the underlying condition is treated, and thus long-term treatment of the mental disorder is unnecessary. However, **short-term comfort measures** (e.g., the judicious use of benzodiazepines in a patient being treated for hyperthyroidism) may be necessary, as the mental symptoms may lag behind the course of the medical condition.

2. **Some general medical conditions are chronic** (e.g., previous stroke or toxic exposures, and degenerative or demyelinating diseases) and little can be done to alter their course. The mental

disorder in chronic medical illness may require **ongoing psychiatric treatment.**

B.   Presence of Psychiatric Symptoms
Psychiatric symptoms should not be considered a normal response to illness (e.g., depression in a patient with cancer or AIDS), but rather a **terrible complication. Mental disorders should be aggressively treated,** regardless of their medical etiology.

C.   Psychosocial Stresses
The psychosocial stresses of chronic or acute medical conditions, as well as other primary mental or personality disorders, **can exacerbate psychiatric symptoms, interfere with treatment, and generally complicate the clinical picture.**

Suggested Readings

American Psychiatric Association: *Diagnostic and Statistical Manual of Mental Disorders,* 4th Edition. Washington, DC: American Psychiatric Association, 1994.

Blumer D, Wakhlu S, Montouris G, Wyler AR: Treatment of interictal psychoses. *J Clin Psychiatry* 2000;61:110–122.

Diaz-Olavarrieta C, Cummings JL, Velazquez J, de la Cadena CG: Neuropsychiatric manifestations of multiple sclerosis. *J Neuropsychiatry Clin Neurosci* 1999;11:51–57.

Geffken GR, Ward HE, Staab JP, et al: Psychiatric morbidity in endocrine disorders. *Psychiatr Clin North Am* 1998;21:473–489.

Hartman DE: Missed diagnoses and misdiagnoses of environmental toxicant exposure. *Psychiatr Clin North Am* 1998;21:659–670.

Hutto B: Syphilis in clinical psychiatry: a review. *Psychosomatics* 2001;42:453-460.

Lambert MV, Sierra M, Phillips M, David AS: The spectrum of organic depersonalization: a review plus four new cases. *J Neuropsychiatry Clin Neurosci* 2002;14:141-154.

Leroi I, O'Hearn E, Marsh L, et al: Psychopathology on patients with degenerative cerebellar diseases: a comparison to Huntington's disease. *Am J Psychiatry* 2002;159:1306-1314.

Racette BA, Hartlein JM, Hershey T, et al: Clinical features and comorbidity of mood fluctuations in Parkinson's disease. *J Neuropsychiatry Clin Neurosci* 2002;14:438-442.

Raymond V, Gultekin SH, Rosenfeld MR, et al: A serologic marker of paraneoplastic limbic and brain-stem encephalitis in patients with testicular cancer. *N Engl J Med* 1999;340:1788-1795.

Skuster DZ, Digre KB, Corbett JJ: Neurologic conditions presenting as psychiatric disorders. *Psychiatr Clin North Am* 1992;15:311–333.

Tager FA, Fallon BA: Psychiatric and cognitive features of Lyme disease. *Psychiatric Annals* 2001;31:173-181.

Tucker GJ: Seizure disorders presenting with psychiatric symptomatology. *Psychiatr Clin North Am* 1998;21:625–635.

Wilkie FL, Goodkin K, van Zuilen MH, et al: Cognitive effects of HIV-1 infection. *CNS Spectrums* 2000;5:33–51.

Wise MG, Rundell JR (eds): *Textbook of Consultation-Liaison Psychiatry: Psychiatry in the Medically Ill*, 2nd Edition. Washington, DC: American Psychiatric Publishing, 2002.

Chapter 9

An Approach to Acute Changes in Mental Status

JOHN QUERQUES, MD

I. Overview

A. **Acute Mental Status Changes**
An acute change in mental status is any alteration of affect, behavior, or cognition that develops over hours to days. Any element of a standard mental status examination (MSE) can be affected: alertness, attention, concentration, memory, orientation, comprehension, constructional ability, language, mood, thought process, thought content, or perception. Impairment of several domains at once is the rule.

B. **Syndromes Manifest by Mental Status Changes**
Delirium is but one syndrome manifest by an **alteration in consciousness and cognition** (Table 9-1). Other terms that are generally considered synonymous with delirium (though some authors argue their distinctions) are **acute confusional state, acute confusion,** and **encephalopathy.**

C. **Psychosis**
Psychosis is a syndrome of altered thinking, perception, and behavior that severely impairs the patient's ability to understand and experience reality; however, it spares consciousness. Its hallmark features are **delusions** (i.e., fixed, false beliefs not shared by other members of the patient's sociocultural group) and **hallucinations** (i.e., false perceptions in any of the five sensory modalities).

D. **Consciousness**
Delirium and psychosis share certain features (Figure 9-1). Agitation, delusions, hallucinations, illusions, and disorders of thought process (e.g., loose associations and circumstantiality) are common to both conditions. Despite this overlap, however, the two syndromes are distinct. The differential diagnosis is aided by a simple dichotomous determination: **consciousness is *always* normal in "functional" psychosis and is *always* abnormal in delirium.** Moreover, save

---

Address for correspondence: Dr. John Querques, 185 Pilgrim Road, Deaconess 1, Boston, MA 02215, email: jquerque@bidmc.harvard.edu.

Table 9-1. DSM-IV Criteria for Delirium

- Disturbance of consciousness with diminished ability to focus, sustain, or shift attention
- Change in cognition or new-onset perceptual disturbance not due to dementia
- Acute development (usually over hours to days) of these alterations with fluctuation during the day
- Historical, physical, or laboratory evidence that these alterations have a medical etiology

Adapted from: American Psychiatric Association: *Diagnostic and Statistical Manual of Mental Disorders*, 4th edition. Washington, DC: American Psychiatric Association, 1994.

for psychosis that develops as a result of intoxication (e.g., cocaine or phencyclidine), most cases of functional psychosis develop insidiously over weeks to months. For these reasons, the often-invoked term **"intensive care unit (ICU) psychosis"** is a regrettable misnomer applied to critically ill patients in ICUs who develop acute mental status changes. Delirium, not psychosis, is the usual cause of

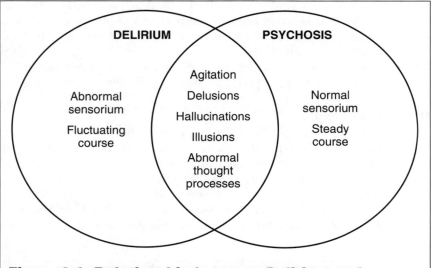

Figure 9-1. Relationship between Delirium and Psychosis

such disturbances, and the causative role of the ICU environment is much less important etiologically than are the nature, severity, and number of the patient's medical morbidities.

II. Delirium

A. **Epidemiology**
Delirium is most common in patients with advanced age; brain impairment (e.g., stroke, dementia, or traumatic brain injury); recent surgery; multiple medical problems, particularly if they are active; extensive medication regimens; a history of delirium; sensory deprivation or overload; impaired vision or hearing; and experience of a recent change in surroundings (e.g., associated with hospitalization). Often, more than one of these risk factors for the development of delirium is present at the same time. Because of its profound effects on levels of arousal and attention, delirium is more commonly diagnosed in medical settings (e.g., medical and surgical units or emergency departments) than in psychiatric venues.

B. **Prevalence**
Estimates of the prevalence of delirium vary according to the population studied. Among hospitalized medical patients, the prevalence of delirium is roughly 10–30%. Higher prevalence figures are usually reported in the elderly and in patients following surgery.

C. **Etiology**
Many roads lead to delirium. The mnemonic **WWHHHHIIMP** (Table 9-2) summarizes the life-threatening causes of delirium that need to be ruled out first. A more comprehensive list of possible etiologies can be divided into the 11 categories recalled by the mnemonic **I WATCH DEATH** (Table 9-3). Frequently more than one etiology is responsible for the delirious state and a combination of minor abnormalities may contribute to alterations in mentation (i.e., the whole is greater than the sum of its parts).

D. **Mechanism**
The pathogenic links between these multifarious etiologies and the ultimate production of delirium are largely unknown. However, consideration of the "wires" (neuroanatomy) and the "juices" (neurochemistry) may yield putative answers. **Alertness is mediated by the ascending reticular activating system (RAS)** and its thalamic projections to both hemispheres; **attention is mediated by neocortical and limbic inputs** to this system. Any structural alteration of these neural fibers theoretically could result in delirium. Moreover,

---

Table 9-2. Life-Threatening Causes of Delirium: WWHHHHHIIMP

Withdrawal
Wernicke's encephalopathy
Hypertensive encephalopathy
Hypoglycemia
Hypoxia
Hypotension/hypoperfusion
Intracranial hemorrhage
Infection
Meningitis/encephalitis
Poisoning

Adapted from: Wise MG, Trzepacz PT: Delirium (confusional states). In Rundell JR, Wise MG (eds): *The American Psychiatric Press Textbook of Consultation-Liaison Psychiatry.* Washington, DC: American Psychiatric Press, 1996:258–274.

---

because the RAS is a cholinergic system, **a deficit in acetylcholine could render this critical arousal network defunct.** This anatomical and chemical hypothesis is consistent with the clinical recognition of **anticholinergic deliria.** Overdose of any agent that has significant anticholinergic properties (e.g., tricyclic antidepressants [TCAs], diphenhydramine, and some neuroleptics) are frequent causes of anticholinergic delirium. A complementary theory posits that delirium is a hyperdopaminergic state. Support for this contention comes from research evidence that stress (e.g., that which ensues postoperatively) stimulates dopamine output in the mesocorticolimbic tract. This hypothesis coincides squarely with the overwhelming success of dopamine-blocking drugs in the treatment of delirium.

E.   **History**
To gather useful history from the delirious patient, the examiner must be fortunate enough to "catch him on the wane," that is, when he is more lucid and coherent. Even then, however, the information he provides may be of dubious reliability and the clinician **may have to rely on collateral sources of information.** Whether from the patient or from these ancillary informants, the crucial questions to ask are:

Table 9-3. Differential Diagnosis of Delirium: I WATCH DEATH

Infection	Any, but especially meningitis, encephalitis, bacteremia, tertiary syphilis, human immunodeficiency virus (HIV) infection, and urinary tract infection (UTI) in elderly patients
Withdrawal	Alcohol, benzodiazepines, or barbiturates
Acute metabolic	Electrolyte derangements, fluid imbalances, renal failure, hepatic failure, or acid-base disorder
Trauma	Head injury, burns, or fractures
CNS pathology	Any
Hypoxia	Anemia, hypotension, hypoperfusion, heart failure, respiratory failure, or carbon monoxide poisoning
Deficiencies	Vitamin B_{12} (cyanocobalamin), folate, or thiamine
Endocrinopathies	Dysfunction (increase or decrease of activity) of pituitary, thyroid, and adrenal glands; hyperglycemia; or hypoglycemia
Acute vascular	Emergent or urgent hypertension, stroke, shock, or myocardial infarction
Toxins/drugs	Any toxin; see also Table 9-4
Heavy metals	Lead, manganese, or mercury

Adapted from: Wise MG, Trzepacz PT: Delirium (confusional states). In Rundell JR, Wise MG (eds): *The American Psychiatric Press Textbook of Consultation-Liaison Psychiatry.* Washington, DC: American Psychiatric Press, 1996:258–274.

---

1. **What is the patient's baseline level of function?** This determination helps ascertain the extent and nature of the deviation from the patient's usual affective, behavioral, and cognitive state.

2. **What are the patient's medical problems?** In addition to inquiries related to the conditions listed in Tables 9-2 and 9-3, specific queries about any brain insults—both remote and recent—should be made. Any brain insult heightens vulnerability to delirium. Moreover, recent head injury, seizure, or stroke may point to an emergent intracranial catastrophe. Brain insults include:

   a. Head injury

    b.   A fall that may have resulted in an occult head injury

    c.   Seizure

    d.   Stroke

    e.   Human immunodeficiency virus (HIV) infection

    f.   Dementia

3. **What medications does the patient take? Were any recently started or discontinued?** A variety of medications have been associated with delirium (Table 9-4). Pharmaceuticals recently added to the patient's regimen can be especially significant, as these would be more likely to cause a mental status change, either by pharmacodynamic or pharmacokinetic means. Frequently overlooked are drugs newly removed from the patient's drug regimen. Withdrawal from certain medications (e.g., benzodiazepines, opiates, or barbiturates) can lead to delirium. Moreover, when cytochrome P450 inducers (e.g., carbamazepine, steroids, or tobacco [of particular relevance in hospitalized patients who may be barred from smoking]) are stopped, levels of drugs (e.g., benzodiazepines, cyclosporine, or clozapine) metabolized through this pathway may increase in serum level. When P450 inhibitors (e.g., azole antifungals, or selective serotonin reuptake inhibitors) are discontinued, levels of remaining drugs (e.g., benzodiazepines or TCAs) may decrease. Either of these alterations in the patient's medication regimen can precipitate mental status changes.

4. **Does the patient abuse alcohol or other drugs? Has he recently stopped using these substances?** Intoxication and abrupt withdrawal are frequent causes of delirium. Intoxication with ethanol substitutes (e.g., ethylene glycol or methanol) should also be considered, as these compounds may be exploited for their inebriating properties or to effect suicide.

F.   **Physical Examination**

A general physical examination, targeting the physical findings expected in the conditions listed in Tables 9-2 and 9-3, is critical to the prompt and proper identification of the etiology of delirium. Such an evaluation has typically been completed before the psychiatrist is called to assess the patient. The psychiatrist's contribution is performance of a comprehensive MSE, which is no different from that discussed in Chapter 3. A few key points about the evaluation of the delirious patient warrant elaboration.

1.   **Observation**

Much **critical data can be gleaned by simply observing the patient.** While perusing the record, the clever examiner gathers much useful information by keeping the patient in his visual

Table 9-4. Some Medications and Medication Classes Associated with Delirium

Analgesics	**Antineoplastics**
Corticosteroids	Asparaginase
Nonsteroidal anti-inflammatory	Cytarabine
drugs	Ifosfamide
Salicylates	Interleukin-2
Antiepileptics	**Antiparkinsonians**
Antimicrobials	Levodopa
Acyclovir	Selegiline
Chloroquine	**Cardiac medications**
Efavirenz	Acetazolamide
Fluoroquinolones	Beta-adrenergic blockers
Ganciclovir	Calcium channel blockers
Mefloquine	Digoxin
Metronidazole	Propafenone
Nevirapine	Quinidine
Sulfonamides	**Histamine (H_2-receptor) blockers**
	Miscellaneous
	Baclofen
	Pilocarpine
	Sildenafil

Adapted from: Drugs that may cause psychiatric symptoms. *Med Lett Drugs Ther* 2002;44:59–62.

field and noting: **coarse motor activity** (e.g., picking at the sheets, thrashing, or near stillness); **verbal output** (e.g., loud or vulgar utterances); and **cooperation with staff.** Before greeting the patient or otherwise attracting his notice, the examiner should observe him more closely and note, in addition to the above: **general appearance** (does the patient look comfortable in the bed?; are the sheets and blankets in disarray?); **fine motor activity** (e.g., tremor, myoclonus, or adventitious orobuccal movements); **skin** (e.g., diaphoretic, dry, or red); and **pupils** (e.g., mydriasis or miosis). Only then does the clinician greet the patient and note his response: Does he turn toward the examiner? Does he make eye contact? Does he track as the examiner walks farther into the room? Does he greet the clinician in return? Note that even in a heavily sedated intubated patient, all of these observations are still possible.

Levels of **alertness** and **attentiveness** must be assessed first because the remainder of the examination requires that the patient's full attention be focused on the prescribed questions and tasks. Patients who lack full alertness can be assessed using the Glasgow Coma Scale (Table 9-5), which assesses eye opening, verbal output, and motor activity, and rates alertness on a scale from 3 to 15. Additionally, a narrative comment about the patient's response to various stimuli should be documented. For example: *The patient's eyes were closed on approach and did not open upon verbal stimulus, nor did they open with vigorous shaking of his shoulder. Only when sternal pressure was applied did his eyes open—and even then only for a second—and he mumbled a few incomprehensible sounds.* Such a description clearly communicates the patient's status, which can then be easily compared to subsequent observations.

Attention refers to the ability to focus awareness on a particular stimulus and to exclude all competing stimuli. The patient who focuses on all manner of stimuli (e.g., the examin-

---

Table 9-5. Glasgow Coma Scale

Category	Response	Points
Eye opening	Spontaneous	4
	To verbal command	3
	To pain	2
	None	1
Best verbal output	Oriented, converses	5
	Disoriented, converses	4
	Inappropriate words	3
	Incomprehensible sounds	2
	None	1
Best motor output	Obeys command	6
	Localizes pain	5
	Withdraws from pain	4
	Abnormal flexion (decorticate)	3
	Abnormal extension (decerebrate)	2
	None	1

Adapted from: Teasdale G, Jennett B: Assessment of coma and impaired consciousness, a practical scale. *Lancet* 1974;2:81–84.

er, the nurse walking by the door, or the soft whir of the intravenous pump) can be described as distractible, hyperalert, and inattentive. More subtle cases of inattention can be identified by specific tests (e.g., digit span).

G.   **Laboratory Assessment**

A routine work-up for delirium includes: a complete blood count (CBC), comprehensive chemistries, levels of vitamin B_{12} and folate, a rapid plasma reagin (RPR) test, urinalysis (U/A), chest radiograph (CXR), and electrocardiogram (ECG). Thyroid-stimulating hormone (TSH) is also commonly ordered as part of a general screen, but it is frequently abnormal in a critically ill patient, even one without intrinsic thyroid disease, rendering its utility questionable. The need for additional diagnostic testing is dictated by the history, the physical examination, the initial laboratory test results, and the patient's response to treatment. These supplementary procedures often include: computed tomography (CT) of the head, magnetic resonance imaging (MRI) of the brain, electroencephalogram (EEG), cerebrospinal fluid (CSF) analysis, and cultures of various fluids.

H.   **Pharmacological Treatment**

The definitive therapy for delirium is treatment of its underlying cause(s); it is usually left to the ministrations of medical and surgical personnel. If the patient's affective, behavioral, or cognitive disturbance is severe enough to put him or others at risk, additional treatment with a neuroleptic medication is indicated. For example, a delirious patient with a persecutory delusion that the medical and nursing staff are trying to harm him may refuse necessary diagnostic tests and therapeutic interventions. He may even disconnect himself from various monitors, remove catheters, and attempt to leave the hospital prematurely. Some clinicians argue that delirium per se is neurotoxic, and even in the absence of such florid derangements prescribe a neuroleptic medication.

1.   Based on decades of clinical experience, **haloperidol is the treatment of choice for the adjunctive therapy of delirium.** For acute or florid agitation, haloperidol should be administered intravenously (though this route is not approved by the U.S. Food and Drug Administration), starting with a dose of 1–5 mg, which is successively doubled every 30 minutes until agitation resolves. Once calm, the patient can be maintained on an intravenous (IV) haloperidol drip, or more commonly on a standing regimen of IV or oral haloperidol. For less severe agitation, haloperidol can be administered orally; a typical starting dose is 1–5 mg two or three times a day.

2. With the burgeoning popularity of the **atypical antipsychotic agents,** these pharmaceuticals are increasingly being used for treatment of delirium. Some small studies have shown them to be safe and effective.

I. **Psychological Treatment**
    Frequent reassurance, explanation of the patient's circumstances, and orientation to time and place should be provided to the patient in clear, simple language, especially during more lucid phases of the delirium. He should be approached and spoken to with the assumption that he registers some measure of external reality, in much the same way a comatose patient may be treated. Once the delirium has resolved, a brief explanation of the episode should be offered and the patient permitted to talk about his or her experience. Throughout the encounter, the psychiatrist should be available to the patient's visitors and caretakers to explain delirium, to answer questions, and to provide support, as the experience of delirium can be frightening to the patient and to those around him or her.

J. **Behavioral Treatment**
    Acute and florid agitation often requires application of soft or leather restraints of two, three, or all limbs. When two limbs are restrained, one arm and the contralateral leg should be selected, as other combinations are more dangerous to the patient. Concomitant treatment with a sedating medication is almost always in order when restraining patients, as the discomforting experience of physical restraint is akin to that of pharmacological paralysis. Soft vests around the patient's torso prevent thrashing about in the bed and the attendant risk of injury (e.g., by dislodging vital medical equipment, incurring blunt force trauma, or falling out of bed). Hand mitts can be used to hamper the patient's attempts to remove various catheters and wires. The patient who wanders or whose agitation or confusion may be quelled simply by the presence of another person often benefits from constant observation.

III. Acute Psychosis

Psychosis shares a variety of features with delirium. However, functional psychosis always occurs within a clear sensorium (i.e., the patient is fully awake, alert, and attentive), whereas by definition delirium involves a beclouding of consciousness. In a general medical setting, the development of psychotic symptoms over hours to days is rare and should always raise suspicion of delirium; an assessment of the patient's levels of alertness and attention should be made urgently. Once delirium has been excluded, attention should focus on illicit drug use and withdrawal phenomena.

Suggested Readings

American Psychiatric Association: *Diagnostic and Statistical Manual of Mental Disorders,* 4th edition. Washington, DC: American Psychiatric Association, 1994.

Burns A, Gallagley A, Byrne J: Delirium. *J Neurol Neurosurg Psychiatry* 2004;75: 362–367.

Crippen DW: Pharmacologic treatment of brain failure and delirium. *Crit Care Clin* 1994;10:733–766.

Drugs that may cause psychiatric symptoms. *Med Lett Drugs Ther* 2002;44:59–62.

Gleason OC: Delirium. *Am Fam Physician* 2003;67:1027–1034.

Meagher DJ: Delirium: optimising management. *BMJ* 2001;322:144–149.

Misra S, Ganzini L: Delirium, depression, and anxiety. *Crit Care Clin* 2003;19: 771–787.

Practice guideline for the treatment of patients with delirium. *Am J Psychiatry* 1999; 156(5 Suppl):1–20.

Strub RL, Black FW: *The Mental Status Examination in Neurology,* 3rd edition. Philadelphia: F. A. Davis, 1993.

Teasdale G, Jennett B: Assessment of coma and impaired consciousness, a practical scale. *Lancet* 1974;2:81–84.

Wise MG, Trzepacz PT: Delirium (confusional states). In Rundell JR, Wise MG (eds): *The American Psychiatric Press Textbook of Consultation-Liaison Psychiatry.* Washington, DC: American Psychiatric Press, 1996:258–274.

Chapter 10

An Approach to the Patient with Neuropsychiatric Dysfunction

ANTHONY P. WEISS, MD

STEPHAN HECKERS, MD

> *Psychiatry has undergone a transformation in its relationship to the rest of medicine. . . . This transformation rests principally on the realization that patients with so-called "mental illnesses" are really individuals with illnesses of the nerves and brain.*
> —Wilhelm Griesinger, 1868

I.   Introduction

The brain is a complex organ with many functions. **Disease processes that affect the brain do not always recognize the (somewhat) arbitrary boundaries that divide the treatment domains of neurology and psychiatry.** Although neurologists generally treat patients with sensory-motor dysfunction, and psychiatrists generally treat patients with affective, behavioral, or cognitive dysfunction, there exists a large intermediate group of patients with dysfunction in both of these realms. Indeed, these patients with neuropsychiatric dysfunction comprise a considerable portion of the clinic population for both neurologists and psychiatrists.

In addition to the prevalence of these patients, developing the skills to assess neuropsychiatric symptomatology is important for several reasons. First, **psychiatric symptoms may result directly from underlying neurological damage** (e.g., traumatic brain injury causing disinhibition). It is the associated sensory-motor findings on examination that will uncover the root cause of these symptoms. Second, **psychiatric symptoms are commonly seen in the context of neurological disorders** (e.g., depression in Parkinson's disease). In some cases, the psychiatric symptoms will predate or predominate over the other features of the illness; a thorough examination by the psychiatrist may therefore lead to early recognition and treatment. Third, **knowledge of the neurological exam is crucial in distinguishing "real" neurological deficits from simulated deficits associated with conversion disorders or malingering.** The psychiatrist will often be called upon to clarify this diagnostic dilemma. Finally, the psychiatrist must be aware of the numerous ways in which **psychotropic medications can affect the sensory and motor systems of the brain** (e.g., dystonias and other movement disorders) and be capable of assessing the severity of these adverse effects.

Address for correspondence: Dr. Anthony P. Weiss, Charlestown Navy Yard, Building 149, 149 13th St., Charlestown, MA 02129-2000, email: weiss. anthony@a1.mgh.harvard.edu.

This chapter will provide an outline for the assessment of these patients, with a focus on the mental status and neurological exams. By first reviewing the relevant neuroanatomy, it is hoped that the rationale for the individual components of this assessment will become clear. To close, a brief discussion of the clinical intersection between "neuro" and "psychiatric" will then be provided for illustrative purposes.

II.   Organization of the Nervous System

The role of the nervous system is to act as an interface between the internal milieu and the external environment. At its very core, this interaction involves three components: **input from the environment, evaluation of this incoming information, and output of a response (Figure 10-1; stimulus → evaluation → response).** Remembering this wonderful simplicity is an important first step in reducing the potentially overwhelming complexity of the nervous system's multiple nuclei and pathways. Understanding these three basic roles also serves as an aid in comprehending the organization of the standard neurological exam.

A   **Input from the Environment**
        We experience the world through our five senses, which serve as the input channels for information to access the brain.

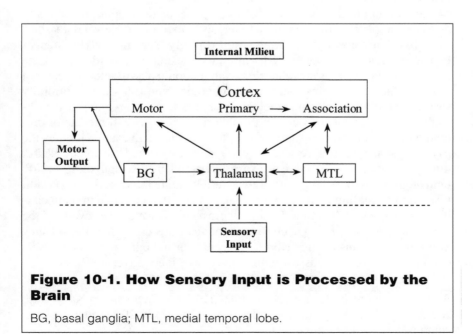

Figure 10-1. How Sensory Input is Processed by the Brain

BG, basal ganglia; MTL, medial temporal lobe.

1. In neuroanatomic terms, this **occurs through the peripheral nervous system** (touch), and through those cranial nerves with sensory components (CN I, smell; CN II, sight; CN V, touch; CN VII, taste; and CN VIII, hearing).
2. The **information from these channels gets routed through separate nuclei within the thalamus,** an area of the brain often called the "gateway," on the way to the primary sensory areas of the cerebral cortex. These primary sensory regions include:
   a. S1 (somatosensory touch) in the postcentral gyrus,
   b. A1 (auditory) in the superior temporal gyrus, and
   c. V1 (visual) in the occipital lobe.

B.   **Evaluation of Incoming Information**
To this point, these sensory inputs remain segregated. **Integration and evaluation of this sensory input occurs in successive steps.**
1. First, the different features of a single sensory modality are brought together in areas called **unimodal association cortex.** In the visual association cortex, for example, the color, intensity, and motion of an object are brought together as one.
2. From there, admixing of the different sensory modalities occurs in regions known as **heteromodal association cortex.**
3. An additional level of integration is provided by **input from limbic and paralimbic regions** of the brain, including the cingulate cortex and regions of the medial temporal lobe (hippocampus and amygdala).
   a. It is at this third level of integration that **the brain creates a representation of experience that is imbued with emotion** and viewed in the context of prior experience.
   b. Evaluation and interpretation involves the comparison of new information with previously stored information and current expectations or desires. This allows the brain to classify information as new or old, and threatening or nonthreatening.

C.   **Output of a Response**
Based on the result of evaluation and interpretation, the brain then creates a response. This may involve a subtle change in internal hormonal milieu, a shift in neurotransmitter balance, or something more overt, such as bodily movement.
1. The regions involved in generating this motor response include **motor cortex, motor nuclei of the thalamus, the basal ganglia, and the cerebellum.**

a.   The basal ganglia, which includes the striatum (caudate + putamen) and the globus pallidus, is charged with the role of integrating and coordinating this motor output.

b.   The striatum receives input from the motor cortex and it projects to the globus pallidus.

c.   The globus pallidus in turn relays the neostriatal input to the thalamus.

d.   The thalamus then projects back to the cortical areas that gave rise to the cortico-striatal projections, thereby closing the cortico-striato-pallido-thalamo-cortical loop.

III.   Evaluating the Nervous System: The Neurological Exam

Even for experienced clinicians, the neurological exam is perhaps the most intimidating component of the standard physical assessment of the patient. While this may be related to the bewildering array of eponymous signs and mysterious maneuvers (cf, the palmomental reflex), it is more likely due to confusion regarding the purpose of the components of the exam. Just as we test the fitness of the heart or lungs, the neurological exam is nothing more than a fitness test for the brain. **Given the component functions of input, evaluation, and output described above, it should be no surprise that the standard neurological exam sets out to probe the integrity of these three domains.** While the precise details regarding the conduct of the exam are beyond the scope of this guidebook, below are some basic principles that should help in conceptually organizing the overall process.

A.   **Assessing Input**
During every waking moment the environment bombards our bodies with an abundant array of stimuli, including light waves, sound waves, vibrations, and odors to name just a few. Our nervous system is arranged in such a manner that specialized detection systems exist for each of these stimuli.

1.   Within the peripheral nervous system, for example, separate **specialized nerve endings exist to detect pain, temperature, light touch, deep pressure, and vibration.**

2.   Our cranial nerves are similarly specialized to provide a channel for the other **four types of stimuli that we call senses.**

3.   To test the integrity of these sensory inputs, the examiner needs to provide the appropriate stimulus (sometimes called an "adequate stimulus") for each and every component described above.

a.   In the tactile domain, for example, one must **test for the intactness of temperature** sense (with a cold tuning fork),

b. **light touch** (with the sweep of your hand across the skin),

c. **pain** (with a pinprick), and

d. **vibration sense** (with a vibrating tuning fork).

e. Similar principles hold true for testing **visual, auditory, olfactory,** and **gustatory acuity.**

4. Note that **even when testing sensory inputs, we actually rely on some type of output to assess integrity.** When we conduct each aspect of this sensory exam, we are asking in essence "Can you feel/see/hear/smell/taste this?" Even for those components of the exam that do not require verbal feedback (e.g., the corneal reflex or the pupillary light reflex), some type of motor response is in fact required.

a. To be confident that an abnormal finding on sensory exam is truly due to aberrant sensory input, this additional complexity must be kept in mind, and the source of pathology determined based on the exam in its entirety.

B. Assessing Integration and Evaluation

Even the simplest unicellular organisms have means by which they can sense and react to the environment. These responses are automatic and limited; the same stimulus will result in the same response regardless of context. There are a number of these **automatic or reflexive responses** that can be tested in the human, **including the corneal reflex and the pupillary light reflex** discussed above. Three additional sets of reflexes are commonly probed in a standard neurological exam:

1. **Proprioceptive reflexes:** These reflexes, also known as **deep tendon reflexes (DTRs),** are based on the simple reflex arcs that are activated by stretching (or tapping). Since they are influenced by the descending corticospinal tracts, DTRs can provide important information on the integrity of this pathway at several levels.

2. **Nociceptive reflexes:** These reflexes are based on **reflex arcs located in the skin** (rather than muscle tendons) and **are therefore elicited by scratching or stroking.**

a. These include the **abdominal reflexes, cremasteric reflex, and anal wink,** none of which is extensively used clinically.

b. The major nociceptive reflex of clinical value is the **plantar reflex.** Stroking the sole of the foot should elicit plantar flexion of the toes.

c. Babinski's sign, marked by an extensor response (i.e., dorsiflexion) of the toes, often with fanning of the toes and flexion of the ankle, is seen in pyramidal tract disease.

3. **Primitive reflexes (release reflexes):** These reflexes are present at birth but disappear in early infancy. Their reappearance later in life is abnormal and is often reflective of frontal lobe disease. Among others, they include **the grasp reflex** (stroking the patient's palm will lead to an automatic clutching of your finger between his or her thumb and index finger) and **the snout reflex** (gentle tapping over the patient's upper lip will cause a puckering of the lips). Note that this may also elicit a **suck response,** or a turning of the head toward the stroking stimulus (**root reflex**).
4. The brains of higher mammals, particularly in the human, have the added capacity to integrate sensory information across domains, evaluate this information, and react in a manner consistent with past experience, current context, or future expectations. The ability to use these higher-level faculties is often considered a part of the **mental status examination.** While this component of the assessment may be as brief as the Folstein Mini-Mental State Exam, or as extensive as a full-day neuropsychological battery, the core aspects of the mental status examination remain the same:
    a. consciousness,
    b. attention,
    c. memory,
    d. language,
    e. organization/planning, and
    f. visuospatial skill.

    Each of these cognitive domains is critical in moving from a stimulus to a situationally appropriate response. Given the importance of language as an example of this input-to-output bridge, we have included a table outlining the various types of aphasia and their detection (Table 10-1). For specific details on carrying out the other components of the mental status exam, the reader is directed to other chapters in this text.

C. **Assessing Output**
    Although there are many potential responses to environmental stimuli, including subtle changes in the internal hormonal or neurochemical milieu, most often the response will require some type of motor output. **The examination of this output can be divided into a motor (or muscular) component and a coordination component.**
    1. **Observation of gait** is an excellent screening test for the patient without focal weakness. If the patient is able to rise briskly and

Table 10-1. Basic Aphasiology

Type	Repetition	Comprehension	Speech
Global	Impaired	Impaired	Nonfluent
Wernicke's	Impaired	Impaired	Fluent
Broca's	Impaired	Intact	Nonfluent
Conduction	Impaired	Intact	Fluent
Transcortical			
Motor	Intact	Intact	Nonfluent
Sensory	Intact	Impaired	Fluent

independently from a seated position and walk independently, gross motor deficits can be confidently ruled out.

2. **The ability to walk on heels and toes** further assures distal lower-extremity strength.

3. In addition, walking is an extraordinarily complex motor skill that requires significant coordination of the trunk and limbs. Its actual complexity makes it an ideal screening **test for coordination ability.**

   a. The human has a particularly narrow base when standing upright; with any degree of incoordination (**ataxia**), the patient will need to widen the base to remain upright.

   b. Balance becomes even more difficult when other sensory information is removed, forming the basis for **the Romberg maneuver.**

   c. The sensitivity of screening is further increased by having the patient **walk heel to toe** (as on a tightrope). The ability to do this smoothly and quickly rules out any major impairment in coordination.

IV. Neuropsychiatric Dysfunction in Clinical Practice: Input Problems

As **the majority of conditions involving impaired sensory input are due to peripheral (rather than central) nervous system dysfunction,** the psychiatrist will not often be called upon to evaluate or treat these abnormalities.

A. **Somatized Symptoms**

The one input condition that the psychiatrist will see is the patient with suspected somatized sensory symptoms.

1. The numb hand or arm, hysterical blindness, and burning sensations in the mouth are but a few of the presentations that will often lead to psychiatric consultation.
2. The ability to competently evaluate these patients with a thorough neurological exam and psychiatric interview is an important skill that will improve the chances of proper care.

V. Neuropsychiatric Dysfunction in Clinical Practice: Evaluation Problems

The majority of patients that fall under the treatment domain of the psychiatrist **will demonstrate dysfunction in the integration or evaluation stages of information processing.** By definition, patients with dementia demonstrate difficulties in multiple realms of cognitive functioning.

A. Cognitive Problems
1. In addition, other patients with psychiatric illness, including depression, post-traumatic stress disorder, and schizophrenia, have now been shown to have objective deficits in cognition.
2. Given the importance of cognitive function on overall psychosocial performance, the skilled psychiatrist should have a working knowledge of the different cognitive domains and be adept at screening to probe the integrity of these domains.

VI. Neuropsychiatric Dysfunction in Clinical Practice: Output Problems

A. Disorders of Motor Output or Coordination
There are several disorders of motor output or coordination that also have prominent affective, behavioral, or cognitive sequelae. This list includes **Parkinson's disease and Huntington's disease** among others.
1. In Parkinson's disease, for example, depression can occur in up to 40% of all patients and behavioral disturbances can result from the disease and/or its treatment.
2. Psychiatrists will often be called upon to work in tandem with their neurologist colleagues to provide care for these patients.
3. In addition, a number of **psychotropic medications can cause motor output problems.**
   a. **Chief among them are the conventional antipsychotics** (e.g., chlorpromazine and haloperidol). While the development of newer medications without this adverse event profile (i.e., the atypical neuroleptics) has limited the use of the older medications, the psychiatrist must remain proficient

in the standard motor exam for evaluating those patients still at risk.

b. The **abnormal involuntary movement scale (AIMS)** is one example of a battery that has standardized the motor exam for this purpose.

VII. Conclusion

As evidence accumulates implicating brain physiology in psychiatric disorders, the gap between psychiatry and neurology will continue to narrow. The preponderance of cases with sensory-motor and behavioral deficits that simply represent dysfunction in these two separate domains of cerebral processing may attest to that fact. **The practicing psychiatrist must have at least a basic understanding of how to assess the integrity of brain function in each of the three main functional realms: input, evaluation, and output.**

Suggested Readings

DeGowin RL, Brown DD: *DeGowin's Diagnostic Examination,* 7th edition. New York: McGraw-Hill, 1999.

Glick TH: *Neurologic Skills.* Boston: Blackwell Scientific, 1993.

Haerer AF: *DeJong's The Neurologic Exam,* 5th edition. Philadelphia: Lippincott Williams & Wilkins, 1992.

Heimer L: *The Human Brain and Spinal Cord: Functional Neuroanatomy and Dissection Guide,* 2nd edition. New York: Springer-Verlag, 1995.

Lishman WA: *Organic Psychiatry,* 3rd edition. Oxford: Blackwell Science, 1998.

Mesulam MM: *Principles of Behavioral and Cognitive Neurology,* 2nd edition. Oxford: Oxford University Press, 2000.

Samuels MA: *Videotextbook of Neurology for the Practicing Physician, Vol. 2: The Neurologic Exam.* Boston: Butterworth-Heinemann, 1996.

Samuels MA, Feske S, Livingstone C: *Office Practice of Neurology.* Philadelphia: Saunders, 2003.

Chapter 11

Dementia and Cognitive Impairment

JOSHUA L. ROFFMAN, MD

I.   Overview

Among the disorders of cognitive impairment, dementia has received the most attention and has generated the most apprehension. Dementia is characterized by more than just a significant decline in memory; it also involves at least one other area of cognitive function. A syndrome marked by clinical and pathophysiologic heterogeneity, dementia is usually irreversible, but it is always treatable. This contrasts with many conditions that must be considered in the differential diagnosis of dementia (most notably delirium and depression), most of which are reversible if they are readily identified (see Table 11-1). Although dementia is not considered a normal consequence of the aging process, the incidence of dementia increases with age. Moreover, as the geriatric population swells and the prevalence of dementia grows, effective diagnosis and management of dementia will become increasingly important for the clinician.

A.   **Definition**
1.   DSM-IV defines dementia as the presence of an **acquired deficit in memory and at least one other impaired higher cortical function:**
    a.   **Aphasia,** a difficulty with any aspect of language;
    b.   **Apraxia,** an impaired ability to perform motor tasks despite intact motor function;
    c.   **Agnosia,** an impairment of object recognition despite intact sensory function; or
    d.   **Executive dysfunction,** a difficulty with abstracting, planning, organizing, sequencing, monitoring, or initiating or stopping complex behaviors.
2.   A diagnosis of dementia requires a **change from baseline;** deficits must be **significant enough to detract from social or occupational function.** These deficits **cannot occur exclusively during an episode of delirium,** and they **cannot be accounted for by another Axis I diagnosis,** such as major depressive disorder.

Address for correspondence: Dr. Joshua L. Roffman, Massachusetts General Hospital, Wang Ambulatory Care Center 812, 15 Parkman St., Boston, MA 02114, email: jroffman@partners.org.

Table 11-1. Differential Diagnosis of Dementia

Nonreversible Causes	*Potentially Reversible Causes*
Degenerative	*Psychiatric*
Alzheimer's disease	Depression
Frontal lobe dementia	*Obstructive*
Pick's disease	Normal pressure hydrocephalus
Dementia with Lewy bodies	Obstructive hydrocephalus
Corticobasal degeneration	*Neoplastic*
Huntington's disease	Tumors (malignant or benign)
Parkinson's disease	Paraneoplastic encephalitis
Wilson's disease	Carcinomatous meningitis
Progressive supranuclear palsy	*Infectious*
Amyotrophic lateral sclerosis	Chronic meningitis
Vascular	(e.g., tuberculous)
Vascular dementia	HIV dementia
Stroke	Neurosyphilis
Diffuse white matter disease	Postherpes encephalitis
Postanoxic injury	Lyme encephalopathy
Traumatic	*Demyelinating/autoimmune/*
Dementia pugilistica	*inflammatory*
Postconcussion syndrome	Multiple sclerosis
Infectious	Vasculitis
Creutzfeldt-Jakob disease	Systemic lupus erythematosus
Progressive multifocal	Polyarteritis nodosa
leukoencephalopathy	*Endocrine*
Metabolic	Hypothyroidism
Korsakoff syndrome	Adrenal insufficiency
	Cushing's syndrome
	Hyper/hypoparathyroidism
	Hepatic failure
	Renal failure
	Metabolic
	Wernicke's encephalopathy
	Vitamin B_{12} deficiency
	Toxic/pharmacologic
	Drug/medication effects
	Heavy metals, organophosphates
	Chronic alcoholism
	Vascular
	Chronic subdural hematoma

3. **Mild cognitive impairment** can be viewed as a related entity that occurs in older individuals who exhibit some slowing of the ability to learn new information. However, unlike patients with dementia, for those with mild cognitive impairment once information is retained, memory degradation does not occur; fortunately, occupational and social function remain intact. Mild cognitive impairment can represent a precursor to dementia and should be monitored for progression over time.

B.   Epidemiology

1. The overall prevalence of dementia in people over the age of 60 is estimated at 15%. While the **prevalence at age 60 is 1%, it doubles every 5 years** after the age of 60; **by age 85, the prevalence of dementia approaches 50%.** Dementia affects approximately 4 million people in the United States and is associated with an estimated cost of $113 billion each year.
2. The most common form of dementia, **Alzheimer's disease,** accounts for up to 50–70% of cases; other common etiologies include **Lewy body dementia** (which occurs in up to 25% of cases) and **vascular dementia** (which occurs in up to 20% of cases).
3. While the overall incidence of dementia is equivalent in men and women, men exhibit higher rates of vascular dementia and lower rates of Alzheimer's disease than do women.

C.   Clinical Phenomenology

1. **Alzheimer's disease** is characterized by a **slow, steady cognitive decline.** The disorder typically presents initially with **loss of short-term memory.** Subsequent symptoms include **word-finding and naming difficulty** with associated circumlocution and use of clichés, and **apraxias** that affect a variety of activities, such as dressing, eating, and driving. When individuals have advanced Alzheimer's disease, they develop **impaired judgment** and can manifest personality changes (including **apathy, hostility, or social withdrawal**). The average survival after the onset of symptoms is **8 to 10 years.**
2. **Dementia with Lewy bodies,** which is more prevalent than previously thought, **shares features of both Alzheimer's disease and Parkinson's disease.** Patients exhibit **progressive cognitive decline** with at least two of the following additional features:
    a. **Recurrent visual hallucinations;**
    b. **Parkinsonism;** or

    c. **Fluctuating cognition,** with variation in attention and alertness.

Afflicted patients frequently experience repeated falls and exhibit an unusual sensitivity to the extrapyramidal side effects of antipsychotic medications.

3. **Vascular dementia** is typically associated with a **stepwise progression of cognitive deficits** that is thought to be linked with ischemic events. Affected persons often exhibit associated **focal deficits in sensory or motor function,** as well as **laboratory evidence of cerebrovascular disease.**

4. Less common dementias (from a variety of causes) are reviewed below:

    a. **Frontotemporal dementias,** including **Pick's disease,** present with **insidious behavioral changes that precede cognitive decline.** Behavioral changes can include **disinhibition, impulsivity, inflexibility, and stereotypy;** language impairments are also seen and can include **increased verbal output and echolalia.**

    b. Dementia associated with **normal pressure hydrocephalus (NPH)** presents with a **"magnetic gait"** followed by **urinary incontinence.** Symptoms improve rapidly following a therapeutic lumbar puncture (the **Miller Fisher** test).

    c. Dementia associated with **movement disorders** (e.g., Parkinson's disease, Huntington's disease, Wilson's disease, progressive supranuclear palsy, and corticobasal degeneration) are often associated with the late stages of dementia.

5. **In all cases,** an underlying diagnosis of dementia may predispose a patient to **delirium and perceptual disturbances, depression, and anxiety.**

D.   **Etiology and Risk Factors**

The pathophysiologies of dementia are a subject of ongoing research; the depth of our current understanding varies by subtype. While for most dementias advanced age places patients at greater risk, additional risk factors vary across the dementia subtypes.

1. In **Alzheimer's disease,** postmortem examination of the brain reveals diffuse **amyloid plaques** and **neurofibrillary tangles.** Loss of neurons in the basal forebrain results in prominent reductions of acetylcholine; neurons in the hippocampus also appear vulnerable to damage. **Multiple genetic abnormalities** (including trisomy 21 and mutations on chromosomes 1, 14, and 21) have been clearly associated with the disease; however, to date these mutations account for fewer than 5% of cases. The

ApoE-4 **allele** has also been linked with an increased risk of Alzheimer's disease and with an earlier age of onset.

2. Progression of **vascular dementia** is related to cerebrovascular disease, vasculitis, or embolic disease (including atrial fibrillation). Contributing risk factors include hypertension, hyperlipidemia, diabetes mellitus, obesity, and smoking.

3. The diagnosis of **Lewy body dementia** is confirmed by the presence of **Lewy bodies,** which are round, eosinophilic intraneuronal inclusions that appear in cortical and subcortical structures; at present these can be detected only in postmortem examination. The relationship between Lewy bodies and neuronal degeneration is uncertain. Some studies suggest that a genetic predisposition may play an important role; moreover, the disease is twice as prevalent in males.

II. The Evaluation

Thorough evaluation of new-onset dementia is often a time-consuming process that reflects the difficulty of obtaining historical information from cognitively impaired patients and the considerable work-up necessary to rule out reversible etiologies. In most cases, the final diagnosis relies on clinical assessment, as laboratory and neuroimaging tests rarely confirm the presence of a primary dementia.

A. **Gathering History**
1. **General approach**
    a. Although the patient with cognitive impairment can provide valuable information via self-reporting, it is likely that inaccuracies will emerge because of memory-related or other cognitive deficits. **Obtaining collateral information** from family members, close friends, and established treaters is therefore essential.
    b. To minimize patient distress, the clinician should conduct at least a portion of the interview with friends or family members away from the patient.
2. **The cognitive history**
    a. The interviewer should determine whether deterioration has occurred **precipitously or insidiously,** and whether the decline has been **gradual or stepwise.** The course of illness can be helpful in creation of a differential diagnosis, as described elsewhere in this chapter.
    b. A detailed description of the nature of altered behaviors should be obtained; this should include **changes in the ability to remember new information, disinhibited or inap-**

propriate behaviors, paranoia, hallucinations, or changes in personality.

   c. Functional status can be assessed using the **Activities of Daily Living Scale,** which evaluates basic areas of function (including bathing, dressing, toileting, transferring, continence, and feeding). The ability to perform more complex tasks can be determined using the **Instrumental Activities of Daily Living Scale,** which includes ambulating, using the telephone, shopping, preparing meals, performing housework, doing laundry, self-administering medication, and paying bills (Table 11-2).

3. **The psychiatric history**

The presence of a premorbid psychiatric diagnosis should be evaluated. This becomes important for three reasons:

   a. Risk factors for certain types of dementia can be elicited (e.g., alcohol abuse and Wernicke-Korsakoff syndrome);

   b. Certain primary psychiatric syndromes can mimic aspects of dementia (e.g., depression or psychosis); and

   c. Conversely, dementia can place a patient at risk for another psychiatric problem (e.g., depression or anxiety).

4. **The medical history**

   a. **Medical illnesses** (including stroke, head trauma, hypertension, hyperlipidemia, lupus, and human immunodeficiency virus or other chronic infectious agents affecting the central nervous system) **that might contribute to manifestations of cognitive dysfunction** should be elicited.

   b. **Nutritional status, a history of drug or alcohol use**

Table 11-2. Activities of Daily Living	
Basic	**Instrumental**
Bathing	Shopping
Dressing	Cooking
Walking	Managing finances
Toileting/continence	Housework
Feeding	Using telephone
Transfers (to/from bed, chair)	Traveling outside of home
	Making simple home repairs
	Doing laundry
	Self-administering medications

> **or abuse, and exposure to cigarettes and other toxins** should be established.
>
> c. **A review of systems** should encompass presence of urinary symptoms, vision or hearing loss, gait disturbance, falls, or signs of occult infection or neoplasm.
>
> d. **A medication history is essential as medications are implicated in up to 30% of cases of dementia.** Common offenders include anticholinergics, antihistamines, antihypertensives, psychotropics, sedative-hypnotics, and narcotic analgesics.

5. **A family history** can be useful, especially in cases of Alzheimer's disease and frontotemporal dementia.

6. **A social and occupational history** will serve to establish premorbid intelligence and education, as well as changes in the level of function.

B.   Physical Examination

1. **A general medical assessment** should be carried out; particular emphasis should be placed on the cardiovascular system. The clinician should be mindful of physical signs that suggest endocrine, inflammatory, and infectious processes that may be contributing to cognitive symptoms.

2. **A careful neurological examination** should be completed with attention paid to focal motor or sensory signs, altered reflexes (including frontal release signs), gait, and coordination. The presence of cogwheeling, tremor, or rigidity may be consistent with a parkinsonian process, while paralysis of vertical gaze can be consistent with progressive supranuclear palsy. Funduscopic examination can indicate vascular damage as well as increased intracranial pressure. Screening of vision and hearing can reveal losses that can mimic or exacerbate cognitive decline.

C.   The Mental Status Examination and Cognitive Testing

1. On mental status examination, questions that pertain to **mood and neurovegetative symptoms** may indicate whether a treatable depression is contributing to cognitive difficulties. An elevated mood or an expansive affect can signal manic symptoms associated with frontal lobe syndromes. Psychotic symptoms (e.g., delusions of infidelity or theft) should also be addressed.

2. The **Folstein Mini-Mental State Examination (MMSE)** is a short, structured instrument that can elicit problems with orientation, attention, calculation, language, and memory (Table 11-3). The instrument can also be used to document changes seen over time. Of note, the MMSE has poor specificity for demen-

Table 11-3. Folstein Mini-Mental State Examination

Task	Scoring
Orientation	1 point each for year, season, date, day of the week, month, state, county, town, building, floor/room
Registration	1 point each for 3 objects
Calculation	1 point each for correct serial 7 subtractions, or for each letter in "WORLD" spelled backwards correctly
Recall	1 point each for the 3 objects from before
Naming	1 point each for correctly naming a watch and a pen
Repeating a phrase	1 point if patient successfully repeats "No ifs, ands, or buts"
Verbal commands	1 point each for taking a piece of paper with right hand, folding it in half, and putting it on the floor
Written commands	1 point if eyes close on written command "CLOSE YOUR EYES"
Writing	1 point if patient writes a complete sentence
Drawing	1 point if patient copies intersecting pentagons with ten corners and two intersecting lines
	Total score out of 30 points

tia, and it may exhibit poor sensitivity in highly intelligent or in well-educated patients.

3. Additional cognitive testing can unmask deficits in **executive function, abstraction, praxis, and visuospatial performance.** These tasks include **clock-drawing** ("Draw a clock face and set the hands to 'ten to two' "), **word fluency** ("List as many animals as you can in one minute"), **proverb interpretation, and simple tasks of praxis** (e.g., brushing teeth and combing hair).

4. A referral for **formal neuropsychological testing** can be useful when deficits are mild or difficult to characterize after an initial encounter.

D.   Laboratory Assessment

1. Routine laboratory studies are listed in Table 11-4. The American Academy of Neurology recommends obtaining **serum elec-**

Table 11-4. Laboratory Investigations

Routine Studies
Blood studies
  Complete blood count
  Electrolytes
  Glucose
  Blood urea nitrogen
  Creatinine
  Liver function tests
  Thyroid stimulating hormone
  Syphilis serology (e.g., rapid plasmin reagin)
  Vitamin B$_{12}$
  Folate
  Calcium
  Phosphorus
  Magnesium
Urine studies
  Urinalysis
Neuroimaging
  Noncontrast head computed axial tomography scan
Additional Studies (Based on History and Physical Findings)
Blood studies
  Sedimentation rate
  Human immunodeficiency virus testing
  Rheumatoid factor
  Antinuclear antibody and other autoimmune disorder screens
  Drug levels
  Heavy metal screening
  Lipid profile
Imaging studies
  Brain magnetic resonance imaging
  Positron emission tomography scan
  Noninvasive carotid studies
  Chest x-ray
Electrophysiology
  Electrocardiogram
  Electroencephalogram
Other
  Lumbar puncture

trolytes, serum glucose, blood urea nitrogen, creatinine, liver function tests, a complete blood count, thyroid function tests, a vitamin B$_{12}$ level, and syphilis serology as part of the dementia evaluation; however, the likelihood of detecting a reversible cause of dementia with this screen is less than 10%. A **noncontrast computed axial tomography (CT) scan** of the brain can detect subdural hematoma, hydrocephalus, stroke, or tumors, as well as region-specific atrophy (as in frontotemporal dementia). A **urinalysis** should be performed to rule out a urinary tract infection that may be otherwise asymptomatic in elderly patients.

2. Several additional tests may be useful; these are ordered as a consequence of clinical suspicion:

    a. **Brain magnetic resonance imaging (MRI)** should be ordered in a patient with focal neurologic deficits; this modality is more sensitive for recent stroke than CT. MRI is contraindicated in patients with pacemakers or metallic implants.

    b. An **electroencephalogram (EEG)** can identify a toxic-metabolic encephalopathy, partial complex seizures, or Creutzfeldt-Jacob disease.

    c. A **lumbar puncture** is indicated for suspicion of hydrocephalus, vasculitis, cancer, or a tumor of the central nervous system.

    d. Additional serum testing can include **human immunodeficiency virus (HIV)** and **heavy metal screening** for patients with potential exposure to these agents, as well as testing for autoimmune diseases.

E.   Differential Diagnosis

History combined with physical examination, mental status and cognitive examinations, and laboratory studies will be useful in differentiating reversible and nonreversible causes of dementia as listed in Table 11-1. **Particular attention should be given to ruling out depression and delirium,** two of the most common treatable causes of cognitive dysfunction in elderly patients. **Even for patients with a non-reversible dementia, determination of a specific diagnosis is essential to optimal management and the assessment of prognosis.**

III. Treatment

The first step in the management of dementia involves the **treatment of reversible etiologies and the minimization of aggravating factors** (such as comorbid depression or sensorium-altering medications). A combination of psychosocial, behavioral, and pharmacological interventions can then be employed to target specific symptoms, to provide an optimal environment for patients and caregivers, and in some cases to slow progression of the disease.

A.   Treatment of Reversible Etiologies
1.   When a reversible medical etiology is identified and treated, cognitive function can usually be expected to improve. In some cases, it may be too late for restoration to a premorbid baseline; however, further decline may be prevented.
2.   Surgical interventions (such as shunting of cerebrospinal fluid in normal pressure hydrocephalus and evacuation of subdural hematomas) should be considered if appropriate.

B.   Minimization of Aggravating Factors
1.   The **reduction or elimination of drugs that affect the CNS** (see the section on the medical history above) should be attempted. Consideration should also be given to over-the-counter medications such as diphenhydramine.
2.   Certain **coexisting medical conditions** (such as urinary tract infections, atrial fibrillation and other conditions that cause cerebral hypoperfusion, and disorders that cause pain) can significantly exacerbate cognitive and behavioral symptoms; rapid diagnosis and treatment can substantially improve function in these areas among patients with an underlying dementia.
3.   If present, **major depressive disorder** can be treated with **selective serotonin reuptake inhibitors, mirtazapine, or buproprion,** all of which have favorable side effect profiles. Tricyclic antidepressants can cause orthostatic hypotension and cardiotoxicity, while venlafaxine can cause or exacerbate hypertension; these agents should therefore be used with caution in the geriatric population. When lack of energy and low motivation are especially prominent, a trial of a **psychostimulant** (e.g., methylphenidate) can be attempted; however, clinicians should be vigilant for the emergence or exacerbation of psychotic symptoms with this medication class.

C.   Pharmacotherapy
Pharmacotherapy for dementia can be divided into agents that improve cognitive function or slow the rate of cognitive decline, and those that target symptoms (such as agitation and hallucinations).
1.   **Acetylcholinesterase inhibitors** (e.g., tacrine [Cognex®], donepezil [Aricept®], rivastigmine [Exelon®], and galantamine

[Reminyl®]) have been approved by the U.S. Food and Drug Administration (FDA) for cognitive enhancement of persons with with Alzheimer's disease. None will stop the progression of dementia, but each may slow the decline by 6 months to a year. All can have cholinergic side effects, such as nausea, headaches, and bradycardia. While donepezil is the preferred agent in terms of once-a-day dosing (5 mg daily for 4 to 6 weeks followed by 10 mg daily thereafter), rivastigmine (dosed at 2–6 mg twice daily, increased gradually) avoids hepatic metabolism, and thus potential drug-drug interactions.

2. **Memantine** (Namenda®), an NMDA-receptor antagonist, was recently approved by the FDA for use in moderate to severe Alzheimer's disease. Recent clinical trials have demonstrated improved outcome on cognitive and behavioral measures both with memantine alone and in combination with donepezil. The dose is slowly titrated up to 10 mg twice daily; side effects include constipation, dizziness, headache, and confusion.

3. There is some evidence that **vitamin E** (2000 IU daily) and selegeline may slow progression of Alzheimer's disease.

4. For **hallucinations and delusions, low doses of atypical antipsychotics** (such as risperidone, olanzapine, and quetiapine) may be useful. While risperidone is less sedating than olanzapine or quetiapine, it is more likely to exacerbate extrapyramidal symptoms in patients with parkinsonism. When these agents fail, high potency typical neuroleptics, such as haloperidol, are generally effective, but also significantly increase the risk of extrapyramidal effects. Low-potency neuroleptics, such as thioridazine and chlorpromazine, should be avoided due to their sedative effects and their effects on postural hypotension.

5. **Agitation** can be manifest by motor restlessness, verbal outbursts, or physical aggression. Once a medical or pharmacological etiology has been ruled out, pharmacotherapy can be used along with behavioral interventions (see below). The best-studied intervention, **the use of neuroleptics, appears to have only moderate efficacy in the treatment of acute agitation in patients with dementia.** Case reports have indicated promise for several other agents, including trazodone, lithium carbonate, carbamazepine, and valproic acid. **Benzodiazepines can worsen cognitive impairment and induce oversedation, especially in the elderly, or may paradoxically result in marked disinhibition; therefore this class of medication should be avoided.**

6. **For vascular dementia, a mainstay of pharmacotherapy is the control of hypertension and other modifiable risk fac-**

tors. Anticoagulation (with aspirin or warfarin) is often utilized, although the risk of falls and other conditions that lead to hemorrhage should be taken into account.

D. **Behavioral and Psychosocial Interventions**
   1. **Patient and family education** is critical to the creation and maintenance of a trusting and supportive environment. Collaboration with family members is often crucial to keep the patient informed. When addressing a patient, content should be kept simple and to the point.
   2. **Frequent reorientation to their environment** will provide demented patients with reassurance and avoid escalation of anxiety and agitation.
   3. **Address behavioral and safety problems** (e.g., wandering, agitation, screaming, incontinence, and aggression); behavioral control of these symptoms is likely to prevent early nursing home placement. For paranoid symptoms, **reassurance and distraction** are often preferred responses.
   4. **Address legal issues** (such as the establishment of wills, health care proxies, and durable power of attorney) **early in the course of the illness, and suggest that the patient receive assistance with financial management.**
   5. **Continue routine health maintenance visits** every 3 to 6 months, and consider **referral to a neuropsychiatric consultant** when psychiatric or behavioral symptoms do not respond to commonly effective treatments, or when a patient presents with unusual symptoms or a rapid progression.
   6. **Refer caregivers and family members to support groups** and to other sources of information. Remember that care providers for demented patients are at significant risk for anxiety and depression.

Suggested Readings

Cummings JL, Vinters HV, Cole GM, Khachaturian ZS: Alzheimer's disease: Etiologies, pathophysiology, cognitive reserve, and treatment opportunities. *Neurology* 1998;51:S2–S17.

Daly EJ, Falk WE, Brown PA: Cholinesterase inhibitors for behavioral disturbance in dementia. *Curr Psychiatry Rep* 2001;3:251–258.

Falk WE: The patient with memory problems or dementia. In Stern TA, Herman JB, Slavin PL (eds): *The Massachusetts General Hospital Guide to Primary Care Psychiatry,* 2nd edition. New York: McGraw-Hill, 2004:197–212.

Felician O, Sanderson TA: The neurobiology and pharmacotherapy of Alzheimer's disease. *J Neuropsychiatry Clin Neurosci* 1999;11:19–31.

Folstein MF, Folstein SE, McHugh PR: "Mini-mental state." A practical method for grading the cognitive state of patients for the clinician. *J Psychiatr Res* 1975;12: 189–198.

Geldmacher DS, Whitehouse PJ: Evaluation of dementia. *N Engl J Med* 1996;335: 330–336.

Helmuth L: New Alzheimer's treatments that may ease the mind. *Science* 2002;297: 1260–1263.

Papka MP, Rubio A, Schiffer RB: A review of Lewy body disease, an emerging concept of cortical dementia. *J Neuropsychiatry Clin Neurosci* 1998;10:267–279.

Peterson RC, Stevens JC, Ganguli M, et al: Practice parameter: Early detection of dementia: Mild cognitive impairment (an evidence-based review). *Neurology* 2001;56:1133–1142.

Tariot PN, Farlow MR, Grossberg GT, et al: Memantine treatment in patients with moderate to severe Alzheimer's disease already receiving donepezil: A randomized controlled trial. *JAMA* 2004;291:317–324.

Chapter 12

An Approach to the Patient with Disordered Sleep

PATRICK SMALLWOOD, MD
THEODORE A. STERN, MD

I.   Introduction

Sleep is an active biochemical process complete with various physiological markers, stages, and patterns that provide a basic indication of overall well-being. In this chapter, normal sleep is examined, followed by a brief discussion of the diagnosis and treatment of the three major classes of sleep disorders recognized by the *Diagnostic and Statistical Manual of Mental Disorders*, 4th ed., Text Revision (DSM-IV-TR).

II.   Normal Sleep

A.   **Polysomnography**
Sleep is defined objectively through polysomnography, which **involves the simultaneous recording of multiple physiological parameters in a standardized fashion** known as a polysomnogram (PSG). The **parameters recorded by a PSG include an electroencephalogram (EEG), electrooculogram (EOG), electrocardiogram (ECG), electromyogram (EMG), respiratory effort, pulse oximetry, and snore monitoring.** Once completed, the PSG provides objective data by which the stages, architecture, and amount of sleep can be defined and examined in order to determine the presence or absence of a sleep disorder. Table 12-1 describes the salient PSG findings that define the various sleep stages.

B.   **Sleep Cycle and Architecture**
There are two major types of sleep defined by the PSG: (1) non-rapid eye movement (NREM) sleep, and (2) rapid eye movement (REM) sleep, also known as *paradoxical sleep*. NREM sleep is further divided into four additional stages, NREM 1 through 4.
1.   NREM and REM alternate in a rhythmic fashion known as the **NREM-REM cycle.** In normal healthy individuals, this cycle begins with NREM 1 and progresses to NREM 2, 3, 4, 3, 2, and then REM. The **NREM-REM cycle generally repeats itself at**

Address for correspondence: Dr. Theodore A. Stern, Massachusetts General Hospital, Fruit Street, Warren Building, Room 605, Boston, MA 02114, email: TStern@Partners.org.

Table 12-1. Human Sleep Stages and Distribution Across the Night

	EEG Findings	EMG Findings	EOG Findings	Distibution Over the Night
Wake	Alpha waves (8–14 Hz)	Muscle tone and activity present	Variable eye movements	<5%
NREM 1	Theta waves (4–7 Hz)	Muscle tone and activity present	Slow rolling eye movements	2–5%
NREM 2	Theta waves (4–7 Hz); sleep spindles (12–14 Hz ≥0.5 seconds); K-complexes (triphasic)	Muscle tone and activity present, but slowing	Slow rolling eye movements	45–55%
NREM 3 & 4	Delta waves (0.5–2 Hz) present ≥50% of the time	Marked decrease in muscle tone and activity	Slow rolling eye movements	13–23%
REM	Relatively low-voltage mixed-frequency waves	Absence of muscle activity	Conjugate rapid eye movements	20–25%

NREM, non-rapid eye movement; REM, rapid eye movement; Hz, Hertz; EEG, electroencephalogram; EMG, electromyogram; EOG, electrooculogram.

90- to 120-minute intervals three to four times a night; this pattern is known as the **sleep cycle.**

2. Of note, NREM 3 and 4 (also known as delta sleep) are most prominent in the first half of the night, and REM sleep becomes increasingly more prominent as the night progresses.

3. **Sleep latency,** usually 10–20 minutes, is the time from lights out until the first NREM period.
4. **REM latency,** usually 90–100 minutes, is the time from sleep onset until the first REM period.
5. **Sleep efficiency** is calculated thusly: [(total sleep time)/(total sleep record time)] x 100.
6. **Sleep architecture** is the pattern and distribution of sleep stages across an average night and is summarized in Table 12-1.

C. **Sleep Across the Life-span**
The amount of time spent in the different stages of sleep varies with age. **As we age, we experience a reduction in the intensity, depth, and continuity of sleep.** Specific findings in the elderly include:
1. Increased sleep latency
2. Reduced NREM 3 and 4
3. Decreased REM latency
4. Reduced total REM amount
5. Frequent awakenings, and
6. Decreased sleep efficiency.

III. Sleep Disorders: Overview

The DSM-IV-TR divides sleep disorders into three major categories: Primary Sleep Disorders, Sleep Disorders Related to Another Mental Disorder, and Other Sleep Disorders. Of the three, Primary Sleep Disorders are the most common, and are therefore emphasized here.

A. **Primary Sleep Disorders**
DSM-IV-TR subdivides the primary sleep disorders into the **dyssomnias** and the **parasomnias.**
1. **Dyssomnias** are primary sleep disorders that result in complaints of either sleeping too little (insomnia) or too much (hypersomnia). The DSM-IV-TR subcategorizes dyssomnias into six groups.
    a. *Primary insomnia.* Insomnia is the subjective complaint of deficient, inadequate, or unrefreshing sleep. **To qualify as a primary insomnia, there must be objective daytime sleepiness and/or subjective feelings of not being rested, and an absence of psychiatric or medical conditions that better account for it.** With **primary insomnia,** the classic form of insomnia, sufferers complain of decreased daytime functioning, and are frequently overaroused and anxious at bedtime. **Sleep-state misperception** is a primary insomnia in which sufferers complain of inadequate and/or poor

sleep, but objective findings on the polysomnogram are lacking. **Idiopathic insomnia** is chronic insomnia present from childhood and is most likely the result of an underlying innate process.

b. *Primary hypersomnia.* The **hallmark of all primary hypersomnias is the complaint of somnolence and excessive daytime sleep.** In addition, they are not the direct result of underlying medical or psychiatric conditions, and they are confirmed by objective PSG findings. One type of primary hypersomnia, known as **recurrent hypersomnia or Kleine-Levin syndrome,** primarily affects adolescent males, with symptoms including hypersomnia, hyperphagia, and hypersexuality. It often follows an acute viral infection.

c. *Narcolepsy.* Narcolepsy is **defined by the tetrad** of **sleep paralysis** upon falling asleep or waking, brief (10–15 minutes) **sleep attacks** occurring in inappropriate circumstances, **cataplexy** (a condition of sudden and transient bilateral weakness or paralysis) triggered by strong emotion (such as laughter, anger, or surprise), and **hypnagogic hallucinations.** It is a rare condition, with an incidence of 0.07%. The onset of this disorder is usually in the late teens and early 20s, and its course is chronic. Genetic factors play a role in the etiology.

d. *Breathing-related sleep disorders.* The **hallmark of sleep-related breathing disorders is** *apnea,* **the cessation of nasobuccal airflow for greater than 10 seconds.** The most commonly encountered breathing-related sleep disorder is **obstructive sleep apnea (OSA),** which affects 1–2% of the adult male population in the United States, increasing to 8.5% of men between the ages of 40 and 65 years. Women account for 12–35% of OSA patients, with the majority of them being postmenopausal. Nocturnal symptoms of OSA include snoring, choking, enuresis, reflux, and cardiac dysrhythmias, and daytime symptoms include headaches, hypersomnolence, automatic behavior, and neuropsychiatric abnormalities. Risk factors include male sex, age 40–65 years, obesity, smoking, alcohol use, and poor physical health. **The principal defect is occlusion of the upper airway at the level of the pharynx** during wake-sleep transitions and sleep proper. Two other breathing-related sleep disorders include **central sleep apnea** and **mixed sleep apnea.** With central sleep apnea, there is cessation of airflow without an attempt to initiate thoracoabdominal respiratory effort; the etiology of this is felt to lie in abnormal CNS processes. With mixed sleep apnea, there are combined repetitive central and obstructive apneas. Symptoms and treatment for both central and mixed sleep apnea are similar to those of OSA.

e. *Circadian rhythm disorders.* **Circadian rhythm is an endogenous rhythm of bodily functions that is influenced by environmental cues, or** *zeitgebers.* It is unique to each person, averaging 25 hours, but can be as long as 50 hours for some. **With circadian rhythm sleep disorders, the timing of sleep, not its quality and architecture, is adversely affected.** These disorders are self-limited and resolve as the individual adjusts to the new sleep-wake schedule. The most commonly encountered disorders include **jet lag syndrome, shift-work sleep disorder, delayed sleep phase disorder** ("night owls"), and **advanced sleep phase disorder** ("larks").

f. *Dyssomnia not otherwise specified.* The three most common disorders in this class include **periodic limb movement disorder (PLMD), restless leg syndrome (RLS),** and **idiopathic hypersomnia.**

   i. **PLMD** is quite a common dyssomnia, affecting up to 40% of people over the age of 65 years. Symptoms include brief (0.5–5 seconds) stereotypic contractions of the lower limbs at intervals of 20–60 seconds, unrefreshing sleep, and daytime hypersomnia.

   ii. **RLS** is a movement disorder characterized by deep sensations of creeping or aching inside the legs and calves when lying or sitting that produce an overwhelming urge to move them. Patients with RLS often suffer from PLMD.

   iii. **Idiopathic hypersomnia,** as the name implies, is a hypersomnia of unknown origin. It is frequently confused with narcolepsy, but is distinguished from it by the absence of cataplexy and immediate-onset REM sleep.

2. **Parasomnias** are sleep disorders in which undesirable events arise during specific sleep stages or at the transition between wakefulness and sleep. Children are affected more often than adults, and several different parasomnias may occur in the same individual. **Typically, individuals are difficult to arouse during an episode and often have poor recall of the episode.** The most common parasomnias include sleep-talking, sleepwalking, sleep terror disorder, nightmare disorder, and enuresis. Although

not a common parasomnia, *REM behavior disorder* is of clinical interest and included in this discussion.

a. **Sleeptalking** (somniloquism) arises during NREM 1 and 2. It involves vocalizations ranging from simple words and phrases to complete conversations. It is frequently spontaneous, but may be elicited by speaking to the sleeper. It is a benign condition that warrants no treatment.

b. **Sleepwalking** (somnambulism) arises during NREM 3 and 4. It occurs predominantly during the first third of the night and upon partial emergence from delta sleep. Sufferers may walk for some distance and carry out semipurposeful activities, such as running and eating. Serious accidents, such as tripping or falling out of open windows, have been reported. Sufferers are frequently unresponsive to efforts to wake them, and once awakened are amnestic to the event. Sleepwalking begins in childhood and often resolves spontaneously by adolescence.

c. **Sleep terror disorder** (pavor nocturnus) occurs during NREM 3 and 4, often during partial arousal from delta sleep. Symptoms include screaming, flailing about, sitting up in bed, and autonomic activity, including tachypnea, tachycardia, and mydriasis. Episodes, often 1–10 minutes in duration, take place early in the night, when NREM duration is at its longest. Because night terrors are a NREM phenomenon, and therefore not associated with dreaming, patients are often amnestic to the episode.

d. **Nightmare disorder** occurs during REM sleep, frequently late in the night as REM intervals increase. Sufferers experience terrifying dreams whose content is often remembered. Unlike sleep terrors, nightmares lack autonomic arousal, as well as motor activity due to REM-related muscle atonia.

e. **Nocturnal enuresis** arises during any or all sleep stages. The main symptom is involuntary micturition occurring without conscious arousal.

f. **REM behavior disorder** occurs during the second half of the night during REM sleep. Patients recall their dreams in vivid detail, and appear to be acting them out through simple to quite complex movements that result from the loss of muscle atonia that is normally present during REM sleep. While 60% of cases are idiopathic, up to one-third are due to brainstem pathology and alcoholism. Males are affected nine times more frequently than females.

B. **Secondary Sleep Disorders**

The DSM-IV-TR subdivides the secondary sleep disorders into those related to another mental disorder, those related to a general medical condition, and those that are substance-induced.

1. **Sleep disorders related to another mental disorder.** As a general rule, sleep disorders resulting from psychiatric disorders most often present with insomnia, rather than hypersomnia, as a chief complaint.

   a. *Psychotic disorders.* Common findings include difficulty with sleep initiation and maintenance, decreased total sleep time and sleep efficiency, and disrupted REM sleep early in the episode.

   b. *Mood disorders.* With depression, common findings include early morning awakening, decreased delta sleep, decreased REM latency, long first REM period, increased REM density, and nocturnal restlessness. With bipolar disorder, the percentage of REM sleep increases during the depressed phase and decreases during the manic phase.

   c. *Anxiety disorders.* Anxiety disorders are the most common psychiatric cause of insomnia. Sleep findings include increased pre-sleep worry with difficulty initiating sleep, decreased sleep efficiency, and poor sleep maintenance.

2. **Sleep disorder due to a general medical condition.** The most common sleep complaint with sleep disorders resulting from a general medical condition is insomnia. While virtually any medical condition can disrupt sleep, the most common ones include seizures, cluster headaches, abnormal swallowing, cardiovascular disease, metabolic disorders, pain, asthma, and gastroesophageal reflux.

3. **Substance-induced sleep disorder.** The general rule regarding substance-induced sleep disorders is that if the substance is a CNS depressant, intoxication causes sedation and withdrawal causes insomnia. If the substance is a CNS stimulant, intoxication results in insomnia and withdrawal results in sedation.

   a. Alcohol, the most commonly encountered substance that affects sleep, has the following effects:

      i. *Small to moderate* amounts result in sedation and frequent awakenings.

      ii. *Acute intoxication* results in decreased REM and increased delta sleep.

      iii. *Acute withdrawal* results in insomnia, increased REM sleep, and decreased delta sleep.

      iv. *Chronic use* results in insomnia that may persist for months or up to a year after detoxification.

IV.   Approach to the Patient with Disordered Sleep

A.   **Sleep History**
The first step in diagnosing a sleep disorder is to obtain a detailed sleep history. This can be accomplished through direct inquiry of the patient and his or her bed partner, or with a standardized sleep questionnaire. All patients should be urged to keep a 2-week sleep diary that details the time and amount of sleep, the number and length of any naps, the number of awakenings, wake-up times, any medications taken, and subjective mood during the day. For patients in whom hypersomnia is the major complaint, an Epworth Sleepiness Scale (ESS), a simple self-administered questionnaire that requires patients to rate their degree of sleepiness in a variety of routine situations, is often given.

B.   **Physical Examination and Laboratory Testing**
Prior to laboratory work-up, all patients should receive a physical examination. For patients complaining of hypersomnia, special focus is placed on the distribution of obesity, the respiratory system, the cardiovascular system, and the oronasomaxillofacial region. Basic labs, if indicated, should include CBC, blood gases, pulmonary function tests, an ECG, thyroid function tests, serum iron, and electrolytes. Cephalometric x-rays of the skull and neck may also be obtained to evaluate for skeletal discrepancies if craniofacial malformations are suspected as a possible etiology for any breathing-related sleep disorder. Once completed, the patient must be referred to a sleep disorder clinic for polysomnography, which often confirms the diagnosis.

C.   **Treatment**
Table 12-2 summarizes the nonpharmacological and pharmacological treatments for the most commonly encountered primary sleep disorders. For secondary sleep disorders, definite treatment is aimed at the underlying condition causing the sleep disturbance.

Suggested Readings

Aldrich MS: Cardinal manifestations of sleep disorders. In Kryger MH, Roth T, Dement WC, (eds): *Principles and Practice of Sleep Medicine,* 2nd edition. Philadelphia: WB Saunders, 1994:418–434.

American Psychiatric Association: *Diagnostic and Statistical Manual of Mental Disorders*, 4th edition, Text Revision. Washington: American Psychiatric Association, 2000:597–661.

Table 12-2. Treatment Options for Frequently Encountered Primary Sleep Disorders

Primary Sleep Disorder	Nonpharmacologic Treatment	Pharmacologic Treatment
Dyssomnias		
Primary insomnia	Sleep hygiene; stimulus control; sleep restriction; biofeedback; relaxation training; paradoxical intention; cognitive therapy; psychotherapy	*Benzodiazepines* Triazolam (0.125–0.25 mg/hs) Temazepam (15–30 mg/hs) Oxazepam (15–30 mg/hs) Lorazepam (1–2 mg/hs) Diazepam (2.5–10 mg/hs) Clonazepam (0.5–2 mg/hs) *Imidazopyridines* Zolpidem (10–20 mg/hs) *Pyrazolopyrimidines* Zaleplon (10–20 mg/hs) *Antihistamines* Diphenhydramine (25–50 mg/hs) *Sedating antidepressants* Amitriptyline (10–75 mg/hs) Imipramine (25–100 mg/hs) Doxepin (10–75 mg/hs) Trazodone (25–100 mg/hs)
Primary hypersomnia	Regular bedtime; avoid daytime naps	*Amphetamines* Dextroamphetamine (5–60 mg/d) Methamphetamine (5–40 mg/d) Methylphenidate (5–80 mg/d) *Nonamphetamines* Pemoline (18.75–112.5 mg/d) Modafinil (200–400 mg/d)
Narcolepsy	Regular bedtime; daytime naps	*Amphetamines* Dextroamphetamine (5–60 mg/d) Methamphetamine (5–40 mg/d) Methylphenidate (5–80 mg/d) *Nonamphetamines* Pemoline (18.75–112.5 mg/d) Modafinil (200–400 mg/d) *Tricyclic antidepressants* Imipramine (25–100 mg/d) Desipramine (25–100 mg/d)

continued

Table 12-2. Treatment Options for Frequently Encountered Primary Sleep Disorders (continued)

Primary Sleep Disorder	Nonpharmacologic Treatment	Pharmacologic Treatment
Breathing-related sleep disorders	Weight loss; avoidance of sedating substances; positional therapy; UPPP; tracheostomy; CPAP; BiPAP	? Protriptyline (5–20 mg/d) ? Fluoxetine (20–40 mg/d)
Periodic limb movement disorder and restless leg syndrome	None	*Dopaminergic agents* Carbidopa/levodopa (12.5/50 mg/hs) Pergolide (0.05–1 mg/hs) Pramipexole (0.125–1.0 mg/hs) *Benzodiazepines* Clonazepam (0.5–2 mg/hs) *Opioids* Codeine (15–30 mg/hs) Oxycodone (5–10 mg/hs) *Others* Gabapentin (100–800 mg/hs)
Parasomnias		
Sleepwalking disorder	Reassurance; maintenance of safe environment; psychotherapy; hypnosis	Diazepam (2.5–10 mg) Clonazepam (0.5–2.0 mg)
Sleep terror disorder	Reassurance; stress reduction	Diazepam (2.5–5 mg/hs) Clonazepam (0.5–2.0 mg/hs)
Nightmare disorder	Reassurance; stress reduction; psychotherapy; desensitization; rehearsal therapy	None
REM behavior disorder	Reassurance; maintenance of safe environment	Clonazepam (0.5–2.0 mg/hs)

BiPAP, bilevel positive airway pressure; CPAP, continuous positive airway pressure; REM, rapid eye movement; UPPP, uvulopalatopharyngoplasty.

Bootzin RR, Lahmeyer H, Lillie JK (eds): *Integrated Approach to Sleep Management: The Healthcare Practitioner's Guide to the Diagnosis and Treatment of Sleep Disorders.* Belle Mead, NJ: Cahners Healthcare Communications, 1994.

Carskadon MA, Dement WC: Normal human sleep: an overview. In Kryger MH, Roth T, Dement WC (eds): *Principles and Practice of Sleep Medicine,* 3rd edition. Philadelphia: WB Saunders, 2000:15–25.

Johns MW: A new method for measuring daytime sleepiness; the Epworth sleepiness scale. *Sleep* 1991;14:540–545.

Moore CA, Williams RL, Hirshkowitz M: Normal sleep and sleep disorders. In Sadock BJ, Sadock VA (eds): *Kaplan and Sadock's Comprehensive Textbook of Psychiatry,* 7th edition. Baltimore: Lippincott Williams & Wilkins, 2000: 1677–1700.

Smallwood P: Obstructive sleep apnea revisited. *Med Psychiatry* 1998;1:42–52.

Stern TA: Sleep disorders. In: Hyman SE, Jenike MA (eds): *Manual of Clinical Problems in Psychiatry.* Boston: Little, Brown, 1990:140–150.

Weilburg, JB, Richter JM: Approach to patients with disordered sleep. In: Stern TA, Herman JB, Slavin PL (eds): *MGH Guide to Psychiatry in Primary Care.* New York: McGraw-Hill, 1998:67–77.

Chapter 13

An Approach to the Substance-Abusing Patient: Affective, Behavioral, and Cognitive Impairment Associated with Intoxication, Withdrawal, and Chronic Use

BRIAN P. BRENNAN, MD

I. Overview of Alcohol Abuse and Dependence

A. Epidemiology

    1. **Alcohol abuse varies from brief episodes of excessive drinking to a chronic pattern of regular drinking that causes significant problems.** However, by definition, drinking with this condition never progresses to either psychological or physical dependence.

    2. **Alcohol dependence is defined as the excessive and recurrent use of alcohol despite medical, psychological, social, or economic problems.** Tolerance and withdrawal symptoms are included in the diagnostic criteria, but they are not required to make the diagnosis.

B. Prevalence

    1. **The lifetime prevalence for alcohol abuse is 6% in women and 12% in men. The lifetime prevalence for alcohol dependence is 8% in women and 20% in men.**

    2. Roughly one-third of individuals with an alcohol disorder have at least one other psychiatric disorder. The psychiatric conditions most commonly comorbid with alcohol-use disorders are abuse of a second substance, antisocial personality disorder, conduct disorder, bipolar disorder (mania), and schizophrenia. Other frequently comorbid disorders include major depressive disorder (MDD), anxiety disorders, attention-deficit/hyperactivity disorder (ADHD), and posttraumatic stress disorder (PTSD).

    3. Approximately 25–50% of suicides involve alcohol.

    4. Alcohol-related medical problems affect more than 10% of drinkers and are the third leading cause of death in the U.S.

Address for correspondence: Dr. Brian P. Brennan, McLean Hospital, Admissions Building, 1st Floor, 115 Mill Street, Belmont, MA 02478, email: bbrennan@partners.org.

C.   **Etiology and Mechanism**
1.   The positive reinforcement associated with alcohol use appears to be mediated by:
    a.   Activation of γ-aminobutyric acid A ($GABA_A$) receptors
    b.   Release of opioid peptides and dopamine
    c.   Inhibition of glutamate N-methyl-D-aspartate (NMDA) receptors
    d.   Interaction with the serotonin system
2.   Chronic alcohol use results in upregulation of excitatory glutamate NMDA receptors and the downregulation of inhibitory neuronal GABA receptors.
3.   Termination of alcohol consumption results in central nervous system (CNS) hyperactivity due to a lack of opposition to an alcohol-induced excitatory state.

II.   The Evaluation of Alcohol-Related Disorders

A.   **History**
1.   **Screening for alcohol-related problems should be mandatory for all psychiatric patients.** This should involve questioning about the quantity and the frequency of drinking. In addition, several screening instruments are helpful in detecting less overt problems:
    a.   **CAGE questionnaire**
    b.   **Michigan Alcoholism Screening Test (MAST)**
    c.   **Alcohol Use Disorders Identification Test (AUDIT)**
2.   Individuals with known alcohol problems should be **screened for the use of other drugs** (both legal and illegal), given the high rate of abuse of other substances in this population.
3.   A full psychiatric evaluation should be performed to assess for other **comorbid psychiatric disorders** (see I.B.2).
4.   A **detailed social history** should be performed to evaluate for social problems commonly associated with alcoholism, including erratic school or employment history, domestic violence, or marital problems.

B.   **Physical Examination**
1.   **Signs of alcohol intoxication**
    a.   Mild: disinhibition, slurred speech, a staggering gait, and euphoria
    b.   Severe: confusion, stupor, coma, respiratory paralysis, and death

2. **Alcohol withdrawal syndromes**
   a. Signs and symptoms of **minor withdrawal** present within 6 hours of the last drink and resolve within 24–28 hours and include insomnia, tremulousness, anxiety, GI upset, headache, diaphoresis, nystagmus, and hyperreflexia.
   b. **Withdrawal seizures** may occur within 2 hours of the last drink and generally occur within the first 48 hours after cessation of alcohol use; generalized tonic-clonic seizures are seen predominantly in chronic alcoholics who suddenly stop drinking.
   c. **Acute alcoholic hallucinosis** develops within 12–24 hours of the last drink and resolves within 24–48 hours; hallucinations (generally auditory or visual and paranoid in nature) in the absence of associated delirium, tremor, or autonomic hyperactivity.
   d. **Delirium tremens** (DTs) typically develops between 48 and 96 hours after the last drink and lasts 1–5 days; it is a syndrome characterized by hallucinations, profound disorientation, autonomic hyperactivity (tachycardia and hypertension), low-grade fever, agitation, and diaphoresis. Risk factors for the development of DTs include: a history of sustained drinking, previous DTs, age >30, concurrent illness, and a greater number of days since the last drink.
3. **Wernicke's encephalopathy:** This is a common acute neurological disorder in chronic alcoholic patients **caused by thiamine deficiency.** The classic triad involves a mental status change, ophthalmoplegia, and ataxia.
4. **Korsakoff's syndrome:** This is a neuropsychiatric disorder of selective anterograde and retrograde amnesia most frequently seen in alcoholic patients after an episode of Wernicke's encephalopathy (approximately 80% of patients recovering from Wernicke's encephalopathy exhibit the memory disturbance of Korsakoff's syndrome). It is characterized by marked deficits in anterograde and retrograde memory, apathy, an intact sensorium, and relative preservation of long-term memory and other cognitive skills. Confabulation may be present.

C. **Review of Systems**
   Medical problems commonly seen in alcohol-use disorders include GI bleeding, pancreatitis, cirrhosis, hepatitis, cardiomyopathy, labile hypertension, electrolyte abnormalities, anemia, intracranial hemorrhage and/or history of recurrent trauma, sleep disorders, peripheral neuropathy, and an increased incidence of cancer (e.g., esophageal, liver, stomach, colon, and lung).

D.   Laboratory Assessment
1.   No single test is diagnostic for alcoholism. Several laboratory abnormalities are commonly found including: an elevated γ-glutamyl transpeptidase (GGT) (>30 U/L), an elevated mean corpuscular volume (MCV) (>95 mm^3 in males and >100 mm^3 in females), and elevated liver function tests (aspartate aminotransferase [AST] and alanine aminotransferase [ALT]).

E.   Differential Diagnosis
1.   Other medical problems must be ruled out before a diagnosis of alcoholism can be made.
   a.   **Alcohol intoxication** presents with disinhibition, and in more severe cases, delirium, ataxia, and coma. Other life-threatening conditions with this clinical presentation need to be considered and evaluated (e.g., head trauma, stroke, and hypoglycemia).
   b.   **Alcohol withdrawal** can also be mimicked by other conditions (e.g., infection, trauma, metabolic disturbances, drug overdose, hepatic failure, and GI bleeding); therefore extensive testing is required to exclude these (and other) diagnostic considerations.
   c.   **Alcoholism** can cause a variety of medical complications for which evaluation and, if needed, treatment, needs to be carried out.
2.   Several psychiatric disorders coexist with alcoholism. However, a definitive diagnostic assessment cannot be accomplished while an individual is actively drinking. This makes distinguishing primary from secondary psychiatric disorders particularly difficult in the alcoholic patient. **Several criteria suggest the presence of a primary, or non–alcohol induced, psychiatric disorder.** These include:
   a.   The presence of psychiatric symptoms prior to alcohol use.
   b.   Symptoms greater than what would be expected given the duration and the amount of drinking.
   c.   Symptoms that last longer than 4 weeks following detoxification.
3.   Common presentations that can complicate the diagnostic process include:
   a.   The drinking patient with mood symptoms: **More than 60% of alcoholics are clinically depressed when admitted for detoxification.** In most cases, depressive symptoms should clear within 2 weeks of sobriety. If not, evaluation for a comorbid depressive disorder should be performed.

    b. The drinking patient with anxiety symptoms: **Alcoholics frequently complain of generalized anxiety symptoms or panic attacks.** These patients require a comprehensive evaluation after achieving sobriety.

    c. The drinking patient with psychotic symptoms: **The hallucinations associated with delirium tremens or alcoholic hallucinosis are often confused with schizophrenia or other psychotic disorders.**

III. The Treatment of the Patient with Alcohol Problems

A. **Pharmacological**

  1. **Thiamine,** 100 mg PO or IV/IM in the acute setting, should be administered before any glucose-containing solutions are administered, to decrease the risk of precipitating Wernicke's encephalopathy or Korsakoff's syndrome. In addition, multivitamins and folate should be given routinely and electrolyte abnormalities should be corrected.

  2. **Alcohol withdrawal**

    a. Patients with a low risk of seizures or DTs: Oral benzodiazepines, such as chlordiazepoxide 25–50 mg every 2 hours as needed for withdrawal symptoms.

    b. Patients with a history of seizures, DTs, or prolonged heavy consumption: Oral benzodiazepines such as chlordiazepoxide (50–100 mg initially, then 50–100 mg every 2 hours as needed) for withdrawal symptoms with a hold for sedation (an alternative agent is diazepam 10–20 mg initially, with 10–20 mg every 2 hours as needed). This can be tapered slowly on a daily basis. These patients require frequent monitoring to prevent falling behind in their treatment for withdrawal.

    c. The short-acting benzodiazepine **lorazepam is preferable in patients with significant liver damage, cognitive impairment, unstable medical problems, or age >65.** This drug is rapidly metabolized and excreted by the kidney, allowing more flexibility in the management of unstable patients.

    d. Delirium tremens: IV **diazepam,** 5–10 mg IV every 5 minutes until a calm but awake state is achieved. Continue parenteral benzodiazepines until the patient is no longer delirious or at high risk for aspiration. Haloperidol may also be helpful in controlling psychotic and agitated behavior.

   3.   **Detoxification:** Long-acting benzodiazepines (such as chlordiazepoxide and diazepam) are the standard agents.

   4.   **Long-term treatment**

      a.   **Naltrexone** is an opiate antagonist shown to decrease craving and relapse in alcoholics. It is given in doses of 50 mg orally per day and is contraindicated in patients taking opiates or those with acute hepatitis or liver failure.

      b.   **Disulfiram** inhibits alcohol metabolism and leads to increased levels of acetaldehyde and symptoms of tachycardia, dyspnea, nausea, and vomiting if the patient drinks. Generally, disulfiram is given in doses of 250 mg orally per day.

         i.   It works best in stable, motivated patients.

        ii.   **Liver function tests must be followed routinely** given the risk of disulfiram-induced hepatitis.

       iii.   It may exacerbate psychosis in some schizophrenics due to inhibition of dopamine β-hydroxylase. Consider reducing the dose to 125 mg daily and adding a high-potency antipsychotic, such as haloperidol.

      c.   Ondansetron: A selective $5\text{-}HT_3$ antagonist shown to reduce alcohol consumption in early-onset alcoholics. It has not been effective in late-onset alcoholics.

      d.   Acamprosate: A derivative of the amino acid taurine that acts at the glutamate receptor and has been found to increase abstinence in recent trials. It is available in Europe and is awaiting Food and Drug Administration (FDA) approval in the U.S.

B.   **Behavioral**

   1.   An understanding of the **stages of behavioral change** (see Table 13-1) that patients with addictive disorders must pass through on the road to recovery is crucial for the clinician.

   2.   Successful treatment involves helping the patient move from one stage to the next through the use of the interventional techniques that are most effective at each stage. Typically, **patients cycle through this process several times before achieving stable sobriety.**

   3.   This approach works best when the clinician recognizes the importance of stepwise progression through the stages of change rather than instant recovery.

C.   **Psychological**

Many treatment options exist to reduce the amount and frequency of drinking in patients willing to accept treatment.

Table 13-1. The Stages of Behavioral Change

1. Precontemplation

The drinker is unaware that alcohol use is a problem, or has no interest in changing the drinking pattern.

2. Contemplation

The drinker becomes aware of problems, but is still drinking and is usually ambivalent about stopping.

3. Preparation

The previous pattern persists, but the drinker now makes the decision to change. The drinker may initiate small changes.

4. Action

Behavioral change begins; it is typically a trial and error process with several initial relapses.

5. Maintenance

A new behavior pattern is consolidated; relapse prevention techniques help to maintain change.

6. Relapse

Efforts to change are abandoned. The cycle may be repeated until permanent sobriety is established.

Adapted from Prochaska J, DiClemente C, Norcross J: In search of how people change: Applications to addictive behaviors. *Am Psychologist* 1992;47:1102–1114.

---

1. **Substance abuse counseling**
   a. **Directive behaviorally-based therapy:** Specific prescriptions for gaining and maintaining sobriety (e.g., going to Alcoholics Anonymous, stopping vigorous socializing with other drinkers, regular follow-up with a counselor and sponsor).
   b. **Avoidance of passive nondirective forms of psychotherapy.**
   c. **Cognitive-behavioral therapy** (CBT) is aimed at relapse prevention and helps alcoholics identify high-risk situations and their predictors of relapse. Make distinctions between lapses (brief slips) and full relapses. CBT is most effective with patients who have achieved an initial period of sobriety.
   d. **Group therapy**

2. **Self-help programs:** Alcoholics Anonymous is the primary treatment resource for most alcoholics.
3. **Family counseling**

D. **Criteria for Referral for Inpatient Detoxification**
1. A history of failure in outpatient detoxification or multiple relapses.
2. Active suicidal ideation or acute psychosis.
3. A history of DTs or alcohol withdrawal seizures.
4. Comorbid medical problems that require frequent daily monitoring detoxification.
5. Severe withdrawal symptoms that have not responded adequately to initial oral doses of benzodiazepines.
6. Lack of a sober and safe environment for outpatient detoxification.

E. **Criteria for Referral for Specialized Long-Term Alcoholism Treatment**
1. A history of multiple treatment failures.
2. Alcoholics with a serious comorbid psychiatric condition, especially if they have not responded to initial efforts at psychiatric management.
3. Alcoholics who also abuse other drugs (polysubstance abuse).
4. Homeless persons or alcoholics living in very unstable environments.

IV. Overview of Cocaine-Related Disorders

A. **Diagnostic Criteria**
1. **Criteria for substance abuse** include continued substance use despite one of the following: failed obligations at home, work, or school; hazardous use; substance-related legal problems; substance-related social and interpersonal problems.
2. **Criteria for substance dependence** include continued maladaptive use of a substance that causes impairment and distress with ≥3 of the following in a 12-month period):
   a. **Tolerance:** one needs more substance to achieve the same effect or the usual amount of substance has less effect.
   b. **Withdrawal:** development of withdrawal symptoms characteristic for the given substance.
   c. **Use of larger amounts and for longer periods than intended.**
   d. **Inability to cut down.**

      e. **Excessive time spent obtaining, using, or recovering from use of the substance.**
      f. **Activities given up because of substance use.**
      g. **Continued use despite knowledge of problems.**

B.   **Prevalence**
    1. **A community survey from 1991** demonstrated that 12% of the population had used cocaine at least once during their lifetime, that 3% had used cocaine within the last year, and that 1% had used cocaine in the last month.
    2. Data from the National Institute of Drug Abuse (1997) demonstrated that **55% of drug-abusing patients are dependent on cocaine.**

C.   **Mechanism**
Cocaine blocks the uptake of dopamine, serotonin, and norepinephrine from each of their neuron terminals by binding to the presynaptic transporter complexes.

V. The Evaluation of the Cocaine-Abusing Patient

A.   **History**
Determine the route, pattern, links to drug access, and use of other substances.

B.   **Physical Examination**
    1. **Signs of chronic use** include weight loss, anorexia, needle tracks, evidence of skin-popping (small marks resembling insect bites secondary to intradermal injection), fresh or scarred bite marks on lips or tongue, worn teeth, nosebleeds, and nasal septum ulceration.
    2. **Signs of acute intoxication** include evidence of an adrenergic surge (tachycardia with risk of arrhythmias, increased blood pressure, and vasoconstriction), chest pain, pupillary dilation, diaphoresis or chills, nausea and vomiting, euphoria, hypervigilance, anxiety, decreased appetite, hypersexuality, and psychosis (including paranoid and persecutory delusions, or formication [i.e., "bugs crawling on my skin"]).
    3. **Signs of cocaine withdrawal** include dysphoric mood, fatigue, vivid and unpleasant dreams, insomnia or hypersomnia, increased appetite, as well as agitation or psychomotor retardation.

C.   **Laboratory Assessment**
A urine toxicological screen can detect cocaine in the urine for up to 36 hours.

D.   **Differential Diagnosis**
Acute cocaine intoxication may mimic acute mania. Intoxication with several other substances (e.g., amphetamines and phencyclidine [PCP]) may present in a similar fashion. These agents can be distinguished only by urine toxicological screen.

VI.   The Treatment of Cocaine-Related Disorders

A.   **Pharmacological**
1. **For acute intoxication:**
    a. For mild agitation: diazepam 5–10 mg PO; IV for seizure (5 mg/min)
    b. For a severe β-adrenergic state: propranolol 1 mg IV every minute up to 8 minutes or labetalol 2 mg IV every minute.
2. **For cocaine craving and withdrawal:**
    a. **Desipramine:** more than five controlled trials indicate that desipramine is efficacious for cocaine dependence.
    b. **Dopamine agonists:** acute use decreases craving.
        i.   Bromocriptine: controlled trials show mixed efficacy; gradual initiation is required to prevent headache, nausea, or psychosis; the dose is 0.625 mg three times a day, which can be increased to 7.5 to 12.5 mg/d as tolerated.
        ii. Amantadine has an unclear efficacy but it is better tolerated. The dose is 200 mg/d for the first 2 weeks, then it is given twice a day.

B.   **Psychological**
Disruption of the binge cycle requires 2 to 7 treatment contacts per week; initially, it is helpful to be in a drug-focused multimodal program that includes:
1. **Individual, family/couples, and group therapy.**
2. **Peer support and 12-step groups:** Alcoholics Anonymous, Narcotics Anonymous, Cocaine Anonymous, and Rational Recovery.
3. **Educational sessions** including family meetings.

C.   **Behavioral**
See section III.B.1 in Alcohol-Related Disorders.

1. Urine testing (with contingencies)
2. Restricting money, access, and social activity
3. Monitoring by a significant other
4. Frequent, immediate contact with support as needed for cravings

VII. An Overview of Narcotics-Related Problems

A. **Prevalence**
   1. A United States community survey from 1991 demonstrated that 6% of the population had used analgesics for nonmedical reasons, 2.5% had used them within the last year, and 0.7% used them within the last month.
   2. The death rate among opioid addicts is 20 times that in the general population due to increased rates of overdose, AIDS, suicide, homicide, and trauma.
   3. Studies show that 80–90% of opioid-addicted individuals receive a psychiatric diagnosis during their lifetime. The most common psychiatric conditions are MDD (25% current and 50% lifetime) and antisocial personality disorder (25–40%).

B. **Mechanism**
   1. **Opiates bind to three different endogenous opioid receptors in the brain:**
      a. **Mu and delta:** These receptors influence mood, reinforcement, analgesia, respiration, blood pressure, GI function, and endocrine function.
      b. **Kappa** receptors produce dysphoria and analgesia.
   2. **Opiates are categorized as to how they bind to and activate receptor types:** agonists, antagonists, and partial agonists.
   3. Examples:
      a. Morphine, methadone, and fentanyl are pure mu agonists.
      b. Buprenorphine and pentazocine are mu partial agonists.
      c. Naloxone and naltrexone are mu antagonists.
   4. A positive reinforcing effect of opiates is mediated through the ventral tegmental area (VTA), dopamine projections to the nucleus accumbens, and the direct effects of mu and delta agonists on neurons in the nucleus accumbens.

VIII. The Evaluation of the Narcotic-Abusing Patient

A. **History**

One should evaluate for comorbid substance use (alcohol, benzodiazepines, and cocaine are the most common).

B. **Physical Examination**

1. **Signs of opiate intoxication** include initial euphoria followed by apathy, pinpoint pupils, dysphoria, lethargy, drowsiness, mental clouding, psychomotor retardation or agitation, impaired judgment, and impaired social and occupational functioning.

2. **Signs of opiate withdrawal:**

   a. Mild signs include sweating or piloerection, yawning, lacrimation or rhinorrhea, tremor, marked irritability, muscle aches, dilated pupils, and increased respiratory rate.

   b. Severe signs include (48–72 hours after last dose) tachycardia, hypertension, nausea, vomiting, abdominal cramps, and diarrhea that may lead to dehydration.

3. **Signs of heroin overdose** include constricted pupils, bradycardia, depressed respirations, cyanosis, stupor/coma, hypothermia, and noncardiogenic pulmonary edema.

4. **Medical complications of intravenous opioid use:**

   a. Infections (most frequently due to *Staphylococcus aureus*, beta-hemolytic streptococci, and anaerobes) include cellulitis, skin abscesses, endocarditis, osteomyelitis, pulmonary emboli, and pneumonia.

   b. Liver disease (e.g., hepatitis A, B, C, and D).

   c. HIV infection: According to one study, two-thirds of IV drug users in the northeastern U.S. are HIV-positive.

   d. Pulmonary disease: tuberculosis and pneumonia.

   e. Renal disease: Focal or diffuse glomerulosclerosis and subsequent nephritic syndrome and end-stage renal disease.

E. **Laboratory Assessment**

Check urine toxicological screening tests. Most short-acting opioids are detectable in the urine for 12–36 hours after administration. Poppy seed consumption may result in a false-positive result.

F. **Differential Diagnosis**

Comorbid psychiatric diagnoses are common. It is often difficult to distinguish between a primary mood disorder and an opiate-induced mood disorder.

IX. The Treatment of the Narcotics-Abusing Patient

A. **Pharmacological**

1. **Heroin overdose:** Administration of naloxone, a pure opiate antagonist, 0.4 mg (1 mL), repeated every 5 minutes as needed, or IV drip of 4 mg/L in 5% dextrose in water at a rate of 100 mL/h. Overdose symptoms may last 1–4 hours, requiring that an antagonist be administered as needed. Note: Naloxone may also precipitate withdrawal.

2. **Rapid detoxification:** Four different strategies:

    a. **Methadone substitution** (in licensed clinics or during medical/surgical hospitalization only): The starting dose of methadone (usually 15–30 mg) is determined by a 24-hour observation period and is based on signs and symptoms of withdrawal. Methadone can be tapered at a rate of 5–10% per day for inpatients and 10% per week for outpatients (given the greater availability of opioids in an ambulatory setting, a slower taper is important to provide a more comfortable detoxification).

    b. **Buprenorphine,** a partial mu agonist, is very effective for opioid detoxification. It is available in both a parenteral and sublingual form, and a sublingual form that combines it with naloxone. It causes fewer withdrawal symptoms and has less potential for abuse. It is safe in overdose and it exhibits little respiratory depression due to the "ceiling effect" of being a partial mu agonist.

    c. **Clonidine** is an α_2-adrenergic agonist that suppresses withdrawal symptoms of tachycardia and hypertension. However, it has no effect on craving, muscle aches, insomnia, nausea, or abdominal cramping (but one can use nonsteroidal anti-inflammatory drugs [NSAIDs], trazodone, prochlorperazine, and dicyclomine, respectively, for these). Side effects are sedation and hypotension; vital signs should be checked before each dose.

        i. On day 1: 0.1–0.3 mg every 4–6 hours (not to exceed 1 mg)

        ii. On days 2–4: increase the dose to control withdrawal symptoms (not to exceed 1.3 mg)

        iii. On day 5: taper by 0.2 mg/d

    d. **Ultrarapid detoxification:** This involves a combination of clonidine 0.1–0.2 mg four times a day with doses given as needed for vital sign elevations, followed by naltrexone 12.5 mg on day 1 and increasing over days 2–5 to 50 mg/d.

One may also use clonidine (same doses) with buprenorphine (2 mg sublingual) followed by a naltrexone induction
from 12.5 mg (day 1) to 50 mg (day 2) with discontinuation
of clonidine and buprenorphine on day 3 (O'Connor et al,
1995).

B.   Psychological
Several psychotherapeutic interventions (including CBT, behavioral
therapy, family therapy, and group therapy) have been shown to
improve the outcomes for opioid addicts.

C.   Behavioral
See section III.B.1 in Alcohol-Related Disorders and Table 13-1.
Self-help groups such as Narcotics Anonymous and therapeutic
communities have been especially helpful in highly-motivated individuals.

X.   Benzodiazepine-Related Problems

A.   Intoxication
1. Signs and symptoms of benzodiazepine intoxication are similar
   to those of alcohol intoxication (see section II.B.1).
2. Benzodiazepine intoxication can be differentiated from alcohol
   intoxication by the lack of odor on the breath and by the results
   of the serum and urine toxicological screens.
3. **Flumazenil,** a specific benzodiazepine antagonist, can reverse
   the life-threatening effects of benzodiazepine overdose. An initial IV dose of 0.2 mg can be given over 30 seconds, to be followed by a second 0.2-mg IV dose if no response is seen after
   45 seconds. This can be repeated at 1-minute intervals up to a
   total dose of 5.0 mg. Note: Flumazenil is contraindicated in
   patients dependent on benzodiazepines or those taking tricyclic
   antidepressants, as flumazenil may precipitate seizures in these
   patients.

B.   Withdrawal
1. Symptoms of benzodiazepine withdrawal include anxiety, insomnia, irritability, depression, tremor, nausea or vomiting, and
   anorexia. In severe cases seizures are possible.

C.   Detoxification
1. A gradual reduction in the dose is recommended; the taper may
   be extended over several weeks or months.

    2. After use of high-potency, short-acting agents (e.g., alprazolam), a switch can be made to a high-potency, long-acting agent (e.g., clonazepam) in the ratio of 0.5 mg of clonazepam to 1.0 mg of alprazolam and then tapered over 1–3 weeks.

XI. Amphetamine-Related Problems

A. **Intoxication**
1. Signs and symptoms are similar to those of cocaine intoxication (see sections V.B.1 to 3).
2. A paranoid psychosis without disorientation can also occur. Most frequently it is seen in young adults who abuse IV methamphetamine hydrochloride or individuals who use oral amphetamines on a chronic basis.
3. Most signs of intoxication clear in 2–4 days.

B. **Detoxification**
1. Amphetamines can be withdrawn abruptly.
2. If sedation is necessary, benzodiazepines are the drugs of choice.
3. Be watchful for symptoms of depression; it can be severe with suicidality for as long as 3–6 months after cessation of chronic amphetamine abuse.

XII. Club-Drug–Related Problems

A. **Ecstasy**
3,4-Methylenedioxymethamphetamine (MDMA), also known as ecstasy, has both amphetamine-like and hallucinogenic effects. In toxic amounts, it produces distorted perceptions, confusion, hypertension, hyperactivity, and potentially fatal hyperthermia.

B. **Gamma-hydroxybutyrate**
Gamma-hydroxybutyrate (GHB) is a CNS depressant which, in overdose, can produce coma and death. It is FDA-approved for the treatment of narcolepsy.

C. **Ketamine**
Ketamine has been used as an anesthetic. It can produce delirium, amnesia, and respiratory depression in overdose.

Suggested Readings

American Psychiatric Association: *Diagnostic and Statistical Manual of Mental Disorders,* 4th ed., Text Revision. Washington: American Psychiatric Press, 1995.

Gastfriend DR, O'Connell JJ: The cocaine or opiate-abusing patient. In Stern TA, Herman JB, Slavin PL (eds): *The MGH Guide to Primary Care Psychiatry,* 2nd ed. New York: McGraw-Hill, 2004:513–519.

Gastfriend DR, Renner JA, Hackett TP: Alcoholic patients—acute and chronic. In Stern TA, Fricchione GL, Cassem NH, et al, (eds): *Massachusetts General Hospital Handbook of General Hospital Psychiatry,* 5th ed. Philadelphia: Mosby, 2004:203–216.

Matthews J: Substance-related disorders: cocaine and narcotics. In Stern TA, Herman JB (eds): *Psychiatry Update and Board Preparation.* New York: McGraw-Hill, 2000:85–96.

O'Connor PG, Fiellin DA: Pharmacologic treatment of heroin-dependent patients. *Ann Intern Med* 2000;133:40–54.

O'Connor PG, Waugh ME, Carroll KM, et al: Primary care-based ambulatory opioid detoxification: the results of a clinical trial. *J Gen Intern Med* 1995;10:255–260.

Renner JA: Alcoholism and alcohol abuse. In Stern TA, Herman JB (eds): *Psychiatry Update and Board Preparation.* New York: McGraw-Hill, 2000:73–84.

Renner JA, Bierer MF: The alcoholic patient. In Stern TA, Herman JB, Slavin PL (eds): *The MGH Guide to Primary Care Psychiatry,* 2nd ed. New York: McGraw-Hill, 2004:499–512.

Renner JA, Gastfriend DR: Drug-addicted patients. In In Stern TA, Fricchione GL, Cassem NH, et al, (eds): *Massachusetts General Hospital Handbook of General Hospital Psychiatry,* 5th ed. Philadelphia: Mosby, 2004:217–229.

Chapter 14

An Approach to the Patient with Schizophrenia and Other Psychotic Disorders: Delusions, Hallucinations, Disorganized Speech, or Grossly Disorganized Behavior

Dost Öngür, MD, PhD

I.   Psychotic Symptoms

Psychosis is a gross impairment in reality testing. As such, it can be seen in several different psychiatric (e.g., schizophrenia) and medical conditions. Psychosis is manifest by:

A.   Delusions

Delusions are **fixed, false beliefs that are not in keeping with a person's culture or background.** They can be nihilistic, persecutory, somatic, sexual, or religious. The delusions most typical of schizophrenia are of thought withdrawal, thought insertion, or thought broadcasting. Bizarre delusions are ones that involve beliefs that could not possibly be based in reality (e.g., the belief in having birds fly inside one's head), while nonbizarre delusions are physically possible (e.g., the delusion of infidelity by a spouse).

B.   Hallucinations

Hallucinations are **sensory perceptions in the absence of an inciting external stimulus;** they can occur in all five sensory modalities. The hallucinations most commonly experienced by a person with schizophrenia are human voices.

C.   Disorganized Speech

Disorganized speech is caused by a disorder of thought; manifestations include tangentiality, loosening of associations, word salad, neologisms, illogical thinking, and thought blocking.

D.   Disorganized Behavior and Catatonia

Disorganized behavior can include childlike silliness, agitation, poor hygiene, unusual dress, or inappropriate sexual behavior. Catatonia

---

Address for correspondence: Dr. Dost Öngür, PhD, Massachusetts General Hospital, Wang Ambulatory Care Center 812, 15 Parkman St., Boston, MA 02114-3117, email: DOngur@Partners.org.

can be characterized by mutism, waxy flexibility, extreme negativism, echolalia, or echopraxia.

E.   **Negative Symptoms**
Poverty of speech (in content and amount), affective flattening, anhedonia, and avolition comprise negative symptoms.

II.   Drugs and Medical Conditions Associated with Psychosis

A.   **Clinical Manifestations**
Many of the agents and conditions listed in Table 14-1 present with psychosis, as well as more specific manifestations.
1.   For example, **alcoholic hallucinosis** typically involves visual and tactile hallucinations of insects that crawl on the bed and on one's skin.
2.   By contrast, **complex partial seizures** may involve olfactory hallucinations (e.g., of burning rubber) and disorganized and stereotyped behaviors, or irritability.
3.   Finally, use and abuse of **cocaine and amphetamines** are linked with paranoia and hallucinations, but not a formal thought disorder.
4.   **Alzheimer's disease** is characterized by progressive cognitive decline, as well as by other types of cortical dysfunction.
5.   **Vitamin B_{12} deficiency** is manifest by megaloblastic anemia.
6.   **Infectious diseases** are typically heralded by fever and by elevations of the white blood cell count.

III.   Schizophrenia

A.   **Overview**
Schizophrenia is a common, debilitating illness whose hallmark is psychosis. It causes an enormous burden to individuals, to families, and to society at large.

B.   **Diagnosis**
A DSM-IV-TR diagnosis of schizophrenia rests on:
1.   **An active phase.** Psychotic symptoms last at least 1 month (less if treated), and include two or more of the following (only one is required if delusions are bizarre or if voices are conversing or maintaining a running commentary):
     a.   Delusions
     b.   Hallucinations
     c.   Disorganized speech

Table 14-1. Medications and Medical Conditions Associated with Psychosis

Drugs of abuse	**Infectious diseases**
Alcohol	Brain abscess
Amphetamines	Herpes encephalitis
Barbiturates	Infectious mononucleosis
Caffeine	Malaria
Cannabis	Meningitis
Cocaine	Syphilis
Hallucinogens	**Endocrine disorders**
(LSD, PCP, MDMA)	Addison's disease
Inhalants	Cushing's syndrome
Opioids	Hypo/hyperthyroidism
Sedative-hypnotics	Hypo/hyperparathyroidism
Neurological disorders	Nutritional deficiencies
Alzheimer's disease	Niacin deficiency (pellagra)
Complex partial seizures	Thiamine deficiency
Huntington's disease	(Korsakoff's psychosis, beriberi)
Hydrocephalus	Vitamin B_{12} (pernicious anemia)
Lupus cerebritis	**Others**
Parkinson's disease	Neoplasms
Pick's disease	Heavy metal exposures
Wilson's disease	Prescription medications

LSD, lysergic acid diethylamide; PCP, phencyclidine; MDMA, methylene-dioxymethamphetamine.
Modified from Henderson and Goff, 2000.

    d. Disorganized or catatonic behavior
    e. Negative symptoms
2. Major social or occupational dysfunction (at work, in relationships, or with self-care).
3. An illness of at least 6 months (including the prodromal and residual phases).
4. Not all patients with schizophrenia present with the same symptoms. Indeed, the DSM-IV-TR recognizes five subtypes:
    a. **Catatonic type:** see above for catatonia
    b. **Disorganized type:** manifest by disorganized speech or behavior and negative symptoms

    c. **Paranoid type:** characterized by delusions and hallucinations

    d. **Undifferentiated type:** with a mixture of psychotic symptoms

    e. **Residual type:** no active psychotic symptoms, with a chronic course of illness

C.   **Course of Illness**

Although the DSM-IV-TR criteria are time-limited, schizophrenia is a lifelong illness. The typical course of illness is comprised of an acute phase, followed by stabilization (which is punctuated by psychotic exacerbations), and then a resolution into a residual state of deficient social and cognitive function. About one-third of patients do better than expected and live independently; however, being asymptomatic is a rarity for those with schizophrenia. Many patients are chronically impaired; they are unable to hold jobs or to engage in stable relationships.

D.   **Epidemiology, Etiology, and Mechanism**

1. **Prevalence**

    a. The prevalence of schizophrenia is **1% worldwide,** with a few isolated regions showing higher rates.

    b. Some studies have found higher rates in immigrant populations (e.g., Afro-Caribbeans in Britain) and the urban poor; this may be in part related to "downward economic drift" of patients.

    c. Males manifest illness earlier (between the ages of 18 and 25 years) than do females (26–45 years).

    d. There is **no gender difference** in the overall rates of illness.

    e. At-risk children typically manifest subtle cognitive, affective, and diffuse developmental abnormalities prior to the onset of illness.

    f. Schizophrenia is also associated with a typical **prodrome** that can last from a few months to 2 years. It is characterized by social withdrawal, impaired hygiene, depression, anxiety symptoms, and by odd thoughts, behaviors, and affect.

    g. Disorders of substance abuse and dependence are commonly comorbid with schizophrenia. They reduce medication compliance and complicate treatment and symptomatology.

    h. The vast majority of patients with schizophrenia smoke cigarettes. This contributes to increased rates of cardiopulmonary disease in this patient population.

2. **Etiology**
   a. Schizophrenia has a significant **genetic component,** as illustrated by the 50% concordance rate of monozygotic twins for the diagnosis, as opposed to the 15–20% concordance rate for dizygotic twins, who substantially share the same environment.
   b. However, **no single genetic factor can be identified for the illness;** rather, multiple genes and other etiologic agents interact in complex ways in the pathogenesis of the illness.
3. **Mechanism**
   a. The **neurodevelopmental hypothesis of schizophrenia** states that abnormalities during development of the fetal brain, as well as perinatal and postnatal insults, cause lasting changes in the brain that manifest themselves as psychosis in early adulthood. Increased rates of perinatal complications in schizophrenics, an increased rate of winter births (consistent with exposure to viral infections during the second trimester), as well the **neurological soft signs** (such as impaired stereognosis and graphesthesia) seen in patients with schizophrenia are all consistent with abnormalities in the developing brain.
   b. The **dopamine hypothesis of schizophrenia** revolves around the notion that patients with schizophrenia manifest increased levels of mesolimbic dopamine activity. This hypothesis draws on the dopamine-blocking properties of antipsychotic medications and the ability of dopaminomimetic agents to induce psychosis. However, abnormalities in the serotonergic, glutamatergic, and probably other neurotransmitter systems also contribute to the pathogenesis of schizophrenia.
   c. **Reduced frontal lobe activity** is hypothesized to underlie the negative symptoms and cognitive deficits seen in schizophrenia. Specific cellular changes have been described in the frontal lobes as well as in the medial temporal lobes of patients with schizophrenia. These changes may indicate reductions in glutamatergic activity in schizophrenia.

E.   **Evaluation of Psychosis**
The differential diagnosis of schizophrenia includes other psychiatric illnesses (see Table 14-2), a variety of drugs, and medical conditions (see Table 14-3). Organic etiologies for psychosis can often be ruled out based on the clinical context, on the constellation of symptoms, as well as on the results of laboratory and imaging studies.

Table 14-2. The Differential Diagnosis of Psychosis Without an Apparent Organic Etiology

- Schizophrenia spectrum disorders:
  Schizophreniform disorder (similar to schizophrenia, but with a
    duration of less than 6 months)
  Brief reactive psychosis (duration less than 1 month)
  Schizotypal personality disorder (no active phase of schizophrenia)
- Bipolar disorder
- Major depression with psychotic features
- Schizoaffective disorder
- Delusional disorder

---

1. **Brain imaging** is recommended for patients with first-break psychosis, an atypical psychosis, or treatment-refractory psychotic symptoms.
2. **Neuropsychological testing** is helpful in evaluating psychotic symptoms and cognitive impairment.
3. The major challenge facing the clinician presented with a psychotic patient without an organic etiology is to distinguish **affective psychoses** (as in bipolar disorder and major depression) from schizophrenia.

Table 14-3. The Evaluation of Psychosis

- Complete physical and neurological examination
- Mental status examination (supplemented by neuropsychological testing as needed)
- Full laboratory screen (basic chemistry panel, calcium, CBC, thyroid panel, LFTs, VDRL, vitamin B_{12}, folate, HIV when indicated)
- Toxicological screen
- Brain imaging (CT or MRI)
- EEG if clinically indicated

CBC, complete blood cell count; CT, computed tomography; EEG, electroencephalogram; HIV, human immunodeficiency virus; LFT, liver function test; MRI, magnetic resonance imaging; VDRL, Venereal Disease Research Laboratory test (syphilis).
Modified from Henderson and Goff, 2000.

    a. A **careful history** from the patient and caregivers about mood symptoms and particularly about **episodes of major depression or mania,** is invaluable.

    b. A psychotic presentation with prominent manic symptoms (e.g., grandiosity, pressured speech, impulsivity, and increased goal-directed behavior) may indicate an underlying bipolar disorder, which in the acute manic phase can be indistinguishable from schizophrenia.

    c. However, in affective psychoses, psychotic symptoms are found mainly during episodes of dysregulated mood. Therefore, the presence of psychotic symptoms at baseline indicates that a schizophrenia spectrum disorder or **schizoaffective disorder** (see below) is present.

    d. Patients with schizophrenia can have an episode of major depression or mania and this does not automatically qualify them for **schizoaffective disorder.** However, if mood episodes exist for a significant portion of illness duration, then a diagnosis of schizoaffective disorder should be entertained.

4. **Negative symptoms, poor premorbid functioning, insidious onset, and the absence of remissions predict a poor outcome from schizophrenia.**

    a. Patients with schizophrenia, paranoid type, have a later age of onset and better overall prognosis.

    b. Generally, the outcome for schizophrenia is poor, but newer antipsychotic medications have led to increased functionality. For reasons that are not clear, the outcome is generally better in underdeveloped countries.

    c. The **suicide rate for individuals with schizophrenia is 10%.**

    d. Patients with schizophrenia also have an **increased rate of violence,** particularly if they are paranoid or disorganized. Both the presence of delusions, which promote violence, and auditory command hallucinations are risk factors for violence.

    e. More than half of patients with schizophrenia have **impaired insight** into their illness.

F. **Treatment: Pharmacological, Psychological, and Behavioral**
1. **Pharmacotherapy**

    a. The mainstay of treatment of patients with schizophrenia is **antipsychotic medications.** These are generally grouped into first- and second-generation antipsychotics (FGAs and SGAs).

i. All **antipsychotics block the dopamine D_2 receptor** and this is at least part of the reason for their efficacy.

ii. SGAs also block other receptors, especially the serotonin $5\text{-}HT_2$ receptors, and this may account for their different efficacy and side-effect profile. SGAs also block histaminergic and adrenergic receptors, which accounts for their metabolic side effects.

iii. **FGAs and SGAs are equally efficacious for positive symptoms** of schizophrenia, but SGAs are likely to be better for **negative symptoms** and have a more favorable side-effect profile.

iv. One significant complication with FGA treatment is **tardive dyskinesia (TD),** which emerges late in the course of treatment, or is unmasked during termination of FGA treatment. No established treatments exist, but vitamin E, melatonin, and clozapine have been tried.

v. **Extrapyramidal symptoms (EPS) are effectively treated with anticholinergic medications,** such as benztropine or diphenhydramine (see Table 14-4).

vi. FGAs are also associated with an elevated risk of **neuroleptic malignant syndrome (NMS),** a potentially fatal condition associated with muscular rigidity, hyperthermia, tremor, incontinence, mental status changes, and elevations of vital signs, white blood cell (WBC) counts, or serum creatine phosphokinase (CPK).

Table 14-4. Side Effects Commonly Associated with First-Generation Antipsychotics

Side Effect	Description
Extrapyramidal symptoms (EPS)	*Hours:* Acute dystonic reaction *Days:* Akathisia (subjective sense of discomfort relieved by getting up and walking around) *Weeks/months:* Parkinsonism (masked facies, pill-rolling tremor, bradykinesia, and rigidity)
Tardive dyskinesia (TD)	Late emerging choreiform, involuntary movements of the lips, tongue, jaw, upper extremities; may be irreversible
Other	QTc prolongation with thioridazine; hyperprolactinemia

vii. Two FGAs, **haloperidol and fluphenazine, are available as long-acting, intramuscular decanoate preparations** that are administered biweekly or monthly. They appear useful in patients with chronic noncompliance.

viii. Several recent guidelines recommend treatment with an adequate dose of an SGA medication as first-line treatment for schizophrenia. Lack of response to one SGA should be followed by a trial of a second SGA, then a FGA or clozapine.

ix. **Clozapine was the first SGA** to become available. It is the only antipsychotic medication found **effective in treatment-resistant patients with schizophrenia,** but blood draws to monitor WBCs and a significant side-effect profile caused clozapine to be classified as a second-line agent. Blood draws are weekly for first 6 months and biweekly thereafter. Medication should be discontinued if the WBC count falls below 3000 cells/mL^3 or drops by 3000 cells on any given test result.

x. Meta-analyses have found **no clear differences in efficacy among the remaining SGAs;** choice of medication depends on comorbidity, side-effect profile, and other considerations (Davis et al, 2003). SGAs can be associated with NMS, EPS, or TD, but they occur at a much lower frequency than with FGAs (see Table 14-5).

xi. As a group, **SGAs are associated with a metabolic syndrome consisting of weight gain, glucose intolerance, and hyperlipidemia.**

xii. **Aripiprazole may be different from the other SGAs since it is a partial agonist** at the D_2 dopamine receptor site. It is bound to the receptor and provides low-level stimulation; thus it may be associated with fewer side effects arising from dopamine blockade. Due to their relatively safe side-effect profile and multiple pharmacodynamic effects, low-dose SGAs are commonly used for irritability, impulse control, and anxiolysis in clinical practice.

b. **Augmentation treatments** involving more than one antipsychotic medication, one antipsychotic and another psychotropic medication, or one antipsychotic and another class of medication aimed at treatment of side effects can be considered. Depending on the symptomatology of the indi-

Table 14-5. Side Effects and Typical Dosing Schedules for Second-Generation Antipsychotics

Medication	Year	Starting Dose	Target Dose	Side Effects	Comment
Clozapine	1989	25 mg/d	200–600 mg/d	Agranulocytosis, seizures, sedation	Weekly/biweekly blood draws for WBC count
Risperidone	1994	0.5 mg/d	4–6 mg/d	Hyperprolactinemia	Available as long-acting intramuscular preparation
Olanzapine	1996	2.5 mg/d	15–20 mg/d	Weight gain, NIDDM	Available as a sublingual wafer
Quetiapine	1998	25 mg/d	600–800 mg/d	Sedation	
Ziprasidone	2000	20 mg twice a day	80 mg twice a day	QTc prolongation (~15-20 ms)	Give with food to improve absorption
Aripiprazole	2002	15 mg/d	15–30 mg/d	Psychomotor activation	Partial agonist

NIDDM, non–insulin dependent diabetes mellitus; WBC, white blood cell.

vidual patient, antidepressants, mood stabilizers, benzodi-azepines, or psychostimulants can be used adjunctively.

    i.   Several recent studies indicate that **lamotrigine may be beneficial for an adjunctive antipsychotic effect.** Finally, electroconvulsive therapy (ECT) can be a useful adjunct to treat partially-responsive patients, especially if it is used early in the course of the illness.

  c. **Acute treatment in the emergency and inpatient setting includes containment, reduction in stimulation, and development of an alliance.** Medication side effects should be avoided.

    i.   Education and support for the patient and the patient's family is vital.

    ii. Long-term treatment should include individual supportive and problem-solving therapy.

    iii. Recent studies indicate some benefit from **CBT for reality testing around delusions, as well as for smoking cessation.**

    iv. Family work should include development of realistic expectations. **Stable housing, improved vocational skills/supportive employment programs, and medication compliance all reduce hospitalization rates.**

IV. Schizoaffective Disorder

A.   **Overview**

A large number of patients with chronic psychotic illnesses also experience significant mood episodes (major depression or mania); if these episodes of affected individuals are present for a substantial portion of the illness, then the patients will qualify for a DSM-IV-TR diagnosis of schizoaffective disorder.

1.   Typically, patients diagnosed with schizoaffective disorder have psychotic symptoms that are indistinguishable from schizo-phrenic symptoms.

2.   However, the clinical presentation can be quite variable depending on whether the patient presents during a mood episode, or with baseline psychotic symptoms without mood symptoms.

B.   **Epidemiology**

1.   **The prevalence of schizoaffective disorder has not been well-described,** but appears to be less common than that of schizophrenia. In epidemiology, as in symptomatology, schizoaffective disorder has characteristics which lie between schizophrenia and mood disorders with psychotic features.

2.   The prognosis for schizoaffective disorder is better than that for schizophrenia, but worse than that for mood disorders. Large epidemiological studies have found that **patients with schizoaffective disorder can be divided into two groups: a depressive type and a bipolar type.**

    a.   Interestingly, for those patients with schizoaffective disorder, the individuals with a depressive type have a course more reminiscent of schizophrenia (with a chronic deterioration and disability) than a mood disorder.

3.   Patients with schizoaffective disorder have similar rates of suicide and violence as those with schizophrenia.

C.   **Etiology**
Genetic studies indicate that relatives of patients with schizoaffective disorder have an increased risk of schizophrenia and mood disorders. Debates about whether schizoaffective disorder is mechanistically closer to schizophrenia or to mood disorders have not been resolved.

D.   **Evaluation**
When evaluating a person for schizoaffective disorder, the same considerations should apply as in the evaluation for schizophrenia (described above) and in the mood disorders chapter (elsewhere in this volume); brain imaging, neuropsychological testing, and standard laboratory tests are likely to be of help.

E.   **Differential Diagnosis**
Because substance abuse and dependence are common among patients with schizophrenia, and because these are frequently associated with depressive or manic symptoms, it is important for the clinician to establish that the patient's mood symptoms are not secondary to substance-related problems prior to the diagnosis of a schizoaffective disorder.

F.   **Treatment: Pharmacological, Psychological, and Behavioral**
Treatment for schizoaffective disorder involves the use of antipsychotic medications, similar to treatment for schizophrenia. Lack of insight into their illness is a problem for this population, as it is for patients with schizophrenia.

1.   Treatment of episodes of dysregulated mood in bipolar disorder is similar to the strategy applied for major depression.

2.   Typically, patients are maintained on an antipsychotic and a mood stabilizer or antidepressant medication.

    3.   Nonpharmacological treatments are as essential in the treatment of schizoaffective disorder as they are in schizophrenia.

V.   Mood Disorders with Psychotic Features

A.   **Overview**

Both major depressive disorder (MDD) and bipolar disorder can be accompanied by psychotic symptoms. Indeed, **about 25% of consecutive hospital admissions with MDD and as many as 50% of all patients with bipolar disorder exhibit psychotic symptoms.** The hallmark of these psychotic symptoms is that they improve significantly when mood episodes are treated.

    1.   **Psychosis in MDD often takes the form of delusions of guilt or somatic decay** and dysfunction, as well as auditory hallucinations, while **mania is frequently accompanied by delusions of grandeur and thought disorder.**

    2.   Classic studies of mania indicated that psychotic symptoms typically emerge at the height of disorganization, in a quasi-delirious manic state.

    3.   There is a growing realization, however, that many patients with bipolar disorder have lingering delusions and a subtle thought disorder at baseline.

B.   **Treatment: Pharmacological, Psychological, and Behavioral**

    1.   The current first-line treatment for MDD with psychotic features is combined use of SSRIs and second-generation antipsychotic therapy.

    2.   However, there should be a low threshold for referring these patients for ECT, as this condition is **exquisitely responsive to ECT** (Rothschild, 2003). The best long-term maintenance following an episode of MDD with psychotic features is under debate, but the judicious use of antidepressants and antipsychotics demonstrates the lowest rates of relapse.

    3.   For the treatment of psychotic symptoms in the context of bipolar disorder, combination of a second-generation antipsychotic medication with a mood-stabilizing medication is efficacious.

VI.   Delusional Disorder

A.   **Overview**

Delusional disorder is quite distinct from all the conditions discussed so far in this chapter. The core feature of delusional disorder is that **one or more nonbizarre delusions** are present for more than 1 month. Hallucinations, if present, are not prominent. **Psychosocial**

functioning is usually well preserved, except for the direct impact of the delusions.

1. The most common subtype of delusional disorder is the persecutory type, where the individual believes he or she is being conspired against, cheated, spied upon, followed, drugged, harassed or obstructed in the pursuit of long-term goals.
2. Affected persons may engage in repeated attempts to remedy the injustice that they perceive to suffer through legal action, and they are typically resentful and angry.

B.   **Epidemiology, Etiology, and Mechanism**
Delusional disorder is not seen frequently in the psychiatric setting for several reasons.

1. First, it is **less common than the major psychoses.** Estimates of its lifetime prevalence range from 0.03–0.1%.
2. Second, **the age of onset of delusional disorder is later than that for schizophrenia;** most patients are diagnosed in their 40s, 50s, or even later.
3. Third, individuals with delusional disorder typically do not show insight into their disorder, and they tenaciously hold onto their account of events.
4. Finally, because psychosocial functioning is usually intact, only rarely are cases that cause major disruption in the individual's life brought to medical attention. As a result, little systematic study of delusional disorder has been carried out.

C.   **Course**
Delusional disorder tends to run a chronic and stable course. Most patients never fully recover from their delusions, although some can begin to reality-test more successfully with treatment.

D.   **Evaluation**
In evaluating an individual for delusional disorder, the same considerations apply as with any patient who presents with psychotic symptoms: brain imaging, neuropsychological testing, and standard laboratory tests to rule out an organic etiology should be considered.

E.   **Diagnosis**
When considering the diagnosis, the differential diagnosis includes dementia, substance-induced psychosis, MDD with psychotic features, a shared psychotic disorder (folie-à-deux), and hypochondriasis.

1. The presence of cognitive impairment distinguishes dementing illnesses from delusional disorder.
2. The chronological relationship of delusions with substance use or mood symptoms helps to clarify whether the delusions are secondary to substance use or to a mood episode.
3. Shared psychotic disorders involve more than one individual.
4. Patients with hypochondriasis have more insight into their preoccupations with health than do those with delusional disorder, somatic type.
5. Uncommon but specific forms of delusional disorder exist, including Capgras syndrome, in which the individual believes that a person close to them has been replaced by a double, and Fregoli syndrome, in which the individual identifies a familiar person in various other people he or she encounters. Subtypes include:
   a. Erotomania, in which a person believes an important person is in love with him or her
   b. Grandiosity
   c. Jealousy, in which one's lover or spouse is believed to be unfaithful
   d. Persecution
   e. Somatic
   f. Mixed

F.   **Treatment: Pharmacological, Psychological, and Behavioral**
Recommendations for treatment are based on clinical observation, not on empirical evidence. Unfortunately, there is little systematic data that compares treatments for patients with delusional disorder. Tact and skill may be necessary to **persuade patients to accept treatment,** and to **begin discussing the ways in which delusions are disruptive to their lives.** The physician must **neither condemn not collude with the patient's beliefs,** and must **emphasize the confidential nature of the physician-patient relationship.**
1. **Antipsychotic medications are usually ineffective in treating the delusions** at the core of the presentation. Nonetheless, they should be tried, as they may help relieve the agitation and anxiety that accompany the delusions.
2. Anxiolytics and antidepressants may be useful depending on the presentation, but ECT has no role in the treatment of delusional disorder.

Selected References

Davis JM, Chen N, Glick ID: A meta-analysis of the efficacy of second generation antipsychotics. *Arch Gen Psychol* 2003;60:553–564.

Henderson DC, Goff DC: Psychosis and schizophrenia. In Stern TA, Herman JB (eds): *Massachusetts General Hospital Psychiatry Update and Board Preparation*, New York: McGraw-Hill, 2000:97–103.

Hirsch SR, Weinberger D (eds): *Schizophrenia*, 2nd edition. Boston: Blackwell Publishing, 2003.

Miyamoto S, Duncan GE, Goff DC, Lieberman JA: Therapeutics of schizophrenia. In Davis KL, Charney D, Coyle JT, Nemeroff C (eds): *Neuropsychopharmacology, the Fifth Generation of Progress*. Philadelphia: Lippincott Williams & Wilkins, 2002:775–809.

Norquist GS, Narrow WE: Schizophrenia: epidemiology. In Sadock BJ, Sadock VA (eds): *Comprehensive Textbook of Psychiatry,* Philadelphia: Lippincott Williams & Wilkins, 1999:1110–1117.

Rothschild AJ: Challenges in the treatment of depression with psychotic features. *Biol Psychiatry* 2003;53:680–690.

Schatzberg AF: Non-schizophrenic psychoses: common and distinguishing features. *J Psychiatr Res* 2004;38:1–2.

Chapter 15

An Approach to the Patient with Disordered Mood: Depression, Irritability, or Elevated Mood

JEFF C. HUFFMAN, MD

I. Overview

Having disordered mood—whether elated, sad, irritable, or angry—is a normal part of human existence; as such, it is not pathologic. However, **when mood symptoms persist, affect function, or are associated with abnormalities of behavior or judgment, such symptoms are considered abnormal and require assessment.**

In this chapter, syndromes associated with depressed mood (e.g., major depression, dysthymia, and grief), and with irritable, expansive, or elated mood (e.g., bipolar disorder and cyclothymia) will be described.

II. Syndromes Associated with Depression

A. **Major Depressive Disorder (MDD)**
   1. **Definition: MDD is a syndrome that involves 2 weeks of either depressed mood or anhedonia (i.e., loss of interest in formerly pleasurable activities) plus four associated symptoms.** Such symptoms must occur most of the day, nearly every day for 2 weeks, and must result in diminished function (Table 15-1).
   2. **Epidemiology: Approximately 15% of the population has had an episode of major depression.** MDD is about twice as common in women; the mean age of onset is approximately 30 years. Recurrence is common; the risk of recurrence is 50% in those with one episode of MDD, and 90% in those with three or more episodes. The risk of MDD is increased two- to threefold in those having a first-degree relative with MDD.

B. **Dysthymia**
   1. **Definition:** Dysthymia is more chronic but requires fewer depressive symptoms than MDD. **Dysthymia consists of depressed mood, more days than not, for 2 years, with no**

Address for correspondence: Dr. Jeff C. Huffman, Massachusetts General Hospital, 55 Fruit Street, Warren 605, Boston, MA 02114, email: Jhuffman@partners.org.

Table 15-1. Diagnostic Criteria for Major Depressive Episode

A. Five of the following nine symptoms must have been present most of the day, nearly every day, for 2 weeks, and must include depressed mood or anhedonia as one of the five symptoms:
   1. Depressed mood
   2. Anhedonia (loss of pleasure in most activities)
   3. Significant change in appetite or change in weight
   4. Insomnia or hypersomnia
   5. Psychomotor agitation or retardation
   6. Decreased energy
   7. Guilt or feelings of worthlessness
   8. Decreased concentration
   9. Recurrent thoughts of death or suicidal ideation

B. These symptoms must result in impaired function or clinically significant distress.

C. These symptoms are not due to a mixed episode, grief, or the physiological effects of substance use or a general medical condition.

Adapted from American Psychiatric Association: *Diagnostic and Statistical Manual of Mental Disorders,* 4th ed. Washington, American Psychiatric Association, 1994.

---

   symptom-free period of 2 months or longer. In addition, two or more additional symptoms are needed, and function must be impaired (Table 15-2).

   2. **Epidemiology: The lifetime prevalence of dysthymia is approximately 6%.** It can coexist with MDD; when it does the syndrome is called *double depression*. Like MDD, dysthymia is more common in women and in those with a family history of depressive syndromes.

C. **Adjustment Disorder with Depressed Mood**

   1. **Definition: An adjustment disorder with depressed mood is diagnosed when a person exhibits symptoms of depression in response to a stressor.** These symptoms are judged to be out of proportion to what would normally be expected in such circumstances (or the symptoms significantly impair function); however, they do not meet criteria for another depressive syndrome (e.g., MDD).

Table 15-2. Diagnostic Criteria for Dysthymia

A. Depressed mood, most of the day, more days than not, for at least 2 years.

B. Two or more of the following symptoms during depressed mood during this period:

1. Decreased concentration
2. Decreased appetite (or overeating)
3. Insomnia or hypersomnia
4. Decreased energy
5. Decreased self-esteem
6. Feelings of hopelessness

C. There have been no persistent depression-free periods for 2 months or longer during this period; furthermore, a major depressive episode cannot have been present during the first 2 years of this episode.

Adapted from American Psychiatric Association: *Diagnostic and Statistical Manual of Mental Disorders,* 4th ed. Washington, American Psychiatric Association, 1994.

---

   2. Epidemiology: Adjustment disorder has been less rigorously studied than other depressive syndromes; thus **less is known about the prevalence, the genetic influence, and the recurrence rate of this disorder.** However, approximately 3% of psychiatric outpatients receive this diagnosis, and 10–20% of hospitalized medical inpatients seen in psychiatric consultation are diagnosed with an adjustment disorder.

D.   **Grief**

   1. **Definition: Grief is diagnosed when a person experiences depressed mood and has associated symptoms in the context of a significant loss,** frequently the death of a loved one. The depressed mood and associated symptoms do not meet criteria for another depressive syndrome, such as MDD.

   2. **Epidemiology:** Grief and major depression have superficial similarities, with depressed mood, guilt, and changes in energy, sleep, and appetite being common to both. However, there are a number of important differences between normal grief and abnormal major depression in response to the loss of a loved one (Table 15-3).

Table 15-3. Distinguishing Bereavement from Major Depression

Bereavement	Major Depression
Sadness is intermittent and comes in waves	Sadness is persistent and un-remitting
Mood is reactive to pleasurable events	Mood unreactive to pleasurable events
Passive wishes to join deceased loved one	Active thoughts of suicide
Self-esteem intact	Self-esteem impaired, with feelings of worthlessness

Both conditions may be characterized by profound sadness; frequent crying spells; decreased interest; impaired energy, appetite, and sleep; and feelings of guilt.

E. **Substance-Induced Mood Disorder**
1. **Definition: Depressive syndromes may result from intoxication with, chronic use of, or withdrawal from substances, both illicit and prescribed.** This disorder is diagnosed when depressed mood and associated symptoms are considered to be the result of substance use or withdrawal.
2. **Epidemiology:** At times this diagnosis may be difficult to make, as patients with primary depressive symptoms may turn to the use of illicit substances for temporary relief of their symptoms, only to have a worsening of symptoms as the result of the substance use or withdrawal. Substance-induced mood disorder resulting from illicit substances is most commonly caused by chronic use of alcohol or benzodiazepines, or by withdrawal from cocaine or amphetamines. In addition, medications (e.g., steroids and interferon-alpha) prescribed for medical illnesses can result in depressive symptoms (Table 15-4).

F. **Depression Due to a General Medical Condition**
1. **Definition: Depression due to a general medical condition is diagnosed when the symptoms of a depressive syndrome are considered to be the direct physiological result of a medical illness.** This does not include depressive episodes that occur as the result of psychosocial stress caused by development of medical illness; rather, it is only diagnosed when the illness itself

---

Table 15-4. Selected Medications and Illicit Substances Associated with Mood Episodes

Depressed mood:

Illicit substances
- Chronic alcohol or benzodiazepine use
- Withdrawal from cocaine or amphetamines

Other medications
- Corticosteroids
- Interferon-alpha
- Isotretinoin
- Methyldopa

Elevated mood:

Illicit substances
- Phencyclidine (PCP) intoxication
- Cocaine or amphetamine intoxication

Other medications
- Corticosteroids
- Thyroid hormone
- Sympathomimetics
- Antidepressants and psychostimulants (in those with underlying bipolar illness)

(e.g., hypothyroidism) is felt to be the physiological cause of depressed mood and neurovegetative symptoms.

2. **Epidemiology:** A number of general medical conditions have been associated with the development of depressive syndromes. Table 15-5 lists the most common of these conditions.

III. Evaluation of the Patient with Depressed Mood

A. **History of Present Illness**

1. A careful determination of the onset, course, and severity of mood symptoms is essential for accurate diagnosis. One begins by determining the characteristics of the episode:

   a. When did it begin? (to determine the duration of an episode)

   b. What was the precipitating event, if any? (to determine if grief, an adjustment disorder, substance use or withdrawal, or medical illness may be playing a role)

Table 15-5. Selected General Medical Conditions Associated with Mood Episodes

Depressed mood:
- Hypothyroidism
- Cushing's syndrome
- Multiple sclerosis
- Huntington's disease
- Parkinson's disease
- Stroke (especially left frontal lobe)
- Traumatic brain injury
- Epilepsy
- Neoplasm (especially pancreatic and central nervous system)
- Systemic lupus erythematosus (SLE)
- Vitamin B$_{12}$ deficiency

Elevated mood:
- Hyperthyroidism
- Wilson's disease
- Multiple sclerosis
- Stroke (especially right-sided)
- Traumatic brain injury
- Epilepsy (especially complex partial seizures)
- Tertiary syphilis
- Encephalitis

    c.   Has depressed mood been persistent throughout the episode? (i.e., is depressed mood present most of the day, nearly every day, as is required for MDD, or has depressed mood been less pervasive, as in dysthymia?)

    d.   What associated symptoms are present (i.e., have interest, energy, appetite, sleep, and concentration been affected, as required for MDD?)

2. **Suicidality should be assessed in any patient with depressed mood.** Key points of the assessment for the risk of suicide include:

    a.   Does the person have passive wishes to be dead, known as *passive suicidal ideation:* "Do you feel that your life is not worth living?" "Do you ever wish that you would go to sleep and not wake up?"

        b.   Does the person have active plans to end his or her life, known as *active suicidal ideation?* If so, does the person have a plan and the means to carry out such a plan? Does the person have intent to carry out this plan presently? If so, what, if anything, would need to change to reduce these feelings?

        c.   In addition to questioning about current thoughts of suicide, a suicide assessment should include questions about prior suicide attempts, psychotic symptoms, substance use or abuse, and demographic variables (e.g., living alone, being unemployed, being unmarried, and being elderly or an adolescent), as each of these factors is associated with increased risk of suicide attempt.

        d.   If thoughts of suicide are present, the physician should carefully consider treatment options and disposition plans to maximize the patient's safety and reduce the risk of incipient harm.

B.   **Past Psychiatric History and Family History**

    1.   **A review of the past psychiatric history should focus on the number, length, and course of prior depressive episodes, and on prior treatment trials (and their effectiveness).** This should significantly aid in treatment planning and help the patient and the physician learn what to expect with regard to the episode length and which treatments may be helpful.

    2.   **The interviewer should also inquire about current or past symptoms of mania or hypomania** (as patients with bipolar disorder require different treatments for depressive syndromes than do those without bipolar illness).

    3.   **Finally, a review of the family psychiatric history may be helpful,** given the genetic contribution of most mood disorders. Assessment of family members' response to specific treatments is also useful (e.g., "which antidepressant was most helpful to your mother when she had similar symptoms?"), as there is some indication that treatment response may also be genetically determined.

C.   **Physical Examination and Laboratory Data**

    1.   **Physical examination should focus on specific abnormal findings** that may suggest a substance- or illness-associated cause for depression.

        a.   Thinning of hair (especially of the lateral third of the eyebrows), dry skin, and coarse voice suggest hypothyroidism.

    b.   Cushingoid phenomena (e.g., central obesity, moon facies, and hirsutism) suggest hypercortisolism.

    c.   Track marks may suggest the use of intravenous drugs.

  2. **The gathering of laboratory data should be driven by information gleaned by history-taking and the physical examination.**

    a.   **A thyroid-stimulating hormone level** should be obtained if hypothyroidism is a possibility.

    b.   **Levels of vitamin B_{12} and folate** should be obtained if malnutrition appears present or if the patient has neurological symptoms suggestive of B_{12} deficiency.

    c.   **Serum and urine toxicology screens** should be obtained if there is a question of substance use.

IV. Treatment of the Patient with Depressed Mood

Treatment begins with accurate diagnosis. Based on the diagnosis and severity of symptoms, the treatment may include therapy, medications, or simply reassurance and monitoring. For patients with a current episode of major depression or dysthymia, antidepressants are the treatment of choice.

Averaged over large populations, **all antidepressants appear to be equally efficacious, with approximately 70% of patients having a response** (i.e., a 50% reduction of symptoms) to a given antidepressant. However, individuals respond differently to different agents, even within the same class. It may take trial and error to find an agent that is both well tolerated and effective for a given individual.

In general, antidepressants work slowly; they take up to 6 weeks to show a significant effect on depressive symptoms. Therefore a trial of an antidepressant should be no shorter than 6 weeks if the agent is well-tolerated. If a patient has a partial response to a treatment after 4–6 weeks, the dose of the agent should be increased until either remission is achieved or side effects become intolerable.

A.   **Selective Serotonin Reuptake Inhibitors (SSRIs)**

SSRIs are generally **considered the first line of treatment for these disorders.** Table 15-6 lists available SSRIs and the common dosage ranges for each of these agents. In general, these agents are well tolerated and safe. They are much less dangerous in overdose than older agents (e.g., tricyclic antidepressants [TCAs]).

Table 15-6. Selective Serotonin Reuptake Inhibitors (SSRIs) and Their Dosage Ranges

Antidepressant	Initial Target Dose	Dosage Range
Citalopram	20 mg/d	20–80 mg/d
Escitalopram	10 mg/d	10–20 mg/d
Fluoxetine	20 mg/d	20–80 mg/d
Fluvoxamine	50–100 mg/d	50–300 mg/d
Paroxetine	20 mg/d	20–80 mg/d
Sertraline	50–100 mg/d	50–300 mg/d

1. **Common side effects** include headache, nausea, diminished appetite, diarrhea, anxiety, sedation, and insomnia. These side effects usually diminish or disappear after several days, but if they persist, a switch to another agent may be necessitated.
   a. **Sexual dysfunction occurs in at least 15–20% of patients taking SSRIs.** Such symptoms range from a mild decrease in libido to anorgasmia or ejaculation abnormalities. Sexual side effects are reversed by discontinuation of the agent, and the use of some other pharmacological agents (e.g., bupropion, methylphenidate, sildenafil, and buspirone) may help to diminish these side effects.

B. **Other First-Line Treatments for Depression**
   1. **Venlafaxine:** a dual serotonin and norepinephrine reuptake inhibitor; it has a similar side effect profile to the SSRIs.
   2. **Bupropion:** an agent that has effects on norepinephrine and dopamine. Side effects include anxiety, insomnia, tremor, and headache. This agent should be avoided in patients with bulimia, or a history of head trauma or seizure, as seizures are slightly more common with this antidepressant.
   3. **Mirtazapine:** an agent that blocks 5-HT$_2$ and 5-HT$_3$ receptors, it also has effects on serotonin and norepinephrine. It can lead to weight gain and sedation, making it useful in patients with weight loss and insomnia, but less attractive to patients who wish to avoid these effects.

C. **Older Agents for Treatment-Refractory Depression**
   1. **Tricyclic antidepressants (TCAs):** these agents block reuptake of serotonin and norepinephrine, and have been used effective-

ly for years. Their use is limited by side effects (e.g., anti-cholinergic effects, sedation, and orthostatic hypotension) and by the development of cardiac conduction abnormalities that may be particularly dangerous in overdose.

2. **Monoamine oxidase inhibitors (MAOIs):** these agents inhibit the enzyme monoamine oxidase, which degrades serotonin, norepinephrine, and dopamine. Their use is most often limited by the need for a tyramine-free diet while taking these agents, with a risk of hypertensive crisis if foods with tyramine are ingested.

D.   **Psychotherapeutic Approaches**
Talking therapies are also effective in the treatment of MDD and dysthymia, either in combination with medications or alone.

1. **Cognitive-behavioral therapy (CBT)** is the best studied therapeutic treatment of depression. It appears to be as effective as medications for mild to moderate depression. CBT involves modification of behaviors associated with depression and restructuring of maladaptive automatic thoughts that perpetuate depression.

2. **Other psychotherapeutic modalities** (e.g., interpersonal therapy [IPT] and psychodynamic psychotherapy) can also be used in the treatment of depression.

E.   **The Passage of Time**
Depressed mood as the result of grief or adjustment disorder often resolves with time; afflicted patients should be monitored closely for the development of more severe depressive syndromes. Patients with depressive syndromes associated with substance use or general medical conditions require treatment of their substance use disorder or medical illness, with ongoing monitoring for residual depression during treatment.

V. Syndromes Associated with Irritable, Expansive, or Euphoric Mood

Clinically important syndromes associated with elevated or irritable mood usually involve a hypomanic, manic, or mixed episode. Therefore, to understand syndromes associated with elevated or irritable mood, one must first understand the criteria for these episodes (Table 15-7).

A manic episode is diagnosed when there is euphoric, expansive, or irritable mood along with associated manic symptoms, lasting 1 week or more. Manic episodes are frequently associated with psychotic symptoms, reckless or dangerous behavior, and im-

Table 15-7. Diagnostic Criteria for Manic, Mixed, and Hypomanic Episodes

Manic episode:

A. A distinct period of 1 week or more of euphoric, expansive, or irritable mood.

B. During this period, three or more of the following symptoms are present (four or more if mood is only irritable):
  1. Increased self-esteem or grandiosity
  2. Decreased need for sleep
  3. Racing thoughts or flight of ideas
  4. Easy distractability
  5. Increased rate of speech or loquacity
  6. Increased goal-directed activity or psychomotor agitation
  7. Increased reckless behavior (e.g., spending, sexual indiscretions, reckless driving)

C. There is marked impairment of function, impairment in interpersonal relationships, need for hospitalization, or psychotic symptoms.

D. Symptoms are not accounted for by a mixed episode and are not the direct physiological effects of substance use or a general medical condition.

Hypomanic episode:
Criteria are the same as for manic episode except that:
  1. Symptoms are required for only 4 days
  2. Function and relationships are not markedly impaired
  3. Hospitalization is not required and psychotic symptoms are not present

Mixed episode:
Criteria are simultaneously met for a manic episode and a major depressive episode (except for time duration) nearly every day for at least 1 week.

paired function. Patients with mania usually require hospitalization to avoid harm that results from impaired judgment.

The symptoms of a hypomanic episode are similar to those of mania; however, symptoms are only required for 4 days, function is not abnormally affected, psychosis is not present, and hospitalization is not required. Hypomania can be a time of high productivity and improved short-term function; however, it is frequently followed by a depressive episode of longer duration.

A mixed episode is diagnosed when criteria are simultaneously met for a manic episode and for a major depressive episode (except for time criteria) for a period of 1 week. In such cases, irritable mood often predominates.

A. **Bipolar I and Bipolar II Disorders**
1. **Definition: Bipolar I disorder is diagnosed when a person has one or more manic (or mixed) episodes.** Depressive episodes are common in bipolar I disorder; however, a depressive episode is not required to make the diagnosis. In contrast, bipolar II disorder requires both a hypomanic episode and a major depressive episode during one's lifetime (Table 15-8).
2. **Epidemiology:** Bipolar disorder is **present in approximately 2–3% of the population** and it is equally common in men and women. The mean age of onset is approximately 20 years. **The rapid cycling subtype of bipolar disorder is diagnosed when a person has four or more mood episodes in 12 months** (such patients frequently have mood states that switch rapidly). Rapid cycling bipolar disorder is often refractory to treatment and is more common in women. Bipolar illness has a stronger genetic component than MDD; persons with a first-degree relative with bipolar disorder have a seven- to tenfold increase in the risk of developing this disorder.

B. **Cyclothymia**
1. **Definition:** A diagnosis of **cyclothymia requires 2 years of recurrent hypomanic symptoms and recurrent depressive symptoms that do not meet criteria for MDD.** No manic

Table 15-8. Differences among Bipolar Disorders and Cyclothymia

	Manic Episodes	Hypomanic Episodes	Major Depressive Episodes
Bipolar I disorder	Yes	May have; not required	May have; not required
Bipolar II disorder	No	Yes	Yes
Cyclothymia	No	Yes	No

episodes or major depressive episodes are present (as these would generate a diagnosis of bipolar I or II disorder). Over this 2-year span, there is no symptom-free period lasting 2 months or more.

2. **Epidemiology:** Cyclothymia has been less extensively studied than bipolar disorder. Some feel it to be a less severe form of bipolar disorder; this is supported by the fact that one-third of patients with cyclothymia go on to develop full-blown bipolar disorder. Furthermore, people with cyclothymia have an elevated rate of bipolar disorder among first-degree family members.

C. **Substance-Induced Mood Disorder (with Mixed or Manic Features)**
1. **Definition:** This disorder is diagnosed when a manic or mixed episode is thought to result from the direct effects of intoxication with, chronic use of, or withdrawal from a substance.
2. **Epidemiology:** Table 15-4 lists illicit substances and medications associated with the development of irritable, expansive, or euphoric mood. In particular, patients taking cocaine and amphetamines may appear manic, and only toxicology screens can differentiate symptoms of intoxication from primary mania. Among prescribed substances, corticosteroids are the medications most frequently associated with development of mixed or manic symptoms. Antidepressants may induce mixed or manic symptoms in patients with preexisting bipolar disorder.

D. **Mood Disorder Due to a General Medical Condition (with Manic or Mixed Features)**
1. **Definition:** This disorder is **diagnosed when a manic or mixed episode results from the direct physiological effects of a general medical condition.**
2. **Epidemiology:** Table 15-5 lists the most common general medical conditions associated with the development of mixed or manic symptoms. Of these, hyperthyroidism may be the most common cause.

VI. Evaluation of the Patient with Irritable, Elevated, or Expansive Mood

Patients with elevated mood may be more difficult to interview than those with depressed mood because of uncooperativeness and disorganization of thought processes; furthermore, they may have less insight into their mood state. Therefore information from collateral sources is especially important in these patients.

A.   History of Present Illness
1. Because all diagnoses listed above are based on the development of hypomanic, manic, or mixed episodes, the initial goal is to determine whether the patient with irritable, expansive, or euphoric mood is currently having one of these mood episodes.
2. Initial questions (to both patients and their friends and family) should be focused on determining the patient's mood status.
    a. As with depressive episodes, **the length of the episode, any precipitating factors, and any history of such episodes should be determined.** Medical conditions, recent medication changes, and use of illicit substances should be addressed to determine if these factors are related to the development of the episode.
    b. **The specific symptoms of the episode should then be determined**—the interviewer should inquire about changes in sleep, energy, speech, self-esteem (grandiosity), thought processes ("do your thoughts seem to be racing at times?"), and other associated symptoms.
    c. **Behavioral changes** can be an important part of mood episodes that are associated with elevated mood. Has the person had markedly increased productivity? Has he or she acted more spontaneously or recklessly than usual, especially with regard to spending, sudden travel, or hypersexuality?
    d. The interviewer should ask about both **psychotic and depressive** symptoms. Psychotic symptoms can be an important part of manic or mixed episodes, and may be associated with dangerous or harmful behavior. Likewise, depressive symptoms are present in a mixed episode.
    e. An assessment for **suicide risk** should be performed.

B.   Past Psychiatric History and Family History
1. **Past history of both depressive episodes and episodes involving elevated mood should be determined.** Because those suffering from manic and mixed episodes often have limited insight into their mood state, the gathering of collateral information is important. Helpful questions for determining a history of mania include:
    a. "Have you ever been so 'hyper' that you have gotten into trouble or not been your usual self?"
    b. "Have you ever gone days without sleep and found that you didn't need it?"
    c. "Has anyone ever said that you were 'revved up' or seemed manic?

    2. **Knowing about a family history of mood disorder**—especially bipolar disorder—can be useful; a family history of response or nonresponse to specific treatments (e.g., lithium) may also help to guide treatment.

C. **Physical Examination and Laboratory Data**
    1. **Physical examination should focus on the stigmata** (e.g., goiter, fine tremor, and track marks) **that may suggest a substance- or illness-related cause for symptoms.**
    2. Similarly, laboratory examinations should be performed based on information from the history and the physical examination. Toxicological screens are frequently indicated for patients with mood episodes that involve elevated mood.

VII. Treatment of Mood Episodes Associated with Irritable, Expansive, or Euphoric Mood

As with depressive mood episodes, treatment varies according to diagnosis. Patients with elevated mood states usually require both acute treatment with medication to rapidly reduce symptoms and maintenance medication to prevent recurrence. Some types of therapy may help to reduce recurrence of symptoms once the patient has been stabilized.

A. **Acute Treatment of Mood Episodes in Patients with Bipolar Disorder or Cyclothymia**
    1. **The initial first-line treatment of any mood episode in a patient with bipolar disorder** (or cyclothymia) **is a mood stabilizer** (e.g., lithium or valproic acid; Table 15-9).
    2. **Patients in mixed or manic states, especially with severe symptoms or psychosis, often require the short-term addition of an antipsychotic** to reduce symptoms acutely.
    3. Patients in depressive states may require the addition of an antidepressant (or a second mood stabilizer) in the short-term if a single mood stabilizer alone is ineffective.

B. **Maintenance Treatment of Mood Episodes in Patients with Bipolar Disorder or Cyclothymia**
    1. Long-term treatment with a mood stabilizer is required for most patients with bipolar disorder or cyclothymia.
    2. Patients whose illness recurs despite an adequate dose of a mood stabilizer and good mood hygiene may require addition of a second mood stabilizer or an antipsychotic medication.

Table 15-9. Treatment of Acute Manic Episodes
Mild to moderate symptoms without psychosis: Lithium or valproic acid (VPA)
Severe or psychotic symptoms: Lithium or VPA plus an atypical antipsychotic (olanzapine or risperidone)

Refractory manic symptoms:
  1. Increase the dose of the antipsychotic
  2. Check lithium or VPA levels and increase the dose if the level is submaximal
  3. Re-evaluate for substance-related or general medical conditions
  4. Consider the addition of a benzodiazepine or a typical antipsychotic
  5. Consider the addition of a second mood stabilizer

For mixed episodes, episodes associated with rapid cycling bipolar disorder, or dysphoric mania, preferentially use VPA and other anticonvulsant mood stabilizers.

3. **In general, maintenance treatment with antidepressants should be avoided,** as long-term use of antidepressants may increase the frequency of mood episodes. However, individual patients may require antidepressants if depressive episodes cannot be prevented with other agents.

C. **Treatment of Mood Episodes Related to Substance Use or a General Medical Condition**
   1. This primarily requires cessation of substance abuse or treatment of the illness. However, mood stabilizers or antipsychotics may be required acutely if patients have severe symptoms that impair judgment or imperil safety.
   2. Maintenance treatment may be required if the medical illness related to the mood episode is chronic or refractory to treatment (e.g., systemic lupus erythematosus [SLE]) or requires long-term treatment with a medication (e.g., corticosteroids) associated with mania/hypomania.

D. **Mood-Stabilizing Medications Used in the Treatment of Bipolar Disorder and Cyclothymia**
   A mood stabilizer is defined most broadly as an agent that effectively treats at least one type of mood episode (mania or depression)

without precipitating or worsening the other type of mood episode (Table 15-10). Lithium, a number of anticonvulsants, and possibly some atypical antipsychotics (e.g., olanzapine) appear to meet these criteria; antidepressants (which can precipitate mania) and typical antipsychotics (which have been associated with development of depression) are not considered mood stabilizers.

1. **Lithium** is the best established mood stabilizer. It is the only mood stabilizer found to reduce suicide risk, and is the only mood stabilizer effective for both acute mania and acute depression; it is also effective for the maintenance treatment of bipolar disorder (and cyclothymia). Its use can at times be limited by its narrow therapeutic index. It requires titration of dosage, and in acute mania additional agents are often required until therapeutic levels are achieved.

   a. **Common side effects** include tremor, sedation, GI effects, and hypothyroidism. Renal insufficiency can occur with chronic use.

Table 15-10. Selected Medications Used in the Treatment of Bipolar Disorder

Medication	Initial Target Dose	Therapeutic Level	Initial Lab Monitoring	Chronic Lab Monitoring
Lithium	900–1200 mg/d	0.6–1.2 mEq/L	CBC, Cr, TSH, ECG	Lithium level, Cr, TSH
Valproic acid	1000–1500 mg/d	50–120 mEq/L	CBC, LFTs	CBC, LFTs, VPA level
Carbamazepine	800–1200 mg/d	8–12 µg/L	CBC, LFTs	CBC, LFTs, CBZ level
Lamotrigine	100–200 mg/d	n/a	None; monitor for rash	None
Oxcarbazepine	1200–1600 mg/d	n/a	Electrolytes (sodium)	Sodium level
Olanzapine	10–20 mg/d	n/a	None	Consider a fasting glucose
Risperidone	2–3 mg/d	n/a	None	None

CBC, complete blood cell count; CBZ, carbamazepine; Cr, creatinine; ECG, electrocardiogram; LFT, liver function tests; TSH, thyroid-stimulating hormone; VPA, valproic acid.

    b. **Lithium toxicity** may occur when the serum lithium level exceeds 1.5 mEq/L. Symptoms can include delirium, stupor, severe tremor, renal failure, and seizures. Treatment includes discontinuation of lithium, infusion of normal saline, and when symptoms are severe, dialysis.

2. **Several anticonvulsants** have also been used as mood stabilizers. Of these, valproic acid, carbamazepine, and lamotrigine are most frequently used. Anticonvulsants may be more effective than lithium in the treatment of mixed episodes and in the maintenance treatment of rapid cycling bipolar disorder.

    a. **Valproic acid** is effective in the acute treatment of mania and for prevention of manic recurrence; it is less effective in the treatment of depression. It may be rapidly loaded (20 mg/kg per day). Side effects include sedation, gastrointestinal upset, tremor, and weight gain. Liver function tests should be monitored with valproic acid due to the risk of elevation of transaminases, and rarely hepatotoxicity.

    b. **Carbamazepine** is also effective for treatment and prevention of mania; it is less effective for depression. Side effects include sedation, gastrointestinal upset, and rash. Complete blood count should be monitored because of the risk of aplastic anemia. Carbamazepine also induces hepatic metabolism, reducing the serum concentration of certain other agents metabolized through the liver. Oxcarbazepine, a metabolite of carbamazepine without such effects on liver metabolism, has also been used to treat mania.

    c. **Lamotrigine** is effective in the treatment of bipolar depression and the maintenance treatment of rapid cycling bipolar disorder. Its acute use is limited by the requirement for slow titration (over 6 weeks or more) to reduce the risk of dangerous dermatological disorders (e.g., Stevens-Johnson syndrome). Side effects include headache, dizziness, and tremor.

    d. **Atypical antipsychotics** are becoming more frequently used in the treatment of acute mania; in addition, olanzapine has recently been approved for use in the maintenance treatment of bipolar disorder. These agents are useful because they may be rapidly titrated in acute mood states, and they appear to treat symptoms of dysregulated mood and psychosis. Of these agents, olanzapine has been most frequently used; risperidone and quetiapine have also received Food and Drug Administration approval for the treatment of acute mania. Chronic use of atypical antipsychotics may be somewhat limited by the risk of weight gain and the development of type II diabetes mellitus (especially with olanzapine) and the risk of extrapyramidal symptoms (especially with risperidone).

E.   **Antidepressants**
Antidepressants may also be used in the treatment of depressive episodes in bipolar disorder when monotherapy with a mood stabilizer has failed.

1. **Antidepressants should not be used alone because of the risk of inducing mania and the cycling of mood episodes.** When used, standard doses of antidepressants should be prescribed, and the dosages increased until symptoms are reduced or intolerable side effects develop. Antidepressants should be tapered (if possible) once a period of stability of at least 4–8 weeks has resulted.

2. Based on the limited data available, bupropion and paroxetine appear to be the antidepressants associated with the lowest rate of switching to mania; therefore these are the antidepressants of choice for patients with bipolar disorder.

F.   **Other Agents Used in the Treatment of Refractory Mood Episodes**

1. **Typical antipsychotics** are effective in the reduction of symptoms during acute mania, though they are not indicated for maintenance treatment.

2. **Benzodiazepines,** especially clonazepam, may be used in refractory mixed or manic symptoms.

3. **Electroconvulsive therapy (ECT)** is effective for refractory symptoms of manic, mixed, or depressive episodes.

G.   **Psychotherapeutic Approaches**
While generally not effective during acute mixed or manic episodes, psychotherapeutic approaches can be effective during acute depression and in the maintenance treatment of bipolar disorder to reduce the rate of recurrence.

Standard psychotherapeutic approaches (e.g., CBT) are effective in the treatment of depressive episodes.

In the maintenance treatment of bipolar disorder, psychotherapeutic interventions frequently focus on enhancing good mood hygiene. Such treatment focuses on the maintenance of a regular sleep schedule, stress reduction, provision of psychoeducation, avoidance of maladaptive approaches to mood symptoms (e.g., substance use), and identification of specific factors that have previously contributed to relapse.

Suggested Readings

American Psychiatric Association: Practice guideline for the treatment of patients with bipolar disorder (revision). *Am J Psychiatry* 2002;159(Suppl 4):1–50.

American Psychiatric Association: Practice guideline for the treatment of patients with major depressive disorder (revision). *Am J Psychiatry* 2000;157(Suppl 4): 1–45.

Cassem NH, Papakostas GI, Fava M, Stern TA: Mood-disordered patients. In Stern TA, Fricchione GL, Cassem NH, et al (eds): *Massachusetts General Hospital Guide to General Hospital Psychiatry,* 5th edition. Philadelphia: Mosby, 2004:1–50.

Morrison J: *The First Interview: Revised for DSM-IV.* New York: Guilford Press, 1994.

Sachs G, Huffman JC, Stern TA: Approach to the patient with elevated, expansive, or irritable mood. In Stern TA, Herman JB, Slavin PL (eds): *Massachusetts General Hospital Guide to Primary Care Psychiatry,* 2nd edition. New York: McGraw-Hill, 2003:181–196.

Chapter 16

An Approach to the Anxious Patient: Symptoms of Anxiety, Fear, Avoidance, or Increased Arousal

DAN V. IOSIFESCU, MD
MARK H. POLLACK, MD

I.   Overview

Anxiety is an expected, normal, and transient response to stress; it may be a necessary cue for adaptation and for coping. Pathologic anxiety results from an unknown internal stimulus, or is inappropriate or excessive when compared to the existing external stimulus.

A.   **Features of Pathological Anxiety**
Pathologic anxiety is distinguished from a normal emotional response by four criteria:
1.   **Autonomy:** it has no or minimal recognizable environmental trigger.
2.   **Intensity:** it exceeds the patient's capacity to bear discomfort.
3.   **Duration:** the symptoms are persistent rather than transient.
4.   **Behavior:** anxiety impairs coping, and results in disabling behavioral strategies, such as avoidance or withdrawal.

B.   **Manifestations of Anxiety**
1.   **Physical symptoms** (e.g., tachycardia, tachypnea, diaphoresis, diarrhea, and lightheadedness) are related to autonomic arousal.
2.   **Affective symptoms** range in severity from mild (e.g., edginess) to severe (experienced as terror, the feeling that one is "going to die" or "losing control").
3.   **Behavior** that is characterized by avoidance (e.g., noncompliance with medical procedures) or compulsions.
4.   **Cognitions** include worry, apprehension, obsessions, and thoughts about emotional or bodily damage.

II.   Epidemiology and Prevalence

Anxiety disorders are among the most prevalent psychiatric disorders in the general population. **Approximately one-quarter of the United States population experiences pathologic anxiety over the course of their lifetime** (Table 16-1).

Address for correspondence: Dr. Dan V. Iosifescu, Massachusetts General Hospital, 50 Staniford Street, S50-401J, Boston, MA 02114, email: Diosifescu@Partners.org.

Table 16-1. Prevalence of Anxiety Disorders in the United States Population

Disorder	Lifetime Prevalence (%)	Prevalence per Year (%)
Any anxiety disorder	24.9	17.2
Panic disorder	3.5	2.3
Agoraphobia	5.3	2.8
Social phobia	13.3	7.9
Simple phobia	11.3	8.8
Generalized anxiety disorder	5.1	3.1

First-degree relatives of patients with anxiety disorders **have a significantly increased risk for anxiety disorders** compared with those in the general population. For first-degree relatives of patients with panic disorder the risk is increased four- to eightfold. Limited data from twin studies are also **consistent with a genetic contribution.**

III. Etiology

A.   Neurophysiology

A variety of central nervous system (CNS) structures and their related neurotransmitter systems generate and modulate anxiety symptoms. **Central noradrenergic systems,** including the **locus ceruleus (LC),** a small retropontine nucleus that is the major source of the brain's adrenergic innervation, are involved in triggering panic attacks. LC blockade (e.g., by tricyclic antidepressants [TCAs] or alprazolam) decreases panic attacks. The **γ-aminobutyric acid (GABA)** neurons from **the limbic system,** especially the septohippocampal areas, mediate generalized anxiety, worry, and vigilance. The highly concentrated GABA receptors in those structures bind benzodiazepines to reduce this heightened state of vigilance. Neuronal connections exist between the LC and limbic structures (including the amygdala). **Serotonergic systems and neuropeptides** are important modulators of the two systems outlined above. The interconnections of these neuronal systems explain the efficacy of clinical interventions (serotonergic and noradrenergic antidepressants, benzodiazepines, and cognitive-behavioral therapy [CBT]) with diverse mechanisms of action on pathologic anxiety.

B. **Cognitive-Behavioral Formulations**
Cognitive-behavioral formulations of anxiety focus on the information-processing and behavioral reactions that characterize the anxiety experience. The emphasis is placed on the role of thoughts and
beliefs (cognitions) in activating anxiety, as well as on the role of
avoidance or other escape responses in the maintenance of both fear
and dysfunctional thinking patterns. Faulty cognitions are often
characterized by overprediction of the likelihood, or the impact, of
negative events. Attempts to neutralize anxiety with avoidance or
compulsive behavior serve to "lock in" anxiety reactions and contribute to the chronic arousal and anticipatory anxiety that mark anxiety disorders.

IV. Work-Up of the Anxious Patient

The work-up of the anxious patient should rely primarily on the medical and
psychiatric history, the medication and drug history, and on the appropriate
physical and neurological examinations. One should consider the anxiogenic
effects of existing medications and medical conditions, as well as the effects
of substance use and withdrawal (see below). Targeted physical examination,
as well as laboratory and clinical tests are employed based on clinical
assessment, patient characteristics, and the focus (e.g., cardiac, pulmonary,
gastrointestinal, neurological) of the patient's somatic complaints.

V. Anxiety Associated with a General Medical Condition

Anxiety is particularly common in the general medical setting. The National
Ambulatory Medical Care Survey (1980–1981) revealed that **anxiety is the
presenting problem for 11% of the patients visiting primary care physicians (PCPs),** and is the most common psychiatric problem seen by PCPs. In
a patient with a known medical illness, the condition, its complications, and
its treatment should be suspected as potential causes of anxiety. For example
a patient's anxiety may be due to chronic obstructive pulmonary disease
(COPD), hypoxia, respiratory distress, or the use of sympathomimetic bron-
chodilators. A patient with an organic cause of anxiety may not otherwise
meet criteria for panic disorder or generalized anxiety disorder; there is often
a significant lack of **psychological** symptoms in the context of severe physical symptoms.

A. **Factors Associated with an Organic Anxiety Syndrome**
The **presence of certain factors** can help differentiate an organic
anxiety syndrome from a primary anxiety disorder:

    1.   Onset of symptoms after the age of 35 years
    2.   Lack of personal or family history of an anxiety disorder
    3.   Lack of a childhood history of significant anxiety, phobias, or separation anxiety
    4.   Absence of significant life events generating or exacerbating the anxiety symptoms
    5.   Lack of avoidance behavior
    6.   A poor response to anxiolytic agents

B.   **Diagnostic Criteria for an Anxiety Disorder Due to a General Medical Condition (DSM-IV-TR)**
    1.   Prominent anxiety, panic attacks, or obsessions and compulsions dominating the clinical presentation.
    2.   Evidence from history, physical examination, or laboratory findings that the disorder is a direct physiological consequence of a general medical condition.
    3.   The disturbance is not better accounted for by another mental disorder.
    4.   The disturbance does not occur exclusively during the course of delirium.
    5.   The disturbance causes clinical distress or impairment in social, occupational, or other important areas of functioning.

C.   **Common Medical Conditions Associated with Anxiety**
Anxiety disorders frequently complicate medical illness. More than 90% of the patients with anxiety disorders present primarily with somatic complaints. Moreover, most patients with anxiety disorders first seek help in primary care settings or emergency rooms. The majority of heavy users of primary care services (including patients with chronic illness) have significantly higher rates of mood and anxiety disorders than do less frequent visitors to PCPs. High rates of anxiety disorders are found in patients who present with chest pain, dizziness, dyspnea, and symptoms of irritable bowel syndrome. The presence of anxiety disorders represents a negative risk factor for the outcome of treatment of the medical illness. Several conditions linked with anxiety include:
    1.   **Endocrine:** e.g., hyperadrenalism (pheochromocytoma), hypothyroidism, and hyperparathyroidism
    2.   **Drug-related:**
        a.   **Intoxication:** e.g., with caffeine, cocaine, sympathomimetics, theophylline, corticosteroids, and thyroid hormones
        b.   **Withdrawal:** e.g., from alcohol, narcotics, or sedative-hypnotics

3. **Hypoxia:** all causes of **cerebral anoxia,** including **cardiovascular** (arrhythmias, angina, congestive heart failure, anemia) and **respiratory** (COPD, pulmonary embolism) conditions
4. **Metabolic:** acidosis, hyperthermia, electrolyte abnormalities (e.g., hypercalcemia)
5. **Neurological:** vestibular dysfunction, seizures (especially temporal lobe epilepsy)

D. **Treatment**

In anxiety associated with a general medical condition, recognition of the medical illness is a very important first step. However, treatment of the anxiety disorder is also important, and it could potentially improve morbidity and mortality. Although no randomized trials have been conducted in subjects with anxiety disorders and comorbid medical illness, treatment strategies offered successfully in open trials include use of selective serotonin reuptake inhibitors (SSRIs) and CBT. The doses of antidepressants and the CBT interventions employed are similar to those used for anxiety disorders without medical comorbidity (see below).

VI. Substance-Induced Anxiety

As discussed above, anxiety is commonly triggered by intoxication or by withdrawal from a variety of drugs or substances of abuse. Anxiety can be induced by intoxication with drugs (e.g., caffeine, cocaine, sympathomimetics, theophylline, corticosteroids, or thyroid hormones) while withdrawal from alcohol, opiates, benzodiazepines, barbiturates, other sedative-hypnotics can also trigger anxiety.

A. **Diagnostic Criteria for Substance-Induced Anxiety Disorder (DSM-IV-TR)**

1. Prominent anxiety, panic attacks, or obsessions and compulsions that dominate the clinical presentation.
2. Evidence from the history, physical examination, or laboratory findings that either the symptoms developed during or within 1 month of substance intoxication or withdrawal, or that medication use is etiologically related to the disturbance.
3. The disturbance is not better accounted for by an anxiety disorder that is not substance-induced.
4. The disturbance does not occur exclusively during the course of delirium.
5. The disturbance causes clinical distress or impairment in social, occupational, or other important areas of functioning.

B.   **Treatment of Substance-Induced Anxiety**

Appropriate treatment of withdrawal and long-term substance abuse treatment is essential to management of substance-induced anxiety (see Chapter 13 for details). While a history of substance abuse does not represent an absolute contraindication to the use of benzodiazepines, it warrants particular caution on the part of the clinician, given the potential for abuse and dependence. Anxiolytic medications that have been used successfully in subjects with current or past substance abuse include antidepressants (in doses similar to those used for other anxiety disorders, see below), as well as anticonvulsants (valproate [Depakote®], 250 mg twice a day or gabapentin [Neurontin®], 300 mg two to three times a day) and small doses of antipsychotic medications (quetiapine [Seroquel®] 25 mg three times a day).

VII. Panic Disorder and Agoraphobia

Panic disorder is a syndrome characterized by recurrent unexpected panic attacks about which there is persistent concern. Panic attacks are discrete episodes of intense anxiety that develop abruptly and **peak within 10 minutes; they are associated with at least four other symptoms of autonomic arousal.** Whereas the initial panic attack is usually spontaneous, subsequently apprehension frequently develops about future attacks (**anticipatory anxiety**). **Agoraphobia,** a complication of panic disorder, involves anxiety about, or avoidance of, places or situations from which ready escape might be difficult, or from which escape might be embarrassing, or where help may be unavailable in the event of a panic attack. Agoraphobia can significantly restrict a patient's daily activities, to the point where he or she becomes dependent on companions to face situations outside the home; some individuals become home-bound.

A.   **Symptoms Associated with Panic Disorder**
1. **Cardiac symptoms** (e.g., palpitations, tachycardia, chest pain, or discomfort)
2. **Pulmonary symptoms** (e.g., shortness of breath or a feeling of choking)
3. **Gastrointestinal symptoms** (e.g., nausea or abdominal distress)
4. **Neurological symptoms** (e.g., trembling, shaking, dizziness, lightheadedness, faintness, or paresthesias)
5. **Autonomic arousal** (e.g., sweating, chills, or hot flashes)
6. **Psychological symptoms** (e.g., derealization, depersonalization, a fear of losing control or going crazy, or a fear of dying)

B.   **Epidemiology**
     Panic disorder has a lifetime prevalence of 1.5–3.5%; it is more commonly diagnosed in women (2:1 female:male ratio). This difference may reflect a true gender difference or the observation that men tend to self-medicate with alcohol and are less likely to seek treatment. Many affected individuals recall a significant life event in the year before onset of the disease. **The age of onset is typically between late adolescence and the third decade of life,** but many affected individuals experience anxiety dating back to childhood, in the form of inhibited, anxious temperament or childhood anxiety disorders. Panic disorder tends to run in families; however, determining the relative contribution of genetic and environmental factors is an area of active research interest.

C.   **Diagnostic Features of Panic Disorder**
     Based on DSM-IV-TR, the diagnosis requires:
     1. Recurrent, unexpected panic attacks. A large number of patients experience **limited symptom attacks,** where only one or two of the panic symptoms are experienced. Limited symptom panic attacks are also anxiated with significant morbidity.
     2. At least one of the attacks is followed by more than a month of:
         a. Persistent concern about additional attacks
         b. Worry about the implications of the attack and its consequences
         c. A significant change in behavior related to the attacks
     3. There is no organic factor (e.g., general medical condition or substance use) that generates these symptoms.
     4. Panic attacks are not accounted for by any other mental disorder.
     5. The presence or absence of agoraphobia is specified.

D.   **Disease Course and Treatment**
     Panic disorder is often a chronic disease, with high rates of relapse after discontinuation of treatment. **Panic disorder is associated with marked impairments in physical and psychosocial function, as well as in quality of life.** Untreated panic disorder is often complicated by persistent anxiety, avoidant behavior, social dysfunction, marital problems, alcohol and drug abuse, increased utilization of medical services, and increased mortality (from cardiovascular complications and suicide). Avoidant behavior can lead to a progressive constriction of a patient's social interactions, and restricts the individual from the places where panic attacks have occurred or places where easy escape may be difficult or assistance unavailable. Affected patients may experience chronic distress and demoralization

which can trigger depression. While alcohol can temporarily alleviate the anxiety symptoms, patients who abuse it may experience
rebound anxiety, tolerance, and withdrawal, which may each exacerbate anxiety. **Patients with panic disorder lose workdays twice
as often as do those in the general population,** with 25% of panic
patients becoming chronically unemployed; up to 30% of patients
with panic disorder receive public assistance or disability payments.

VIII. Treatment of Panic Disorder

**Treatment of panic disorder has focused on the blockade of panic
attacks, the diminuition of anticipatory or generalized anxiety, and the
reversal of phobic avoidance.** At the same time, comorbid conditions, of
which depression and alcohol abuse are particularly relevant, need to be
treated.

A.   **Pharmacotherapy**
         The pharmacotherapy of panic disorder aims to prevent panic at-
         tacks and to treat comorbid conditions, such as depression. The goal
         of treatment is to reduce both the patient's distress and impairment
         to the point of remission, or to the point where the patient is capable
         of participating in other forms of therapy (e.g., cognitive-behavioral
         therapy). See Table 16-2 for recommended dosages of the most com-
         monly prescribed medications.
         1.   **Antidepressants.** The first medications shown to be effective in
              panic disorder were tricyclic antidepressants (TCAs); mono-
              amine oxidase inhibitors **(MAOIs),** and selective serotonin re-
              uptake inhibitors **(SSRIs)** are also efficacious.
              a.   **Selective serotonin reuptake inhibitors (SSRIs)** are now
                   first-line treatment of panic disorder, a condition that likely
                   involves dysregulation of the central serotonergic system.
                   Currently, paroxetine and sertraline are FDA-approved for
                   the treatment of panic disorder, though other SSRIs (e.g.,
                   fluoxetine, fluvoxamine, and escitalopram) have also
                   demonstrated antipanic efficacy, both in double-blind and
                   open trials. However, direct comparison among different
                   SSRIs in the treatment of panic disorder is lacking. The
                   serotonin-norepinephrine reuptake inhibitors (SNRI) also
                   appear to be comparably effective to SSRIs for the treat-
                   ment of panic disorder.
                   i.   **Advantages of SSRIs** include a favorable side-effect
                        profile, a broad spectrum of efficacy for comorbid dis-
                        orders, a low potential for abuse, safety in overdose,
                        and once-daily dosing.

Table 16-2. Recommended Dosage of the Most Commonly Prescribed Antianxiety Medications

Drug	Daily Dose Range (mg)	Initial Dose (mg)	Dosing Schedule
SSRIs			
Paroxetine (Paxil®)	10–50	10	qd
Paroxetine CR (Paxil® CR)	12.5–50	12.5	qd
Sertraline (Zoloft®)	25–200	25	qd
Fluvoxamine (Luvox®)	50–300	50	qd
Fluoxetine (Prozac®)	10–80	10	qd
Citalopram (Celexa®)	20–60	10–20	qd
Escitalopram (Lexapro®)	10–30	10	qd
TCAs			
Imipramine (Tofranil®)	100–300	10–25	qd
Clomipramine (Anafranil®)	100–250	12.5–25	qd
Amitriptyline (Elavil®)	100–300	10–25	qd
MAOIs			
Phenelzine (Nardil®)	60–90	15	bid
Tranylcypromine (Parnate®)	30–60	10–60	bid
Atypical antidepressants			
Venlafaxine (Effexor®-XR)	75–300	37.5	qd
Nefazodone (Serzone®)	300–600	50	bid
Benzodiazepines			
Alprazolam (Xanax®)	2–10	0.25–0.5	qid
Clonazepam (Klonopin®)	1–5	0.25	bid
Diazepam (Valium®)	5–40	2.5	bid
Lorazepam (Ativan®)	3–16	1.0	tid–qid
Azapirones			
Buspirone (Buspar®)	15–60	5	bid–tid
Beta-blockers			
Propranolol (Inderal®)	10–60	10–20	bid
Anticonvulsants			
Valproate (Depakote®)	500–2000	250	bid
Gabapentin (Neurontin®)	300–5400	300	bid–tid

MAOI, monoamine oxidase inhibitor; SSRI, selective serotonin reuptake inhibitor; TCA, tricyclic antidepressant.

      ii. **Disadvantages of SSRIs** include restlessness, "jitteriness," increased anxiety on initial dosing, sexual dysfunction, and a delayed onset of action (3–6 weeks). The SNRI venlafaxine may be associated with increased blood pressure in some individuals, generally at doses >225 mg/d.

      iii. Given the fact that SSRIs have the potential to cause initial restlessness, insomnia, and increased anxiety, and that panic patients are sensitive to somatic sensations, the starting doses should be low (e.g., paroxetine 10 mg/d, paroxetine controlled-release 12.5 mg/d, sertraline 25 mg/d, fluvoxamine 50 mg/d, fluoxetine 10 mg/d, citalopram 10 mg/d, and escitalopram 10 mg/d). SSRI doses can then be titrated up, based on clinical response and side effects.

      iv. The average effective doses of SSRIs are in the typical antidepressant range, and sometimes higher (e.g., paroxetine 20–40 mg/d, paroxetine controlled-release 25–50 mg/d, sertraline 50–150 mg/d, fluvoxamine 150–200 mg/d, fluoxetine 20–40 mg/d, citalopram 20–40 mg/d, and escitalopram 10–20 mg/d). Venlafaxine is generally efficacious in individuals with panic disorder at doses between 75 and 300 mg/d; its starting dose is 37.5 mg/d.

  b. **Tricyclic antidepressants (TCAs).** Imipramine was the first pharmacological agent shown to be efficacious in panic disorder. Clomipramine is now considered to have superior antipanic properties when compared with other TCAs (possibly related to its selectivity for serotonergic uptake).

      i. **Advantages of TCAs** include their lower cost (when compared to SSRIs), the fact that they are well studied, their efficacy in SSRI nonresponders, and once-daily dosing.

      ii. **Disadvantages of TCAs** include a wide range of adverse effects (with anticholinergic effects, orthostatic hypotension, effects on the cardiac conduction system, weight gain, restlessness, and "jitteriness"), heightened anxiety on initial dosing, a delayed onset of action (3–6 weeks), cardiotoxicity in overdose, and a total cost of care that may be higher than that associated with SSRIs.

      iii. **The impact of side effects.** The adverse effect profile of TCAs accounts for a high drop-out rate (30–70%) in published studies. Treatment should be initiated with lower doses (e.g., 10 mg/d for imipramine) to minimize the "activation syndrome" (restlessness, "jitteriness," palpitations, and increased anxiety) noted upon initiation of treatment. Typical antidepressant doses (e.g., 100–300 mg/d for imipramine) may ultimately be used to control the symptoms of panic disorder. Blood levels of TCAs, especially for imipramine, nortriptyline, and desipramine, can be checked after achievement of a steady state (about 5 days after a dose change), and may be useful in cases of poor response.

   c. **Monoamine oxidase inhibitors (MAOIs),** such as phenelzine and tranylcypromine, are potent antipanic agents.

      i. **Advantages of MAOIs** include their efficacy in treatment-resistant patients.

      ii. **Disadvantages of MAOIs** include their adverse effects profile (orthostatic hypotension, weight gain, and sexual dysfunction), the need for dietary restrictions (to prevent hypertensive crisis), drug interactions, and their toxicity in overdose.

      iii. Optimal dosage. Due to the danger associated with drug interactions, with toxicity in overdose, and with consumption of tyramine-containing foods while taking a MAOI, MAOIs are usually reserved for panic-disordered patients who remain symptomatic after treatment with safer and better-tolerated agents. Optimal doses for phenelzine range between 60 and 90 mg/d, while doses of tranylcypromine generally range between 30 and 60 mg/d.

   d. **Other antidepressants.** Nefazodone, a 5-HT$_2$ antagonist, has not demonstrated robust efficacy for panic disorder. It is efficacious and generally well tolerated for the treatment of depression at doses between 300 and 600 mg/d. Since cases of life-threatening hepatic failure have been reported, liver function tests should be monitored during treatment with nefazodone. Bupropion has been considered ineffective for the treatment of panic disorder based on a small prior report, although it did show efficacy in a more recent study. Treatment is typically initiated at low doses (i.e., 50–100 mg/d) to minimize early activation, with a usual target dose of 100–200 mg twice a day.

 2. **Benzodiazepines**

   a. **Initiation of treatment.** Benzodiazepines are **frequently used in the treatment of panic disorder, due to their efficacy, their rapid onset, and their favorable side effect**

profile. Common side effects noted at the beginning of treatment include sedation and ataxia that can be minimized by initiating treatment with low doses and by gradually titrating the dose upward. Treatment with benzodiazepines is associated with lower drop-out rates than with use of TCAs.

    i.   **Advantages** of benzodiazepines include being highly efficacious and rapidly-acting, and having a favorable side-effect profile.

    ii. **Disadvantages** of benzodiazepines include the propensity to develop a withdrawal syndrome, a potential for abuse, initial sedation and ataxia, increased sedation in the elderly, interactions with alcohol, and impairment of short-term memory.

  b. **Pharmacokinetics.** High-potency benzodiazepines (e.g., alprazolam and clonazepam) are as effective as TCAs and often better tolerated during the treatment of panic disorder. Both clonazepam and alprazolam are FDA-approved for the treatment of panic disorder.

    i.   **Treatment with alprazolam** should be started with 0.25–0.5 mg two to three times a day, and then gradually increased to maintenance doses (0.5–3 mg four times a day). However, alprazolam's short half-life may generate interdose rebound anxiety and withdrawal symptoms. The need to treat interdose anxiety with extra medication may foster a cognitive dependence on the medication. Therefore, a longer-acting high-potency benzodiazepine, such as clonazepam, may be preferred.

    ii. **Treatment with clonazepam** is also effective in the treatment of panic-disordered patients and its antipanic benefits are sustained over time without escalation of dose. Usually an initial bedtime dose of 0.25–0.5 mg is gradually titrated up to 1–3 mg/d, which may be given on a twice a day schedule.

    iv. **Treatment with low-potency benzodiazepines** may also be effective for panic disorder at equivalent doses (e.g., 40 mg/d for diazepam).

  c. **Discontinuation syndromes. Treatment with benzodiazepines should be discontinued gradually,** sometimes over a period of several months. The taper should be slower near its end. Rapid taper of benzodiazepines or abrupt discontinuation is frequently followed by a withdrawal syndrome, associated with rebound anxiety, weakness, and insomnia. The withdrawal syndrome, which has been described after treatments as short as 4–8 weeks, can be sufficiently severe to cause seizures, confusion, and psychotic symptoms; it is more intense with shorter-acting agents (e.g., those with a half-life of 10–20 hours). One strategy to minimize withdrawal is to convert shorter-acting agents to longer-acting benzodiazepines (e.g., clonazepam) prior to the initiation of a taper. Symptoms that persist for more than 2 weeks after discontinuation of a benzodiazepine are often interpreted as a return of the original anxiety disorder.

d. **Abuse and dependence.** Clinicians should consider the **potential for abuse and dependence** when prescribing benzodiazepines, especially in patients with a history of alcohol or substance abuse. A history of substance abuse does not represent an absolute contraindication to benzodiazepine treatment, but caution is warranted on the part of the clinician.

e. **Use in the elderly. Benzodiazepines should be used cautiously in elderly patients,** who, due to less efficient drug metabolism, may be more sensitive to sedation and ataxia, as well as prone to falls and memory impairment. The elderly also experience paradoxical agitation on benzodiazepines more often than do younger patients.

3. **Other agents**
   a. **Buspirone** has antianxiety properties but does not appear to be effective in panic disorder.
   b. **Beta-blockers** are not useful as primary treatment of panic, but they may reduce some somatic symptoms of autonomic arousal and may be used as adjuvants to other agents.
   c. **Some anticonvulsants** (valproate and gabapentin) have been successfully used in typical, atypical, and treatment-resistant panic disorder.

B.   **Cognitive-Behavioral Therapy**
CBT models of panic disorder focus on the information-processing and behavioral reactions that characterize the experience of panic attacks. Initial episodes of panic episodes typically emerge at a time of intense stress; this activates the firing of the fight-or-flight alarm system. In vulnerable individuals, the somatic sensations experienced during the initial panic episodes become cognitively associated with intense stress and danger. Subsequently, catastrophic misinterpretations of the meaning of somatic sensations (e.g., "I'm going to have a heart attack") may trigger similar alarm reactions, even in the absence of danger. The misinterpretations trigger

intense anxiety, which further intensifies somatic sensations in a positive feedback loop and results in a dramatic increase of anxiety into full panic. Later in the course of panic disorder, the alarm reactions (panic attacks) themselves may become the focus of fear.

CBT for panic disorder aims to eliminate catastrophic misinterpretations and the conditioned fear of somatic sensations, as well as to eliminate avoidance behavior. Most CBT for panic disorder typically lasts 12–15 sessions; it includes four components:

1. **Informational interventions** (i.e., explanations about the nature of the disorder) aim to demystify the somatic sensations experienced during panic attacks and to instruct patients about self-perpetuating patterns that maintain the disorder.

2. **Cognitive restructuring** aims to de-catastrophize beliefs about the meaning and the consequences of somatic symptoms. The catastrophic misinterpretations often distort the meaning of somatic sensations (e.g., "I'm going to have a heart attack"), or overestimate the probability or the degree of severity of feared outcomes (e.g., "I'm going to lose control"). The patients are asked to record their thoughts in panic diaries and to later analyze these thoughts as hypotheses, evaluating the evidence for or against them. The goal is to help patients reduce catastrophic interpretations and bring their thoughts in accordance with actual consequences.

3. **Exposure interventions** attempt to extinguish the conditioned response (fear) to certain somatic sensations or external situations in which panic may occur (i.e., agoraphobia). **Interoceptive exposure** is designed to induce somatic sensations usually associated with panic (e.g., running up the stairs to induce tachycardia). **In vivo exposure** targets patients suffering with agoraphobic avoidance, by exposing patients to the avoided situations. The exposure methods are carried out in a gradual manner.

4. **Anxiety management skills** (e.g., slow breathing techniques and muscle relaxation training) provide patients with skills for prevention of anxious responses to initial anxiety sensations. CBT is efficacious as an initial treatment for panic disorder, or as an adjuvant to pharmacological treatment. CBT can also be used for patients who failed pharmacotherapy or who wish to discontinue it. The integration of pharmacotherapy and CBT may produce a better outcome for some patients.

IX. Generalized Anxiety Disorder (GAD)

A. **Overview**

Patients with GAD suffer from excessive anxiety or worry that is out of proportion to situational factors; it occurs more days than not for more than 6 months. These patients are often considered "worriers" or "nervous" by their families and friends. The anxiety is usually associated with muscle tension, restlessness, insomnia, difficulty concentrating, easy fatigability, and irritability. Affected patients typically experience persistent anxiety rather than discrete panic attacks, as in panic disorder.

B. **Epidemiology**

The prevalence of GAD is about 5% in community samples; it is more typically diagnosed in women (2:1 female:male ratio). The age of onset is frequently in childhood or adolescence, with some patients having an onset in their twenties. GAD is frequently comorbid with other anxiety disorders (e.g., panic disorder and social phobia), depression, and with alcohol and drug abuse. The course of the disease is chronic but it fluctuates in its severity; it is frequently worsened during periods of stress.

C. **Diagnostic Criteria (DSM-IV-TR)**

1. Excessive anxiety and worry regarding a number of events or activities, that occurs more days than not for at least 6 months.
2. The individual finds it difficult to control the worry.
3. Three out of six symptoms (restlessness, easy fatigability, difficulty concentrating, irritability, muscle tension, and insomnia) are present.
4. The worry is unrelated to other disorders.
5. The anxiety causes significant distress or impairment in function.
6. The anxiety is not attributed to an organic cause (e.g., substance use or a medical condition).

D. **Pharmacotherapy**

Most pharmacological agents used in panic disorder are also effective in GAD. However, there are some differences:

1. **Benzodiazepines** have been the mainstay of treatment for GAD, although most current guidelines suggest initiation of treatment with an antidepressant that can treat both the anxiety symptoms and depression that often present comorbidly. However, benzodiazepines remain widely prescribed either as cotherapy or monotherapy for GAD because of their overall

anxiolytic effect, rapidity of therapeutic onset, and favorable side-effect profile. There is no evidence that any benzodiazepine is more effective than any others in the treatment of GAD. However, longer-acting benzodiazepines (e.g., clonazepam and diazepam) should generally be preferred for maintenance therapy given the risk for rebound anxiety associated with short-acting benzodiazepines (e.g., alprazolam). The characteristics of treatment with benzodiazepines discussed for panic disorder also apply for GAD.

2. **Antidepressant agents** (SSRIs, TCAs, and MAOIs) are also effective treatment for GAD. SSRIs and SNRIs (e.g., venlafaxine) have become first-line treatment for GAD. Paroxetine, venlafaxine, and escitalopram are FDA-approved for the treatment of GAD. Considerations in the use of antidepressants for GAD are similar to those for panic disorder.

3. **Buspirone,** a 5-HT_{1A} partial agonist, has shown efficacy in the treatment of GAD in a number of studies; however, results in practice have been considered less favorable by many clinicians. It has a gradual onset of effect and a generally favorable side-effect profile. The starting dose is usually 5 mg twice a day, which is then gradually increased to the average therapeutic dose of 10–30 mg twice a day (20–60 mg/d).

4. **Beta-blockers** (e.g., propranolol and atenolol) are useful as adjuvants to other agents, though they are not indicated as monotherapy for anxiety; they may reduce some somatic symptoms of autonomic arousal. When effective, beta-blockers may begin to work within the first week of treatment.

E.   Cognitive-Behavioral Therapy
Many of the same CBT interventions discussed for panic disorder also apply in GAD.

1. Informational interventions identify maladaptive cognitions and the worry process as a primary cause of anxiety.

2. Cognitive restructuring. Patients are asked to record their maladaptive cognitions as they occur in high-anxiety situations. Later, they analyze these thoughts logically, as hypotheses, evaluating the evidence for and against them. As patients get better at evaluating the content of their thoughts, specific "worry times" may be assigned to help them gain control over the constant tendency to worry.

3. Exposure interventions. Imaginary exposure to core worries is used to help patients decrease their worries about specific concerns.

4. Anxiety management skills. Relaxation training (e.g., slow breath-

ing techniques, muscle relaxation training) is used to decrease the arousal that accompanies worry and provides patients with coping tools to use in high-anxiety situations.

X. Specific Phobia

A. **Definition**
Patients with specific phobia have marked and persistent fear of circumscribed situations or objects (e.g., heights, closed spaces, animals, or the sight of blood). Exposure to the phobic stimulus results in intense anxiety and avoidance that interferes with the patient's life.

B. **Epidemiology**
The lifetime prevalence of phobias is about 10% in the general population. The age of onset varies depending on the subtype. Phobias to animals, natural environments (e.g., heights, storms, or water), blood, and injections each have an onset in childhood. Situational phobias (e.g., those triggered by airplanes, elevators, or enclosed places) have a bimodal distribution; one peak occurs in childhood and another peak develops in the mid-twenties.

C. **Diagnostic Criteria (DSM-IV-TR)**
1. Persistent, excessive unreasonable fear of an object or situation.
2. Exposure to a feared stimulus invariably provokes anxiety, including panic.
3. Recognition that the fear is excessive or unreasonable.
4. The phobic stimulus is avoided or endured with dread.
5. The fear and the avoidant behavior interferes with the person's normal routine or causes marked distress.
6. In a patient under the age of 18 years, symptoms last longer than 6 months.
7. The symptoms are not better accounted for by another disorder (e.g., obsessive-compulsive disorder or panic disorder).
8. Specific subtypes (e.g., animal, natural environment, blood-injection-injury, or situational) should be specified.

D. **Treatment**
1. **Exposure-based interventions,** a form of CBT, **are the mainstay of the treatment for specific phobia. The treatment consists of systematic desensitization and participant modeling.** The systematic desensitization consists of relaxation training combined with gradual exposure (frequently imaginary) to the feared stimulus. In participant modeling, the therapist enacts a

behavior and then encourages the patient to repeat that behavior.
2. **Benzodiazepines** are useful acutely to decrease phobic anxiety and to facilitate exposure (e.g., to take an airplane flight). Benzodiazepine treatment may be used to help an individual cope with an occasionally encountered feared event (e.g., flying in an airplane).

XI. Social Phobia

A. **Overview**
Patients with a social phobia fear being exposed to public scrutiny; they fear that they will behave in a way that will be humiliating or embarrassing. This perception leads to persistent fear and ultimately to avoidance or endurance with intense distress of the social situation. The anxiety can be limited to circumscribed performance situations, i.e., "performance anxiety" (e.g., speaking, eating, using a public bathroom, or writing in public), or can affect more general social interactions. Although discomfort related to public speaking is a relatively frequent occurrence in the general population, a significant degree of distress or the presence of impairment is necessary to warrant the diagnosis of social phobia.

B. **Epidemiology**
The prevalence of social phobia varies between 3% and 13%. In epidemiological and community studies the prevalence is greater in females than in males; however, the prevalence is greater for males in clinical samples. This may be the result of males experiencing more pressure for social performance and thus becoming aware of existing pathology. The onset of social phobia is usually in adolescence, although most affected individuals have a history of anxiety dating back to childhood.

The symptoms of social phobia may overlap with those of panic disorder, avoidant personality, and shyness. Social phobia is frequently comorbid with depression and with alcohol and drug abuse. The course of the disease is chronic but it fluctuates; it is frequently worsened during periods of stress.

C. **Diagnostic Criteria (DSM-IV-TR)**
1. Fear of showing anxiety symptoms or acting in a way that will be embarrassing or humiliating when scrutinized by others.
2. The presence of a situation almost invariably provokes anxiety.
3. Recognition by the patient that the fear is excessive or unreasonable.
4. The phobic stimulus is avoided or endured with intense anxiety.

5. The fear and the avoidant behavior interfere with the person's normal routine or cause marked distress.
6. In a patient under the age of 18 years, symptoms last longer than 6 months.
7. The symptoms are not better accounted for by an organic condition or by another mental disorder (e.g., trembling in Parkinson's disease or stuttering).
8. The subtype ("performance anxiety" vs. generalized) should be specified.

D. Treatment
   1. **Pharmacotherapy**
      An increasing number of studies have examined the efficacy of pharmacological agents for the treatment of social phobia. **Medications with demonstrated efficacy in social phobia include MAOIs, benzodiazepines, SSRIs, venlafaxine-XR, beta-blockers, and gabapentin.**
      a. **MAOIs.** In double-blind studies, phenelzine has proven effective in the treatment of social phobia. Doses used are similar to those used for depression and for panic disorder.
      b. **High-potency benzodiazepines,** especially alprazolam and clonazepam, are effective in social phobia.
      c. **Beta-blockers** have been used with mixed results in the treatment of social phobia. Doses (10–40 mg) of propranolol or 50–150 mg/d of atenolol have been shown to benefit patients with performance anxiety, but beta-blockers are not effective for the generalized subtype of social phobia.
      d. **SSRIs.** All SSRIs, as well as venlafaxine XR, have been reported as efficacious in the treatment of social phobia at typical antidepressant doses. Paroxetine is the first agent to receive FDA approval for this indication. Of note, TCAs are not generally effective for the treatment of social phobia.
      e. **Gabapentin** (dose range, 300–3600 mg/d) demonstrated efficacy in the treatment of social phobia in a randomized placebo controlled trial.
   2. **Cognitive-Behavioral Therapy**
      Fear of critical evaluation by others in social interactions is the key cognitive aspect of social phobia. This fear motivates avoidance of social situations and ultimately prevents the acquisition of social confidence and skills. The CBT for social phobia includes:
      a. **Informational interventions,** which are designed to clarify to the patient the anxiogenic nature of their thoughts and the role of avoidance in heightening socially phobic patterns.

    b. **Cognitive restructuring,** which is designed to modify the maladaptive cognitions that detract from competent social performance. Typical cognitive distortions include negative expectations of social performance ("I will not know what to say"), distorted evaluations of the self ("Everyone can do it but me"), and distorted anticipation of the reaction of others ("They will think I'm stupid"). Patients are taught to self-monitor their cognitive distortions and to analyze them logically, as hypotheses, evaluating the evidence for and against them.

    c. **Exposure interventions,** which aim to provide patients with the ability to practice in social situations and to evaluate their cognitions in that context. Patients rehearse feared interactions in group and homework assignments.

    d. **Social skills training** includes instructions and programmed practice in a role-playing format.

XII. Obsessive-Compulsive Disorder

A.   Overview

Obsessive-compulsive disorder (OCD) is characterized by recurrent, intrusive, unwanted thoughts (i.e., obsessions, such as fears of contamination), or compulsive behaviors or rituals (e.g., repetitive hand-washing).

  1. **Obsessions** are recurrent, persistent thoughts, impulses, or images characterized by four criteria:

    a. They are experienced as intrusive and inappropriate and cause marked anxiety and distress.

    b. They are not simply worries about real-life problems.

    c. Attempts are made to ignore obsessions or neutralize them with some other thought or action.

    d. The person recognizes the obsession as a product of his or her own mind, rather than imposed from the outside as in thought insertion.

  2. **Compulsive behaviors** take place in response to obsessions or rigid rules. Compulsive behaviors are aimed at reducing distress or preventing a dreaded event; they are clearly excessive or unconnected in a realistic way with the event they are trying to neutralize.

B.   Epidemiology

The lifetime prevalence is 2–3% in the general population. The mean age of onset is in the mid-twenties; less than 5% of patients develop the disease after the age of 35 years. The disease has a chronic course.

C. **Diagnostic Criteria (DSM-IV-TR)**
1. The presence of obsessions or compulsions.
2. The patient is (or was) able at some point to recognize that the obsessions or compulsions are excessive or unreasonable.
3. The obsessions or compulsions cause marked distress, are time-consuming (more than 1 hour/day), or significantly interfere with the person's normal routine.
4. The content of the obsessions or compulsions is not restricted to the features of any concomitant Axis I disorder.
5. The obsessions or compulsions cannot be attributed to an organic cause (e.g., substance use or medical condition).

D. **Differential Diagnosis**
The differential diagnosis includes obsessive-compulsive personality disorder, phobic disorders, depression, schizophrenia, and Tourette's disorder.

E. **Pharmacotherapy**
1. **Antidepressants. Agents that inhibit serotonin reuptake are the pharmacological treatments of choice for OCD.** Clomipramine, a TCA with potent serotonin reuptake inhibition, has been studied for more than 20 years and has been proven efficacious in the treatment of OCD. The effective doses tend to be high, up to 250 mg/d.

   More recently, several SSRIs (e.g., fluvoxamine, fluoxetine, sertraline, paroxetine, and citalopram) have been shown to provide safe and effective treatment for OCD. Fluvoxamine, sertraline, and paroxetine have been FDA-approved for the treatment of OCD. SSRIs are generally effective in OCD at higher doses compared with antidepressant doses: fluvoxamine (up to 300 mg/d), fluoxetine (up to 80 mg/d), sertraline (up to 200 mg/d), and paroxetine (up to 60 mg/d).

   Few OCD patients achieve a symptom-free state in response to therapy with serotonergic agents alone; partial relief from obsessional thinking is the more usual outcome. Most patients who respond to SSRI therapy obtain partial relief from obsessional thinking; their subjective experience of anxiety and their use of compulsive behaviors to decrease anxiety are often reduced but not eliminated.

Response to SSRI therapy may require 8–10 weeks of treatment. Failure to respond to SSRI therapy may reflect inadequate dosing or inadequate duration of treatment. If a patient does not respond to an SSRI at adequate high doses, use of an alternative SSRI may be successful.

2. **Buspirone,** a 5-HT$_{1A}$ partial agonist, has been helpful in treatment-refractory OCD, as an adjuvant to SSRIs. The medication is started at a dose of 5 mg twice a day, then gradually increased to the average therapeutic dose of 10–30 mg twice a day (20–60 mg/d).

3. **Benzodiazepines** (e.g., clonazepam) have been used successfully to treat comorbid anxiety in the OCD patient. However, benzodiazepines are not effective when used alone in the treatment of OCD. Some benzodiazepines (e.g., diazepam and alprazolam) are reported to have increased plasma levels when used in combination with SSRIs (such as fluvoxamine).

4. Other agents (e.g., trazodone, lithium, pindolol [a beta-blocker with intrinsic sympathomimetic activity], and risperidone [an antipsychotic]) have sometimes proven effective as adjuvants to potentiate the effect of SSRIs for the treatment of OCD.

F. **Cognitive-Behavioral Therapy**
The goal of CBT for OCD patients is to interrupt the chronic cycles of intrusive concerns and the compulsive rituals used by patients to ameliorate their obsessions. CBT is very effective in OCD, especially in combination with pharmacological treatment. The CBT methods utilized in OCD involve exposure and cognitive interventions.

1. **Exposure and response prevention.** The exposure consists of gradually confronting the patient with situations which are likely to trigger obsessive thoughts and compulsive rituals. For example, patients who fear contamination might be given a "dirty" hand towel and encouraged to hold the "contaminated" towel for an hour or longer. The response prevention used at the time of exposure requires patients to resist performing their compulsive rituals, such as hand-washing, for a progressively longer period of time. The repeated exposure without performing the compulsive rituals gradually decreases anxiety.

2. **Cognitive interventions** provide patients with additional skills for breaking the link between intrusive thoughts and compulsive responses.

XIII.   Post-Traumatic Stress Disorder (PTSD)

A.   Overview

Patients with PTSD have experienced an event that involved the threat of death, injury, or severe harm to themselves or others; their response involved intense fear, helplessness, or horror. Patients frequently re-experience the traumatic event in the form of nightmares or flashbacks, or by marked arousal when exposed to situations reminiscent of the event. PTSD patients avoid situations that remind them of the trauma; they may become emotionally numb, irritable, hypervigilant, or have difficulties with sleep and concentration.

B.   Epidemiology

The syndrome was initially described long before the Vietnam War; for those who had combat injuries the prevalence of PTSD is about 20%. PTSD can also occur in civilians who suffer life-threatening accidents or assaults; **the lifetime prevalence of PTSD in the general population is about 8%.** The syndrome may occur at any age. Symptoms usually begin within the first 3 months after trauma, although symptoms can be delayed for months or years. The course is varied; complete recovery occurs within 3 months in only half of those affected. Many others experience symptoms for more than a year after the trauma.

The complications of PTSD include social withdrawal, depression, and thoughts of suicide, as well as abuse of alcohol and other drugs. Psychosocial risk factors for PTSD include previous personality disorder, early trauma, a chaotic childhood, and previous mental illness. Protective factors include good self-esteem, external control, and social support.

C.   Diagnostic Criteria (DSM-IV-TR)

1.   The patient must have experienced, witnessed, or confronted an event that involved actual or threatened death, serious injury, or threat to the physical integrity of self or others. The person's response involved intense fear, helplessness, or horror.

2.   Persistent re-experience of the trauma in the form of intrusive recollections, nightmares, flashbacks, psychological distress and psychological reactivity occurs on cue exposure.

3.   Persistent avoidance of stimuli (thoughts and activities) associated with the trauma; numbing of general responsiveness (detachment or estrangement from others or sense of shortened future).

4. Symptoms of increased arousal (sleep disturbance, irritability, anger, difficulty concentrating, hypervigilance, and a startle response).
5. Symptoms last for more than 1 month.
6. Symptoms cause significant distress and impairment. Subtypes: acute (symptoms for less than 3 months), chronic (symptoms for more than 3 months), and delayed-onset (onset more than 6 months after trauma).

D.   Differential Diagnosis
The differential diagnosis includes acute stress disorder, in which symptoms occur within 4 weeks of the traumatic event and persist for less than 4 weeks.

E.   Pharmacotherapy
Pharmacological treatment targets reduction of prominent symptoms (e.g., antidepressants for depression). A number of studies have demonstrated the efficacy of the SSRIs for the treatment of the general PTSD syndrome. Exposure-based CBT is very effective for PTSD. Also important is psychotherapy aimed at survivor guilt, anger, and helplessness. Affected patients may benefit from family therapy and from vocational rehabilitation in the context of their significant impairment in social and professional functioning. The role of pharmacotherapy in PTSD has traditionally been related to symptomatic relief and facilitation of the onset of trauma-focused psychotherapy. However, SSRIs have recently demonstrated efficacy for reducing the range of core symptoms of PTSD.

1. **Antidepressants.** TCAs (e.g., amitriptyline and imipramine) have effectively reduced PTSD symptoms in double-blind studies. SSRIs (e.g., fluoxetine, sertraline, and paroxetine), bupropion, nefazodone, and MAOIs (e.g., phenelzine) have all been reported to have some efficacy in PTSD. Sertraline and paroxetine are the only pharmacological agents that have received FDA-approval for PSTD. The drugs are used in doses similar to those listed in Table 16-2; the doses for bupropion are 225–450 mg/d.

2. **Buspirone** has been reported to reduce the anxiety and increased arousal in PTSD patients at doses of 30–60 mg/d. When used, it is typically coadministered with an antidepressant.

3. **Mood stabilizers including lithium and anticonvulsants (such as carbamazepine, valproate, gabapentin, lamotrigine, and topiramate) in typical therapeutic doses have demonstrated efficacy for the treatment of PTSD.** One hypothesis

for the positive effects of these medications on PTSD symptoms relates to a reduction of kindling.

4. **Beta-blockers** (e.g., propranolol, nadolol, and atenolol) may be useful in some patients with PTSD to decrease persistent symptoms of autonomic hyperarousal. **Clonidine** at doses of 0.2–0.6 mg/d may also be beneficial.

5. **Benzodiazepines** can reduce anxiety and improve sleep in PTSD, but may have negative therapeutic effects (including disinhibition, irritability, and forestalling recovery).

6. **Neuroleptics** may reduce psychosis and impulsiveness in PTSD patients.

F.   Individual Psychotherapy

General support, informing patients about the typically time-limited nature of post-trauma symptoms (such as sleep disturbance), providing symptomatic relief, and making patients aware of the availability of mental health resources (should symptoms worsen or persist) are reasonable management strategies for most individuals exposed to trauma. Accruing evidence suggests that broadly applied critical incidence stress debriefing in the aftermath of a trauma may not be beneficial for most patients and may actually increase the likelihood of developing PTSD. For the chronic PTSD patient, exposure-based therapies, such as CBT, appear to be the most successful.

G.   Cognitive-Behavioral Therapy

CBT interventions aim to disrupt the link between trauma-related cues and severe anxiety responses and hypervigilance that characterize PTSD.

1. **Informational interventions** aim to help patients understand their symptoms. Discussion of dissociation and flashbacks may normalize and decrease the fear triggered by these symptoms.

2. **Cognitive restructuring** aims to help patients identify distortions in their thoughts that may have been generated by trauma (e.g., "The world is an unsafe place" or "I am helpless").

3. **Exposure interventions** aim to help patients control their emotional reactions associated with trauma. PTSD patients experience a diffuse association with objects and situations which are only remotely linked to the trauma. With repeated exposure, patients learn to differentiate between the diffuse, exaggerated fears generated by trauma and the actual safety of current situations. The intensity of exposure therapy can vary. Implosive therapy, a more intense form of exposure therapy, is effective but depends on the ability of the patient to tolerate intense lev-

els of arousal. Systematic desensitization involves a more gradual exposure and can be beneficial in overcoming the phobic
avoidance related to trauma.

4. **Relaxation training** may be used as it is in other anxiety disorders to provide patients with skills for preventing anxious
responses to initial stages of exposure treatment.

H.   Group Therapy
Patients involved in group therapy experience the understanding and
support provided by fellow victims; also, groups can sometimes
generate and process more intense effects than individual therapy.
Some researchers also report a greater effect of group therapy on
avoidance and the numbing symptoms present in PTSD, but no con-
clusive comparisons have yet been made.

XIV. Adjustment Disorder with Anxious Mood

A.   Overview
**Adjustment disorders are characterized by the development of
emotional or behavioral symptoms in the context of identified
psychosocial stressor(s).** The presence of symptoms also induces
marked distress that is in excess of what would be expected from the
exposure to the stressor, and/or impairs the patient's social and occupational function. The symptoms occur within 3 months of the
occurrence of the stressor and remit within 6 months of the cessation
of the stressor. Adjustment disorder with anxious mood is a subtype
of adjustment disorder where the predominant manifestations are
nervousness, worry, jitteriness, or in children, fear of separation
from major attachment figures.

B.   Epidemiology and Prevalence
In children, the prevalence rate of adjustment disorders has been
reported as being between 4.3% and 7.6%. Rates of adjustment disorders of 13–16% have been reported in clinical samples.

C.   Diagnostic Criteria (DSM-IV-TR)
1. The development of emotional or behavioral symptoms in response to identifiable stressor(s) occurring within 3 months of
the onset of the stressor(s).
2. Symptoms or behaviors that are clinically significant as evidenced by either marked distress that is in excess of what would
be expected from the exposure to the stressor, and/or significant
impairment in the patient's social and occupational (academic)
function.

3. The stress-related disturbance does not meet criteria for another Axis I disorder and is not merely an exacerbation of a pre-existing Axis I or Axis II disorder.
4. The symptoms do not represent bereavement.
5. Once the stressor(s) (or its consequences) have terminated, the symptom(s) do not persist for more than an additional 6 months.

D. **Differential Diagnosis**
The **differential diagnosis** includes PTSD, bereavement, and anxiety disorder not otherwise specified.

E. **Treatment**
Treatment of this condition is typically aimed at reducing the impact of the known stressor, primarily through psychosocial interventions, including crisis interventions. Short-term interventions, including CBT involving desensitization to the psychosocial stressor, may be sufficient in a significant number of cases. There are no randomized studies assessing the effects of psychopharmacological interventions in adjustment disorders. However, symptomatic relief with a benzodiazepine or antidepressant treatment can markedly improve the patient's quality of life and prevent complications.

XV. Conclusions

Anxiety disorders are a group of psychiatric disorders associated with high morbidity and with significant mortality (through suicide, comorbid substance abuse, and from cardiovascular problems). Given the similarities in presentations between certain medical conditions and anxiety disorders, a comprehensive medical, psychiatric, and substance use history is very important in the diagnostic process. Since most anxiety disorders tend to be chronic, many patients will benefit from ongoing pharmacotherapy and/or psychosocial interventions to optimize and to maintain benefit.

Anxiety disorders benefit from a range of psychopharmacological and psychotherapeutic interventions. For many patients, a combination of treatment modalities is the most effective treatment solution, although this issue requires further study. High rates of relapse (20–50%) after discontinuation of pharmacotherapy support the need for maintenance therapy for many individuals.

Suggested Readings

American Psychiatric Association: *Diagnostic and Statistical Manual of Mental Disorders,* 4th Edition, Text Revision. Washington: American Psychiatric Association, 2000:429–468.

Fyer AJ, Gabbard GO, Pine DS, et al.: Anxiety disorders. In Sadock BJ, Sadock VA (eds): *Comprehensive Textbook of Psychiatry,* 7th edition. Baltimore: Williams & Wilkins, 2000:1457–1489.

Hyman SE, Arana GW, Rosenbaum JF: *Handbook of Psychiatric Drug Therapy,* 4th editon. Boston: Little, Brown, 2000.

Otto MW, Reilly-Harrington NA, Harrington JA: Cognitive-behavioral strategies for specific disorders. In Stern TA, Herman JB, Slavin PL (eds): *The MGH Guide to Primary Care Psychiatry,* 2nd edition. New York: McGraw-Hill, 2004:75–84.

Pollack M, Smoller J, Lee D: The anxious patient. In Stern TA, Herman JB, Slavin PL (eds): *The MGH Guide to Primary Care Psychiatry,* 2nd edition. New York: McGraw-Hill, 2004:137–152.

Pollack M, Otto M, Bernstein J, Rosenbaum J: Anxious patients. In Stern TA, Fricchione GL, Cassem NH, Jellinek MS, Rosenbaum JF (eds): *Massachusetts General Hospital Handbook of General Hospital Psychiatry,* 5th edition. Philadelphia: Mosby, 2004:175–201.

Taylor CB: Treatment of anxiety disorders. In Schatzberg AF, Nemeroff CB (eds): *The American Psychiatric Press Textbook of Psychopharmacology.* Washington: American Psychiatric Press, 1995:641–655.

Chapter 17

An Approach to the Patient with Physical Complaints or Irrational Anxiety About an Illness or Their Appearance

Terry Rabinowitz, MD, DDS
Joseph Lasek, MD

I. Introduction

The patient referred for evaluation and treatment of a physical or psychiatric complaint for which no cause can be found is often vexing, even for experienced clinicians. Some of these patients feign symptoms for secondary gain or to attain the "patient role;" others suffer a great deal.

Many of these unfortunate patients are preoccupied by their symptoms (e.g., pain, or gastrointestinal or genitourinary difficulties) or by perceived defects in their appearance. They may get angry at or devalue a physician whom they believe is not doing enough to find the cause of their problems. They may "doctor-shop" in a futile search to find the "right" physician who will appropriately diagnose and treat their condition. Many become so disabled by their symptoms that they live marginal, unfulfilled lives: they lose or relinquish their jobs, their scholastic performance is often compromised, and their relationships often end because their partner becomes so frustrated or feels so inadequate as to make a relationship impossible.

This chapter addresses a collection of disorders that have in common symptoms or signs that cannot be explained by a purely physical cause. Included here are somatization disorder, undifferentiated somatoform disorder, conversion disorder, pain disorder, hypochondriasis, body dysmorphic disorder, malingering, dissociative disorders, factitious disorders, and psychological factors affecting a medical condition.

II.   Somatoform Disorders

The somatoform disorders comprise a collection of disorders characterized by bodily symptoms that suggest a physical disorder, but for which no physical cause can be found. The term "somatoform" has roots in Greek and Latin: *somato* (body) + *form* (having the shape of). Therefore, a person with a somatoform disorder has symptoms that appear related to the body as opposed to the mind.

The symptoms of somatoform disorders are not intentionally produced; moreover, they must be of sufficient magnitude or intensity to

Address for correspondence: Dr. Terry Rabinowitz, Fletcher Allen Health Care, 111 Colchester Ave., Burlington, VT 05401-1473, email: Terry.Rabinowitz @vtmednet.org.

cause significant impairment in function in occupational, scholastic, social, or other important domains. In addition, affected persons must seek medical treatment for their symptoms.

To reach a diagnosis of a somatoform disorder or any other disorder, it is essential to systematically rule out conditions that may in fact be responsible for the symptoms reported. In other words, a diagnosis of one of these disorders is predicated on the notion that a true physical cause of the symptoms has been ruled out beyond a reasonable doubt. Table 17-1 lists the somatoform disorders that appear in DSM-IV-TR.

A.   **Somatization Disorder**

The patient with somatization disorder (originally termed *hysteria* or *Briquet's syndrome*) has a pattern of recurring clinically significant somatic complaints. These complaints cause the afflicted individual to seek some form of medical treatment, or to cause significant impairment in one or more important domains.

For somatization disorder to be diagnosed, the symptoms must have begun before the age of 30 years and must occur over a period of several years. As is true for all somatoform disorders, the symptoms reported cannot be explained by a general medical condition or by the direct effects of a substance. If the symptoms occur in the presence of a general medical condition, the complaints must be in excess of what would be expected from that condition.

For somatization disorder to be diagnosed, an extensive set of criteria (including four pain symptoms, two gastrointestinal symptoms, one sexual symptom, and one pseudoneurological symptom) must be met. These criteria serve as a safeguard against the premature or incorrect diagnosis of the disorder.

The prevalence of somatization disorder ranges from 0.2–2% among women; it is less than 0.2% in men. Roughly 10–20% of first-degree female relatives also have the disorder. Male relatives of women with somatization disorder have an increased risk of antiso-

---

Table 17-1. The Somatoform Disorders in DSM-IV-TR

- Somatization disorder
- Undifferentiated somatoform disorder
- Conversion disorder
- Pain disorder
- Hypochondriasis
- Body dysmorphic disorder
- Somatoform disorder not otherwise specified

cial personality disorder and substance-related disorders. Women with the disorder often have a history of missing, disturbed, or defective parents and of sexual or physical abuse; although it may be decades since the abuse, the "trauma" may still play an important role in setting the stage for symptoms in the present.

Patients with somatization disorder often describe their symptoms in a dramatic fashion; however, their descriptions are often lacking in detail. They may seek help concurrently from multiple physicians, and they may have impulsive or antisocial behaviors as well as anxiety and depression symptoms. Common comorbid Axis I or II disorders include major depressive episode, dysthymia, personality disorder, and substance abuse. Prevalence rates of one or more comorbid psychiatric disorders may be as high as 75%.

The patient's culture and ethnicity may also have a significant influence on the report of symptoms. **As well, the culture and ethnicity of the examining clinician may color his or her understanding and interpretation of the symptom complex reported.** Therefore, it is important to consider each patient's heritage when contemplating this diagnosis. It occurs more frequently in those who are in lower socioeconomic groups and in whites more than non-whites. Some general medical conditions that might be confused with somatization disorder include multiple sclerosis, systemic lupus erythematosus, acute intermittent porphyria, and hemochromatosis.

Somatization disorder is a chronic condition. Complete remissions are the exception rather than the rule. Treatment should focus on support and reassurance, as well as on appropriate treatment (behavioral and pharmacological) of comorbid conditions. The differential diagnosis includes general medical condition, schizophrenia, delusional disorder, anxiety disorders (e.g., panic disorder and generalized anxiety disorder), and mood disorders.

Clues to diagnosis include an early onset, a chronic course without the development of physical signs or structural abnormalities, and the absence of characteristic laboratory values or diagnostic findings suggestive of a physical disorder.

B.   Undifferentiated Somatoform Disorder
This disorder has criteria similar to those for somatization disorder; however, symptoms need to be present for at least 6 months and the physical symptoms are below the threshold for a diagnosis of somatization disorder.

C.   Conversion Disorder
This fascinating disorder has as its essential feature a loss of, or deficit in, sensory or motor function that is suggestive of a neu-

rological or other general medical condition and which occurs in relation to psychological stress. In this disorder, a patient "converts" his or her psychological distress into physical or neurological symptoms. Common symptoms among those with conversion disorder include paralysis, aphonia, seizures, gait or coordination disturbances, blindness or tunnel vision, or anesthesia; however, virtually any motor or sensory complaint may occur, and symptoms or deficits cannot be limited to complaints of pain or sexual dysfunction per DSM-IV-TR.

Conversion disorder has a prevalence of 0.3% in the general population, of 1–3% in a general medical outpatient setting, and of 1–4.5% in inpatient medical settings. The female-to-male ratio ranges from 2:1–10:1, depending on the cohort studied. It occurs more commonly in men in military settings or in those who were involved in industrial accidents. Symptoms may be precipitated by exposure to others with similar symptoms.

Conversion disorder occurs with greater frequency in those of lower socioeconomic status, with less education and psychological sophistication, and in those from rural settings. Prior medical illness is commonly found. Associated psychiatric conditions include depression, anxiety, and schizophrenia, as well as histrionic and dependent personality disorder.

Clues to the diagnosis include symptoms that do not conform to known anatomical pathways or to physiological mechanisms. In addition, persons with conversion disorder often view their symptoms with significant detachment. For instance, they may be remarkably unconcerned by paralysis on one side of their body or by loss of vision. This response has been termed *la belle indifference* to connote a lack of concern about symptoms that would normally cause great consternation in an affected patient. Some patients may move a "paralyzed" extremity unconsciously or may mysteriously avoid obstacles despite their blindness; others with blindness may break out in a broad uncontrollable smile when a silly gesture is made in front of their "blind" eyes.

In general, symptoms of conversion disorder develop rapidly and are of short duration; first onset is usually in adolescence or childhood. Predisposing risk factors include physical disorders, the presence of stressors (including grief), rape, incest, or warfare. Good prognostic factors include a more acute onset, stressors occurring at onset of symptoms, previous good health, absence of other disorders, and symptoms of paralysis, aphonia, or blindness. Symptoms with a worse prognosis include pseudoseizures, tremor, and amnesia.

D.   Pain Disorder
The key feature in pain disorder is the occurrence of chronic, severe, preoccupying pain (without a detected physical cause or one that is far out of proportion to existing pathology and that is significant enough to cause impairment in multiple domains). Psychological factors are considered to play a significant role in the onset, severity, exacerbation, or maintenance of the pain.

For each of the somatoform disorders, but especially for this one, it is important to remember that the symptoms are neither intentionally produced nor feigned. Patients with pain disorder experience pain; however, compared with others who have pain of similar magnitude and duration, these patients are significantly more disabled.

There are three diagnostic subtypes in pain disorder: psychological (where psychological factors play a significant role in the symptom complex), nonpsychiatric pain associated with a general medical condition (where psychiatric factors play a minor role in the condition), and a combined form with elements of the preceding two varieties.

In pain disorder, associated symptoms or complications can be recalled by use of the mnemonic, "9 Ds": **d**isability, **d**isuse, **d**rug misuse, **d**octor-shopping, **d**ependency, **d**emoralization, **d**epression, **d**ramatic accounts of illness, and **d**epression.

Little is known about its clinical course or prevalence, but poorer outcomes are associated with a long period of no treatment before presentation, somatization, unemployment, and receipt of compensation for injuries or disability. For most patients pain resolves quickly and without complication; however, there is tremendous variability in the time to resolution. DSM-IV-TR reports that depressive disorders, alcohol dependence, and chronic pain may be more common in first-degree biological relatives of persons with pain disorder.

E.   Hypochondriasis
A preoccupation with the fear or belief of having a serious disease, based on a misinterpretation of benign physical signs or symptoms, characterizes the hypochondriac. An affected patient may present with a single recurrent symptom or with many during the course of the illness; it is accompanied by profound bodily preoccupation, a persistent fear of disease, and a strong but **nondelusional** conviction of having an illness. These symptoms of hypochondriasis are differentiated from those of somatization disorder by virtue of the heightened concern or preoccupation about the body

and function. Hypochondriacs are preoccupied with bodily function, fear disease, and are convinced they have an illness.

The prevalence of hypochondriasis in the general population is 1–5%, and up to 36% in inpatient medical settings; men and women are equally affected.

The origins of the disorder are unclear; however, positive predictors include disease or significant stressors at an early age (where the patient had or witnessed disease in a family member, had childhood adversity, or had neglectful or abusive parents). The first onset may occur in the context of a real illness—in fact, the key differential diagnostic consideration in hypochondriasis is an underlying general medical condition (e.g., myocardial infarction, congestive heart failure, or stroke)—or following the death of a loved one ("overidentification"). Hypochondriasis is a chronic condition with about 25% of patients having a poor prognosis, 65% having a chronic but fluctuating course, and 10% recovering.

F.   **Body Dysmorphic Disorder**

Persons with body dysmorphic disorder (previously called dysmorphophobia) have an imagined defect or deformity in appearance despite an unremarkable appearance. Most often the face, breasts, or genitals are felt to be defective. This causes significant anguish and leads to the persistent seeking of medical and surgical treatment in hope of effecting an acceptable change in appearance.

The disorder is quite resistant to psychiatric treatment; it leads to significant social withdrawal and disability. Anxiety, depression, and paranoia are common associated conditions.

True prevalence rates for body dysmorphic disorder are unknown. Reported rates in those with anxiety or depressive disorders range from 5% to approximately 40%; in settings dominated by cosmetic surgery and dermatological care, reported rates range from 6–15%.

Comorbid major depressive disorder is seen in 80% of afflicted patients. Other comorbid disorders include social anxiety disorder, substance abuse, and obsessive-compulsive disorder. Social dysfunction is present in up to 97% of affected individuals.

G.   **Somatoform Disorder Not Otherwise Specified (NOS)**

As is true for all DSM-IV-TR diagnostic categories, somatoform disorder NOS describes disorders with somatoform symptoms that do not meet full criteria for any of the other somatoform disorders. Included here are pseudocyesis (the false belief that one is pregnant); a disorder involving nonpsychotic hypochondriacal symptoms of less than 6 months' duration; and a disorder involving unexplained physical complaints of less than 6 months' duration that are not due to another mental disorder.

H. **Malingering and the Factitious Disorders**
Malingering involves the conscious feigning of physical or psychological symptoms for secondary gain. It is not considered a psychiatric disorder per se, but it may be the only reason a patient seeks or is referred for psychiatric evaluation and treatment. Malingering may be very difficult to diagnose; it may be even more difficult for the examining physician to report because of worry that patients so diagnosed will take legal action against them for insinuating that they might be receiving secondary gain for their invented symptoms. Szasz (1956) has said malingering is not a diagnosis but an accusation.

Moreover, some malingerers feign symptoms to avoid life-threatening or noxious tasks, such as might be required of a prisoner of war or a hostage. Thus, there are times when malingering is not performed for typically selfish secondary gain.

Ford and Feldman (2002) reported on four categories of malingered symptoms: production or simulation of an illness, exacerbation of a previous illness, exaggeration of symptoms of a previous or concurrent illness, and falsification of laboratory samples or medical reports.

In contrast with those who malinger, those with factitious disorders are characterized by the intentional production of physical or psychological signs or symptoms and they are motivated by a desire to assume the sick role, and not to receive secondary gain. Factitious disorders are referenced in DSM-IV-TR under three separate subtypes: with predominantly psychological signs and symptoms, with predominantly physical signs and symptoms, and with combined psychological and physical signs and symptoms.

The term *Munchausen syndrome* describes a chronic factitious disorder in which faking illness becomes the focus of a person's life. It was named for the protagonist in the book *Baron Munchausen's Narrative of His Marvelous Travels and Campaigns in Russia,* by R.E. Rapse (1784). Munchausen told fantastic stories; hence the name of this disorder and the historical descriptors associated with it: *peregrination*—wandering from hospital to hospital, and *pseudologia fantastica*—the telling of tall tales (i.e., pathological lying). Persons with Munchausen syndrome rarely if ever stop their behaviors until they are discovered.

A troubling variant of Munchausen syndrome is Munchausen syndrome by proxy. This form of child or adult abuse is

characterized by a caregiver's (usually the mother's) claim, or production of, illness in the ward. Although the disorder is most common in the mothers of children, it may also occur as a consequence of induced or feigned illness in an adult.

Ford and Feldman (2002) suggested four methods by which factitious disorders can be diagnosed: the patient is fortuitously discovered while engaging in factitious illness behavior (e.g., injecting feces under the skin, dropping blood from a cut finger into a urine specimen, or injecting a nondiabetic child with insulin); by the presence of incriminating paraphernalia seen among the patient's belongings; by laboratory findings that suggest a factitious etiology (high insulin levels with low C-peptide level or no drug level detected in a patient claiming severe drug reaction); and when no known disease that can explain current signs and symptoms is present.

Other keys to diagnosis include: a history presented dramatically, but with details lacking; failure of symptoms to respond as expected to usual therapies; indifference or marked acquiescence to invasive or painful procedures; and fleeing the scene when definitive tests are recommended or refusal to have certain tests or studies or to have a psychiatry consultation, and a lack of cooperation with evaluation, noncompliance with treatment, or becoming argumentative or uncooperative when old records and/or confirmatory tests are requested. This information may also be useful when malingering is suspected.

Because of the secretive, misleading, and disingenuous nature of most persons who malinger or who have factitious disorders, there is a paucity of data on prevalence of these disorders; however, prevalence rates of 0.6–10% have been reported, and vary according to the patient population studied and the study site. Frequently, those with Munchausen syndrome are unmarried middle-aged men who are estranged from their families; many others with factitious disorders are women, aged 20–40 years, who work in medical occupations (e.g., nursing or medical technology) (Ford and Feldman, 2002).

Prevalence rates for malingering also vary. Rates may be lower in populations where there are lower payments for malpractice and for disability settlements or litigation rates.

I.   **Dissociative Disorders**
       Included in this diagnostic category are dissociative amnesia, dissociative fugue, dissociative identity disorder (formerly called *multiple personality disorder*), **depersonalization disorder, and dissociative disorder not otherwise specified.**
       The common feature of these disorders is a disruption in

consciousness, memory, identity, or perception, but with preserved reality testing. Symptoms may appear suddenly or develop more gradually, and may persist or show rapid resolution; a history of trauma is strongly correlated with dissociation.

When considering a diagnosis of a dissociative disorder, it is important to remember that **dissociative disorders are not considered psychotic disorders.** That is, reality testing remains preserved in these disorders. Therefore, if psychosis is present, another psychiatric disorder should be considered. Furthermore, a person's ethnicity and culture should be considered when contemplating a diagnosis of any dissociative disorder. Some members of certain religious denominations (e.g., Pentecostal Christians) may experience dissociative symptoms during religious ceremonies or at other times. As an expected occurrence for some "believers," the experience should not be considered pathologic.

Prevalence rates for the dissociative disorders are roughly equal in men and women; a higher prevalence rate has been noted among younger individuals. The combined prevalence rate all for all dissociative disorders is about 10%.

1. **Dissociative amnesia. An inability to recall important personal information is the essential feature of dissociative amnesia.** The personal information is often related to a traumatic event. Amnesia may be present for only specific areas or it may be global in nature. Severe stress may cause symptoms in large groups of men and women. Three-quarters of cases last between 24 hours and 5 days.

2. **Dissociative fugue. In dissociative fugue, sudden, unexpected travel away from home or one's customary place of daily activities, with an inability to recall some or all of one's past are the predominant features.** In some cases, patients with dissociative fugue assume entirely new identities. During a fugue state, patients may appear entirely normal and may fool even experienced clinicians. This disorder has a prevalence rate of about 0.2% and it occurs primarily in adults between the second and fourth decades.

3. **Dissociative identity disorder (DID) is characterized by the presence of two or more distinct identities or personalities.** When present, one of the personalities predominates over all others. The mean number of personality states in dissociative identity disorder is 13, but the reported range is from 2 to 100. It occurs more frequently in women than in men, with a reported maximum prevalence rate of about 1%.

This disorder is quite controversial; in many cases, borderline personality disorder or another disorder (instead of dissociative identity disorder) has been diagnosed, perhaps because patients with borderline personality disorder may have dissociative episodes.

However, DID may be diagnosed in patients with borderline personality disorder when they demand an alternative diagnosis that they feel is more appropriate—this may be a way for a patient to "blame the other guy" for actions (e.g., self-mutilation, suicidal gesture, or public intoxication) that are unacceptable or humiliating.

Prevalence rates of DID are nine times higher in females than in males, and it is strongly associated with a history of sexual abuse. Increased and more severe symptoms are associated with an earlier and more frequent abuse history. Symptoms usually develop between adolescence and the third decade of life. Comorbid psychiatric disorders include depression, substance abuse, borderline personality disorder, somatization disorder, sleep disorders, and sexual disorders.

Risk factors for borderline personality disorder with dissociation include inconsistent treatment by caregivers, sexual abuse by caregivers, witnessing sexual violence as a child, and being raped as an adult.

4. **Someone with depersonalization disorder has the feeling of being detached or disconnected from his or her body or from his or her mental processes.** As for all dissociative disorders, reality testing is intact.

It is estimated that as many as 50% of the adult population experience at least one episode of depersonalization in a lifetime. Prevalence rates for men and women are equal.

5. **Among dissociative disorders not otherwise specified, Ganser's syndrome (also called *the syndrome of approximate answers*) is probably best known. It is characterized by a person responding to a question with obvious, not-quite-correct answers.** Such an answer would be "3" in response to, "What is 1 plus 1?" and "April" when asked the month, even though it is really May, and "13" when asked, "How many eggs are in a dozen?" This disorder was originally described in prisoners but is not restricted to this population. Some patients with this disorder may have schizophrenia or an underlying brain disease, and many patients with Ganser's syndrome may be motivated to appear psychotic, incompetent, or cognitively impaired. Thus, malingering should be suspected in patients in whom Ganser's syndrome is present. In fact, malingering should be ruled out before any dissociative disorder diagnosis is made.

J. **Psychological Factors Affecting a Medical Condition**
Virtually any general medical condition may be adversely affected by a concurrent psychological disorder. This may occur in one of several ways, paraphrased from DSM-IV-TR: The factors can influence the course of the general medical condition, the factors may interfere with treatment of the general medical condition, the factors may constitute an additional health risk for the individual (e.g., continued overeating in an individual with weight-related diabetes), the factors may precipitate or exacerbate symptoms of the general medical condition by eliciting stress-related physiological responses (e.g., causing chest pain in individuals with coronary artery disease, or bronchospasm in individuals with asthma).

The adverse psychological factor(s) may be the result of an Axis I or II disorder, symptoms or personality traits that do not meet criteria for a bona fide Axis I or II disorder, maladaptive health behaviors, or physiological responses to environmental or social stressors.

K. **Sexual Dysfunction or Complaints**
DSM-IV-TR contains a separate category for sexual and gender identity disorders (see Chapter 21). However, **sexual dysfunction may be a component of any of the disorders covered in this chapter.** Thus, these disorders may be real or feigned, depending on the primary psychiatric diagnosis.

A wide range of sexual dysfunction may accompany these disorders. On one end of the spectrum may be unwillingness to engage in sexual contact, which is accompanied by feigning headache, backache, or dyspareunia (malingering). On the other end may be intense unremitting pain in the sex organs for which no physical cause can be found, but which makes sexual contact impossible (somatization disorder), loss of sensation in the sex organs following sexual assault of a close friend (conversion disorder), or psychogenic impotence in a man who has just learned that he has contributed to an unplanned pregnancy.

Filling the gap in this continuum may be problems such as a feeling of detachment during sexual intercourse in a woman with a history of being sexually assaulted (depersonalization disorder), impotence secondary to diabetes in a patient with characterological traits that caused him to be noncompliant with his prescribed insulin regimen (psychological factors affecting a general medical condition), and refusal to have sexual contact in a man of normal body habitus who believes he has a grossly misshapen body (body dysmorphic disorder).

III.   Treatment

The disorders described in this chapter may cause significant, long-lasting, and treatment-refractory problems for afflicted patients. Thus, it is not only important to diagnose them accurately, it is **equally important** to ensure that a thorough assessment of other psychiatric and nonpsychiatric disorders that may be more amenable to treatment (and which may reflect a more accurate diagnosis) has been performed. Once you are sure that your diagnosis is accurate, treatment options for these disorders include pharmacological interventions and psychotherapy, as well as supportive care. **The aim of treatment should be management, not cure.**

Pharmacological treatments for these disorders are, in general, less effective than are psychotherapy and support, except for the management of comorbid symptoms (such as depression, anxiety, psychosis, and fear). However, comorbid symptoms and disorders may be the greatest source of distress for these patients. For instance, patients with conversion disorder may be so distressed by their paralysis that they become depressed and despondent. If the symptoms last for more than a few weeks, depressive symptoms and major depression may be present and should be treated.

A.   **Consultation**

Psychiatric consultation for some somatoform disorders can decrease health care costs. **Possible approaches (Abbey, 2002) to these patients include:**

1.   **Reattribution approach:** a three-step process that links psychosocial stressors to physiologic mechanisms, then to physical symptoms. This generally works best with patients in primary care settings who have good insight.

2.   **A psychotherapeutic approach,** which focuses on developing a close therapeutic relationship with the patient. This may be appropriate for patients with more intense symptoms.

3.   **A directive approach,** comprised of interventions put forth in a medical framework, which may be effective for patients who are not psychologically minded.

B.   **Management**

The principles of management for somatization and somatoform disorders, recommended by Abbey (2002), will serve patients with any of the disorders in this chapter well. These principles, adapted from Abbey, include:

1.   **Emphasize explanation**

Provide the patient with tangible mechanisms, exculpation, and encouraging self-management. Do not reject the patient's explanations or collude with the patient's ideas of illness.

Try to understand the meaning of the patient's symptoms and tailor explanations to these meanings.

2. **Arrange for regular follow-up visits**
3. **Treat mood, anxiety, or other comorbid disorders**
4. **Avoid polypharmacy**
   This may cause an increased intensity of symptoms rather than an attenuation, or may cause **new** symptoms.
5. **Provide specific therapy when indicated** (e.g., physical therapy, massage therapy, hypnotherapy, or biofeedback)
6. **Change the social dynamics**
7. **Resolve difficulties in the doctor-patient relationship**
   Recognize and control negative reactions and countertransference. Recognize guilt, anger, dismissiveness, and collusion with patient. Find something likeable or interesting about the patient, even if it is simply amazement at their level of somatization. Set clear limits on your availability (Abbey, 2002).

For all of these disorders, a nonconfrontational approach is strongly recommended. This is especially true if malingering is suspected, when confronting someone with antisocial traits might lead to violence. In addition, this approach allows many patients an opportunity to "save face," thereby avoiding humiliation that might occur in response to being told their symptoms "are all in your head."

Suggested Readings

Abbey SE: Somatization and somatoform disorders. In Wise MG, Rundell JR (eds): *Textbook of Consultation Liaison Psychiatry. Psychiatry in the Medically Ill,* 2nd edition. Washington: American Psychiatric Publishing, 2002:361–392.

American Psychiatric Association: *Diagnostic and Statistical Manual of Mental Disorders,* 4th edition, Text Revision. Washington: American Psychiatric Association, 2000:485–512.

Barsky AJ, Stern TA, Greenberg DB, Cassem NH: Functional somatic symptoms and somatoform disorders. In Stern TA, Fricchione G, Cassem NH, et al (eds): *Massachusetts General Hospital Handbook of General Hospital Psychiatry,* 5th edition. Philadelphia: Mosby/Elsevier Science, 2004:269–292.

Brusco C, Geringer E: Somatoform disorders. In Stern TA, Herman JB (eds): *Massachusetts General Hospital Psychiatry Update and Board Preparation,* 2nd edition. New York: McGraw-Hill, 2004:137–144.

Calabrese L, Stern TA: The patient with multiple physical complaints. In Stern TA, Herman JB, Slavin PL (eds): *Massachusetts General Hospital Guide to Primary Care Psychiatry,* 2nd edition. New York: McGraw-Hill, 2004:269–278.

Ford CV, Feldman MD: Factitious disorders and malingering. In Wise MG, Rundell JR (eds): *Textbook of Consultation Liaison Psychiatry. Psychiatry in the Medically Ill,* 2nd edition. Washington: American Psychiatric Publishing, 2002:519–534.

Strub RL, Black FW: *The Mental Status Examination in Neurology,* 4th edition. Philadelphia: FA Davis, 2000:74–92.

Szasz TS: Malingering: "diagnosis" or social condemnation? *Arch Neurol Psychiatry* 1956;76:432–443.

Yutzy, SH: Somatoform disorders. In Hales RE, Yudofsky SC (eds): *The American Psychiatric Publishing Textbook of Clinical Psychiatry,* 4th edition. Washington: American Psychiatric Publishing, 2003:659–690.

Chapter 18

An Approach to the Patient with Disordered Eating or Appetite

JENNIFER L. DERENNE, MD

I. Anorexia Nervosa

A. Overview

Anorexia nervosa (AN), a syndrome affecting 0.5% of young women, is **characterized by a disturbance in body image that leads to a refusal to maintain a minimally normal weight for one's height and frame.** The DSM-IV-TR defines "minimally normal" as **less than 85% of ideal body weight (IBW) or a body mass index (BMI) below 17.5 kg/m^2.** Afflicted individuals are intensely afraid of gaining weight; they employ severe measures (including caloric restriction, purging, and compulsive exercise) to prevent weight gain. Despite the fact that they are emaciated, many have markedly distorted perceptions of their bodies and feel that they are fat or that certain parts of their bodies (e.g., the thighs, abdomen, or buttocks) are abnormally large.

1. Epidemiology

a. **The lifetime prevalence of AN is estimated to be around 0.5%** and its incidence appears to be increasing.

b. Most anorexic women become symptomatic between the ages of 15 and 30.

c. While previously thought to be a disorder of affluent Caucasian women, cases of AN have been reported all over the world and in all socioeconomic groups. However, anorexia tends to be more prevalent among women in industrialized societies and in women who participate in activities (such as gymnastics, ballet, figure skating, and long-distance running) that value thinness.

d. Certain personality traits (e.g., perfectionism, rigidity, and competitiveness) are common in these patients.

e. Males account for only 5–10% of patients with eating disorders and homosexual men may be more susceptible to the disorder than heterosexual men.

Address for correspondence: Dr. Jennifer L. Derenne, Massachusetts General Hospital, 15 Parkman WACC 812, Boston, MA 02114, email: JDerenne @Partners.org.

2. **Etiology**

The etiology of AN is not entirely clear, although **genetic, psychological, and environmental contributions, such as the media and societal expectations, are thought to play a role.** The evidence for a strong biologic component to the illness is clear.

a. **Women with a family history of eating disorders are three times more likely to develop AN than their counterparts,** and many patients (as well as their family members) carry comorbid diagnoses (e.g., other anxiety disorders, mood disorders, and substance abuse disorders).

b. Many young women develop AN after a loss or a psychosocial stressor, such as going away to school.

c. Others, who are overweight or see themselves as overweight, will start a diet that spirals into malnutrition and develop an obsession with being thin. Many will deny feeling hungry, but most who have recovered admit that they were nearly always ravenous when they were restricting severely. The primary focus is on losing weight or preventing weight gain.

d. Women with AN of the restricting subtype typically restrict calories and exercise excessively, while those of the binge-eating/purging subtype regularly binge and then purge using laxatives, emetics, or diuretics to prevent weight gain.

e. Many develop obsessive-compulsive rituals around eating. Fatalities often result from cardiac arrhythmias, which are usually secondary to electrolyte abnormalities.

B. **The Evaluation**

1. **The interview and clinical history**

Patients with eating disorders are often not forthcoming about their symptoms and behaviors; concerned family members or friends often bring them to medical attention. In addition, their perception of normal weight, food intake, and exercise habits is distorted; moreover, they typically deny that their behavior is problematic. Therefore, **the evaluating clinician must obtain a detailed history, asking specific questions to establish the nature of the disorder and the length of the illness.** After discussion with the patient, family members, friends, and other treatment providers should corroborate the history. A complete history of abnormal eating behavior should include the following components:

a. Duration of symptoms

    b. Weight history (highest and lowest lifetime weights, usual adult weight)

    c. Food intake with calorie counts

    d. Purging history (e.g., the frequency, method, and amount of time spent engaging in purging behaviors)

    e. Medication use (including use of ipecac, laxatives, diuretics, enemas, and diet pills; be sure to specify the frequency and the amount used)

    f. Exercise history (e.g., the frequency and the duration of workouts)

    g. Menstrual history (e.g., the age at menarche, fertility, and length of amenorrhea)

    h. Full medical and psychiatric review of systems, including gastrointestinal symptoms (e.g., abdominal discomfort and constipation), neurovegetative symptoms of depression, suicidal ideation, and substance abuse.

2. **The physical examination**

    a. **Height and weight:** the treating clinician should weigh the patient in a hospital gown facing away from the scale. The same scale should be used at each visit, and the patient should not be told his or her weight.

        i. **A urine specific gravity** should be obtained to rule out water-loading, and one should ensure that the patient is not hiding weights under the gown. A weight that is <75% of one's IBW is a criterion for hospitalization.

    b. **Vital signs** (pulse, temperature, respiratory rate, and orthostatic blood pressure) should be recorded at the initial evaluation and on every follow-up visit. Hypothermia, hypotension, or bradycardia indicates medical instability and possibly the need for hospitalization.

    c. **Dermatological signs,** e.g., dry or yellow-tinged skin (carotenemia), and fine, downy hair on the trunk and extremities (lanugo), hand abrasions from self-induced vomiting (Russell's sign), and alopecia should be assessed.

    d. **Examination of the head, eyes, ears, nose and throat** may reveal an enlargement of the parotid gland and dental erosions secondary to vomiting.

    e. **The examination of the chest:** cardiac arrhythmia and mitral valve prolapse should be ruled out. Pulmonary edema can signify heart failure secondary to cardiac muscle atrophy.

    f. **The gastrointestinal tract** may manifest decreased bowel sounds and rectal prolapse may result from chronic laxative abuse.

      g. **The neurological system** may manifest a peripheral neuropathy secondary to nutritional deficiency.

      h. **The musculoskeletal system** may be afflicted by hypoalbuminemia and right heart failure that induces peripheral edema.

3. **The laboratory assessment**

      a. Electrolytes should be checked initially and periodically, as hypokalemia and hypomagnesemia can precipitate life-threatening arrhythmias.

      b. Hypoglycemia is common in nutritionally compromised patients

      c. A complete blood count with differential (e.g., leukopenia, neutropenia, anemia, and thrombocytopenia) can be associated with AN.

      d. A thyroid-stimulating hormone level should be taken.

      e. Order a serum β-human chorionic gonadotropin (β-hCG) level; many patients are amenorrheic secondary to AN, but pregnancy should be ruled out. Postpubertal women become amenorrheic secondary to low estrogen levels from diminished pituitary secretion of luteinizing hormone (LH), and follicle-stimulating hormone (FSH).

      f. Obtain an electrocardiogram to assess heart rate, rhythm, and the QT interval in patients who are to be treated pharmacologically.

      g. Use dual-energy x-ray absorptiometry to evaluate the bone density of the lumbar spine to assess osteopenia, which can predispose patients with AN to fractures.

4. **Differential diagnosis**

      a. Weight loss secondary to a general medical disorder (such as diabetes mellitus, Addison's disease, a brain tumor involving the hypothalamic-pituitary axis, cancer, a malabsorption syndrome, or dysphagia).

      b. Major depression

      c. Psychosis with delusions about food

      d. Obsessive-compulsive disorder

      e. Substance abuse

      f. An anxiety disorder

      g. A personality disorder

C.   **Treatment**

Because eating disorders are difficult to treat, afflicted **patients usually require a multidisciplinary treatment team** that includes the primary care physician (PCP), psychologist, psychiatrist, and nutritionist. It is crucial that team members have clearly defined roles and are in close communication with each other to best coordinate care.

1. **Medical stabilization is the first priority.**
   a. **Assess the degree of malnutrition, the laboratory values, and the vital signs;** hospitalization may be needed for weight restoration. The primary care physician and the nutritionist should coordinate plans for safe refeeding with gradual weight gain. For the first 3 weeks, the internist should be alert for refeeding syndrome in which phosphate depletion can lead to cardiac arrest and death.
   b. **Perform frequent weight checks.**
   c. **Order daily multivitamin infusion and calcium 1500 mg daily plus vitamin D 400 IU daily.**

2. **Education of the patient and the family**
   It is essential that the health care provider explain all of the risks of malnutrition, including death. Many patients are unaware that cardiac toxicity can develop with use of ipecac. The dangers of hypokalemia secondary to purging should also be explained repeatedly. Anorexics who purge are at high risk for developing medical complications.

3. **Nonpharmacological therapies**
   a. **Partial hospitalization or day treatment** relies upon intensive programs that provide supervised meals, group therapy, and skills training for patients deemed stable enough to step down from inpatient level of care.
   b. **Cognitive behavioral therapy (CBT)** done in both group and individual settings is very directive; it focuses on changing cognitive distortions as well as on teaching the patient self-monitoring skills.
   c. **Psychodynamic therapy** is a traditional open-ended, insight-oriented measure that can be helpful for motivated patients.
   d. **Group therapy,** whether it be psychodynamic or skills-based, can be especially helpful for patients who have difficulty with interpersonal interactions.
   e. **Successful family therapy** requires the cooperation of all members of the family, but can be very helpful in focusing on dynamics that may contribute to the patient's underlying problem.

4. **Pharmacological care**
   a. Selective serotonin reuptake inhibitors (SSRIs) (e.g., fluoxetine, paroxetine, and sertraline) may decrease symptoms of depression that can exacerbate eating-disordered behaviors.

   b. Benzodiazepines: low-dose lorazepam or clonazepam can reduce premeal anxiety, and enable a patient to consume enough calories to restore weight to a healthy range.
   c. Antipsychotics such as risperidone or olanzapine can reduce anxiety and treat delusional thoughts regarding weight or food. However, these medications should be prescribed only after an honest discussion with the patient, as many will feel betrayed if they later learn that atypical antipsychotics are associated with weight gain.

II. Bulimia Nervosa

A. Overview

Bulimia nervosa (BN) is a condition in which a person consumes a large number of calories in a short period of time. Typically, she will report feeling a loss of control over her eating. As anxiety sets in over the consequences of her actions, the patient purges by inducing vomiting or taking laxatives, or compensates for the binge by fasting or by exercising heavily. To meet full diagnostic criteria, **the patient must binge and compensate for the binge at least twice a week for a period of 3 months.** Patients may be further categorized into purging and nonpurging categories. As one might expect, there is considerable overlap between AN and BN, with some patients experiencing symptoms of both illnesses at different points in their lives. Usually, a patient with a history of AN will develop bulimic symptoms when allowing herself to eat previously forbidden foods. Women who do not meet full DSM-IV-TR criteria for either illness, but who have significant issues surrounding eating, are lumped into the Eating Disorder, Not Otherwise Specified category.

1. Epidemiology
   a. **BN affects about 3% of women,** although the number of cases on college campuses is thought to be significantly higher.
   b. **Male patients comprise only 10% of the eating disorder population.**
   c. BN tends to be more prevalent in industrialized societies and in women who participate in activities that value thinness.
   d. Some women with BN are competitive, obsessional, and rigid, while others tend to be more impulsive.
   e. Gambling, binge-drinking, self-mutilation, and other im-

pulse control disorders tend to be more common in patients with bulimia.

    f.   Many patients with BN have a history of sexual abuse.

  2. **Etiology**

As with AN, BN is thought to be **multifactorial in origin,** with both biologic and environmental components.

    a.   Patients with BN tend to carry comorbid diagnoses and many have a family history of eating disorders, mood disorders, and substance abuse.

    b.   Bulimia nervosa often develops after a period of stress.

    c.   Bulimics almost uniformly have difficulty with assertiveness and mutuality in relationships, as well as allowing themselves to feel and to appropriately express emotion.

    d.   In addition, they may feel enormous societal and self-imposed pressure to be thin.

    e.   As such, many sharply curb consumption between binges; the combination of high emotion and deprivation inevitably leads to another binge. As purging cannot completely rid the body of calories, the patient's weight either increases or remains steady and the cycle continues.

B.   **Evaluation**

The history, physical exam, interview, and laboratory assessment, and differential diagnosis for patients with BN is nearly identical to that for anorexics. Because most patients are of normal weight, they often do not appear ill. **Particular attention should be focused on weight, vital signs, dentition, cardiac and GI exams, and potassium level.**

C.   **Treatment**

  1. **Medical stabilization**

    a.   Frequent weight checks and vital sign monitoring are important even if the patient does not appear to be underweight. Referral to a nutritionist specializing in eating disorders may be particularly helpful.

    b.   Potassium should be checked frequently and repleted as necessary. However, providing patients with standing potassium supplements can actually do more harm than good. If the patient varies the frequency of bingeing/purging or stops all together, she becomes susceptible to hyperkalemia with high risk of potentially fatal arrhythmias.

  2. **Education of the patient and the family**

The clinician should focus a lot of energy on the education of these women, about the medical complications of BN, including esophageal stricture, Mallory-Weiss tears, stomach rupture, parotid enlargement, and dental erosion. Laxative abuse may cause enough damage that the bowels will not move without artificial stimulants. Patients who induce vomiting should be instructed to gargle with bicarbonate of soda immediately after vomiting, then wait about 30 minutes before brushing their teeth to neutralize stomach acid and decrease the likelihood of further dental erosion. All patients with bulimia should receive dental care referrals. Finally, a good deal of attention should be focused on educating patients about potassium and risk of death when levels are not within the narrow therapeutic range.

3. **Therapy**

CBT is thought to be the most helpful treatment modality for BN. Several structured groups specialize in the integrative treatment of BN, drawing on psychoeducation, CBT, and interpersonal effectiveness training to reduce symptoms.

4. **Pharmacological care**

a. SSRIs (such as sertraline, fluoxetine, and paroxetine) are the treatment of choice for BN, as they are thought to decrease symptoms of both anxiety and depression that may exacerbate the eating disorder. Bupropion should be avoided in patients with active bingeing and purging, as seizures appear to be more common in this population.

b. Topiramate has shown promise in the treatment of many impulse-control disorders and may help reduce urges to binge and purge.

c. Antipsychotics may help to decrease delusions about body image or weight, but should be prescribed only after discussing the risks of weight gain.

III.   Obesity

A.   Overview

Obesity is defined as BMI [weight in pounds x 703/(height in inches)^2] of 30 kg/m^2 or greater. Costing more than \$100 billion annually in associated health care costs, obesity is currently the most expensive preventable disorder in the United States. Modest weight loss (around 10% of body weight) can significantly reduce morbidity and mortality from diabetes mellitus, obstructive sleep apnea, hypertension, and hyperlipidemia. Consumers in the United States spend about \$45 billion per year on weight loss services; despite initial success, long-term weight loss is successfully maintained in only 5% of patients. A large percentage of obese patients suffer from binge eating disorder (BED), which is defined as bingeing at least twice per week for at least 6 months. As in BN, patients consume large amounts of food in a discrete period of time. They often feel as though they have lost control of their eating. However, in BED, patients do not engage in compensatory measures to prevent weight gain.

1. **Epidemiology**

   More than 30% of Americans meet criteria for obesity, and more still are overweight (BMI >27). BED has a prevalence of 1–4% with a female:male ratio of 1.5:1. BED is by far the most common eating disorder in men.

2. **Etiology**

   Like the other eating disorders, **the etiology of obesity** is multifactorial with **genetic predisposition to body size, sedentary lifestyle, and eating behaviors** that contribute to excess body weight. **Hyperphagia** is a well-known symptom of atypical depression, while dysregulation of satiety centers can occur in those with organic brain disease. Environmental and psychological triggers can influence caloric consumption and exercise habits. Weight accumulates when more calories are taken in than are expended in a given period of time. Many obese people struggle with self-esteem issues and depression that stem from their body size; others overeat to deal with anxiety or overwhelming affect and subsequently become obese.

B. Evaluation

1. **History**

   As cultural attitudes continue to suggest that people struggling with obesity are lazy, morally deficient, or lack self-control, the evaluating clinician must be careful to approach the history in a nonjudgemental, empathic manner. Many obese patients find the process of providing a medical history and a physical humiliating. A complete history in an obese patient should also include the following:

   a. **The past medical history and review of systems** should focus on medical diseases (e.g., including hypothyroidism, Cushing's disease, and polycystic ovary syndrome) that are known to cause obesity. Patients should be screened for symptoms of diabetes, sleep apnea, and cardiac disease.

   b. A variety of **medications** (e.g., steroids, hormone replacement, oral contraceptives, antipsychotics, valproic acid, lithium, antidepressants, and insulin) are associated with weight gain.

   c. **The weight history,** including the highest and lowest weights, past efforts at weight loss (e.g., exercise, diets, pharmacological interventions, and surgery), and the age of onset of obesity should be determined.

d. **Exercise habits** and circumstances that may interfere with increased physical activity should be reviewed.

e. **Food logs** with calorie counts should be maintained.

f. A past or present **history of disordered eating** (including bingeing, purging, or restricting calories) should be uncovered. What triggers bingeing? If one is purging, the amount and frequency should be clarified. Also ask about a preoccupation with food and one's body image. What does the patient believe is a realistic and achievable weight loss goal?

g. **A personal and family psychiatric history of depression, bipolar disorder, substance abuse, or psychosis** may underlie obesity.

h. The **motivation for weight loss** should be assessed. It is important to note the psychosocial context of the patient's weight problem (including discrimination, family dynamics, relationships, and self esteem).

2. **Physical examination**
   a. Careful measurement of weight and height should be made and the BMI calculated (<19 is underweight, 19–25 is healthy, 25–30 is overweight, and >30 is obese).
   b. Vital signs
   c. Assess for signs associated with BN (e.g., Russell's sign, parotid enlargement, altered bowel sounds, or rectal prolapse).
   d. Perform a complete exam to rule out medical complications of obesity.

3. **Laboratory studies**
   a. Check the TSH.
   b. Obtain electrolytes (low potassium can indicate surreptitious purging by vomiting or by use of laxatives).
   c. Glucose (screen for diabetes mellitus).
   d. Determine the results of the liver function tests.
   e. Obtain a lipid panel.
   f. Obtain an electrocardiogram and exercise tolerance test, if indicated.
   g. Perform an arterial blood gas or sleep study if indicated, if the patient has symptoms of obstructive sleep apnea.

4. **Differential diagnosis**
   a. A medical problem, such as Cushing's disease, or hypothyroidism

b. Medication effect (e.g., secondary to use of an atypical antipsychotic or a steroid)
c. Atypical depression
d. An anxiety disorder
e. Psychosis (with delusions around the need for increased food intake)

C. **Treatment**
1. **Patient education**
   a. The patient needs to be educated about realistic goals for weight loss. Most patients should expect to lose about a pound per week. The only effective means for weight loss is moderate diet with increased physical activity. Patients should be cautioned against restricting severely, as deprivation leads to bingeing and to continuation of the cycle of symptoms.
   b. The patient also needs to be educated about the risks of obesity, including heart disease, diabetes, and obstructive sleep apnea.
   c. If one is purging, the patient must be educated about the associated risks (see AN and BN).
2. **Diet and exercise**
   a. The patient should work with a nutritionist to compose a sound meal plan with adequate protein, carbohydrates, and fat that will still enable the patient to lose weight. The patient should avoid an overly restrictive diet.
   b. Twenty to thirty minutes of moderate aerobic activity 3–5 times a week, if appropriate from a cardiac standpoint (some patients may need to start out more slowly), is reasonable.
3. **Therapy**
   a. Overeaters Anonymous
   b. Weight loss support groups
   c. Open-ended psychodynamic groups
   d. CBT and dialectical behavioral therapy (DBT) skills groups focused on behavior modification
   e. Individual CBT
   f. Insight-oriented psychodynamic therapy
4. **Pharmacological care**
   Medications should not be used for strictly cosmetic purposes; they are indicated for patients with a BMI >30 or >27 in those with obesity-related medical complications.
   a. Several FDA-approved drugs (e.g., sibutramine and phentermine) suppress appetite and increase energy via their

action on adrenergic receptors. Orlistat inhibits fat absorption but is associated with fat-soluble vitamin deficiency and anal leakage.

   b. Open-label treatment with SSRIs reduce anxiety and depression that may exacerbate overeating. Bupropion also reduces appetite and increases energy; however, it should be avoided in patients who binge and purge. Topiramate is thought to reduce the urge to binge.

5. **Surgical treatment**

   Gastric bypass or banded gastroplasty can be very effective; some patients lose over 50% of their body weight. However, the risk of potential complications (including cardiac arrest, peritonitis, pulmonary embolism, and deep venous thrombosis) must be weighed against the benefits for each patient. Noncompliance with food volume restriction can lead to stomach rupture and death, and some patients rapidly regain weight when they continue to consume large amounts of high-calorie liquids. Surgical interventions are contraindicated in patients with active substance abuse, bulimia, and uncontrolled psychiatric illness.

Suggested Readings

American Psychiatric Association: *Diagnostic and Statistical Manual of Mental Disorders,* Fourth Edition, Text Revision. Washington: American Psychiatric Association, 1994:539–550, 729–731.

Arnold LM, McElroy SL, Hudson JL, et al: A placebo-controlled, randomized trial of fluoxetine in the treatment of binge-eating disorder. *J Clin Psychiatry* 2002;63: 1028–1033.

Becker AE: Eating disorders. In Stern TA, Herman JB (eds): *Massachusetts General Hospital Psychiatry Update and Board Preparation,* 2nd edition. New York: McGraw-Hill, 2004:165–171.

Becker AE, Grinspoon SK, Klibanski A, Herzog DB: Eating disorders. *N Engl J Med* 1999;340:1092–1098.

Becker AE, Hamburg P, Herzog DB: The role of psychopharmacologic management in the treatment of eating disorders. *Psychiatric Clin North Am* 1998;5:17–51.

Becker AE, Kaplan LM: The obese patient. In Stern TA, Herman JB, Slavin PL (eds): *Massachusetts General Hospital Guide to Primary Care Psychiatry,* 2nd edition. New York: McGraw-Hill, 2004:451–465.

Becker AE: Outpatient management of eating disorders in adults. *Curr Womens Health Rep* 2003;3:221–229.

Bremer J, Herzog DB, Beresin EV: The patient with anorexia or bulimia. In Stern TA, Herman JB, Slavin PL (eds): *Massachusetts General Hospital Guide to Primary Care Psychiatry,* 2nd edition. New York: McGraw-Hill, 2004:171–179.

Brownell KD, Fairburn CG (eds): *Eating Disorders and Obesity.* New York: Guilford Press, 1995.

McElroy SL, Arnold LM, Shapira NA, et al: Topiramate in the treatment of binge eating disorder associated with obesity: A randomized, placebo-controlled trial. *Am J Psychiatry* 2003;160:255–261.

Must A, Spadano J, Coakley EH, et al: The disease burden associated with overweight and obesity. *JAMA* 1999;282:1523–1529.

Yanovski SZ, Yanovski JA: Obesity. *N Engl J Med* 2002;346:591–602.

Chapter 19

An Approach to the Patient with Impaired Impulse Control

KATHY SANDERS, MD

I. Introduction

A. Overview

Patients with impaired impulse control frequently come to the attention of physicians. **Impulsive behavior is part and parcel of many psychiatric disorders** (e.g., psychotic disorders, affective disorders, anxiety disorders, and personality disorders). In addition, a host of organic mental disorders (including mental retardation, brain injury, delirium, dementia, and substance abuse disorders) **often present with impulsive behavior.**

This chapter will focus on the specific impulse control disorders as defined by the *Diagnostic and Statistical Manual, Fourth Edition, Text Revision* (DSM-IV-TR). However, **all patients with impulsive behavior impel the clinician to take into account the complex biopsychosocial context of each patient and to create a broad differential diagnosis.** For example, a patient may develop impulsive and aggressive behavior some time after a traumatic brain injury; this may be the first evidence of the patient's trauma history.

B. Impulse Control Disorders Not Otherwise Specified

Impulse-control disorders not otherwise specified (NOS) is **the DSM-IV-TR category for disorders that include intermittent explosive disorder, kleptomania, pyromania, pathological gambling, trichotillomania, and impulse control disorder NOS.** Each of these conditions involves a drive, or a temptation, to perform some act that is harmful to the person or to others, or the failure to resist such an impulse. Other associated features are the experience of increasing tension (e.g., of dysphoria or arousal intensity) before committing the act, that is followed by a release of tension, a sense of gratification, or a sense of pleasure and relief during and after the act. There may or may not be a sense of guilt, regret, or self-reproach following the behavior.

Address for correspondence: Dr. Kathy Sanders, Massachusetts General Hospital, Bulfinch 440, Boston, MA 02114, email: KSanders@Partners.org.

C.   Comorbidity
Whether these conditions are distinct diagnoses or variants of another Axis I disorder is a source of controversy. In some ways they are similar to obsessive-compulsive disorder (OCD), substance dependence, mood disorders, and mental disorders due to a general medical condition. A similar etiology for OCD, eating disorders, mood disorders, paraphilias, and alcohol and substance abuse disorders has been postulated because similar treatments are efficacious for these disorders. Additionally, patients diagnosed with impulse control disorders have an increased risk of being diagnosed with substance abuse disorders, OCD and other anxiety disorders, eating disorders, and mood disorders. Moreover, there is an increased incidence of substance abuse disorders and mood disorders in family members of patients with these impulse control disorders.

D.   Etiology
While in the past these disorders were thought to result from psychodynamic conflicts, more recently, as improvement in impulsive symptoms has accompanied use of the serotonergic antidepressants, biological hypotheses that concern serotonergic pathways are being explored. Interestingly, lowered levels of serotonin in the mesolimbic circuitry are associated with impulsive and violent behaviors. The complexity of these disorders and their relative ubiquity warrants a comprehensive approach that includes psychopharmacology and behavioral techniques, as well as family and social supports.

II.   Intermittent Explosive Disorder

A.   Overview
Episodic violence of any type is common in our society. However, when applying strict diagnostic criteria, this disorder is considered rare; **men account for up to 80% of the cases.** Intermittent explosive disorder and personality change due to a general medical condition (aggressive type) are the diagnoses available for a patient with episodic violent behavior. The **DSM-IV-TR diagnostic criteria for intermittent explosive disorder include:**

1. Several discrete episodes of a failure to resist aggressive impulses that result in serious assaultive acts or the destruction of property.
2. Aggressivity during the episodes is distinctly out of proportion to any precipitating psychosocial stressors.
3. The aggressive episodes are not better accounted for by another mental disorder (e.g., antisocial personality disorder, borderline personality disorder, a psychotic disorder, a manic episode, a

conduct disorder, or attention-deficit/hyperactivity disorder), and they are not due to the direct physiological effects of a substance (e.g., a drug of abuse or a medication) or a general medical condition (e.g., head trauma or Alzheimer's disease).

B.   **The Evaluation**
Violent behavior frequently can be accounted for by psychiatric and medical conditions. Among these diagnoses, **violence is often associated with a personality change due to a general medical condition** (e.g., secondary to seizures, head trauma, a neurological abnormality, dementia, or delirium), aggressive or disinhibited type. Psychosis (from schizophrenia or a manic episode) may also cause impulsive and episodic violence. Finally, personality disorders of the borderline or antisocial type must be considered.

C.   **Treatment**
The acute management of aggressive and violent behavior may involve the use of physical restraint and the rapid administration of a combination of parenteral neuroleptics and benzodiazepines. Psychopharmacological interventions are commonly employed in the chronic management of this disorder. No single approach has been shown effective in intermittent impulsive violence. Anticonvulsants, lithium, β-blockers, anxiolytics, neuroleptics, antidepressants (both serotonergic and polycyclic agents), and psychostimulants have all been used with varying results. Drug selection for the long-term management of violent impulses takes into account the safety of the agent and the side-effect profile. The clinician also considers aspects of temperament, coping style, capacity for stress management, etiology, history, age, and concomitant medical and psychiatric diagnoses, as well as the neurobiology of the patient when selecting a drug or psychotherapy.

III.   Kleptomania

A.   **Overview**
More than 150 years ago, kleptomania was recognized as an out-of-character behavior of **"nonsensical pilfering"** in which worthless items were stolen. A characteristic increase in tension was relieved only by the act of stealing. Individuals with this condition were not known to have a lifestyle of stealing or of premeditated thievery. Since its initial description, few systematic or scientifically rigorous studies have been conducted.

B.   Diagnostic Criteria
Diagnostic criteria from DSM-IV-TR include:
1. A repetitive failure to resist the urge to steal objects that are not needed for personal use or of monetary value.
2. An increase in tension immediately before committing the theft.
3. A sense of pleasure, gratification, or relief associated with the theft.
4. The absence of anger or vengeance while stealing; the thefts are not in response to a delusion or hallucination.
5. Absence of diagnostic criteria for a conduct disorder, a manic episode, or an antisocial personality disorder.

C.   Etiology
Little is known about the epidemiology of kleptomania. Few studies have been published on this subject. It is estimated that the prevalence within the general population is 6 out of 1000. Less than 5% of shoplifters meet criteria for kleptomania. Women are more likely than men to be diagnosed with kleptomania. **Kleptomania tends to have its onset in later adolescence, followed by a course of chronic, intermittent episodes of stealing over many years.** Patients generally come to professional attention via court referral or by disclosure during treatment for a related psychiatric disorder. There is often a lag time of many years (up to several decades) between the onset of the behavior and an individual's presentation for treatment. Women with this disorder on average seek treatment in their 30s, while men seek treatment in their 50s.

D.   The Evaluation
Clinicians should examine the patient for ego-dystonic reactions to the behavior and for the unpremeditated or impulsive nature of the stealing episodes.

E.   Differential Diagnosis
The differential diagnosis includes:
1. Criminal acts of shoplifting or stealing
2. Malingering to avoid prosecution for theft
3. Antisocial personality disorder
4. Conduct disorder
5. Manic episode
6. Schizophrenia
7. Dementia

F.   **Treatment**
Treatment successes for those with kleptomania are hard to pinpoint.
Treatment modalities include:
1.   Insight-oriented psychotherapy
2.   Behavioral therapies that use covert and aversive sensitization
3.   Somatic therapies, including electroconvulsive therapy (ECT)
and pharmacotherapy, particularly with serotonergic antidepressants

IV.   Pyromania

A.   **Overview**
Pyromania is defined as **pathological fire-setting without evidence of intense emotional expression, fire-setting as a criminal act, or secondary, monetary, or political gain.**

B.   **Diagnostic Criteria**
DSM-IV-TR diagnostic criteria include:
1.   The deliberate act of setting a fire in a purposeful manner on more than one occasion
2.   Increasing tension and/or affective arousal associated with the act
3.   Fascination, attraction, and curiosity about fires
4.   Obvious pleasure, gratification, or relief while setting fires, or when witnessing or participating in the aftermath of the fire-setting
5.   The motivation for fire-setting is not monetary gain, an expression of sociopolitical ideology, a means of concealing criminal activity, a means of expressing anger or vengeance, a means of improving one's living circumstances, in response to a delusion or hallucination, or a result of impaired judgment (e.g., from dementia, mental retardation, or substance intoxication).
6.   Conduct disorder, a manic episode, or an antisocial personality disorder must be ruled out.

C.   **Epidemiology**
True pyromania is rare. Pyromania is assumed to have preponderance in males, often with a history of a fascination with fires that dates back to childhood or early adolescence.

D.   **The Evaluation**
Intentional fire-setting for profit, for political interests, or for revenge will exclude a diagnosis of pyromania. Delusions or hallucinations associated with schizophrenia or another psychotic disor-

der must be ruled out. Fire-setting cannot be due to a manic episode with poor impulse control. Dementia or another mental disorder caused by a medical condition may result in behavior due to an impaired ability to acknowledge the consequences of an act. Conduct disorder in children and antisocial personality disorder in adults must be considered in the differential.

E.   **Treatment**
There is no definitive treatment modality for fire-setting. Typically several modalities (such as behavioral therapy, pharmacotherapy, and family therapy [especially where children are concerned]) are used simultaneously.

V.   Pathological Gambling

A.   **Overview**
Pathologic gambling involves a failure to resist the impulse to gamble in the face of severe disruption of personal, family, or vocational functioning. This disorder is most similar to addictive disorders; similarities to alcoholism are also noted.

B.   **Diagnostic Criteria**
DSM-IV-TR diagnostic criteria:
1.   Persistent and recurrent maladaptive gambling behavior as indicated by five (or more) of the following:
      a.   Preoccupation with gambling (e.g., reliving past gambling experiences, planning the next venture, or thinking about ways to get money to continue gambling)
      b.   The need to gamble with increasing amounts of money to achieve the desired excitement level
      c.   Repeated and unsuccessful efforts to control, cut back, or to stop gambling
      d.   Restlessness or irritability during attempts to cut down or to stop gambling
      e.   Gambling as a means to escape from problems or to relieve dysphoric mood (e.g., feelings of helplessness, guilt, anxiety, or depression)
      f.   Increased gambling activity after losing money ("chasing" one's losses)
      g.   Lying to family members, to one's therapist, or to others, to conceal the extent of involvement with gambling
      h.   The commission of illegal acts, such as forgery, fraud, theft, or embezzlement to finance gambling

    i.   Jeopardizing or losing a significant relationship, job, or educational or career opportunity because of gambling

    j.   Reliance on others to provide money to relieve a desperate financial situation caused by gambling

2. The gambling behavior is not better accounted for by a manic episode.

C.   **Epidemiology**

The incidence of pathological gambling may be as high as **3% in the general population.** One-third of pathological gamblers are women, who make up only 2–4% of the membership of Gamblers Anonymous. Cultural and sociological factors play a role in the specific manifestation of behavior in the pathological gambler (e.g., cockfights, horse racing, the stock market, ma jong, pai go, and bingo).

D.   **The Evaluation**

The differential diagnosis must sort out social gambling and professional gambling from the pathological type. **As with all impulse control disorders NOS, the clinician must make sure the behavior is not due to a manic episode or to an antisocial personality disorder.** Since pathological gamblers exhibit tolerance and withdrawal associated with episodes of gambling, evidence of irritability, restlessness, poor concentration, and dysphoria can be detected when a gambling episode is delayed or disrupted. Increasingly higher bets are made and more risks are taken as the need for excitement and arousal is chased. Associated alcoholism, workaholic behavior, mood disorders, and antisocial, narcissistic, and borderline personality disorders may be noted.

E.   **Treatment**

Treatment for compulsive gambling is difficult and the course is characterized by frequent relapses, financial difficulties, and legal problems that work against a commitment to ongoing therapy. No specific treatment modality has been shown to work predictably. Treatment modalities include psychodynamic psychotherapy, behavioral therapy, cognitive therapy, use of psychotropic medications, and electroconvulsive therapy (ECT). The use of Gamblers Anonymous and the associated 12-step programs, Gam-Anon and Gam-a-teen, are important resources in breaking the addiction cycle.

VI.   Trichotillomania

A.   **Overview**
The term *trichotillomania* was introduced to medical literature by the French dermatologist Francois Hallopeau in 1889, and defined as a compulsive urge to pull out one's own hair.

B.   **Diagnostic Criteria**
The DSM-IV-TR defines trichotillomania with the following **diagnostic criteria:**
1.   Recurrent pulling out of one's hair, resulting in significant hair loss
2.   Increased tension immediately before pulling out the hair or when attempting to resist the behavior
3.   The experience of pleasure, gratification, or relief when pulling out the hair
4.   The disturbance is not better accounted for by another mental disorder and is not due to a general medical condition (e.g., a dermatological condition).
5.   The disturbance causes clinically significant distress or impairment in social, occupational, or other important areas of functioning.

C.   **Epidemiology**
Initially considered rare, there is evidence that **1–3% of the population has trichotillomania.** There is a bimodal presentation. Some individuals present before the age of 6 years; in this group, boys and girls are evenly represented and they are managed with behavioral interventions. This type is time-limited and is treatable. The second cluster begins in adolescence, and it is made up predominantly of girls. This disorder is chronic and poorly treated. The site of the hair pulling is commonly the scalp (two-thirds of cases) but can include eyelashes, eyebrows, facial hair, and pubic hair. Comorbidity (with other psychiatric diagnoses) is common. Mood disorders, psychotic disorders, eating disorders, anxiety disorders, and substance abuse disorders are prevalent. Trichotillomania can be a symptom of another major mental illness (e.g., OCD, mental retardation, schizophrenia, depression, and borderline personality disorder). This has raised controversy regarding whether trichotillomania is a separate diagnostic entity or part of a symptom complex.

D.   **The Evaluation**
It is important to differentiate trichotillomania from OCD. One should look for impulsive urges as opposed to goal-associated ide-

ation about the hair pulling. Factitious disorder (which involves a desire for medical attention) should be ruled out. **Alopecia secondary to an organic cause is the most difficult to rule out.** Any Axis I mental disorder that has the symptom of trichotillomania due to command hallucinations or delusional beliefs must be considered.

E.   **Treatment**
      As with many impulse control disorders, different treatment modalities have been used with variable success. Psychodynamic psychoanalytic psychotherapy has been successful in selected case reports. Behavioral treatment has also been successful. Techniques include:
      1. Focus on hair-pulling as a habit and substituting other responses.
      2. Positive reinforcement for not pulling one's hair and negative reinforcement of hair-pulling, aversive conditioning, relaxation, and competing response training are some of the behavioral techniques.
      3. Hypnotherapy
      4. Psychopharmacology with serotonergic antidepressants, neuroleptics, or lithium
      5. Personal appearance problems require attention to both psychotherapeutic and psychopharmacologic interventions for lasting efficacy of treatment.

VII. Impulse Control Disorder Not Otherwise Specified

A.   **Overview**
      This category of disorders does not meet diagnostic criteria for any of the previously discussed impulse control disorders or for another mental disorder having the features involving impulse control. Included in this category are diagnoses such as pathological spending, pathological shopping, repetitive self-mutilation, compulsive sexual behavior, and compulsive face-picking. Most of the literature on this category of impulsivity focuses on repetitive self-mutilation.

B.   **Epidemiology**
      It is more common in women than in men. However, it is considered endemic in male prisons. Two-thirds of self-mutilators have a history of sexual and physical abuse in childhood. The disorder starts in adolescence and is characterized by severe psychosocial morbidity.

C. **The Evaluation**
Theories about the causes of self-mutilation range from psychodynamic to psychobiologic. Self-mutilation gives a quick sense of relief to stress and is often likened to an addiction.

D. **Differential Diagnosis**
The **differential diagnosis includes:**
1. A component of borderline, narcissistic, and antisocial personality disorders
2. Mental retardation, as caused by Lesch-Nyhan and deLange syndromes
3. Hallucinations or delusions from a psychotic disorder
4. Sexual sadomasochism
5. OCD

E. **Treatment**
Multimodal treatment is the current recommended treatment. Prognosis is guarded and worsens when comorbidity with eating disorders and substance abuse disorders exists. Intentional or accidental suicide may occur. Psychopharmacology includes use of serotonergic enhancing drugs, and the narcotic antagonist naltrexone. Other modalities include psychodynamic psychotherapy, behavioral therapy, and involvement in self-help and 12-step programs.

VIII. Conclusion

The approach to the patient with impaired impulse control requires that the clinician evaluate the patient for the presence of organic mental conditions and major psychiatric disorders. Often, impulsivity due to a medical condition as well as psychoses and affective disorders can be managed with the treatment techniques best used in those disorders. To the extent that characterological and sociocultural issues and substance abuse play a role in any particular patient's impulsivity; treatment may include behavioral therapy, dialectical behavioral therapy, and 12-step programs along with the use of psychopharmacology.

Suggested Readings

American Psychiatric Association: Impulse-control disorders not elsewhere classified. In *Diagnostic and Statistical Manual of Mental Disorders, Fourth Edition, Text Revision*. Washington: American Psychiatric Association, 2000:663–677.

Best M, Williams JM, Coccaro EF: Evidence for a dysfunctional prefrontal circuit in patients with an impulsive aggressive disorder. *Proc Nat Acad Sci* 2002;99:8448–8453.

Burt VE, Katzman JW: Impulse-control disorders not elsewhere classified. In Sadock BJ, Sadock VA (eds): *Kaplan and Sadock's Comprehensive Textbook of Psychiatry,* 7th edition. Baltimore: Lippincott Williams & Wilkins, 2000:1701–1713.

Coccaro EF: Intermittent explosive disorder. *Curr Psychiatry Rep* 2000;2:67-71; 2000.

DeCaria CM, Hollander E, Grossman R, et al: Diagnosis, neurobiology, and treatment of pathological gambling. *J Clin Psychiatry* 1996;57(Suppl 8):80–84.

Hollander E, Buchalter AJ, DeCaria CM: Pathological gambling. *Psych Clin North Am* 2000;23:629–641.

Klonsky ED, Oltmanns TF, Turkheimer E: Deliberate self-harm in a nonclinical population: prevalence and psychological correlates. *Am J Psychiatry* 2003;160: 1501–1508.

Marazzit D, Mungai F, Giannotti D, et al: Kleptomania in impulse control disorders, obsessive-compulsive disorder, and bipolar spectrum disorder: clinical and therapeutic implications. *Curr Psychiatry Rep* 2003;5:336–340.

McElroy SL, Hudson JI, Pope HG Jr, et al: The DSM-III-R Impulse Control Disorder not elsewhere classified: clinical characteristics and relationship to other psychiatric disorders. *Am J Psychiatry* 1992;149:318–327.

McElroy, SL, Pope HG Jr, Keck PE Jr, et al: Are impulse-control disorders related to bipolar disorder? *Compr Psychiatry* 1996;37:229–240.

McElroy SL: Recognition and treatment of DSM-IV intermittent explosive disorder. *J Clin Psychiatry* 1999;60(Suppl 15):12–16.

Ninan PT: Conceptual issues in trichotillomania, a prototypical impulse control disorder. *Curr Psychiatry Rep* 2000;2:72–75.

Olvera RL: Intermittent explosive disorder: epidemiology, diagnosis and management. *CNS Drugs* 2002;16:517–526.

Petty F, Davis LL, Kabel D, Kramer GL: Serotonin dysfunction disorders: A behavioral neurochemistry perspective. *J Clin Psychiatry* 1996;57(Suppl 8):11–16.

Scott CL, Hilty DM, Brook M: Impulse control disorders not elsewhere classified. In Hales RE, Yudofsky SG (eds): *The American Psychiatric Publishing Textbook of Clinical Psychiatry,* 4th edition. Washington: American Psychiatric Publishing, 2003:781–802.

Stein DJ, Hollander E, Liebowitz MR: Neurobiology of impulsivity and the impulse control disorders. *J Neuropsychiatr Clin Neurosci* 1993;5:9–17.

Winchel RM, Simeon D, Yovell Y: Impulse control disorders. In Tasman A, Kay J, Lieberman JA (eds): *Psychiatry,* 2nd edition. West Sussex, England: John Wiley & Sons, 2003:1555–1588.

Zonana HV, Norko MA: Sexual predators. *Psych Clinics North Am* 1999;22:109–127.

Chapter 20

An Approach to the Patient with Problematic Interpersonal Relationships: Personality Disorders and Their Manifestations

WILLIAM C. WOOD, MD

I.   Introduction

Patients who have difficult interpersonal styles and deeply ingrained patterns of emotional expression and behavior can be challenging to work with. Frequently, clinicians feel angry, helpless, inadequate, and overwhelmed when treating such patients with personality disorders. For example, an adoring patient who is an expert at getting her caregivers to make her feel special may fly into a rage if she feels insufficiently catered to. Such swings in behavior can be unsettling for unwary practitioners, who may have difficulty dealing with their own frustrations. However, knowledge of the patient's interpersonal style can offer a wealth of information about the internal dynamics and emotional needs of the patient, and this knowledge can help guide treatment. Conversely, a lack of attention to interpersonal dynamics can lead to inappropriate care, to retaliation, and even to professional boundary crossings and violations. This chapter attempts to help the clinician develop a repertoire of skills to help these patients and to avoid destructive acting out by members of the treatment team.

II.   Etiology

Personality is rooted in both biology and experience (Cloninger et al, 1993).

A.   Biological Foundations

Genes serve as a template for biological replication from generation to generation (Kandel, 1998). This template is relatively stable, though mutations can occur. Genes also determine which fraction of the genetic template is expressed and which fraction is repressed. While the template function of genes is not influenced by social experience, the transcriptional function is responsive to environmental factors (Kandel, 1998). Thus gene expression is partly regulated by the influence of social factors. The integration of molecular genetics, neuroscience, and child development holds enormous potential

Address for correspondence: Dr. William C. Wood, Massachusetts General Hospital, Fruit Street, WACC 812, Boston, MA 02114, email: Wwood@ Partners.org.

to advance our understanding of personality as a complex outcome of biology and social experience (National Research Council/ Institute of Medicine, 2000).

B. **Psychosocial Foundations**
    Much has been written regarding the complex interaction of psychosocial factors that contribute to personality development and to personality disorders. It is useful to briefly review some basic concepts and theories of development, particularly because they can inform treatment planning.

    1. **Temperament.** Temperament refers to the **innate behavioral** *style* **of an individual,** and includes characteristics such as tempo, rhythmicity, adaptability, energy expenditure, mood, and focus of attention (Thomas and Chess, 1977). Temperament follows a developmental course. Depending upon environmental influences, temperamental characteristics may be relatively unchanged, reinforced, diminished, or otherwise modified through experience over time (Kagan, 1994). **Goodness of fit** refers to the degree to which the caretakers of a child can match the innate capacities of the child to meet the child's basic and developmental needs (Chess and Thomas, 1999). Goodness of fit is a useful concept to assess many caretaking situations, including the doctor-patient relationship.

    2. **Behavioral and social learning theories** state that individuals learn to respond to situations based on rewards and punishment. Maladaptive interpersonal patterns learned in childhood can persist into adulthood, causing significant distress and disappointment for a patient (Bandura, 1977).

    3. **Family systems theory** says that family relationships and family processes can lead to enduring dysfunctional emotions and behaviors (Glick et al, 2000).

    4. **Psychoanalytic theory** has a rich history that contains many complementary (and at times competing) models of personality development, and it offers many paradigms for defining and treating personality disorders (Mitchell and Black, 1995). It is beyond the scope of this chapter to give a full history of psychoanalytic thought, but it is important to understand certain basic concepts.

        a. **Conflict.** All individuals struggle internally with wishes, restraints, fears, and ambivalence. Conflicts emerge which have to be managed; some individuals choose suboptimal strategies in this process (e.g., "the stoic" who needs help but refuses it, and "the help-rejecting complainer" who appeals for help but then rejects it).

b. **Defense mechanisms.** Defense mechanisms are automatic, unconscious, psychological strategies that a person uses to either ward off intense anxiety or to prevent becoming overwhelmed by emotional conflict. Certain defense mechanisms are adaptive for an individual, while others are clearly not (Vaillant, 1992). A partial list of defense mechanisms is given in Table 20-1.

Table 20-1. Defense Mechanisms

Styles of Defense Mechanism	Definition
1. *Immature and/or psychotic*	
a. Projection	Rejection of unacceptable unconscious mental elements by attributing them as belonging to others; in this way these unacceptable impulses are not seen as part of oneself
b. Distortion	Modification of unacceptable unconscious mental elements so that they are allowed to enter consciousness in a more acceptable but disguised form
c. Denial	Disavowal of the existence of unpleasant aspects of reality
d. Splitting	External objects are divided into "all good" and "all bad," accompanied by the abrupt shifting of the object from one extreme to the other, e.g., idealization shifts to devaluation
e. Fantasy	A form of thinking dominated by unconscious material and primary processes that seek imaginary wish fulfillment and immediate solutions to conflicts
f. Passive aggression	Aggression towards others that is expressed through passivity, masochism, and anger towards oneself
g. Acting out	Behavioral response to an unconscious drive or impulse that brings about temporary partial relief of inner tension, while avoiding awareness of either the true unconscious conflict or the emotions associated with it

(continued)

Table 20-1. Defense Mechanisms (continued)

Styles of Defense Mechanism	Definition
h. Dissociation	Segregation of any group of mental or behavioral activity from the rest of the person's psychic functioning; parts of internal reality are denied or unacknowledged, and there may be psychic separation of an idea from the emotions that accompany it
2. *Neurotic (intermediate level)*	
a. Displacement	Transfer of the emotional component of an unacceptable idea or person onto something or someone that is more acceptable
b. Isolation	Separation of an idea or memory from its attached feeling
c. Intellectualization	Use of reasoning/logic in an attempt to avoid confrontation with an objectionable impulse or feeling, thereby avoiding anxiety
d. Repression	Banishment of unacceptable thoughts or feelings from conscious awareness
e. Reaction formation	Development of a socially acceptable attitude that is the direct antithesis of the true feeling or wish held unconsciously
3. *Mature*	
a. Altruism	Doing for others what one wishes for oneself
b. Sublimation	Diversion of unacceptable impulses and drives into personally and socially accepted channels
c. Suppression	Conscious act of controlling and inhibiting unacceptable impulses, emotions, and thoughts
d. Anticipation	Realistic and affect-laden planning for future emotional discomfort
e. Humor	Overt expression of feelings without individual discomfort or immobilization, and without unpleasant effect on others, thereby allowing an individual to tolerate and focus on events and affects that would otherwise be too painful to bear

Adapted from Vaillant, 1992 and Kaplan & Sadock, 1991.

c. **Object relations theory**

Object relations theory says that individuals internalize models of early relationships into their psychology, and draw on these early models when interacting with others later in life. Psychopathology is expressed when an individual superimposes prior dysfunctional patterns of relating onto current interactions. This distorts the current relationship into a parallel re-living of important aspects of past relationships. Doctors are particularly likely to being drawn into re-enactments of dysfunctional patterns, since the patient's dependence on the doctor can trigger emotional and behavioral responses that are fueled by early childhood fears related to safety and trust in a caregiving environment.

d. **Attachment**

The quality of emotional attachments that infants and young children develop with their caretakers has been shown to influence multiple aspects of childhood mental health and subsequent personality development (Cassidy and Shaver, 1999). Infants who experience a secure attachment with their mothers are more likely to develop an internal sense of emotional security. Moreover, the initial infant-mother bond serves as a model for subsequent attachments. Disturbances in this bond lead to various forms of anxiety related to separation and re-connection with the primary caregiver. Maladaptive and defensive styles of interpersonal relating are a natural outgrowth of inconsistent and disruptive early attachments, and can strongly influence adult interpersonal styles.

C. **The Interplay between Biology and Psychology**

As we explore personality traits and personality disorders, it is helpful to keep in mind the interplay between the biological and psychosocial determinants of personality. Many problematic interpersonal styles can be traced to difficulties in one or several of these areas. Successful identification of specific factors that underlie a patient's personality style may not be critical for good management, but having an idea of "where and why it hurts" can facilitate treatment planning and alleviate distress in both the patient and the caregivers.

III.   Personality Traits, Personalities, and Personality Disorders

A.   **Personality Traits**
Personality traits are the particular mannerisms that a person brings to social situations (e.g., flexibility, emotional connectedness, entitlement, concern, and cooperativeness).

B.   **Personality**
Personality refers to a person's style of being, acting, and relating in the world. It is made up of a relatively fixed constellation of personality traits that leads to habitual ways of responding to given situations (APA, 2000). Personality functioning can change temporarily; regression during periods of high stress is not uncommon.

C.   **Personality Disorders**
A personality disorder exists when an individual experiences *consistent* significant impairment in his or her ability to work, love, and play in a meaningful way because his or her style of dealing with the world causes distress to him- or herself and to others, often in a self-defeating manner. Invariably this is because one or more personality traits are experienced with an intensity that alienates others. The patient with a personality disorder generally has personality traits that are common to all of us, but which the patient consistently experiences with an *abnormal* intensity and with subsequent distress.

IV.   Presentation, Diagnosis, and Management of Personality Disorders

A.   **General Considerations**
1. **Formal diagnostic criteria.** Personality disorders are comprised of a set of 10 discrete, qualitatively distinct syndromes in the *Diagnostic and Statistical Manual of Mental Disorders, Fourth Edition, Text Revision* (DSM-IV-TR; APA, 2000). These diagnoses are based predominantly on expert consensus, with a relatively small body of fiercely debated empirical research regarding validity and prevalence (Westen and Shedler, 1999). The DSM-IV-TR criteria for personality disorders are given in Table 20-2, while the specific criteria for each of the ten personality disorders are detailed in the DSM-IV-TR and discussed below.
2. **Dimensional approaches to personality assessment.** Dimensional models of personality functioning assess personality traits along a continuum from normal to severely disordered. It

---

Table 20-2. General Diagnostic Criteria for a Personality Disorder

---

1. An enduring pattern of inner experience and behavior that deviates markedly from the expectations of the individual's culture. This pattern is manifested in two (or more) of the following areas:
   a. cognition (i.e., ways of perceiving and interpreting self, other people, and events)
   b. affectivity (i.e., the range, intensity, lability, and appropriateness of emotional response)
   c. interpersonal functioning
   d. impulse control

2. The enduring pattern is inflexible and pervasive across a broad range of personal and social situations.

3. The enduring pattern leads to clinically significant distress or impairment in social, occupational, or other important areas of functioning.

4. The pattern is stable and of long duration, and its onset can be traced back at least to adolescence or early adulthood.

5. The enduring pattern is not better accounted for as a manifestation or consequence of another mental disorder.

6. The enduring pattern is not due to the direct physiological effects of a substance (e.g., a drug of abuse or a medication) or a general medical condition (e.g., head trauma).

Adapted from APA, 2000.

---

is useful to keep in mind that specific personality traits can be problematic for an individual, even though the person may not meet criteria for a discrete personality disorder.

3. **Epidemiology.** The prevalence of personality disorders has been difficult to measure (Sater et al, 2001; Westen and Shedler, 1999; Zimmerman, 1994). However, the prevalence of personality disorders is significantly higher on inpatient psychiatric units than it is in the general population.

4. **Comorbidity.** Comorbidity of personality disorders with Axis I mental disorders is high. At times, it is nearly impossible to differentiate between an Axis II personality disorder and an Axis I disorder. In addition, it is common for an individual to meet criteria for several personality disorders. In this instance, multiple diagnoses are given.

5. **Interpersonal styles.** Each personality disorder can be characterized by a particular **interpersonal style.** These interpersonal styles are described in Table 20-3.

6. **Psychotherapy.** Psychotherapy is the cornerstone for treatments that are aimed at a fundamental change in personality functioning. Evidence-based treatments are gaining in popularity; however, limitations in the design of treatment studies make it difficult to assess and compare the efficacy of many forms of psychotherapy.

7. **Psychopharmacology.** Medications can play a role in the treatment of personality disorders by targeting specific symptoms and by treating comorbid Axis I disorders. Symptoms of personality disorders that can be responsive to medications include cognitive-perceptual distortions, behavioral impulsivity, affect dysregulation, and anxiety, as well as a wide array of overlapping symptoms that characterize Axis I disorders (Gabbard, 2000b).

B. Cluster A Personality Disorders

1. **General considerations.** Cluster A personalities are **odd and eccentric.** As a group, there is a temperamental association with **low reward-dependence** (Gabbard, 2000b). Individuals with these personalities are the **least likely to seek mental health treatment.** When they do come for help, it is usually at the urging of someone else.

2. **Paranoid personality disorder**

   a. **Clinical presentation: This disorder is characterized by pervasive distrust and suspicion; moreover, the motives of others are frequently interpreted as malevolent.** This distrust is shown in several ways (e.g., unreasonable expectations of exploitation or harm by others, questioning without justification the loyalty or trustworthiness of friends and associates, reading demeaning or threatening meanings into benign remarks or events, having a tendency to bear grudges and to be unforgiving of insults of injuries, or experiencing unfounded, recurrent suspiciousness about the fidelity of sexual partners) (Edgerton and Campbell, 1994).

   b. **Treatment approaches:** Paranoid patients have a very hard time trusting anyone; therefore, building a therapeutic alliance is crucial early in treatment. The patient may experience the clinician as persecutory and blame the clinician for treating him poorly. The task of the clinician is to accept these projections nondefensively without colluding with the patient's distortions. The primary goal of treatment is to

Table 20-3. Modes of Interpersonal Relatedness in DSM-IV-TR–Defined Personality Disorders

Personality Disorder	Dominant Mode of Interpersonal Relatedness
Paranoid personality disorder	Pattern of distrust and suspiciousness such that others' motives are interpreted as malevolent
Schizoid personality disorder	Pattern of detachment from social relationships and a restricted range of emotional expression
Schizotypal personality disorder	Pattern of acute discomfort in close relationships, cognitive or perceptual distortions, and eccentricities of behavior
Antisocial personality disorder	Pattern of disregard for, and violation of, the rights of others
Borderline personality disorder	Pattern of instability in interpersonal relationships, self-image, and affects, as well as marked impulsivity
Histrionic personality disorder	Pattern of excessive emotionality and attention seeking
Narcissistic personality disorder	Pattern of grandiosity, need for admiration, and lack of empathy
Avoidant personality disorder	Pattern of social inhibition, feelings of inadequacy, and hypersensitivity to negative evaluation
Dependent personality disorder	Pattern of submissive and clinging behavior related to an excessive need to be taken care of
Obsessive-compulsive personality disorder	Pattern of preoccupation with orderliness, perfectionism, and control
Personality disorder not otherwise specified	Pattern of disordered personality functioning that meets general criteria for a personality disorder, but either does not meet full criteria for any single personality disorder despite causing significant impairment in one or more important areas of functioning, or meets the research criteria of depressive personality disorder or passive-aggressive personality disorder

Adapted from APA, 2000.

help the patient shift from seeing his problems as outside of himself to acknowledging his difficulties as coming from an internal process of distorted perceptions (Gabbard, 2000a).

   c. **Special considerations:** Paranoid patients are prone to respond to perceived threats by becoming violent. **Several strategies that prevent the escalation of aggression are available** (Gabbard, 2000a). These include:

   i. **Do everything possible to help the patient save face.** The clinician should avoid statements that may induce shame or humiliation in the patient. Maintenance of the therapeutic alliance should be prioritized.

   ii. **Avoid arousing further suspicions.** The clinician should explain all physical movement, and act slowly and carefully.

   iii. **Help the patient maintain a sense of control.** This is most effectively done by modeling self-control; the clinician should not panic or show fear.

   iv. **Encourage the patient to verbalize rather than to act out anger with violence.**

   v. **Maintain physical distance, so that the patient does not feel physically trapped.**

   vi. **Be attuned to your own countertransference.** It is important that the clinician not deny the fear of impending violence.

2. **Schizoid personality disorder**

   a. **Clinical presentation: This disorder is characterized by a detachment from social relationships and a restricted emotional range in interpersonal settings.** Afflicted individuals may neither desire, nor enjoy, close relationships. They generally prefer solitary activities, appear indifferent to praise or criticism, have no (or only one) close friends or confidants, and are emotionally cold or detached (Edgerton and Campbell, 1994).

   b. **Treatment approaches:** It is rare that schizoid or schizotypal patients present for treatment without pressure from others. Patients can be helped by individual dynamic supportive therapy, by group psychotherapy, and by a combination of these two approaches. The long-term goals often focus on facilitating relatedness with others. Paradoxically, this requires that the therapist accept the patient's characteristic nonrelatedness, especially early on in treatment (Gabbard, 2000a).

3. **Schizotypal personality disorder**
   a. **Clinical presentation: This disorder is characterized by a combination of discomfort with, and a reduced capacity for, close relationships, and by cognitive or perceptual distortions and eccentricities of behavior.** Possible manifestations include odd beliefs or magical thinking that is inconsistent with cultural norms, unusual perceptual experiences that include bodily illusions, odd thinking and speech, eccentricities, no (or only one) close friends because of lack of desire or discomfort with others, and persistent, excessive social anxiety that tends to be associated with paranoid fears rather than negative self-judgments. Some studies have suggested that schizotypal personality disorder might be more properly considered as a schizophrenia spectrum disorder (Edgerton and Campbell, 1994).
   b. **Treatment approaches:** The approach to working with the schizotypal patient is the same as the approach to working with the schizoid patient (see above).

C. **Cluster B Personality Disorders**
   1. **General considerations.** Cluster B personalities are **dramatic and emotional.** Patients with these personality disorders have **dysregulated affects, problematic behaviors, and cognitive distortions.** Therefore, they tend to provoke strong responses in clinicians. As a group, they are likely to be novelty-seeking (Gabbard, 2000b).
   2. **Special management considerations for extreme behaviors.** Unless substance abuse is a factor in the patient's presentation, the most difficult patients carry a Cluster B diagnosis—either borderline, antisocial, or narcissistic personality disorder. Effective treatment of these patients requires keen attention to the establishment of clear communication, realistic patient expectations, consistency in clinician availability, firm limit-setting, and appropriate management of the emotions that are stirred up in the clinician. Such patients frequently induce strong feelings of aversion, rage, and malice in their treaters (Brandchaft and Stolorow, 1994; Groves, 1978; Maltsberger and Buie, 1974). Therefore, it is also important for members of the treatment team to consult frequently so that they can identify and manage strong countertransference feelings rather than act on them to the detriment of the patient.
   3. **Borderline personality disorder**
      a. **Clinical presentation: This disorder is characterized by instability of interpersonal relationships, self-image, af-**

fects, and personal control of behavior. Manifestations include: frantic efforts to avoid real or imagined abandonment; unstable, intense relationships that alternate between extremes of idealization and devaluation (splitting); recurrent self-mutilation or threats of suicide; and inappropriate, intense, or uncontrolled anger (Edgerton and Campbell, 1994).

b. **Treatment approaches:** The individual with borderline personality disorder is the prototypical difficult patient who can act out destructive impulses, decompensate in the face of a perception of abandonment, and provoke counterproductive acting out in the clinician. **It is best to use a team approach that uses clear and uniform limits with the patient, while providing enough support and consistency to foster a sense of emotional containment for the patient.** Treatment plans may include individual outpatient psychotherapy, group therapy, couples/family therapy, pharmacotherapy, partial hospitalization, and inpatient hospitalization (Gunderson, 2001). **Dialectical behavior therapy (DBT) can be used to reduce acts of self-harm, to increase emotional self-regulation, to manage distressed internal states, and to promote self-esteem** (Linehan, 1993).

c. **Special considerations:** Almost 10% of patients with borderline personality disorder commit suicide; therefore, **safety needs to be assessed frequently,** particularly when a patient is experiencing acute emotional dysregulation or impulsivity.

4. **Antisocial personality disorder**
   a. **Clinical presentation: This disorder is characterized by antisocial behavior and/or inadequacies regarding affect and empathic caring in interpersonal relationships.** Common manifestations include: superficiality; a lack of empathy and remorse, with a callous unconcern for the feelings of others; a disregard for social norms; poor behavioral controls, with irritability, impulsivity, and low frustration tolerance; and an inability to feel guilt or to learn from experience or punishment. By definition, there is evidence of a conduct disorder in childhood. Overtly irresponsible behavior in adulthood can include an inability to sustain consistent work behaviors; recurring conflicts with the law; a repeated failure to meet financial obligations; and the repeated lying to, or conning of, others (Edgerton and Campbell, 1994).

b. **Treatment approaches:** Patients with antisocial personality disorder are notoriously difficult to treat successfully on an outpatient basis. Even with inpatient or residential treatment, gains in treatment tend to be modest. The clinician should **expect deception by the patient within the therapy,** particularly in the earlier phases. Basic principles of care include the following (Gabbard, 2000a):
   i. The therapist must be stable, persistent, and incorruptible;
   ii. The patient's denial and minimization of antisocial behavior must be confronted repeatedly and consistently;
   iii. The therapist must help the patient to connect actions with internal states;
   iv. Confrontations of inappropriate behavior in real time are more effective than talking about the past;
   v. The therapist must monitor countertransference to avoid acting out;
   vi. The therapist should avoid excessive expectations for improvement;
   vii. The treatment should include careful identification and treatment of all Axis I disorders.

c. **Special considerations:** Antisocial personality disorder is **frequently comorbid with substance abuse disorders.** The male-to-female ratio is estimated at 4:1 or higher. Links within families have been demonstrated between men with antisocial personality disorder and family members with somatization disorder.

5. **Narcissistic personality disorder**
   a. **Clinical presentation: This disorder is characterized by a pervasive pattern of grandiosity in fantasy or behavior and by an excessive need for admiration.** Manifestations may include having an exaggerated sense of self-importance, having a feeling of being special so that one should only associate with other special people, exploiting others to advance one's own ends, lacking empathy, and often believing that others are envious of oneself (Edgerton and Campbell, 1994).

   b. **Treatment approaches:** Individual psychotherapy or psychoanalysis is the treatment of choice for narcissistic individuals. The goals of treatment will vary depending on the clinician's theoretical perspective. Most approaches seek to help the patient achieve greater identity development, reduced feelings of isolation and depression, an increased capacity for concern and guilt in relation to others, better awareness of unacknowledged feelings, and a greater acceptance of the inherently ambivalent nature of human relationships.

6. **Histrionic personality disorder**

   a. **Clinical presentation: This disorder is characterized by excessive emotional instability and by attention-seeking.** Behavior includes discomfort if one is not the center of attention, an excessive attention to physical attractiveness, rapidly shifting and shallow emotions, speech that is excessively impressionistic and lacking in detail, a view of relationships as being more intimate than they actually are, and a pattern of seeking immediate gratification (Edgerton and Campbell, 1994). It is helpful to differentiate histrionic personality disorder from hysterical personality style. While these two groups are similar and arguably on a continuum with one another, patients with histrionic personality disorder generally use more primitive defense mechanisms, display greater emotionality, show significantly greater separation anxiety, and act more impulsively than those with hysterical personality style (Horowitz, 1991).

   b. **Treatment approaches:** Patients with an hysterical personality style tend to do well in individual psychotherapy or psychoanalysis, while those with histrionic personality disorder tend to struggle with many issues similar to those of the borderline patient. For both types of patient, it is important to **begin any long-term treatment by joining the patient in an examination of his or her cognitive style** (Shapiro, 1965). Without this initial step, the treatment can be undermined by the use of an impressionistic and vague cognitive style that allows the patient to avoid engaging the depths of his or her emotional life. In general, the therapeutic work done within the transference is the primary pathway towards change; the problems that the patient has outside of therapy are reproduced in the relationship with the therapist, which can be explored in the treatment (Gabbard, 2000a).

   c. **Special considerations:** Histrionic and hysterical patients are prone to develop an eroticized transference towards the treating clinician. A nonexploitative acceptance of the erotic transference that allows for this aspect of the therapy to be explored is an important element of a successful treatment. This will require that the therapist examine countertransference feelings, in order to understand the patient and to forestall countertransference enactments.

D. Cluster C Personality Disorders

1. **General considerations:** Cluster C personalities are **anxious and fearful.** As a group, there is a temperamental association with **harm avoidance** (Gabbard, 2000b).

2. **Avoidant personality disorder**

    a. **Clinical presentation: This disorder is characterized by social discomfort and reticence, by low self-esteem, and by hypersensitivity to negative evaluation.** Manifestations may include the avoidance of activities that involve contact with others because of fears of criticism or disapproval; the inhibited development of relationships with others because of fears of feeling foolish or shamed; a lack of friendships despite the desire to relate to others; or a strong reluctance to take personal risks or to engage in new activities because they may prove embarrassing (Edgerton and Campbell, 1994).

    b. **Treatment approaches:** Patients with avoidant personality disorder tend to respond to **a combination of expressive-supportive psychotherapy with measured, repetitive exposure to the feared situation.** The exposure therapy allows the patient to build tolerance for anxieties and fears around what is avoided; the anxieties and fears may increase initially, with the goal that they decrease over time. The expressive component of the psychotherapy allows for exploration of the emotions that emerge during exposure, and for understanding of why the patient seeks to avoid these emotions. The supportive component of psychotherapy provides empathic support as the patient confronts situations and emotions that have been avoided previously (Gabbard, 2000a).

    c. **Special considerations:** This condition is rarely seen in isolation. There are **high rates of comorbidity with many Axis I disorders,** including major depression, bipolar disorder, certain anxiety disorders, and eating disorders.

3. **Dependent personality disorder**

    a. **Clinical presentation: This disorder is characterized by an excessive need for caretaking with a resultant increase in submissive and clinging behavior, and by fears of separation.** Manifestations may include the excessive need for advice and reassurance about everyday decisions, a reliance on encouragement by others to assume responsibility for major areas of one's life, an inability to express disagreement because of possible anger or lack of support from others, and a preoccupation with fears of being left to take care of oneself (Edgerton and Campbell, 1994).

  b. **Treatment approaches:** Psychotherapy with patients with dependent personality disorder begins with an opening paradox—**overcoming dependent personality traits requires that the patient initially develop dependency on the therapist. In working through elements of this dependency on the therapist, the patient is able to internalize increasing autonomy and self-sufficiency.** A difficulty is that some of these patients are content to live out the dependency eternally, rather than working through their dependent longings and achieving greater emotional independence. There is no one correct way to work with a patient with dependent personality disorder. A common approach is to use a time-limited psychotherapy model, in which the fixed duration becomes a central focus of treatment. In theory, patients experience dependency, and obtain greater independence through a working through of the longings and frustration that develop. Another approach is to allow the patient to develop a positive dependent transference over a long-term regimen of therapy. Some patients work through their dependent longings, while others seek to stay in the role of patient indefinitely. In the middle are patients who achieve therapeutic change in their lives outside of therapy, but only with the ongoing support of their therapist (Gabbard, 2000a).

    i. If a patient is treated in a brief situational setting, such as on a medical inpatient unit, then a management approach is needed that satisfies some of the patient's dependency needs to the extent that it is feasible and appropriate for the staff to do so. At the same time, firm and consistent boundaries help contain the patient's longings to drain unlimited support from the staff.

  c. **Special considerations:** Similar to the diagnosis of avoidant personality disorder, the diagnosis of dependent personality disorder is rarely made in isolation. It also shows **high rates of comorbidity with many Axis I disorders,** including major depression, bipolar disorder, certain anxiety disorders, and eating disorders.

4. **Obsessive-compulsive personality disorder**

  a. **Clinical presentation: This disorder is characterized by a preoccupation with perfectionism, by mental and interpersonal control, and by orderliness.** These preoccupations come at the expense of flexibility, openness, and efficiency. Manifestations can include a preoccupation with rules, lists, or similar items; an excessive devotion to work, with insufficient attention paid to recreation and friendships; a limited expression of warm emotions; a reluctance to delegate work; a demandingness that others submit exactly to one's particular way of doing things; and miserliness (Edgerton and Campbell, 1994).

b. **Treatment approaches:** Patients with obsessive-compulsive personality disorder have been shown to **respond well to dynamic psychotherapy.** These patients have deep-seated fears about loss of control. This sets up an interesting paradox, since acknowledgement of unconscious wishes, fears, and motivations implies that there is something beyond the immediate control of the patient. Once the patient achieves some tolerance for this, however, the **therapy can unlock many of the feelings of shame and guilt associated with unacceptable aspects of the self** that have been defended against by obsessive or compulsive processes. As the patient develops greater self-acceptance, the obsessive and compulsive symptoms tend to abate (Gabbard, 2000a).

E. **Personality Disorder Not Otherwise Specified (NOS)**
Personality disorder NOS is applied in two situations (APA, 2000):

1. The personality pattern meets the general criteria for a personality disorder and several traits of specific personality disorders, but does not meet the full criteria of any one personality disorder; or

2. The personality pattern meets the general criteria for a personality disorder, and the individual is considered to meet the criteria of one of the personality disorders under investigation for possible future incorporation in the DSM classification system.

References

American Psychiatric Association: *Diagnostic and Statistical Manual of Mental Disorders, Fourth Edition, Text Revision.* Washington: American Psychiatric Press, 2000:685–729.

Bandura A: *Social Learning Theory.* Englewood Cliffs, NJ: Prentice Hall, 1977.

Brandchaft B, Stolorow RD: The difficult patient. In Stolorow RD, Atwood GE, Brandchaft B (eds): *The Intersubjective Perspective.* New York: Jason Aronson, 1994.

Cassidy J, Shaver PR: *Handbook of Attachment.* New York: Guilford Press, 1999.

Chess S, Thomas A: *Goodness of Fit: Clinical Applications from Infancy through Adult Life.* New York: Brunner/Mazel, 1999.

Cloninger CR, Svrakic DM, Pryzbeck TR: A psychobiological model of temperament and character. *Arch Gen Psychiatry* 1993;50:975–990.

Edgerton JE, Campbell RJ (eds): *American Psychiatric Glossary,* 7th edition. Washington: American Psychiatric Press, 1994.

Gabbard GO: Combining medication with psychotherapy in the treatment of personality disorders. In Gunderson JG, Gabbard GO (eds): *Psychotherapy for Personality Disorders.* Washington: American Psychiatric Press, 2000b.

Gabbard GO: *Psychodynamic Psychiatry in Clinical Practice,* 3rd edition. Washington: American Psychiatric Press, 2000a.

Glick ID, Berman EM, Clarkin JF, Rait DS: *Marital and Family Therapy,* 4th edition. Washington: American Psychiatric Press, 2000.

Groves JE: Personality disorders I: General approaches to difficult patients. In Stern TA, Herman JH, Slavin PL: *The MGH Guide to Psychiatry in Primary Care.* New York: McGraw-Hill, 1998:591–597.

Groves JE: Taking care of the hateful patient. *N Engl J Med* 1978;298:883–887.

Gunderson JG: *Borderline Personality Disorder: A Clinical Guide.* Washington: American Psychiatric Press, 2001.

Horowitz MJ: *Hysterical Personality Style and the Histrionic Personality Disorder,* revised edition. New York: Jason Aronson, 1991.

Kagan J: *Galen's Prophecy: Temperament in Human Nature.* New York: Basic Books, 1994.

Kandel ER: A new intellectual framework for psychiatry. *Am J Psychiatry* 1998;155:457–469.

Kaplan HI, Sadock BJ: *Comprehensive Glossary of Psychiatry and Psychology.* Baltimore: Williams & Wilkins, 1991.

Linehan MM: *Cognitive Behavioral Therapy of Borderline Personality Disorder.* New York: Guilford Press, 1993.

Maltsberger JT, Buie DH: Countertransference hate in the treatment of suicidal patients. *Arch Gen Psychiatry* 1974;30:625–633.

Mitchell SA, Black MJ: *Freud and Beyond.* New York: Basic Books, 1995.

National Research Council/Institute of Medicine: *From Neurons to Neighborhoods.* Washington: National Academy Press, 2000.

Personality disorders. *Harv Ment Health Lett* 2000;16(9):1–5, and 2000;16(10):1–5.

Sater N, Samuels JF, Bienvenu OH, Nestadt G: Epidemiology of personality disorders. *Curr Psychiatry Rep* 2001;3:41–45.

Shapiro D: *Neurotic Styles.* New York: Basic Books, 1999/1965.

Siegel D: *The Developing Mind: Towards a Neurobiology of Interpersonal Experience.* New York: Guilford Press, 1999.

Thomas A, Chess S: *Temperament and Development.* New York: Brunner/Mazel, 1977.

Vaillant GE: Ego Mechanisms of Defense. Washington: American Psychiatric Press, 1992.

Westen D, Shedler J: Revising and assessing Axis II, part I: Developing a clinically and empirically valid assessment method. *Am J Psychiatry* 1999;156:258–272.

Zimmerman, M: Diagnosing personality disorders: A review in issues and research methods. *Arch Gen Psychiatry* 1994;51:225–245.

Chapter 21

An Approach to the Patient with Gender Dysphoria

Laura M. Prager, MD

I. Definitions

To facilitate an understanding of the problems discussed in this chapter, some definitions will be provided at the outset.

A. Gender Identity
One's sense of oneself as male or female in a biologic, social, and psychological sense.

B. Gender Role
Behavior, attitude, and personality traits that are labeled as either masculine or feminine, based on societal norms.

C. Gender Dysphoria
Unhappiness or discontent with one's anatomic sex.

D. Transsexualism
Profound discontent with one's primary and secondary sexual characteristics and the conviction that one is really a member of the opposite sex, which is usually accompanied by a wish for hormonal therapy gender reassignment surgery (GRS).

E. Transvestism
Cross-dressing with the goal of erotic arousal.

II. Overview

The *Diagnostic and Statistical Manual of Mental Disorders, Fourth Edition, Text Revision* (DSM-IV-TR) specifies three disorders of gender identity: **Gender Identity Disorder in Children; Gender Identity Disorder in Adolescents or Adults; and Gender Identity Disorder Not Otherwise Specified (NOS)** (which includes patients with inter-sex conditions).

Address for correspondence: Dr. Laura M. Prager, Massachusetts General Hospital, 15 Parkman Street, WACC 725, Boston, MA 02114, email: LMPrager@Partners.org.

A.   **Transvestic Fetishism**
      Transvestic fetishism is also included in the DSM-IV-TR as one of
      the paraphilias in which the primary focus of cross-dressing is for
      the purpose of sexual arousal. It can be subdivided into two cate-
      gories depending on whether or not the individual also manifests
      gender dysphoria (i.e., a discomfort with gender role or identity).

B.   **Transsexualism**
      Transsexualism as defined above, although previously defined as a
      disorder in the DSM-III-R, is not listed as a disorder in the DSM-IV-
      TR. This represents the general trend in the field of psychiatry
      towards an understanding of the gender identity disorders as occur-
      ring along a spectrum of gender dysphoria that ranges from mild dis-
      content with one's anatomic sex and feelings of distress with one's
      gender role to absolute loathing of one's anatomic sex and a persist-
      ent desire to alter it with hormones or surgery. The DSM-IV-TR
      diagnostic criteria for the Gender Identity Disorders are presented in
      Table 21-1.

III.   Epidemiology

Disorders of gender identity and transsexualism are quite rare. Current
estimates of prevalence are derived from the number of patients who are
receiving hormonal treatment for gender dysphoria at adult gender-identity
clinics in the Netherlands. Such data yield estimates of 1 in 11,000 men and
1 in 30,400 women (Bakker et al, 1993). There are no epidemiologic studies
of prevalence for gender identity disorder in children.

    **There appears to be a bimodal distribution of male patients who
present with disorders of gender identity** (Bradley and Zucker, 1995). The
first group includes men who present in their 20s and who often have a history of childhood gender identity issues and homosexual orientation. The
second group is composed of men in middle-age (30s and 40s) who have a
history of transvestism and of heterosexual orientation.

IV.   Etiology

The etiology of the disorders of gender identity is poorly understood.
Theories abound, but there are insufficient data to support either biological
or psychosocial determinants. There is no scientific evidence to suggest that
persons with gender dysphoria have neuroendocrine feedback mechanisms
that differ from persons without gender dysphoria. Girls with congenital
adrenal hyperplasia have been exposed to high levels of androgen in utero.
Such girls may exhibit behaviors more consistent with a male gender role in
childhood, but there are no data to suggest that these girls suffer ongoing gender dysphoria in adulthood. Several factors, such as **parental ambivalence**

Table 21-1. Gender Identity Disorders

A. A strong and persistent cross-gender identification (not merely a desire for any perceived cultural advantages of being the other sex).

In children, the disturbance is manifested by four (or more) of the following:

1. A repeatedly stated desire to be, or insistence that he or she is, the other sex
2. In boys, preference for cross-dressing or simulating female attire; in girls, insistence on wearing only stereotypical masculine clothing
3. Strong and persistent preferences for cross-sex roles in make-believe play or persistent fantasies of being the other sex
4. Intense desire to participate in the stereotypical games and pastimes of the other sex
5. Strong preference for playmates of the other sex

In adolescents and adults, the disturbance is manifested by symptoms such as a stated desire to be the other sex, frequent passing as the other sex, desire to live or be treated as the other sex, or the conviction that he or she has the typical feelings and reactions of the other sex.

B. Persistent discomfort with his or her sex or sense of inappropriateness in the gender role of that sex.

In children, the disturbance is manifested by any of the following: in boys, assertion that his penis or testes are disgusting or will disappear or assertion that it would be better not to have a penis, or aversion toward rough-and-tumble play and rejection of male stereotypical toys, games, and activities; in girls, rejecting of urinating in a sitting position, assertion that she has or will grow a penis, or assertion that she does not want to grow breasts or menstruate, or marked aversion toward normative feminine clothing.

In adolescents and adults, the disturbance is manifested by symptoms such as preoccupation with getting rid of primary and secondary sex characteristics (e.g., request for hormones, surgery, or other procedures to physically alter sexual characteristics to simulate the other sex) or belief that he or she was born the wrong sex.

C. The disturbance is not concurrent with a physical intersex condition.

D. The disturbance causes clinically significant distress or impairment in social, occupational, or other important areas of functioning.

From American Psychiatric Association: *Diagnostic Criteria from DSM-IV-TR.* Washington: American Psychiatric Press, 2000.

and other social influences on the sex of rearing appear to be more powerful determinants of gender identity. Likewise, psychosocial factors such as **social reinforcement and family psychopathology** may predispose boys to develop gender identity disorder of childhood; however, there are no hard data to support such conclusions (Bradley and Zucker, 1995).

Other explanations for gender dysphoria include a psychoanalytic approach that presumes that males who wish to be females identify with the mother rather than the father, and that females who wish to be males have mothers who lack a cohesive sense of self. The behaviorists suppose that gender identity develops from social reinforcement, particularly parental responses during a critical period of development, most likely before the age of 2 or 3 years.

Almost all researchers in the field agree that **the "core" gender identity is most likely fixed somewhere before the age of 2 years.** Given this, it is reasonable to conclude that **patients who present with some form of gender dysphoria in adulthood have suffered with their feelings, in one form or another, for most of their life.**

V.   Evaluation

Patients with gender dysphoria exhibit all variations of sexual orientation. Questions about sexual orientation and disorders of sexuality are often confused with questions about gender identity or gender role. Moreover, patients who experience gender dysphoria do not necessarily experience conflicts about their sexuality.

The comprehensive evaluation and management of the child or adolescent who presents with symptoms consistent with gender identity disorder is beyond the scope of this chapter.

A.   **Initial Approach**
  1.   When an adult presents with gender dysphoria, one must **first rule out the presence of intersex conditions,** such as congenital adrenal hyperplasia, androgen insensitivity syndrome, congenital abnormalities leading to ambiguous genitalia, or congenital micropenis.
  2.   One must also **rule out the presence of psychotic disorders,** such as schizophrenia or schizoaffective disorder, that could be accompanied by the delusion that one is really a member of the other gender.
  3.   **A complete screen for comorbid Axis I and II diagnoses** is also crucial. Patients with gender dysphoria are often depressed. They may become suicidal in the setting of real or imagined rejection by loved ones, coworkers, or family members. These patients may also suffer from anxiety disorders. Some patients

with gender dysphoria have a history of unstable personal relationships, self-injurious behavior, or substance abuse. If the patient has already been taking either androgens or estrogens, a referral to an endocrinologist familiar with such treatments is necessary.

4. The adult with gender dysphoria requires **a thorough history regarding the onset of symptoms and the ways he has managed his feelings up to this point.** It is important to explore with patients what adaptations they have already made to accommodate their gender dysphoria and what changes they anticipate.

   a. Not every patient with gender dysphoria wishes to change his or her gender role or desires sex reassignment surgery. Many of these patients are married or involved in long-standing relationships with a partner, have children, and may not wish to disrupt their family in any way.

5. **Laboratory studies should be considered;** these include liver function tests (particularly in patients who have been taking hormones), and serum and urine toxicological screens.

VI. Treatment

Treatment for the adult with gender dysphoria depends on his degree of distress and the intensity of his wish for sex reassignment. The goal is not to "cure" the gender dysphoria, but to help the patient negotiate the gender role transition.

A. **Psychotherapy**
   Psychotherapy is almost always indicated as a way to help patients explore and to accept their feelings, to sustain relationships, and to clarify their wishes regarding hormonal or surgical therapies.

B. **Psychopharmacologic intervention**
   Psychopharmacologic intervention is also warranted if there are comorbid diagnoses such as mood disorders or anxiety disorders.

C. **Education**
   Education about and acceptance of transgender behavior is often crucial. Patients often feel alone with their difficulties and it is important to inform them about support groups and gender networks.

D.   Nonsurgical or Hormonal Options for Gender Adaptation
These include:
1. **For biologic males:** cross-dressing, removal of body hair with waxing or electrolysis, and changing vocal expressions.
2. **For biologic females:** cross-dressing, breast-binding, weight lifting to provide muscle definition and mass, theatre make-up for facial hair, and penile prostheses.

E.   Sex Reassignment
Should the patient conclude that sex reassignment is the only way to resolve their dysphoria, he or she should be referred to a psychiatrist or psychologist who specializes in gender identity problems for further evaluation and management. Such professionals are usually associated with hospitals where sex reassignment surgeries are performed. There are international guidelines established by the Harry Benjamin International Gender Dysphoria Association for the standard of care regarding hormonal and surgical gender reassignment. Some patients wish to take hormones and live in the opposite gender role, but not proceed to sex reassignment surgery. After psychological evaluation, such patients can be referred to an endocrinologist who can initiate hormone therapy. Guidelines for the evaluation and treatment of such patients include:
1. The patient is given written material about the procedure and its consequences.
2. The evaluator collects a detailed history including a discussion of motivation.
3. The patient undergoes psychological testing as well as a full medical evaluation.
4. Subsequently, the patient and the therapist discuss the results of the testing and decide together whether the patient is ready to proceed to the next stage.
5. The patient begins hormone therapy and lives for 2 years in his or her desired gender role.
6. The patient has regular check-ups to monitor the physical effects of the hormones.
7. The patient has regular meetings with the psychotherapist.
8. If the patient experiences relief of his gender dysphoria after living as a member of the opposite gender for over 1 year, then he or she is deemed an appropriate candidate for sex reassignment surgery.

References

American Psychiatric Association: *Diagnostic Criteria from DSM-IV-TR*, Washington: American Psychiatric Press, 2000.

Bakker A, van Kesteren PJM, et al: The prevalence of transsexualism in the Netherlands. *Acta Psychiatrica Scandinavia* 1993;87:237–238.

Bradley SJ, Zucker KJ: *Gender Identity Disorders and Psychosexual Problems in Children and Adolescents*. New York: Guilford Press, 1995.

Gooren L: Transsexualism, Introduction and General Aspects of Treatment. www.xs4all.nl/~txtbreed/gender/gooren.html. Accessed 4/11/2004.

Perrin EC: *Sexual Orientation in Child and Adolescent Health Care*. New York: Plenum, 2002.

Yates A (ed): *Sexual and Gender Identity Disorders*. Child and Adolescent Psychiatric Clinics of North America 2003;2(3).

Chapter 22

Psychiatric Disorders Associated with the Female Reproductive Cycle

ADELE C. VIGUERA, MD, MPH

I. Introduction

Fluctuations in reproductive hormones occur at several important times in the female life cycle (e.g., menses, pregnancy, postpartum, and menopause); these changes are often associated with new-onset mood and anxiety symptoms or with an exacerbation of a pre-existing mood or anxiety disorder. While it seems intuitive that abnormalities in reproductive hormones are solely responsible for the manifestation of psychiatric symptoms during these phases, current data do not support this finding; instead, **a more complicated interplay is apparent between biological and psychosocial factors, and an underlying psychiatric diathesis.**

II. Depression During the Female Life Cycle

A. Epidemiology

    1. **In every age group women have higher rates of depression than do men (approximately 2:1).** The National Comorbidity Study reported that **the highest rates of depression cluster in women during their childbearing years.**

B. Etiology for Gender Differences in the Prevalence of Depression

    1. **Biological explanations of differences in gender-based rates of depression have included hormonal factors.** The beginnings of gender-based differences in rates of depression coincide with the onset of menarche at puberty, when the female brain is exposed to monthly fluctuations of estrogen and progesterone. This pattern of hormonal fluctuations persists through the reproductive years and corresponds to the peak risk of depression among women during the childbearing years. With menopause, estrogen and progesterone remain consistently low and the gender difference in rates of depression disappears. **Estrogen and progesterone affect neurons in the opioid, norepinephrine (NE), serotonin (5-HT), dopamine (DA), and γ-aminobutyric acid (GABA) systems.**

Address for correspondence: Dr. Adele C. Viguera, Massachusetts General Hospital, 15 Parkman Street, WACC 812, Boston, MA 02114, email: aviguera@partners.org.

2. **Estrogen and progesterone receptors have been identified in multiple areas of the central nervous system** (CNS) (e.g., the amygdala, hippocampus, cingulate cortex, locus ceruleus, midbrain raphe nuclei, and central gray matter). Animal studies show estrogens to have organizational effects on developing neurons as well as activational effects on mature neurons. Estrogen plays an important neuromodulatory role in the CNS and modulates many neurotransmitter systems including the dopamine, serotonin, norepinephrine, acetylcholine, and glutamate systems. Estrogens also affect neuron growth and synapse formation and interact with nerve growth factor and other neurotrophins. Other important effects of estrogen include: decreasing seizure threshold, increasing cerebral blood flow, augmenting cerebral glucose utilization, blunting hypothalamic-pituitary-adrenal axis reactivity, and enhancing mood state.

3. **Consistent evidence that shows that premenstrual, pregnancy, postpartum, or perimenopausal associated psychiatric symptoms are correlated with abnormal levels of steroid hormones or gonadotropin release is lacking;** rather, it appears that subgroups of women may have an abnormal response to normal fluctuations of hormones. This subgroup of women is more vulnerable to changes in the hormonal milieu and thus may develop mood and anxiety symptoms at these defined periods of hormonal flux. Clinicians should inquire about whether a patient has been prone to mood symptoms around the time of menses or during pregnancy and the postpartum period, or whether she has developed dysphoria with oral contraceptive pill use, since these features suggest that a patient may be more vulnerable to further episodes during future periods of hormonal fluctuation, such as occur during the perimenopausal transition.

4. **A history of a mood and/or anxiety disorder seems to be an important and positive predictor of risk for reproductive-related mood disorders.**

5. Psychosocial and psychodynamic factors also seem to be associated with affective symptoms during different stages of the reproductive cycle.

III. Premenstrual Syndrome and Premenstrual Dysphoric Disorder

A. **Definitions**
   1. **Premenstrual syndrome (PMS)** is a constellation of emotional and physical symptoms that occur during the luteal phase

only (i.e., between ovulation and menses) of the menstrual cycle. Typically, these symptoms (which are experienced by a majority of women) remit within a few days of onset of menses.

2. **By convention, based on a 28-day menstrual cycle, the first day of menses (i.e., day #1) starts on the first day of bleeding; days #1–14 are referred to as the follicular phase; day #14 is the time of ovulation; and days #14–28 are known as the luteal phase, which is the phase in the cycle characterized by PMS/PMDD symptoms.**

3. **Premenstrual dysphoric disorder (PMDD),** however, is a more severe form of PMS that causes significant impairment in daily functioning and quality of life. The DSM-IV-TR has established strict research criteria and includes the following symptoms, timing, and severity parameters:

   a. In most menstrual cycles during the past year, five or more of the following symptoms were present during the last week of the **luteal phase, with partial remission after the onset of the follicular phase, and complete remission in the week postmenses.** One of the symptoms must include (i), (ii), (iii), or (iv) below:

      i. Markedly depressed mood, hopelessness, or self-deprecating thoughts
      ii. Marked anxiety, feeling "keyed up," or "on edge"
      iii. Affective lability
      iv. Marked anger, irritability, or interpersonal conflicts
      v. Decreased interest
      vi. Difficulty concentrating
      vii. Decreased energy
      viii. Changes in appetite, overeating, or specific food cravings
      ix. Sleep disturbance
      x. Feeling out of control or overwhelmed
      xi. Other physical symptoms (e.g., breast tenderness or swelling, joint or muscle pain, or bloating)

   b. Symptoms interfere with social or occupational functioning and are not merely an exacerbation of an Axis I diagnosis (such as major depression, panic disorder, or dysthymic disorder).

   c. Quality and timing of symptoms must be confirmed by prospective daily ratings during at least two consecutive symptomatic cycles.

B.   Epidemiology
1.   PMS is prevalent in the general population. In some reports more than 80% of women experience one or two emotional or physical symptoms premenstrually.
2.   **PMDD** affects far fewer women and **has a prevalence rate of approximately 3–8%** in women in the United States.

C.   Etiology
1.   **Hormone theories**
     a.   The etiology of PMS and PMDD is unknown; **there is no consistent evidence that either PMS or PMDD is associated with abnormal levels of gonadal hormones.**
     b.   Current evidence suggests that there are subgroups of women who have an abnormal response (i.e., they experience severe mood/anxiety symptoms) to normal fluctuations of gonadal hormones across the menstrual cycle.
     c.   Since estrogen interacts with multiple systems, including the brain, cardiovascular, and other regulatory systems, menstrual-related fluctuations may induce a change in the activity of one of these systems that may lead to disruption of homeostasis and pathology.

D.   Assessment of the Patient with Premenstrual Complaints
1.   **Perform prospective daily symptom rating scales throughout the month and assess the reproductive endocrine status.** After ruling out an underlying medical or psychiatric condition, a patient should fill out prospective daily rating scales over two consecutive cycles. The importance of prospective daily rating of symptoms cannot be overstated. Data suggest that 60% of women who present with a chief complaint of "PMS" actually have mood symptoms that **persist** throughout the month and are not restricted to the luteal phase only; this suggests that the most likely diagnosis is a major depression or other Axis I mood disorder. Tracking will also serve as an effective behavioral intervention that empowers the patient to have more control over her situation. Tracking can help the patient predict when she may not feel well and when she must adjust her life activities accordingly. Documentation of persistent symptoms in the follicular phase rules out a diagnosis of PMDD.
2.   Careful prospective documentation of symptoms throughout the cycle can help clarify the diagnosis and lead to appropriate work-up and treatment.
3.   To determine the presence of luteal phase symptoms, one needs to determine whether the patient has regular ovulatory cycles. A

patient with a history of spontaneous, regular menstrual cyclicity likely has normal menstrual function. To confirm regular ovulatory cycles, a woman can chart her basal body temperature to document a rise in temperature just after ovulation. Alternatively, a patient can measure LH in urine using an over-the-counter kit to detect the LH surge prior to ovulation.

4. **Rule out underlying medical conditions.** Review the medical history for syndromes that could mimic PMDD. For example, endometriosis may cause significant mood symptoms as well as pelvic discomfort prior to and during menses. In addition, certain conditions, such as migraines, epilepsy, and herpes, may have premenstrual worsening. Careful screening and a physical examination by an internist or gynecologist should be part of the evaluation of dysmenorrhea.

5. **Rule out underlying psychiatric conditions.** Review of the psychiatric history should include a patient's experience during periods of hormone fluctuations, such as during pregnancy and the postpartum period, which may suggest that she is at increased risk for developing PMDD. In addition, several Axis I or II diagnoses can be exacerbated premenstrually. Excessive use of alcohol or drugs during the cycle may also affect mood and anxiety states. Axis I diagnoses should be treated to see if symptoms resolve in the follicular phase but persist in the luteal phase.

E. **Treatment**
1. **Nonpharmacological treatments**
   a. Nonpharmacological treatments which are not evidence-based include dietary modifications (such as restricting salt, caffeine, and alcohol), exercise, stress management, and supportive therapy.
   b. Evidence-based nonpharmacological treatments for PMS and PMDD include: **calcium** (1200 mg/d in divided doses); **magnesium** (360 mg/d) supplements; **L-tryptophan** (6 g/d) **from ovulation to menses; vitamin E** (400 U/d); and **vitamin B$_6$** (50–100 mg/d). Three published trials of cognitive-behavioral therapy (CBT) suggest that CBT is superior to wait-list control for improving premenstrual psychological and physical symptoms and functioning.
2. **Hormonal treatments**
   a. **Oral contraceptive pills (OCPs) are sometimes used to treat PMDD** with the hope that ovulation suppression and constant levels of estrogen and progestin throughout the menstrual cycle will eliminate premenstrual symptoms.

OCPs may decrease the severity of the physical symptoms, and may not affect, or may even worsen, premenstrual depressive symptoms. There are very few double-blind placebo-controlled trials of OCPs for the treatment of PMS.

b. **OCPs should not be considered first-line treatments, but should be considered as adjuncts to first-line treatment with a selective serotonin reuptake inhibitor (SSRI).** If OCPs are prescribed, **monophasic birth control pills are favored** over triphasic OCPs, since monophasic pills are less likely to cause adverse mood changes. Monophasic OCPs contain a steady dose of estrogen and progestin throughout the cycle, as compared to triphasic pills that have varying doses of estrogen and progestin throughout the cycle.

c. Administration of the OCP in a continuous fashion (i.e., skipping the placebo week of the OCP and delivering the active pill throughout the cycle) may provide further mood benefits since the brain is less likely to experience a drop in hormonal levels during the placebo phase of the OCP regimen. Patients should have a withdrawal bleed at least once every 3 months. New FDA-approved **continuous pills are now available.**

d. Although once a popular treatment for PMDD, progesterone has failed to show consistent superiority over placebo.

e. **Gonadotropin-releasing hormone agonists** and synthetic androgens (to suppress ovulation) may be useful in treating PMDD; however, both have significant side effects that limit long-term treatment.

f. Without further research, no definitive statements can be made about the utility of hormonal treatments for PMDD.

3. **Psychotropic medications**

a. First-line treatment for PMDD involves use of an SSRI; this is based on over 20 combined open and randomized double-blind placebo-controlled trails. While all SSRIs appear to have similar efficacy, the FDA-approved agents include **fluoxetine (average dose 20 mg/d), sertraline (50–100 mg/d)** and **paroxetine controlled-release (12.5–25 mg/d).** Others, however, including venlafaxine, citalopram, paroxetine, and fluvoxamine have also demonstrated efficacy in randomized controlled trials.

b. **SSRIs may be given either in a continuous fashion** (i.e., an SSRI is taken daily throughout the month) or **intermittently** (i.e., during the week or two weeks before the onset of menses only). Intermittent dosing is popular among patients since they are less likely to experience troublesome side effects (such as weight gain and sexual dysfunction). Head-to-head trials comparing intermittent dosing to continuous dosing have demonstrated that both dosage strategies are equally effective. However, the best candidates for intermittent dosing are those with regular periods; being able to predict when PMDD symptoms begin and end is critical to the intermittent administration of an SSRI.

c. **Non-SSRI pharmacological treatments:** Although one small crossover study failed to show a significant difference from placebo, another study found that **alprazolam,** dosed at 0.25 mg four times a day from day 18 to day 2 of the next menstrual cycle was **more effective than placebo and oral micronized progesterone.**

In addition, **buspirone,** a $5\text{-}HT_{1A}$ serotonin receptor partial agonist, at mean doses of 25 mg/d, was effective in a small, placebo-controlled, double-blind study, though larger controlled trials are needed to confirm this finding.

Other non-serotonergic agents such as bupropion and the tricyclic antidepressants (TCAs) do not appear to be effective in the treatment of PMDD, with the exception of the serotonergic TCA clomipramine, dosed at 25–75 mg/d.

IV.   Psychiatric Illnesses During Pregnancy

Despite early assumptions about the protective effects of pregnancy on women's psychological health, **the available data suggest that women with premorbid anxiety and depressive disorders are at high risk for relapse during pregnancy, especially if maintenance antidepressants or antianxiety medications are discontinued. Recent data suggest that nearly 75% of patients with either bipolar or unipolar disorder will experience a relapse in pregnancy if maintenance medications are discontinued. Psychiatrists must help patients weigh the risks of prenatal exposure to psychotropic medications against the risk of unmedicated psychiatric illness.** While there are increasing data to help inform these difficult decisions, there still remain many unanswered questions regarding the risk for relapse in pregnant and postpartum women with and without medications.

A.   **Categories of Risk Associated with Pharmacotherapy**
1.   **Risk of teratogenesis.** Fetal organ formation occurs primarily during the first trimester. **Teratogenesis is the dysgenesis of fetal organs leading to structural or functional anomalies, and a teratogen is any agent that can cause a major malformation during first-trimester exposure.** The baseline risk of

congenital malformations in the general population is estimated at 2–4% and it is important to remind patients of this baseline risk. A medication that increases this baseline risk for major malformation is considered a teratogen.

2. **Risk of perinatal toxicity.** Perinatal syndromes refer to symptoms present in the neonate that are frequently associated with drug exposure at or near delivery. Several syndromes have been described following in utero exposure to antidepressants, antipsychotics, or benzodiazepines. Potential contributing factors include prolonged drug effects (secondary to immature hepatic microsomal activity), or increased free drug levels (from decreased plasma protein and protein binding).

3. **Risk of behavioral teratogenesis.** Behavioral teratogenesis refers to the long-term effects of in utero drug exposure on neurobehavioral development.

B.   **Risk of Untreated Maternal Psychiatric Illness**

1. **Maternal psychiatric symptoms may jeopardize the well-being of both mother and fetus.** For instance, disabling depression and anxiety may lead to decreased self-care, poor appetite, and suicidal ideation, which may all undermine a woman's participation in routine prenatal care.

2. **Untreated depression and anxiety have been associated with poor neonatal outcome and higher rates of obstetrical and neonatal complications,** such as preterm delivery, low birth weight, and lower Apgar scores; moreover, the physiological changes associated with depression and anxiety may also pose risks to fetal development.

3. **Relapse of recurrent affective illness may increase refractoriness to treatment.**

C.   **Psychotropic Medications During Pregnancy**
Patients and physicians commonly underestimate the risks of untreated maternal psychiatric illness and overemphasize the potential teratogenicity of psychotropic medications. In one study, women exposed to nonteratogenic drugs estimated their teratogenic risk as 25%, which is far higher than the baseline risk of 2–4% and more in the range of known teratogens, such as thalidomide. **Misperception about risk can lead both physicians and patients to terminate otherwise wanted pregnancies or to avoid much-needed pharmacotherapy.** By informing patients about the nature and magnitude of drug exposure risk as well as the real risks of untreated illness, psychiatrists can help patients reach their own decisions.

1. All psychotropics diffuse readily across the placenta, and no psychotropic drug has been approved by the U.S. Food and Drug Administration (FDA) for use in pregnancy. The FDA has established a system that classifies medications into five risk categories (A, B, C, D, and X), based on data derived from human and animal studies. Most psychotropic drugs are classified as category C agents, for which adequate human studies are lacking and risk cannot be ruled out. This classification system is often ambiguous, inaccurate, and misleading. Recently, the FDA has decided to revamp the old labeling system and consider adding narrative statements summarizing and interpreting available data on teratogenic risk. At present, physicians must rely on other sources of information when recommending the use of psychotropic medications during pregnancy.

2. **Antidepressants. Reproductive safety data available on the TCAs and SSRIs indicate that they are considered to be the safest antidepressants for use during pregnancy.** Prenatal exposure to these agents does not increase the risk of major congenital malformations from the baseline of 2–4%. There have been case reports of newborns with SSRI- and TCA-withdrawal symptoms (e.g., jitteriness, irritability, and respiratory difficulty). However, these symptoms are transient and tend to resolve within a few days without any long-term negative sequelae. For TCAs there have been a few reports of infant bowel obstruction or urinary retention, presumably due to anticholinergic effects. More recently, the FDA has considered changing the labeling of the SSRIs to include a warning of potential risk of neonatal toxicity/withdrawal symptoms associated with any SSRI exposure, despite limited data on the prevalence and natural course of these symptoms. The clinical implications of this future warning do not necessarily mean that all patients should stop their antidepressants prior to delivery, but rather patients should be aware of this risk and the various options available to her, including remaining on her medication, reducing the dose, or stopping the medication completely. More importantly, this decision needs to be made mutually with the physician and the patient. The decision should consider very carefully the patient's psychiatric history, risk for postpartum relapse, and her risk for morbidity if she were to stop or even reduce her dose of medication prior to delivery.

   Robust prospective data on the reproductive safety of other antidepressants, including nefazodone, mirtazapine, bupropion, monoamine oxidase inhibitors (MAOIs), and stimulants, are lacking.

3. **Mood stabilizers**
    a. **Lithium is one of the oldest known teratogens and initially it was believed to be associated with a high risk (1 of 50 infants) for a rare cardiac anomaly known as Ebstein's anomaly, defined as right ventricular hypoplasia and downward displacement of the tricuspid valve.** However, more recent, controlled epidemiological studies suggest a real but more modest risk for Ebstein's anomaly following first-trimester exposure. With the baseline risk for Ebstein's anomaly at 1 per 20,000, **the risk for Ebstein's anomaly following first-trimester lithium exposure is between 1 per 2000 (0.05%) and 1 per 1000 (0.1%).** Thus, although the relative risk of Ebstein's anomaly is increased, the absolute risk following first-trimester lithium exposure is small.
    b. Prior to discontinuing lithium, one must consider the severity of the illness (e.g., chronicity, severity of particular mood episodes, and the presence of impaired judgment or psychosis). **For women with severe illness, the risk of recurrence of a severe mood episode during pregnancy may overshadow the relatively small risk of Ebstein's anomaly.** For such women, lithium used during pregnancy may be the most appropriate course. For women with less compelling histories, a slow taper off lithium prior to conception and reintroduction of lithium later in the second or third trimester may be the most prudent treatment. **Given that the risk of relapse following lithium discontinuation is estimated at 50–60%, decisions to taper off any mood stabilizer should be made with extreme caution. In addition, given that risk for postpartum relapse in bipolar patients is between 50% and 70%,** women should strongly consider prophylaxis with mood stabilizers during this high-risk period (either initiated earlier in pregnancy or around delivery).
    c. **Valproic acid and carbamazepine have well-established teratogenic risks, most notably risk of neural tube defects (5% and 1%, respectively) following first-trimester exposure.** However, they are also associated with multiple malformations including craniofacial anomalies ("anticonvulsant face"), heart defects, and growth restriction. More recent data suggest that the overall risk for major malformations with first-trimester valproic acid monotherapy exposure was high, at around 9%, and included heart defects and neural tube defects. Given these data, valproic acid

should not be considered a first-line agent among bipolar women of childbearing age.

d. **Of the newer-generation anticonvulsants, reproductive safety data are unknown for topiramate, gabapentin, and zonisamide.** Reproductive safety data, however, are available for lamotrigine monotherapy, and it appears that the risk for major malformations is <3% and falls within the baseline risk of major malformations in the general population (i.e., 2–4%). **Lamotrigine** may be a preferable alternative for lithium nonresponders when compared to other anticonvulsant mood stabilizers. Further data are needed, however, to make definitive recommendations.

e. **Prenatal testing:** For patients taking lithium during the first trimester as well as anticonvulsants, a high-resolution level II ultrasound is recommended at around 16–18 weeks' gestation to evaluate organ morphology.

f. **Discuss contraception and document this discussion in the patient's chart.** As with other psychotropics, psychiatrists should discuss with women with childbearing potential the teratogenic risks and the importance of contraception when taking anticonvulsants. **Valproic acid and carbamazepine treatment during pregnancy should be coadministered with folic acid supplementation to help mitigate the risk of neural tube defects.** While the utility of folic acid in reducing the incidence of neural tube defects for the general population is clearly established, it remains unclear whether or not it reduces risk for women taking anticonvulsants. Ideally, the supplemental folic acid should be given in the preconception phase and continued throughout pregnancy. **Prenatal vitamins contain 1 mg of folic acid. If a patient is on anticonvulsants, the current recommendation is to increase the standard prenatal vitamin dose to around 4 mg.**

The higher teratogenic risk associated with the older anticonvulsants compared to lithium suggests that psychiatrists should consider a lithium trial for their women of reproductive age who plan to conceive. For those patients who do not respond to lithium, lamotrigine may be the best alternative for pregnant women or women planning pregnancy, given its emerging and promising reproductive safety data.

4. **Neuroleptics. High-potency neuroleptics have not consistently demonstrated increased teratogenicity following first-trimester exposure. Low-potency neuroleptics should be**

avoided in pregnancy given their purported association with an increased risk of congenital malformations. The reproductive safety data about the newer atypical antipsychotics (e.g., olanzapine, clozapine, quetiapine, and risperidone) remains sparse. There are no adequate human studies to evaluate the risk for potential teratogenicity of clozapine, olanzapine, risperidone, quetiapine, or ziprasidone. Perinatal toxicity (including motor restlessness, tremor, difficulty with oral feeding, hypertonicity, dystonia, and extrapyramidal symptoms) has been reported following typical neuroleptic exposure. In general, high-potency neuroleptics appear to be safer than lower-potency or atypical antipsychotics.

Like many psychotropic medications, atypical antipsychotics are not absolutely contraindicated in pregnancy. Patients and their psychiatrists have to consider whether discontinuation of these medications poses unacceptable risks for relapse, especially in women with severe mood disorder or a chronic psychotic illness.

5. **Benzodiazepines.** Early studies of first-trimester benzodiazepine use reported a 10-fold increase from baseline risk of oral cleft palate of <1% (i.e., 0.06%). However, significant **controversy exists about the extent of risk associated with benzodiazepine use.** Perinatal toxicity associated with benzodiazepine use around the time of delivery has included reports of temperature dysregulation, apnea, depressed Apgar scores, muscular hypotonicity, and failure to feed. However, several studies of low-dose benzodiazepines given to women around the time of delivery were not associated with significant perinatal toxicity. Long-term neurobehavioral data following in utero benzodiazepine exposure are unavailable.

D. **Nonpharmacological Treatments**

1. **Electroconvulsive therapy (ECT). The safety of ECT during pregnancy has been widely reported in the literature.** ECT has been used during pregnancy for more than 50 years. **For high-risk situations,** such as psychotic depression or mania, which require expeditious treatment to protect both mother and fetus, **ECT is the treatment of choice.** The safe and effective use of ECT during pregnancy requires coordination of care among the patient's psychiatrist, obstetrician, and anesthesiologist.

2. **Psychotherapy. Pregnancy often evokes feelings about one's early life, doubts about one's capacity to mother, and changing family and work roles. Helping women understand these**

conflicting feelings can be important both during and after pregnancy. For mild depression and anxiety, many women benefit from supportive, interpersonal, and integrative psychotherapy. For major depression during pregnancy, patients should strongly consider antidepressants and intensive psychotherapy along with other supportive interventions.

V.   Postpartum Psychiatric Illnesses

The postpartum period represents a period of increased risk for affective illness in certain subpopulations of women. Despite ongoing controversy regarding the nosology of postpartum psychiatric disorders, studies have consistently demonstrated the deleterious consequences of postpartum psychiatric illness on both the mother and the child. Recognition and appropriate treatment of these disorders not only alleviates maternal psychiatric symptoms, but also promotes healthy mother–infant attachment and infant development.

A.   Overview
Postpartum psychiatric illnesses are conceptualized along a continuum from the more mild, subsyndromal postpartum blues to the more severe psychiatric episodes of postpartum depression or psychosis.
1. **Postpartum blues (PPB) are a self-limited constellation of symptoms that affects 50–85% of all women postpartum. These symptoms usually begin 2–3 days after delivery and consist of depressed mood, crying spells, mood lability, irritability, and anxiety.** These symptoms generally represent a normal part of the postpartum period. However, when symptoms persist beyond 2 weeks or significantly impair functioning, they may represent an evolving major depression.
2. **Postpartum depression (PPD) occurs in 10–15% of all postpartum women,** depending on **the diagnostic criteria used. These prevalence rates are similar to those of nonpuerperal cohorts. More than 60% of women have symptom onset within 6 weeks of delivery.** The DSM-IV-TR classifies PPD as major depression that occurs within 4 weeks postpartum. The course of PPD is highly variable and ranges from 3 to 6 months. Clinical features include all the signs and symptoms of major depression. In addition, women with PPD often have prominent anxiety and obsessionality, including intrusive ego-dystonic obsessional thoughts of wanting to harm the infant.
3. **Postpartum psychosis (PPP) is a rare condition that occurs in 1–2 of every 1000 postpartum women. PPP begins acute-**

ly within the first 48–72 hours postpartum and represents a medical emergency. Clinical features can include delirium, memory impairment, irritability, lability, and psychosis. The presumptive underlying diagnosis for a patient presenting with postpartum psychosis is bipolar disorder, and treatment recommendations include ECT and/or a maintenance mood stabilizer for at least 1 year. PPP is a medical emergency that requires immediate hospitalization and treatment to protect both mother and infant.

B.   Risk Factors
Many etiologic theories of postpartum psychiatric illness have centered on the tremendous **hormonal changes** women experience. For instance, levels of estradiol and estriol drop dramatically within the first days postpartum, while other hormones, such as prolactin and cortisol, also change during the course of pregnancy and postpartum. In general, researchers acknowledge the neuromodulatory function of different hormones, but have yet to find consistent associations between different hormones and the emergence of affective symptoms. The multifactorial nature of these illnesses supports a more integrated theory in which hormonal factors play an important causative role only in women with particular vulnerability to psychiatric illness. This predisposition to psychiatric illness may be biological (evidenced by personal or family history of psychiatric illness), psychological (evidenced by character pathology or limited coping skills), or social/environmental (evidenced by lower occupational/social functioning).

While no biological, psychological, or social factors have been implicated unequivocally, **there is good evidence to suggest that the following factors are associated with an increased risk for postpartum psychiatric illness:**
1.   **Psychiatric history of affective illness. Women with a history of postpartum psychosis have a striking 70–90% risk of recurrent postpartum psychosis.** Women with a history of major depression or bipolar disorder have a 30–50% risk for developing a postpartum mood disorder. Another clear predictor of postpartum depression is depression during pregnancy.
2.   **Family history of psychiatric illness**
3.   **Limited social support and interpersonal distress,** such as marital conflict and child-care stress
4.   **Negative life events** during and after pregnancy

C.   Treatment

1. **Postpartum blues.** Women often benefit from education about the normalcy of certain mood symptoms during the postpartum period. They should also be informed of the signs and symptoms of an evolving major depression and the importance of prompt treatment. Most women with the postpartum blues also benefit from reassurance and supportive interventions, such as child-care assistance and referrals to support agencies.

2. **Postpartum depression**

    a. **Supportive interventions.** Grassroots national organizations, such as Depression after Delivery (DAD), Postpartum Support International (PSI), and Visiting Moms, can provide invaluable assistance to women with postpartum depression. Other options for surrogate family support include the services of a doula, a professional caregiver who is trained to help mothers adjust to the responsibilities of motherhood. Some doulas assist in the childbirth, while others provide critical support during the first postpartum weeks by helping with child-care or household tasks.

    b. **Psychotherapy.** Few studies have documented the efficacy of therapy for treating postpartum depression. Pilot studies of interpersonal therapy (IPT) suggest that this time-limited therapy may help treat mild to moderate postpartum major depression. Another small study comparing cognitive-behavioral therapy and fluoxetine found no significant difference in treating postpartum depression. Further research into the efficacy of these nonpharmacological treatments will help broaden the treatment alternatives for women with postpartum depression.

    c. **Pharmacotherapy**

        i. **Antidepressants.** Despite the high prevalence of postpartum psychiatric illness, there are only a limited number of medication treatment studies. Several studies have demonstrated the efficacy of different antidepressants in the treatment of postpartum depression, including fluoxetine, sertraline, venlafaxine, and bupropion sustained-release). Patients with postpartum depression should be treated as if they had an episode of depression at any other time in their life, with adequate doses of antidepressants for an adequate duration. In the absence of other studies, the most prudent antidepressant choice depends on the patient's depressive symptoms and her own history of response to, and tolerance of, different medications.

> **Women at increased risk for postpartum depression (e.g., with a history of recurrent major depression or postpartum depression) should consider initiating prophylactic antidepressants either late in the pregnancy or in the early postpartum period.** Alternatively, women may elect a wait-and-see approach; however, patients, their loved ones, and psychiatrists should be vigilant for early signs of relapse in order to institute prompt treatment.

ii. **Hormonal therapy.** Few studies have examined the efficacy of estrogen and progesterone treatment for postpartum depression. Despite one limited, open study, progesterone has not consistently been shown to be an effective treatment for depressive symptoms. One other study found that estrogen alone or as an adjunct to antidepressants was effective in treating postpartum depression. Both of these studies had significant methodological limitations; however, both highlight the need for further research into hormonal treatments for postpartum depression.

iii. **For severe postpartum depression, inpatient hospitalization and/or ECT may be required** for containment and for prompt treatment.

iv. **Lithium.** Women with a history of bipolar disorder, recurrent major depression, postpartum depression, and postpartum psychosis are at heightened risk for a puerperal affective episode. **Prophylactic treatment with lithium or other mood stabilizer, initiated either before delivery or within several days postpartum, may help reduce this risk for relapse.**

D.   Breastfeeding
All psychotropic medications are secreted in the breast milk at varying concentrations, but exposure to psychotropic medications is significantly less through breast milk than through the placenta. The benefits of breastfeeding are well established and women with mood disorders should not be denied the opportunity to breastfeed. Sleep deprivation should also be factored into the overall risk/benefit assessment of breastfeeding and psychotropics. The accumulated experience based on published case series and case reports on infants exposed to SSRIs and TCAs suggests that there is no increased risk for acute adverse effects to the infants. **Physicians should obtain infant serum drug levels only if clinically indicat-**

ed. For example, finding a high serum antidepressant level in an infant may be helpful if the infant exhibits significant behavior changes, such as poor suck, increased sedation, or other physical symptoms of distress. If high levels are detected in the setting of a change from baseline behavior, then women should strongly consider discontinuing nursing. If levels are not detectable, this does not exclude the presence of trace amounts that potentially may have neurodevelopmental effects on the infant.

1. **Antidepressants.** Despite **anecdotal cases of neonatal toxicity symptoms** (e.g., irritability, colic, and difficulty feeding), reports of adverse consequences **appear limited.** No studies have shown that any one antidepressant has greater safety during breastfeeding. Antidepressant choice should thus be based on the patient's history of response and tolerance of side effects.

2. **Mood stabilizers. Data on the risks associated with breastfeeding with anticonvulsants and neuroleptics are limited.** The American Academy of Pediatrics categorizes valproic acid and carbamazepine as compatible with breastfeeding, while they recommend caution with breastfeeding and use of lithium. Since the data available for breastfeeding and use of mood stabilizers are minimal, clinical infant monitoring is recommended. There are no formal guidelines yet on how best to monitor the infant. Some investigators have proposed the following: if an infant is exposed to an anticonvulsant through breast milk, liver function tests and anticonvulsant levels, as well as a complete blood count should be monitored (i.e., obtain labs at 4–6 weeks of age and then once every 6–8 weeks). For lithium, infant monitoring should include lithium levels, electrolytes, blood urea nitrogen, creatinine, and thyroid-stimulating hormone at 4–6 weeks of age and once every 6–8 weeks.

VI. Menopause

In the United States, more than 1.3 million women are expected to reach menopause every year. One of the most commonly cited myths is that the "change of life" is associated with wide mood swings, anxiety, and depressive illness. While some women experience psychiatric, cognitive, or somatic symptoms during the menopausal transition, **no specific psychiatric disorder has been associated with menopause itself.**

The relationship between declining estrogen levels and mood symptoms remains controversial. Some studies have demonstrated that certain subgroups of women with histories of mood or anxiety disorders may be more vulnerable to relapse during this phase. Women with a history of an earlier age at menarche and a previous history of mood and anxiety disorders may be at particular risk for experiencing mood/anxiety symptoms associated with the perimenopause. As with PMS and postpartum psychiatric disorders, fluctuations in reproductive endocrine function rather than absolute hormone levels may drive this increased risk for affective symptoms in some women.

A.   **Definitions**
   1.   **Menopause** is defined as **the cessation of menses for 12 consecutive months.** Women naturally enter menopause with advancing age, between the ages of 41 and 59 years. The average age of menopause is 51 years. Women can also experience menopause as a result of exogenous hormone treatment or following bilateral oophorectomy.
   2.   **Perimenopause, the transition from regular menstrual functioning to menopause,** usually lasts between 5 and 10 years. The median age of onset of perimenopause is 47.5 years. Hormonal changes during this period include declining estrogen levels, which are increasingly unopposed by progesterone due to anovulatory cycles. The perimenopause has been associated with a higher rate of depressive symptoms; however, there is no increased risk of major depression.
   3.   Following perimenopause, women enter the **postmenopause,** which can account for roughly one-third of a woman's entire life span. Stable low levels of estrogen and progesterone characterize the reproductive endocrine status of postmenopausal women. While the female:male ratio of depression increases after the age of 45 years, the rate of depression in women throughout all ages declines in the postmenopausal period.

B.   **Etiology**
   1.   **Hormonal theories of menopause-associated depression remain controversial.** Support for "estrogen withdrawal" theories include the increased rate of depression after bilateral oophorectomy compared to women undergoing natural menopause. Some emphasize the potential depressogenic effects of an abrupt decline in estrogen, while others counter that, following surgical menopause, many other complicated hormonal changes also occur, including falling testosterone and progesterone levels.
   2.   **The "domino theory" of menopause-related affective disorders suggests that certain somatic symptoms,** such as sleep disturbance from nocturnal hot flushes, **may lead to mood disturbance.** This has led some to wonder whether the positive effect on mood some women experience on hormone replace-

ment therapy (HRT) results from a direct effect or from the psychological relief they experience as their menopausal somatic symptoms abate.

3. **Women with a history of major depression appear to be at greatest risk for perimenopausal depression;** this furthers the debate over whether perimenopause-associated depression represents a separate diagnosis or merely an exacerbation of recurrent major depression.

4. **Psychosocial theories** often indict the stress of the life-changes that mark the perimenopausal transition. Some of these psychosocial factors include: losing one's reproductive potential, changing family roles, aging, and the onset of physical illnesses. While these factors may be associated with perimenopausal depression, a causal role for psychosocial factors in perimenopausal depression has yet to be established. Furthermore, characterizations of menopause are fraught with culturally-bound, pejorative stereotypes (e.g., the "empty nest"), which ignore the positive feelings of personal mastery and maturity some women experience during this life transition.

C.   **Evaluation**
1. **Psychiatric assessment**
    a. **Screen for menopause-associated physical and psychological symptoms,** including whether they reflect minor nuisances or severely impair social and occupational functioning (Table 22-1). Hot flushes are the most common menopausal symptoms, occurring in up to 75% of perimenopausal and recently postmenopausal women. Other common menopausal symptoms associated with hot flushes that lead women to seek medical care include sleep disruption and mood disturbance, primarily depression.
    b. Determine the symptom onset and course relative to the current hormonal status. While clinical history alone can determine whether a woman is in the perimenopause transition, estradiol and follicle-stimulating hormone (FSH) levels are required to document actual menopause.
    c. Consider monthly **mood charts** to determine the severity, stability, and pattern of symptoms. Both affective and somatic symptoms, such as hot flushes and vaginal dryness, should be monitored.
    d. Obtain a thorough psychiatric history since **psychiatric history is the best predictor of relapse in the menopausal period, and rule out other major mood or anxiety disorders as well as substance abuse.**

Table 22-1. Physical and Psychological Symptoms Associated with Menopause

Vasomotor symptoms
  Hot flushes, night sweats, palpitations
Affective symptoms
  Depressed mood, anxiety, mood swings
Cognitive symptoms
  Poor memory or concentration
Somatic symptoms
  Fatigue, headache, joint pain, paresthesias, vaginal dryness,
    dyspareunia

---

    e.   Assess the patient's **ability to function.** Determine how much the reported symptoms—whether physical or emotional—interfere with the patient's ability to function.

    f.   Inquire about **sexual dysfunction.** Determine whether a major mood disorder is contributing to decreased libido or whether physical discomfort (e.g., vaginal dryness, urogenital atrophy, or dyspareunia) is secondary to a low estrogen state.

    g.   **Assess for risk factors that may predispose a patient to perimenopausal and menopausal mood disorders** including a history of depression, a history of PMS/PMDD, postpartum depression, oral contraceptive–induced dysphoria, premature menopause; and psychosocial factors, such as stress and negative expectations about menopause.

2. **Medical assessment**

    a.   **Assess reproductive endocrine status.** Hormonal changes in menopause include a decrease in estrogen with subsequent elevations of luteinizing hormone (LH) and FSH. The endocrine profile of menopause is typically defined as an FSH level above 40 IU/L and an estradiol level below 25 pg/mL. Perimenopausal women typically have FSH levels above 25 IU/L and estradiol levels below 40 pg/mL. However, there may be a significant cycle-to-cycle variation, so the diagnosis of menopausal status should not rely on hormone levels alone, but also on well-established physical symptoms associated with menopause (e.g., vasomotor symptoms such as hot flushes and night sweats).

    b.   **Rule out underlying medical conditions** that can present with anxiety or depression, such as thyroid disease or cardiac arrhythmias. The physical examination should include an assessment of cardiovascular functioning, bone health, and a history of urogenital difficulties including incontinence, prolapse, vaginal dryness, and dyspareunia.

c. **A gynecologic history** should include whether a patient has had a chemically- or surgically-induced menopause versus a natural menopause. Patients who have had bilateral oophorectomy may experience more difficulties with mood and anxiety. Determine whether or not the woman still has her uterus, since estrogen replacement may increase the risk of uterine as well as breast cancer.

D. Treatment Strategies
1. **Pharmacological strategies**
   a. **Hormone therapy (HT). Careful documentation of the onset of symptoms and the initiation of HT should be determined.** HT may alleviate mild mood symptoms, along with certain physical symptoms, such as vaginal dryness and vasomotor symptoms (e.g., hot flushes and cold sweats). These benefits, however, must be carefully weighed against a possible increased risk for cardiovascular events, stroke, and breast cancer in certain subgroups. The use of HT alone to treat major mood or anxiety disorders is not recommended.
   b. The results from the Women's Health Initiative study published in 2002 have generated concern. In light of these recent findings, the FDA has proposed new labeling revisions for both estrogen plus progestogen therapy (EPT), such as Prempro and Premphase, as well as for the estrogen alone therapy (ET), Premarin, which will highlight the increased risk for heart disease, myocardial infarction, stroke, and breast cancer. The labeling is advising that the primary clinical indication for ET or EPT is for the treatment of moderate to severe menopause symptoms (i.e., vasomotor symptoms and sleep disruption due to vasomotor symptoms). Moreover, the FDA recommends that clinicians prescribe the lowest dose for the shortest duration of time (i.e., <5 years). The North American Menopause Society (NAMS) has a helpful educational website that summarizes the complicated findings of the WHI study and how to apply this information in clinical practice. The NAMS position statement can be viewed at www.menopause.org/Htpositionstatement.

  c. Vaginal dryness and urogenital atrophy should be treated with local ET instead of systemic treatment. Some patients may require dose adjustments or alternative forms of estrogen replacement (e.g., estradiol or conjugated estrogen) before mood improves.

  d. **Antidepressants.** For menopause-associated major depression, **standard antidepressant treatment should be initiated.** All antidepressants are equally effective. If, however, a patient has had a good response in the past to a certain antidepressant, this should guide the antidepressant selection. Treatment should include a full therapeutic trial with adequate dose and duration of treatment. While there is evidence to suggest that estrogen may be helpful in the treatment of depressive symptoms, it is not recommended as monotherapy for the treatment of major depression.

  e. **SSRIs for treatment of hot flushes:** Recent data indicate that SSRIs provide an effective treatment option for hot flushes. Studies have included venlafaxine extended-release (doses of 37.5 mg qd, 75 mg qd, or 150 mg qd), paroxetine controlled-release (12.5–25 mg qd), and fluoxetine (20 mg qd). The overall improvement in hot flushes reported in these clinical trials with the use of an SSRI varied from 50–60%.

  f. **Mood or anxiety symptoms may result from HT itself.** Symptoms may remit if a patient is switched from sequential HT to a continuous hormone replacement preparation. If there is no response in the patient's mental status after 2 to 4 weeks, re-evaluate for a primary psychiatric condition and consider the use of a standard antidepressant.

    In addition, while progestin added to estrogen replacement decreases the risk of endometrial cancer, it may worsen mood. A higher estrogen:progestin ratio may attenuate the dampening effect of progestin.

    If there is no improvement after 2–4 weeks, re-evaluate for a primary Axis I condition and consider the use of standard antidepressant treatment.

2. **Psychotherapy strategies.** Supportive cognitive-behavioral therapy and psychodynamic therapy alone or in combination with pharmacotherapy may help alleviate mild depressive or anxiety symptoms.

3. **Psychoeducation.** Patients often benefit from reassurance that menopause is not a disease but a natural stage of women's development. Psychiatrists should also educate patients about the hormonal changes and potential vasomotor, cognitive, and

psychological symptoms that sometimes accompany menopause. Patient education should also include clear distinctions between these normal symptoms and more disabling conditions, such as major depression and Axis I anxiety disorders. Psychiatrists should also make clear that HRT alone may treat hot flushes but does not treat major depression.

Suggested Readings

Burt VK, Suri R, Altshuler L, et al: The use of psychotropic medications during breastfeeding. *Am J Psychiatry* 2001;158:1001–1009.

Cohen LS, Rosenbaum JR: Psychotropic drug use during pregnancy: weighing the risks. *J Clin Psychiatry* 1998;59(Suppl 2):18–28.

Joffe H, Soares CN, Cohen LS: Assessment and treatment of hot flushes and menopausal mood disturbance. *Psychiatr Clin North Am* 2003;26:563–580.

Menopause Core Curriculum Study Guide, 2nd edition. Cleveland: North American Menopause Society, 2002.

Nonacs R, Cohen LS: Postpartum mood disorders: diagnosis and treatment guidelines. *J Clin Psychiatry* 1998;59(Suppl 2):34–40.

Schmidt PJ, Rubinow DR: Menopause-related affective disorders: a justification for further study. *Am J Psychiatry* 1991;148:844–852.

Viguera AC, Cohen LS, Baldessarini RJ, Nonacs R: Managing bipolar disorder during pregnancy: weighing the risks and benefits. *Can J Psychiatry* 2002;47:426–436.

Yerby M: Management issues for women with epilepsy. Neural tube defects and folic acid supplementation. *Neurology* 2003;61(Suppl 2):S23–S26.

Chapter 23

An Approach to the Use of Laboratory Tests

Felicia A. Smith, MD

I. Introduction

Although the diagnosis of psychiatric conditions relies primarily on a careful interview and an examination of the mental status, laboratory tests and neuroimaging often provide important adjunctive information. These tests are used to help distinguish medical and neurological causes of psychiatric symptoms from those produced by psychological conflicts, and to monitor the progression of certain illnesses. Laboratory tests are also important to keep track of blood levels and side effects of an assortment of psychotropic medications. Finally, advances in technology are creating exciting new methods of examination through neuroimaging. This chapter will provide a brief introduction to the many uses of laboratory tests and neuroimaging techniques in psychiatry today.

Since organic causes for psychiatric symptoms run the gamut of medical and neurologic conditions, a systematic review of systems and a physical examination are essential. Table 23-1 outlines potential organic causes of psychiatric symptoms. Moreover, certain clues (such as history of chronic medical illness, the onset of new psychiatric symptoms after the age of 40, and the sudden appearance of symptoms) should put an organic etiology higher on the differential. The following section describes specific laboratory studies and their potential uses in further detail.

II. Screening

The practice of routinely ordering screening tests (e.g., complete blood count [CBC], serum chemistries, vitamin B_{12} level, folate level, thyroid-stimulating hormone [TSH], rapid plasma reagin [RPR], and toxicology screens) for the work-up of new-onset psychiatric symptoms is controversial. **In current clinical practice, tests should be ordered selectively, with an emphasis placed on their sensitivity and specificity, their ease of administration, and their clinical implications (if results are abnormal).** Presence of specific clinical situations should suggest which studies are most appropriate. Some of these distinct presentations are described below.

Address for correspondence: Dr. Felicia A. Smith, Massachusetts General Hospital, Department of Psychiatry, Fruit Street, WACC 812, Boston, MA 02114, email: fsmith2@Partners.org.

Table 23-1. Medical and Neurological Causes for Psychiatric Symptoms

Metabolic	Hyper- or hyponatremia
	Hyper- or hypocalcemia
	Hypoglycemia
	Ketoacidosis
	Uremic encephalopathy
	Hepatic encephalopathy
	Hypoxemia
	Deficiency states (vitamin B_{12}, folate, and thiamine)
Infectious	HIV/AIDS
	Meningitis
	Encephalitis
	Brain abscess
	Sepsis
	Urinary tract infection
	Lyme disease
	Neurosyphilis
	Tuberculosis
Vascular	Vasculitis
	Cerebral vascular accident
	Multi-infarct dementia
	Hypertensive encephalopathy
Neoplastic	Central nervous system tumors
	Paraneoplastic syndromes
	Pancreatic and endocrine tumors
Intoxication or withdrawal	Acute or chronic drug or alcohol intoxication or withdrawal
	Medications (side effects, toxic levels, interactions)
	Heavy metals
	Environmental toxins
Autoimmune	Systemic lupus erythematosus
	Rheumatoid arthritis
	Sjögren's syndrome
Seizure	Post-ictal or intra-ictal states
	Temporal lobe epilepsy
	Complex partial seizures
Structural	Normal pressure hydrocephalus
Degenerative	Alzheimer's disease
	Parkinson's disease
	Pick's disease
	Huntington's disease
	Multiple sclerosis
	Wilson's disease
Traumatic	Intracranial hemorrhage
	Traumatic brain injury

Adapted from Roffman and Stern, 2004.

A.   Psychosis and Delirium
The onset of psychosis or delirium merits a full medical and neurological work-up. Since the differential diagnosis for these conditions is broad, an extensive list of organic causes for psychiatric symptoms is provided in Table 23-1. Having a systematic approach is therefore essential for clinicians and one is outlined in Table 23-2. Additional studies are warranted when the etiology remains unclear after performing a history, a physical examination, and screening laboratory tests as outlined. Further laboratory tests as listed in Table 23-2 should be ordered, based on clinical suspicion. For example, a patient at high risk for sexually transmitted diseases should be tested for human immunodeficiency virus (HIV) infection. The presence of fever or leukocytosis should prompt blood and urine cultures in the work-up of a systemic infection. Analysis of cerebrospinal fluid (CSF) by lumbar puncture (LP) must be considered in patients with fever, headache, or meningeal symptoms (after ruling out increased intracranial pressure). An electroencephalogram (EEG) may be performed to assess brain activity in a patient with a suspected seizure disorder, and it may also be of help in differentiating neurological from psychiatric etiologies in a patient who is unable to communicate. Finally, neuroimaging plays an important role in the work-up of new-onset psychosis or delirium, and it will be discussed later in this chapter.

B.   Mood Disorders
While depression is often of primarily psychological etiology, it may also be linked to certain medical conditions. **Clinical suspicion for thyroid dysfunction, Addison's disease, rheumatoid arthritis, systemic lupus erythematosus, anemia, folate deficiency, neurodegenerative disorders, and pancreatic cancer should drive pertinent further testing.** New-onset mania deserves a medical, neurological, and laboratory work-up on par with that of psychosis described earlier.

C.   Anxiety Disorders
The differential diagnosis of underlying medical conditions that may cause symptoms of anxiety is broad and covers a host of organ systems. A thorough medical and neurological review of systems once again guides diagnostic testing. A sampling of these causes and appropriate diagnostic testing is outlined in Table 23-3.

Table 23-2. Approach to the Initial Evaluation of Psychosis and Delirium

Screening tests
- Complete blood count (CBC)
- Serum chemistry panel
- Thyroid-stimulating hormone (TSH)
- Vitamin B_{12} level
- Folate level
- Syphilis serologies

Further laboratory tests based on clinical suspicion
- Liver function tests
- Urinalysis
- Blood or urine cultures
- Human immunodeficiency virus (HIV) test
- Toxicology (urine and serum)
- Erythrocyte sedimentation rate (ESR)
- Urine or serum β-human chorionic gonadotropin (in women of childbearing age)
- Ammonia
- Calcium
- Ceruloplasmin
- Serum heavy metals

Other diagnostic studies
- Lumbar puncture (cell count, appearance, opening pressure, Gram's stain, culture, specialized markers)
- Electroencephalogram (EEG)
- Electrocardiogram (ECG)
- Chest x-ray (CXR)
- Arterial blood gas

Neuroimaging
- Computed tomography (CT)
- Magnetic resonance imaging (MRI)

D.   **Substance Abuse Disorders**
       Intoxication and withdrawal from drugs are common causes of mental status changes. **Toxicology testing (of serum and urine) is routinely used to identify which substances have been ingested, while breathalyzer testing is also quite helpful in providing a rapid assessment of an alcohol level.** Since chronic alcohol use

Table 23-3. Organic Etiologies of Anxiety and Pertinent Diagnostic Tests

Condition	Screening Test
Hypoglycemia	Serum glucose
Thyroid dysfunction	Thyroid function tests
Parathyroid dysfunction	PTH, ionized calcium
Hyperadrenalism	Dexamethasone suppression test or 24-hour urine cortisol
Seizure	EEG
Head trauma	CT, MRI of brain
Intoxication/withdrawal (alcohol, drugs, medications)	Urine/serum toxicology, vital signs
Cardiac (myocardial infarction, mitral valve prolapse)	ECG, cardiac ultrasound
Menopause	Estrogen, FSH
Respiratory compromise (COPD, asthma)	Pulse oximetry, CXR, pulmonary function tests
Porphyria	Urine porphyrins
Pheochromocytoma	Urine vanillylmandelic acid

COPD, chronic obstructive pulmonary disease; CT, computed tomography; CXR, chest x-ray; ECG, electrocardiogram; EEG, electroencephalogram; PTH, parathyroid hormone; FSH, follicle-stimulating hormone; MRI, magnetic resonance imaging.

may lead to liver damage, liver transaminases, partial thromboplastin time (PTT), and an albumin level should be checked. A macrocytic anemia should prompt measurement of serum vitamin B_{12} and folate levels. While alcohol and benzodiazepine withdrawal are best diagnosed by signs and symptoms (e.g., elevation in heart rate and blood pressure and the presence of tremor and hyperreflexia), the presence of and changes in serum drug levels can be helpful. Hepatitis serologies and HIV testing should be undertaken in intravenous (IV) drug users who share needles. Finally, an electrocardiogram (ECG) should be checked in a cocaine abuser with cardiac symptoms, in a patient being treated with high doses of antipsychotic medications (to monitor for prolongation of the QTc interval), and in a person following a tricyclic antidepressant (TCA) overdose (given the prevalence of conduction system disturbances associated with such an ingestion).

E.   **Eating Disorders**
      **A patient who presents with a significant eating disorder should
      have screening laboratory tests to measure serum electrolytes
      and nutritional status.** Serum albumin levels or pre-albumin levels
      are useful measures in those with anorexia. A patient who purges, on
      the other hand, may show an elevated amylase, an elevated bicar-
      bonate (metabolic alkalosis), hypokalemia, and hypochloremia.
      Serum aldolase levels may be high in an ipecac abuser, while laxa-
      tive abuse may cause hypocalcemia.

F.   **Geriatric Patients**
      The geriatric population deserves special mention since the likeli-
      hood of medical comorbidity is higher in this group. While there is
      no consensus on screening, **the American Academy of Neurology
      recommends that geriatric patients with mental status changes
      have the following tests performed: thyroid function tests
      (TFTs), vitamin B_{12} level, and depression screening.** Others have
      suggested a urinalysis (U/A), chest x-ray (CXR), ECG, and blood
      urea nitrogen (BUN). Further testing as clinically indicated may
      include: computed tomography (CT), EEG, magnetic resonance
      imaging (MRI), and LP. If clinically indicated, HIV testing and
      syphilis testing should not be overlooked in the elderly.

III.   Monitoring Psychotropic Medications

Laboratory testing may also prove helpful in monitoring certain psychiatric
medications. **While some medications require monitoring of blood levels
because of potential adverse effects, levels may also be helpful in cases of
suspected noncompliance, poor response despite taking therapeutic
doses, and drug-drug interactions.** Table 23-4 lists mood stabilizers and
neuroleptics that require monitoring; specific parameters are provided for
each. Although there are no established guidelines for monitoring antidepressants, laboratory tests may be helpful in certain situations. For example,
selective serotonin reuptake inhibitors (SSRIs) and venlafaxine have been
shown to cause hyponatremia (especially in elderly patients); electrolyte
measurements may therefore be helpful based on clinical suspicion. TCAs
may cause arrhythmias and should be monitored with blood levels and an
ECG (especially in those over age 40 and those with a cardiac history).

IV.   Neuroimaging

A.   **Overview**
      Neuroimaging has become a powerful tool in the differential diag-
      nosis of organic causes of psychiatric conditions, and in neuropsy-
      chiatric research. Although neuroimaging alone rarely establishes a

Table 23-4. Monitoring Psychotropic Medications

Drug	Initial Tests	Blood Level Range	Warnings	Monitoring
Lithium	Electrolytes, BUN/Cr, CBC, TSH, U/A, ECG (if ≥35 years of age)	0.5–1.2 mEq/L	Lithium toxicity	Check level 8–12 h post–last dose once a week while titrating, then every 2 mo with electrolytes, BUN, Cr, TSH
Valproic acid	CBC with differential, LFTs	50–150 mEq/L	Hepatotoxicity, teratogenicity, pancreatitis	Weekly LFTs and CBC until stable dose; then monthly for 6 mo, then every 6–12 mo
Carbamazepine	CBC with differential, LFTs	6–12 µg/mL	Aplastic anemia, agranulocytosis, seizures, myocarditis	CBC, LFTs, drug level every 1–2 wk while titrating, then monthly for 4 mo, then every 6–12 mo
Oxcarbazepine	Electrolytes, BUN, Cr	10–35 µg/mL	None	Electrolytes
Clozapine	CBC with differential		Agranulocytosis, seizure, myocarditis	CBC with differential every week for 6 mo (or more frequently if WBC <3500 cells/mm^3), then every other week; weight, glucose
Olanzapine	Weight, glucose		None official (weight gain, diabetes, dyslipidemia)	Weight, glucose, lipid profile

BUN, blood urea nitrogen; CBC, complete blood cell count; Cr, creatinine; ECG, electrocardiogram; LFTs, liver function tests; TSH, thyroid-stimulating hormone; U/A, urinalysis; WBC, white blood cell count.
Adapted from Alpay and Park, 2004; Hirschfeld et al, 2004.

psychiatric diagnosis, its primary clinical utility at present is to rule out treatable brain lesions. Before ordering such testing, consideration must be given to the indications, risks, potential benefits, cost, and limitations of the testing. A careful history, review of systems, and physical examination should always be performed first—laboratory testing and neuroimaging then follow on a case-by-case basis. Table 23-5 outlines general guidelines for when to consider neuroimaging in the psychiatric patient. The following section reviews the pertinent types of neuroimaging and elaborates on the indications and limitations of neuroimaging in psychiatry.

B. Modalities of Neuroimaging

Contemporary modalities described here include structural (CT and MRI) and functional (positron emission tomography [PET] and single photon emission computed tomography [SPECT]) types. Emphasis will be placed on the structural modalities given their greater clinical applications, while the more research-oriented functional modalities will be briefly introduced.

1. **Computed tomography (CT)**

CT scanning uses x-rays to delineate cross-sectional views of the brain. The rays attenuate differently depending on the density of the material through which they pass, with denser areas (e.g., bone) appearing white and those of lower density (e.g., gas) showing up as black. Tumors, bleeds, and abscesses may be visualized through the use of contrast material (that leaks through areas of compromise in the blood-brain barrier). Idiosyncratic allergic reactions (including hypotension, nausea, urticaria, and possible anaphylaxis) occur in 5% of patients who receive contrast material. Chemotoxic reactions to contrast may

---

Table 23-5. Guidelines for Structural Neuroimaging in Psychiatry

- Acute change in mental status and one of the following:
  * Patient 50 years of age or older
  * Neurological abnormalities
  * Significant head trauma
- New-onset psychosis
- New-onset delirium or dementia of unknown etiology
- Prior to initiating electroconvulsive therapy

Adapted from Dougherty et al, 2004.

also occur in the brain and kidney; they may be manifest as seizures or renal insufficiency or failure, respectively. CT scanning is most useful in detecting acute bleeding (i.e., <72 hours old). It is not helpful to visualize subtle white matter lesions, and is contraindicated in pregnancy. CT is generally less expensive and more readily available than is MRI.

2. **Magnetic resonance imaging (MRI)**

MRI uses the magnetic properties of hydrogen (in water in the body) to form a representation of brain tissue. As nuclei are excited and relax, the energy given off constructs images. Since different components of tissue do this at different rates (called T1 and T2), specific imaging parameters may be selected depending on the clinical situation. T1-weighted images are best for viewing normal anatomy, while T2-weighted images highlight pathology. As in CT scanning, contrast material may be used with MRI to highlight areas of pathology where blood vessels or the blood-brain barrier has been compromised. Gadolinium (the contrast medium used with MRI) is safer than is CT contrast; only one death has been reported in over 5 million dosings (Dougherty et al, 2004). Diffusion-weighted imaging (DWI) is a type of MRI that tracks water movement in tissue; it is primarily used to detect ischemia. MRI is superior to CT in visualizing soft tissue (e.g., white matter), and for looking at the posterior fossa and the brain stem. It is preferable to CT in pregnancy, though it is still relatively contraindicated. MRI, however, is contraindicated in patients with metallic implants and is more difficult to tolerate for many patients (because the procedure is longer, louder, and more cramped). Table 23-6 provides a comparison of the benefits and limitations of CT and MRI.

3. **PET and SPECT**

PET and SPECT are forms of functional neuroimaging that use radioactive tracers to show neuronal activity, cellular metabolism, and neuroreceptor profiles. PET uses positron emission from tracers to measure glucose metabolism or blood flow in the brain. It is the gold standard of functional neuroimaging, but it is very expensive and requires access to a cyclotron (for the production of nucleotides). SPECT, on the other hand, measures single photon emission and is more affordable than PET (in large measure because it doesn't require proximity to a cyclotron). However, spatial resolution is inferior with SPECT (especially for deep brain structures). While these modalities are chiefly used for research purposes, a clinical role in psychiatry is emerging in the realms of dementia and seizures. For exam-

Table 23-6. Comparison of CT and MRI

Computed Tomography	Magnetic Resonance Imaging

Better in visualizing:
• Acute hemorrhage
• Acute trauma
• Subacute hemorrhage
No contraindication with
  metallic implants
More economical, available,
  and comfortable
	Better in visualizing:
	• Soft tissue
	• Posterior fossa and brain stem
	Less radiation exposure

ple, functional neuroimaging has been shown to be both sensitive and specific in differentiating Alzheimer's disease from other forms of dementia. In the seizure realm, PET is often able to find deep seizure foci that go undetected by EEG (which measures cortical surface electrical activity). Moreover, since PET is able to measure both ictal and interictal changes in metabolism, diagnosis does not rely on catching the patient during seizure activity as does the routine EEG. Finally, the use of PET in conjunction with an EEG enables more precise localization of seizure foci in a patient with known seizures who must undergo neurosurgical intervention.

V.   Conclusion

The diagnosis of psychiatric conditions continues to rely primarily on a careful interview and mental status examination; however, laboratory tests and neuroimaging often provide important adjunctive information. As discussed in this chapter, these tests may be used to help diagnose medical or neurological causes of psychiatric symptoms and to monitor progression of certain illnesses. Laboratory tests are also important to keep track of drug levels and side effects of some psychotropic medications as well as the function of bodily organs. Finally, neuroimaging provides a noninvasive means of diagnosing organic causes of psychiatric symptoms; it has exciting possibilities in the realm of neuropsychiatric research. Although the implications of both laboratory testing and imaging techniques are broad, responsible use of these modalities requires individualized consideration based on potential benefits, risks, ease of use, cost, and treatment implications.

Suggested Readings

Alpay M, Park L: Laboratory tests and diagnostic procedures. In Stern TA, Herman JB (eds): *Massachusetts General Hospital Psychiatry Update and Board Preparation,* 2nd edition. New York: McGraw-Hill, 2004:249–262.

Dougherty DD, Rauch SL, Luther K: Use of neuroimaging techniques. In Stern TA, Herman JB, Slavin PL (eds): *Massachusetts General Hospital Guide to Primary Care Psychiatry,* 2nd edition. New York: McGraw-Hill, 2004:61–66.

Hirschfeld RM, Perlis RH, Vornik LA: *Pharmacologic Treatment of Bipolar Disorder,* 2004 handbook. New York: MBL Communications, 2004.

Kirby D, Harrigan S, Ames D: Hyponatremia in elderly psychiatric patients treated with selective serotonin reuptake inhibitors and venlafaxine: a retrospective controlled study in an inpatient unit. *Int J Geriatr Psychiatry* 2002;17:231–237.

Knopman DS, DeKosky ST, Cummings JL, et al: Practice parameter: diagnosis of dementia (an evidence-based review). Report of the Quality Standards Subcommittee of the American Academy of Neurology. *Neurology* 2001;56: 1143–1153.

Kolman PB: The value of laboratory investigations of elderly psychiatric patients. *J Clin Psychiatry* 1984;45:112–116.

Roffman JL, Stern TA: Diagnostic rating scales and laboratory tests. In Stern TA, Fricchione GL, Cassem NH, et al (eds): *Massachusetts General Hospital Handbook of General Hospital Psychiatry,* 5th edition. Philadelphia: Mosby, 2004: 37–48.

Smith FA, Querques J, Levenson JL, Stern TA: Psychiatric assessment and consultation in the medical setting. In Levenson J (ed): *American Psychiatric Publishing, Inc./Academy of Psychosomatic Medicine Textbook of Psychosomatic Medicine.* 2004 (in press).

Chapter 24

Approaches to Psychological and Neuropsychological Assessment

MARK A. BLAIS, PSYD

MICHELLE C. JACOBO, PHD

I.   Psychological Assessment

Psychological tests can be conceptualized as standardized evaluation methods that have been **developed to deliver reliable and valid data** regarding many clinically important aspects of human function. **Psychological instruments** differ from clinical interviews in the degree that they **are standardized.** Standardization ensures that all subjects receive the same material (i.e., questions) presented in the same manner, and that responses are scored and interpreted consistently. Standardization also allows psychological tests to achieve greater reliability than clinical interviews.

A.   **Reliability**
      Reliability **represents the repeatability, stability, or consistency of a subject's test score.**
      1.   Reliability is represented as a correlation coefficient ranging from 0 to 1.0. Research instruments can have reliabilities in the low .70s, while clinical instruments should have reliabilities in the high .80s to low .90s.
      2.   An additional important aspect of reliability is that it sets the upper limit for the validity of the test.

B.   **Validity**
      Validity **reflects the degree to which a test measures the construct it was designed to measure.** Establishing the validity of a test is a complex and difficult process.
      1.   Like reliability, measures of validity are also represented as correlation coefficients ranging from 0 to 1.0. Multiple sources of validity data are required before a test and the interpretations made from the test can be considered clinically valid.
      2.   Two important types of validity are **content validity and predictive validity.**
           a.   **Content validity assesses the degree to which an instrument covers the full range of the target construct.**

Address for correspondence: Dr. Mark A. Blais, Massachusetts General Hospital, 55 Fruit Street, Blake 11, Boston, MA 02114, email: MBlais@ Partners.org.

      b. **Predictive validity indicates how well a test predicts future occurrences of the construct (e.g., depression).**

   3. It is important to realize that **no psychological test is universally valid. Tests are considered valid or not valid for a specific purpose.**

II. Types of Psychological Tests

A. Test of Intelligence
   Intelligence can be defined as "the aggregate or global capacity of the individual to act purposefully, to think rationally, and to deal effectively with the environment" (Matarazzo, 1979). Intelligence tests measure an important domain of adaptive functioning. Furthermore, the application of these tests can aid overall clinical assessment, particularly with regard to treatment planning.

   1. **The Wechsler Intelligence Quotient (IQ) tests** are the most commonly used IQ tests, which **assess individuals from early childhood throughout the life span.**

      a. The series starts with the Wechsler Preschool and Primary Scale of Intelligence (ages 4–6 years).

      b. It progresses to the Wechsler Intelligence Scale for Children-III (5–16 years of age).

      c. It ends with the Wechsler Adult Intelligence Scale-III for persons aged 16–89 (Wechsler, 1991 and Wechsler, 1997a).

      d. A new abbreviated version of the Wechsler IQ test is now available (Wechsler Abbreviated Scale of Intelligence [WASI]) (Wechsler, 1999).

   2. All the Wechsler scales provide three major IQ test scores: the Full Scale, Verbal, and Performance IQs. **All three IQ scores have a mean of 100 and standard deviations (SD) of 15.** These statistical features mean that a 15-point difference between a subject's Verbal and Performance IQ is both statistically and clinically meaningful. Table 24-1 presents an overview of the IQ categories.

   3. The Wechsler IQ tests **are composed of either 10 or 11 subtests** that tap into two primary intellectual domains: **verbal intelligence** (as measured by Vocabulary, Similarities, Arithmetic, Digit Span, Information, and Comprehension) and **nonverbal, visual-spatial intelligence** (as measured by Picture Completion, Digit Symbol, Block Design, Matrix Reasoning, and Picture Arrangement).

      a. Empirical studies have suggested that the Wechsler subscales can be reorganized into **four cognitive domains** and these have now been incorporated as supplemental scores provided by the test.

Table 24-1. Intelligence Quotient Categories with Their Corresponding Scores and Percentile Distribution

Full Scale IQ Score	Categories	Normal Distribution Percentile
≥130	Very superior	2.2
120–129	Superior	6.7
110–119	High average	16.1
90–109	Average	50.0
80–89	Low average	16.1
70–79	Borderline	6.7
≤69	Mentally retarded	2.2

      b. These four domains are: verbal ability (Verbal Comprehension Index), visual-spatial ability (Perceptual Organization Index), attention and concentration (Working Memory Index), and perceptual motor speed (Processing Speed Index).

      c. The availability of these empirically based scores (indices) allows clinicians to assess a patient's functioning along more specific and narrowly defined cognitive domains.

  4. All the **Wechsler subtests have a mean score of 10 and SD of 3.** Given this statistical feature we know that if two subtests differ by 3 or more scaled score points that the difference is significant.

      a. All IQ scores and **subtest scaled scores are adjusted for age.**

      b. It is important to understand that **IQ scores represent a patient's ordinal position,** their percentile ranking as it were, on the test relative to the normative sample.

      c. These scores do not represent a patient's innate intelligence and there is no good evidence that they measure genetically determined intelligence. On the other hand, they do to a considerable degree reflect the patient's current level of adaptive functioning.

B.   **Tests of Personality and Psychopathology**
Objective psychological tests, also called self-report tests, are designed to clarify and quantify a patient's personality functioning and psychopathology. Objective tests use a patient's re-

sponse to a series of true-false or multiple-choice questions to broadly assess multiple areas of psychological functioning. These tests are called "objective" because **their scoring involves little speculation.** Objective tests provide excellent insight into how patients see themselves and how they want others to see and treat them.

Validity scales are incorporated into all major objective tests to assess the degree to which a response style may have distorted the findings. The three main response styles are careless or random responding (which may indicate confusion or psychosis), attempting to "look good" by denying even minor psychological problems, and attempting to "look bad" by overreporting pathology (a cry for help or malingering).

1. **Objective psychological tests**
    a. **The Minnesota Multiphasic Personality Inventory-2 (MMPI-2) (Butcher et al, 1989) is a 567-item true-false, self-report test of psychological functioning.** It was designed to provide an objective measure of abnormal behavior (i.e., to separate subjects into two groups, normal and abnormal), and then to further categorize the abnormal group into specific classes (Greene, 2000).
        i.   The MMPI-2 **contains three validity scales, 10 clinical scales, and a number of content and special scales.**
        ii. MMPI scores are **reported as T-scores,** and T-scores ≥65 are taken to indicate clinical levels of psychopathology.
        iii. The MMPI-2 is interpreted by determining the highest two or three scales, called a *code type.* For example, a 2-4-7-code type indicates the presence of depression (scale 2) impulsivity (scale 4) and anxiety (scale 7) along with the likelihood of a personality disorder (Table 24-2; Greene, 2000).
    b. **The Millon Clinical Multiaxial Inventory-III (MCMI-III) is a 175-item true-false, self-report questionnaire designed to identify both symptom disorders (Axis I conditions) and personality disorders (PDs) (Millon, 1994).**
        i.   The MCMI-III is composed of three modifier indices (validity scales), ten basic personality scales, three severe personality scales, six clinical syndrome scales, and three severe clinical syndrome scales.
        ii. One of the unique features of the MCMI-III is that it attempts to assess both Axis I and Axis II psychopathology simultaneously.

Table 24-2. Behavioral Descriptions Associated with MMPI-2 Scale Elevations

Validity

(L) Lie: Unsophisticated effort to deny psychological problems

(F) Infrequency: Excessive endorsement of infrequent symptoms—looking bad

(K) Defensiveness: Sophisticated or subtle efforts to deny psychological problems

Clinical scales

(1) Hs-Hypochondriasis: Excessive concerns about vague physical complaints

(2) D-Depression: General sadness and depressed mood with guilt and isolation

(3) Hy-Conversion hysteria: Lack insight, deny psychological problems, focus on physical complaints

(4) Pd-Psychopathic deviate: Rebelliousness, hostility, and conflicts with authority figures

(5) Mf-Masculinity-femininity: Males passive, aesthetic and sensitive—females not interested in traditional feminine role

(6) Pa-Paranoia: Suspicious, hostile, and sensitive to criticism

(7) Pt-Psychasthenia: Worried, tense, and indecisive

(8) Sc-Schizophrenia: Alienated, remote, poor concentration and logic

(9) Ma-Hypomania: Overactive, emotionally-labile racing thoughts

(0) Si-Social introversion: Introverted, shy, lacking in social confidence

---

      iii. The Axis II scales resemble but are not identical to the DSM-IV-TR Axis II disorders.

      iv. Given its relatively short length (175 items vs. 567 for the MMPI-2) the MCMI-III has an advantage in the assessment of patients who are agitated, whose stamina is significantly impaired, or who are suboptimally motivated.

  c. **The Personality Assessment Inventory (PAI)** (Morey, 1991) is one of the newest objective psychological tests available.

      i. The PAI **uses 344 items and a four-point response format** (False, Slightly True, Mainly True, and Very True) to generate 22 nonoverlapping scales.

    ii.   These 22 scales include four validity scales, 11 clinical scales, five treatment scales, and two interpersonal scales.

    iii. The PAI **covers a wide range of Axis I and Axis II psychopathology** in addition to variables related to interpersonal functioning and treatment planning, including suicidal ideation, resistance to treatment, and aggression.

    iv. The PAI **possesses outstanding psychometric features** and is an ideal test for broadly assessing multiple domains of relevant psychological functioning.

2. **Projective tests of psychological functioning**

These tests differ from objective tests in that they are less structured and require more effort on the part of the patient. Projective tests are more like problem-solving tasks and they provide us with insights into a patient's style of perceiving, organizing, and responding to external and internal stimuli. While data from projective tests (such as the Rorschach) and objective tests (like the MMPI-2) show little correlation with each other, studies show that they add incrementally to the prediction of certain DSM-IV-TR diagnoses (Blais et al, 2001). When combined, data from objective and projective tests provide a complex multilayered description of a patient's functioning.

    a. **The Rorschach Inkblot Test (Rorschach, 1942/1921) consists of 10 cards that contain inkblots** (five black and white; two black, red, and white; and three composed of various pastels) for which the patient is required to say what the inkblot might be.

        i.   The test is administered in two phases. First, the patient is presented with the 10 inkblots one at a time and is asked, **"What might this be?"** Responses are recorded verbatim.

        ii. In the second phase, the examiner reviews the patient's responses and inquires **where on the card the response was seen** (known as *location* in Rorschach language) and what about the blot made it look that way (known as the *determinants*). For example, if a patient responded to Card V with "A flying bat." (Inquiry: "Can you show me where you saw that?") "Here I used the whole card," ("What made it look like a bat?") "The color, the black made it look like a bat to me." The details of this response would be captured in Exner's Rorschach language as follows: Wo FMa.FC'o A P 1.0.

      iii. **Interpretation of the Rorschach is mainly based on ratios and percentages derived from these codes rather than the patient's verbal responses.** Rorschach "scoring" has been criticized for being subjective. However, over the last 20 years, John Exner, Jr. (Exner, 1993) and his colleagues have developed a scoring system, the Comprehensive System, which has demonstrated acceptable levels of reliability. For example, interrater Kappas of $\geq.80$ are required for all Rorschach variables reported in research studies. Rorschach data are particularly useful for quantifying patients' reality contact and determining the quality of their thinking.

      iv. As a result, Rorschach **findings can help identify a subtle thought disorder or differentiate an affective psychosis from schizophrenia.**

  b. **The Thematic Apperception Test (TAT) is useful in revealing a patient's dominant motivations, emotions, and core personality conflicts (Murray, 1938).**

      i. The TAT is a series of **ambiguously drawn cards depicting people in various interpersonal interactions.**

      ii. The TAT is **administered by presenting 8 to 10 of these cards, one at a time,** with the instructions to: "Make up a story around this picture. Like all good stories it should have a beginning, middle, and an ending. Tell me how the people feel and what they are thinking."

      iii. While there is no standard scoring method for the TAT (making it more of a clinical technique than formal psychological test), when a sufficient number of cards are presented, reliable information can be obtained. Psychologists typically assess TAT stories for emotional themes, level of emotional and cognitive integration, interpersonal style, and view of the world (e.g., is it seen as a helpful or hurtful place?). This type of data can be particularly useful in predicting a patient's response to psychotherapy.

  c. Psychologists sometimes use **projective drawings** (free-hand drawings of human figures, families, houses, and trees) as a supplemental assessment procedure.

      i. These are clinical techniques rather than tests, as there are no formal scoring methods.

      ii. Despite their lack of psychometric grounding, projective drawings can sometimes be very revealing. For example, psychotic subjects may produce a human figure drawing that violates reality (i.e., it is transparent and shows internal organs). Still, such procedures are less reliable and less valid than the other tests reviewed in this chapter.

III.   Neuropsychological Assessment

A.   Overview

Many psychiatric conditions, particularly anxiety and depression, can produce transient neuropsychological deficits. Therefore, **a complete neuropsychological assessment should also include a self-report test of psychopathology** (such as the MMPI-2 or the PAI). Including such a test in the battery allows the neuropsychologist to assess the possible contribution of psychopathology to the cognitive profile. One of the main advantages of neuropsychological assessment is the ability to compare a patient's performance to that of a normative sample. This allows one to determine how well the patient performed relative to a comparison group. However, the usefulness of neuropsychological test data can be limited by the quality of such norms. Unfortunately, the quality of norms varies greatly from test to test. Tests like the Wechsler IQ and Memory scales have excellent norms, while other frequently used tests (like the Boston naming test) have severely limited norms. When working with the elderly it is most helpful to have age- and education-adjusted norms, as both of these variables have a substantial mediating effect on the normal (age-appropriate) decline of cognitive function.

Many neuropsychologists use a flexible battery of tests in their day-to-day clinical work. The test battery is usually **composed of an IQ test** (one of the Wechsler scales) and **a number of selected tests matched to the patient and to the disorder being evaluated.** We will review some of the specific neuropsychological tests that might be used in such a battery or to assess specific cognitive functions. (For a description of these tests see Spreen and Strauss, 1998.)

1.   **Intact attention and concentration are central to most complex cognitive processes;** therefore, it is important to adequately measure these functions in a neuropsychological test battery. In fact, some patients who complain of memory disorders will turn out to have impaired attention and concentration, rather than pure memory dysfunction.

a.   **Tests of attention and concentration include: Trail Making Test Parts A & B, Mental control subtests of the**

Wechsler Memory Scale-III, and the WAIS-III Digit Span, Digit Symbol, and Arithmetic Subtests.

2. **Language is assessed from a number of perspectives, including simple word recognition, reading comprehension, verbal fluency, object naming ability, and writing.**

    a. Frequently used measures of language functioning are: the WAIS-III Verbal IQ Subtests; the Boston Naming Test; the Verbal Fluency Test; Reading (word recognition and reading comprehension) and Written Expression (a writing sample).

    b. The accurate measurement of reading ability (often using the North American Adult Reading Tests, NAART) can provide an estimation of premorbid intelligence and allow the examiner to gauge the degree of overall cognitive decline.

3. **The assessment of memory is extremely important, as impaired memory is both a major reason for referral and a strong predictor of poor treatment outcome.**

    a. An evaluation of memory should cover both visual and auditory memory systems, measure immediate and delayed recall, assess the pattern and rate of new learning, and explore for differences between recognition (memory with a retrieval cue) and unaided recall.

        i.   **The Wechsler Memory Scale-III (WMS-III)** (Wechsler, 1997b) is one of the primary memory inventories.

        ii. The WMS-III is comprised of 11 subtests tapping into auditory and visual memory at both immediate and 30-minute delayed recall. It also provides indications of auditory and visual learning efficiency (new learning ability). Like the Wechsler IQ scales, this memory test is well standardized.

        iii. The WMS-III produces three major memory scores that have a mean of 100 with an SD of 15. The memory subscales all have a mean of 10 and an SD of 3. These statistical properties allow for a detailed evaluation of memory function. In fact, the most recent revision of the Wechsler IQ and Memory scales were jointly normed, allowing for more meaningful comparisons between IQ and memory.

        iv. **The Three Shapes and Three Words Memory Test** (Weintraub and Mesulam, 1985) is a less demanding test of verbal (written) and nonverbal immediate and delayed memory.

4. **Visual-spatial tests (usually with a motor component, drawing) help evaluate right hemisphere functions** in most (right-

handed) adults. Because these deficits are nonverbal (sometimes called *silent*) they are often overlooked in briefer nonquantitative cognitive evaluations.

    a. Tests that tap visual-spatial functioning include: the Rey-Osterreith Complex Figure, the Hooper Visual Integration Tests, the Draw-a-Clock Test, and the Performance IQ Subtests of the WAIS-III.

4. **Executive functioning refers to higher-order cognitive processes, such as judgment, planning, logical reasoning, and the modification of behavior based on external feedback.** These functions are thought to be associated with the frontal and prefrontal lobes and are extremely important for effective real-world functioning.

    a. One of the most frequently used tests of executive functioning is the **Wisconsin Card Sorting Test (WCST)**, which requires the patient to match 128 response cards to one of four stimulus cards using three possible dimensions (color, form, and number). A briefer 64-card version of the WCST is now available.

        i. While the patients match these cards, the only feedback they receive is if they are "right" or "wrong."

        ii. After 10 consecutive correct matches, the matching rule shifts to a new dimension (unannounced) and the patient must discover the "new" rule.

        iii. One of the primary scores from the WCST is the number of perseverative errors committed (a perseverative error is scored when the patient continues to sort to a dimension despite clear feedback that the strategy is incorrect).

    b. Other tests of executive functioning include: The Booklet Format Category Test, the Stroop Color Word Test, and the Similarities and Comprehension subtests of the WAIS-III (tapping abstract reasoning).

    c. Measures of tactile sensitivity and motor strength and speed are also important to measure in a neuropsychological examination. Typically, neuropsychologists are interested in both the absolute magnitude of the patient's performance (how well they performed in comparison to the test's norms) and any differences between the two body sides (the left-right discrepancies).

        i. Tests of motor functioning include the **Finger Tapping Test** (the average number of taps per 10 seconds with the index finger of each hand), and a test of grip strength (using the hand dynamometer).

ii. Sensory tests include Finger Localization Tests (naming and localizing fingers on the subject's and examiner's hand) and the **Two-Point Discrimination and Simultaneous Extinction test** (measuring two-point discrimination threshold and the extinction or suppression of sensory information by simultaneous bilateral activation).

B.   Neuropsychological tests and test batteries

1. **The Halstead-Reitan (H-R) Battery** (Reitan, 1986) is the oldest standardized neuropsychological assessment battery currently in use. The H-R battery is an elaborate and time-intensive set of neuropsychological tests.

    a. Analysis of a H-R battery is almost exclusively quantitative.

    b. The H-R profile is interpreted at four levels: an Impairment Index (a composite score reflecting the subject's overall performance); lateralizing signs; localizing signs; and a pattern analysis for inferences of etiology (Spreen and Strauss, 1998).

2. **The Boston process approach** (Milberg et al, 1986) to neuropsychological assessment is a newer and more flexible style of neuropsychological assessment. The Boston process approach starts with a small core test battery (usually containing one of the Wechsler IQ tests); subsequently, hypotheses regarding cognitive deficits are developed, based on the patient's performance.

    a. Other instruments are then administered to test and refine hypotheses about the patient's cognitive deficits.

    b. The Boston approach focuses on both the quantitative and qualitative aspects of a patient's performance. Qualitative refers to the manner or style of the patient's performance, not just the accuracy. In fact, reviewing how a patient failed an item can be more revealing than knowing which items were missed. In this way the Boston approach reflects an integration of features from behavioral neurology and psychometric assessment.

3. A number of **brief neuropsychological assessment tools** are used in clinical practice. Brief assessment tools are not a substitute for a comprehensive neuropsychological assessment, but they can be useful as screening instruments or when patients cannot tolerate a complete test battery.

    a. One such test is the **Dementia Rating Scale-2 (DRS-2)** (Jurica et al, 2001). This test provides a brief but reasonable assessment of the major areas of cognitive functioning (attention, memory, language, reasoning, and construction).

i.   The test employs a screening methodology in evaluating these cognitive domains, with the patient first being presented with a moderately difficult item; if that item is passed, the rest of the items in that domain are skipped (with the examiner moving on to the next domain). However, if the screening item is failed, then a series of easier items are given to more fully evaluate the specific cognitive ability.

ii. The DRS-2 is a useful tool for assessing patients (55 years of age and older) who are suspected of having Dementia of the Alzheimer's Type (DAT).

iii. It takes between 10 and 20 minutes to administer and it provides six scores.

iv. The total score and the scores from the Memory and Initiation/Perseveration subscales have been useful in the identification of patients with DAT. The DRS was designed to have a deep "floor." This means that the test contains many items that tap low levels of function; thus, it tracks patients as their function declines. This quality makes the DRS a useful tool for monitoring patients with DAT along the course of their illness.

IV.   Common Reasons for Neuropsychiatric Testing

A.   **Differentiation between Depression and Dementia**
The differentiation of depression from dementia in the elderly is the most common neuropsychological referral question. Depression in the elderly is often accompanied by mild cognitive deficits, making the diagnostic picture somewhat confused with that of early dementia. By evaluating the profile of deficits obtained across a battery of tests, a neuropsychologist can help distinguish between these two illnesses. For example, depressed patients tend to have problems with attention, concentration, and memory (new learning and retrieval), while patients with early dementia have problems with delayed recall memory (encoding) and word-finding or naming problems. Both groups of patients can display problems with frontal lobe/executive function.

1.   However, the functioning of the depressed patient will often improve with cues or suggestions about strategies; this typically does not help patients with dementia. While this general pattern will not always hold true, it is this type of contrasting per-

formance that allows neuropsychological assessment to aid differential diagnosis.

B.   Determining Capacity for Independent Living
Whether or not a patient is capable of living independently is a complex and often emotionally charged question. Neuropsychological test data can provide one piece of the information needed to make a reasonable medical decision in this area.

1. In particular, neuropsychological test data regarding **memory functioning** (both new learning rate and delayed recall) and **executive functioning** (judgment and planning) have been shown to predict failure and success in independent living.

2. However, any **neuropsychological test data should be thoughtfully combined with information from an Occupational Therapy (OT) evaluation,** assessment of the patient's psychiatric status, and input from the family (when available) before rendering any judgment about a patient's capacity for independent living.

C.   The Diagnosis of Attention Deficit Disorder
Neuropsychological assessment has a role in the diagnosis and treatment of adults and children with Attention Deficit Disorder (ADD). However, as in the question of independent living status, it provides just one piece of the data necessary for making this diagnosis.

1. **The evaluation of ADD should include a detailed review of academic performance, including report cards and school records.** When possible, living parents should also be interviewed for their recollections of the patient's childhood behavior.

2. The neuropsychological evaluation should focus on **measuring intelligence, academic achievement** (expecting to see normal or better IQ with reduced academic achievement), **and multiple measures of attention and concentration** (with tests of passive, active [shifting], and sustained attention). While the neuropsychological testing profile might aid the diagnosis of ADD in adulthood, the diagnosis is usually based on historical data.

3. The neuropsychological test data or profile is often useful in helping the patient, the family, and the treating professional understand the impact of ADD on the patient's current cognitive abilities, as well as ruling out comorbid disorders (such as learning disabilities, which are very common in ADD).

D.   **Neuropsychological Assessments**
        As an Aid in Treatment Planning

Neuropsychological assessments can often aid in treatment planning for patients with moderate to severe psychiatric illness. While this aspect of neuropsychological testing is somewhat underutilized at present, in the years to come this may prove to be the most beneficial use of these tests.

1. **Neuropsychological assessment benefits treatment planning by providing objective data regarding the patient's cognitive skills (deficits and strengths).**

   a. The availability of such data can help clinicians and family members develop more realistic expectations about the patient's functional capacity (Keefe, 1995). Such data can be particularly helpful for patients suffering from severe disorders, such as schizophrenia. The current literature indicates that neuropsychological deficits are more predictive of long-term outcome in schizophrenic patients than are either positive or negative symptoms.

V.   Tips for Ordering and Understanding Test Reports

A.   **An Approach to Referral for Testing**

Referring a patient for an assessment should be approached like referring to any other professional colleague. Psychological and neuropsychological testing cannot be done "blind."

1. The consulting psychologist will want to hear relevant information about the case and will explore with you what question(s) you want answered as a way of developing a referral question.

2. Based on this case discussion the psychologist will select an appropriate battery of tests designed to obtain the desired information.

3. It is helpful if you prepare your patient for the testing by reviewing with him or her why the consultation is desired and telling him or her that it will likely take three or more hours to complete.

4. You should expect the psychologist to evaluate your patient in a timely manner and to provide you with verbal feedback, and an initial impression of the data, within a day or so of the testing.

5. The written report should follow shortly thereafter (inpatient reports should be produced within 48 hours and outpatient reports should be available within 2 weeks).

B.   The Psychological Assessment Report
1. The psychological assessment report is the written statement of the psychologist's findings. **It should be written in a manner that is understandable and it should plainly state and answer the referral question(s).**
    a. The report should contain: relevant background information, a list of the tests used in the consultation, a statement about the validity of the results and the confidence the psychologist has in the findings, a detailed integrated description of the patient based mainly on the test data, and it should close with clear realistic recommendations.
    b. It should contain raw data (e.g., IQ scores) as appropriate to allow for meaningful follow-up testing.
    c. To a considerable degree the quality of a report (and the assessment consultation) can be judged from the recommendations provided.
    d. A good assessment report should contain a number of useful recommendations.
    e. You should never read just the summary of a test report; this leads to the loss of important information, as the whole report is really a summary of a very complex consultation process.
2. In contrast to the written report from a personality assessment, **the written neuropsychological testing report tends to be less integrated.**
    a. Typically the test findings are provided and reviewed for each major area of cognitive functioning (intelligence, attention, memory, language, reasoning, and construction).
    b. These reports often contain substantial amounts of raw data (along with test means and standard deviations) to allow for meaningful retesting comparison.
    c. However, the neuropsychological assessment report should provide a brief summary that reviews and integrates the major findings and also contains useful and meaningful recommendations.
    d. As with all professional consultations, the examining psychologist should be available, within reason, to meet with you and/or your patient to review and explain the findings.

References

Blais M, Hilsenroth M, Castelbury F, et al: Predicting DSM-IV cluster B personality disorders from MMPI-2 and Rorschach data: A test of incremental validity. *J Pers Asses* 2001;76:150–168.

Butcher J, Dahlstrom W, Graham J, et al: *MMPI-2: Manual for Administration and Scoring.* Minneapolis: University of Minnesota Press, 1989.

Exner J: *The Rorschach: A Comprehensive System, Vol. 1 Basic Foundations,* 3rd edition. New York: Wiley & Sons, 1993.

Greene R: *The MMPI-2/MMPI: An Interpretive Manual,* 2nd edition. Boston: Allyn and Bacon, 2000.

Jurica P, Leitten C, Mattis S: *Dementia Rating Scale-2 (DRS-2): Professional Manual.* Odessa, FL: Psychological Assessment Resources, 2001.

Keefe R: The contribution of neuropsychology to psychiatry. *Am J Psychiatry* 1995; 152:6–14.

Matarazzo J: *Wechsler's Measurement and Appraisal of Adult Intelligence.* New York: Oxford University Press, 1979.

Milberg W, Hebben N, Kaplan E: The Boston process neuropsychological approach to neuropsychological assessment. In Grant I, Adams K (eds): *Neuropsychological Assessment of Neuropsychiatric Disorders,* 1st edition. New York: Oxford University Press, 1986.

Millon T: *Millon Clinical Multiaxial Inventory-III Manual.* Minneapolis: National Computer Systems, 1994.

Morey L: *The Personality Assessment Inventory: Professional Manual.* Odessa, FL: Psychological Assessment Resources, 1991.

Murray H: *Explorations in Personality.* New York: Oxford University Press, 1938.

Reitan R: Theoretical and methodological bases of the Halstead-Reitan neuropsychological test battery. In Grant I, Adams K (eds): *Neuropsychological Assessment of Neuropsychiatric Disorders,* 1st edition. New York: Oxford University Press, 1986.

Rorschach H: *Psychodiagnostics.* New York: Grune & Stratton, 1942/1921.

Spreen O, Strauss E: *A Compendium of Neuropsychological Tests,* 2nd edition. New York: Oxford University Press, 1998.

Wechsler D: *Manual for the Wechsler Adult Intelligence Scale-III.* New York: Psychological Corporation, 1997a.

Wechsler D: *Manual for the Wechsler Intelligence Scale for Children-III.* New York: Psychological Corporation, 1991.

Wechsler D: *Wechsler Abbreviated Scale of Intelligence [WASI].* New York: Psychological Corporation, 1999.

Wechsler D: *Wechsler Memory Scale-III.* New York: Psychological Corporation, 1997b.

Weintraub S, Mesulam M-M: Mental state assessments of young and elderly adults in behavioral neurology. In Mesulam M-M (ed): *Principles of Behavioral Neurology.* Philadelphia: FA Davis, 1985.

Chapter 25

An Approach to the Geriatric Patient

M. CORNELIA CREMENS, MD, MPH

I. Assessment of the Geriatric Patient

A. Overview

As the population of persons over 65 years of age grows (reflecting improvements in health, nutrition, and medical care) the burden of caring for these patients by primary care providers (PCPs), psychiatrists, family members, and caregivers is mushrooming. **Despite improvements in care and technology, the prevalence of medical and psychiatric illness increases with age.** Older patients are more susceptible to physical decline and frailty related to superimposed medical or psychiatric illness. In addition, the numerous medications prescribed for comorbid diseases places another layer of complexity into this tenuous mix of variables. With aging there is a greater variability in pharmacodynamics and pharmacokinetics that requires closer monitoring when initiating or discontinuing medications. **Reduced lean body mass and body water, combined with increased body fat, result in greater availability of water-soluble drugs and lower availability of fat-soluble drugs. Diminished hepatic and renal function result in impaired metabolism and excretion of medications.**

B. Evaluation

The most frequent issues encountered in the evaluation of older patients are dementia, delirium, and depression; these conditions are often complicated by medical illness, substance abuse, and anxiety.

1. **Initial evaluation of the geriatric patient begins with the establishment of rapport with the patient and the family.** Usually the elderly have been referred by a medical professional or been brought by their family for evaluation, rather than being self-referred for psychiatric care.
2. **Identifying the presenting problem can be time-consuming; multiple comorbid problems often confound psychiatric complaints.**

Address for correspondence: Dr. M. Cornelia Cremens, 100 Charles River Plaza (CPZ/100-5-502), Boston, MA 02114, email: mcremens@partners.org.

3. **Common geriatric syndromes include: delirium, depression, dementia, falls, immobility, frailty, incontinence, constipation, failure to thrive, impaired capacity, and sensory impairments.** These syndromes are important to identify and to treat. When illness strikes, geriatric patients may rapidly become unable to perform activities of daily living and to remain independent.

II.   Dementia

A.   **Overview**
The prevalence of dementia is increasing as the population ages; **currently approximately 5–15% of patients over the age of 65 and almost 50% of those over the age of 85 have some type of dementia.** Dementia of the Alzheimer's type (DAT), the most common type of dementia, affects 5–10% of the population over the age of 65 years, 15–20% over the age of 75 years, and 25–50% over the age of 85 years.

1. **Dementia, an acquired syndrome, presents with a decline in memory and a decline in at least one other cognitive domain** (e.g., language, visuo-spatial, or executive function that is sufficient to interfere with social or occupational functioning). The decline in intellectual function is slow, yet persistent; eventually the patient is unable to perform activities of daily living. Memory deficits are a principal component of dementia, and the deterioration of intellectual functioning occurs over months to years. Prevalence rates of dementia and cognitive impairment are reported to be higher in women; **rates of DAT are higher in women while rates of vascular dementia are higher in men.** In DAT, the decline is gradual but steady over a period of 8–10 years.

2. *Mild cognitive impairment* **(MCI) describes the functional and cognitive abilities in the state between normal aging and very mild DAT.** It is important to follow MCI, as it predisposes to the development of subsequent dementia. A patient with mild dementia is also at greater risk for delirium and for serious behavioral problems.

B.   **Differential Diagnosis**
Dementia may be due to DAT, vascular dementia, diffuse Lewy body disease, trauma (to the central nervous system), Parkinson's disease, Creutzfeldt-Jakob disease, Huntington's disease, Pick's disease, or human immunodeficiency virus (HIV) infection.

1. **Potentially reversible causes of symptoms that resemble those of dementia include thyroid dysfunction, deficiencies of vitamins (e.g., B$_{12}$ and folate), infections, metabolic abnormalities, and normal-pressure hydrocephalus (NPH).**

C. **Clinical Manifestations**
   1. DAT is the most common type of dementia; vascular dementia is the second most common type, but it often coexists with DAT and they are difficult diagnoses to tease apart.
   2. **Vascular dementia presents with a stepwise decline in function; it is not global.** In this patient population a history of coronary artery disease (CAD) is common; dementia develops in about 8% of patients who have had a stroke.
   3. **Diffuse Lewy body disease (LBD), a type of dementia with more emotional lability and perceptual disturbances,** was diagnosed initially as DAT by many physicians. However, **patients with LBD often present with a Parkinson's-like gait deficit, visual hallucinations, and fluctuations in cognition.** Recognizing LBD is important, as these patients are exquisitely sensitive to the side effects of psychotropic medications.

D. **Treatment**
   Treatment for dementia remains controversial. **Cholinesterase inhibitors are used to treat a variety of dementias, not just DAT.** Prescribing cholinesterase inhibitors to reduce the behavioral symptoms and to improve function with activities of daily living has a dramatic impact on quality of life, and a limited impact on the eventual course of the disease. **Medications currently available are donepezil, rivastigmine, galantamine, and memantine.**
   1. **Donepezil has been the most widely used, as its once-daily dosing is convenient;** all are somewhat effective; their aim is to slow down the rate of cognitive decline. Side effects are minimal with all of these medications; however, in a given individual one medication may be better tolerated than another.
      a. Donepezil, rivastigmine, and galantamine have a cholinomimetic mechanism of action, while memantine has an antiglutaminergic mechanism.
   2. **Memantine is indicated for moderate to severe DAT.** The goal of treatment is to slow the rate of decline; there is no evidence to suggest that these agents provide significant improvement or prevent the ultimate prognosis of death.

III. Depression

A. Overview

Mood disorders, including those that present later in life, are a major public health problem. Moreover, the prevalence of depression in late life is increasing. Unfortunately, depression increases the mortality in elderly persons with comorbid medical illness. Depression in this cohort is associated with the highest rate of suicide of any age group in the United States. Alcohol increases both the risk of depression and suicide in all age groups, especially in the elderly.

B. Epidemiology

1. **Major depression following stroke is common, occurring in one-quarter to one-half of poststroke patients.** Approximately 50% of all patients with neurological diseases, cardiac diseases, and cancer have depressive symptoms.

2. **The prevalence of major depression in DAT is in the range of 10%, and with Parkinson's disease (PD) it is approximately 20%.**

3. However, in the elderly somatic complaints can be the primary manifestation of depression. These physical complaints can mimic a variety of medical problems (e.g., chest pain, headache, joint pain, nausea, dizziness, and weakness). When medications are prescribed for a patient's numerous medical problems, addition of an antidepressant may alter the metabolism and drug levels of other medications.

C. Treatment

1. **Side effects of antidepressants should be reviewed and tailored to treat target symptoms.** For example, if a patient has poor sleep and weight loss, then one can select a sedating medication (to be given at night) that causes weight gain.

2. **Depression complicates recovery from medical or surgical problems, and therefore it should be treated.** Stimulants can be used alone or in conjunction with an antidepressant when a more urgent response is needed. Electroconvulsive therapy (ECT) for refractory patients and for patients with psychosis should be considered and discussed with the patient and the family early in the course of the illness.

IV.   Bipolar Disorder

A.   **Overview**

Many older patients develop bipolar disorder in mid- or late-life and following a neurological insult. Such patients (with comorbid neurological diseases) have a later onset and are less likely to have a family history of affective illness. Biological risk factors for bipolar mood disorders in the elderly include genetic factors and medical illnesses, particularly vascular diseases. Many patients with dementia or delirium present with secondary mania. Treatment of the symptoms of mania is the same for patients with both bipolar illness and secondary mania, but an accurate diagnosis is beneficial for prognosis.

V.   Delirium

A.   **Overview**

Delirium is difficult to diagnose in the elderly due to symptoms suggestive of medical illness and symptoms attributed to aging. The elderly are more vulnerable to delirium because of medical illness, changes in brain function, brain injuries (such as dementia), reduced hepatic metabolism, and reduced sensory input.

B.   **Epidemiology**

Patients at greatest risk for delirium are >65 years of age, brain-injured (including dementia and strokes), post–cardiac surgery, burned, withdrawing from substances, or plagued by autoimmune disorders. Mortality and morbidity are high in elderly patients with delirium; about 30% will die within the year after their illness, often as a result of the problem that is responsible for the delirium.

C.   **Work-Up**

A comprehensive medical evaluation and examination, as well as an assessment of oxygenation, infections (urinary tract infections are common in the elderly), and review of medications and medication compliance are essential to discerning the etiology of the delirium.

D.   **Clinical Manifestations**

1.   **The clinical features of delirium include a prodromal phase, an abrupt onset, a rapidly fluctuating course, disorientation, decreased attention, altered arousal, psychomotor changes, a disturbed sleep-wake cycle, impaired memory, disorganized thinking, disordered speech, hallucinations (usually**

visual), delusions (persecutory), and altered perceptions. Neurological abnormalities include dysphagia, constructional apraxia, dysnomic aphasia, motor abnormalities, and an abnormal EEG. Emotional disturbances can be prominent (e.g., with intense anger or fear, mania, irritability, depression, euphoria, sadness, rage, apathy, anxiety, or panic). Hyperactive, hypoactive, or mixed clinical subtypes of delirium are widely accepted, with the hyperactive type more frequently reported. Motor subtypes are perplexing in that patients with agitation are more often diagnosed, while those with hypoactive or mixed states may go undiagnosed. There is no significant difference in terms of etiology or outcome between clinical subtypes. The variety of presentations of delirium further confuses the diagnosis, hence the discrepancy about diagnosis between neurologists and psychiatrists. As opposed to dementia, delirium has an abrupt onset of symptoms, which can develop over hours to days and rarely weeks.

2. **Patients with dementia may be paranoid, suspicious, and mistrustful of caregivers, even of close family members.** Delusions are common in dementia; they present as fixed, false ideas or beliefs that even persist when given evidence to the contrary. Hallucinations are usually visual; they may range from a dreamlike state to terrifying visions that appear real but may be related to dementia without delirium. Prolonged memory impairment in patients who have had delirium can persist in half of all patients; it may be permanent. Nursing home patients and patients with dementia are at greater risk of delirium due to their impaired status.

3. Symptoms of delirium in the elderly can persist for up to 12 months after the initial hospitalization; mortality rates also increase after an episode of delirium. Patients with an underlying dementia are at greater risk for delirium; the use of cholinesterase inhibitors has been studied to reduce the risk.

E.   **Management**
Management of delirium is multifaceted. **Identification and diagnosis is key; specific treatment of the underlying cause is preferred.**

1. **Contributing factors should be eliminated to avoid worsening of the delirium.** Anticholinergic medications should be avoided, as they are frequently responsible for delirium. Diphenhydramine, a common medication given to patients of all ages for sleep, can be problematic in an elderly patient due to its strong anticholinergic properties.

2. **Low doses of antipsychotic medication, either typical or atypical agents, are usually adequate to treat delirium in the elderly;** the dose should be increased slowly in order not to overshoot the target dosing.

3. **Restraints may be required to prevent a delirious patient from getting out of bed and falling and developing a hip fracture.** Hip fractures are associated with a greater risk of delirium. On the other hand, the risks associated with restraints may be greater among the elderly, and other, less restrictive means to prevent falls should be considered, if possible.

4. **Whenever possible a family member or another familiar person should stay with the patient to reorient them;** this may obviate the need for medications or restraints. However, in a patient with significant delirium, both restraint and medication may be indicated.

5. **When patients are uncooperative or unable to take oral medications, intravenous haloperidol can be used** to sedate and to reduce the psychotic symptoms of the delirium. Elderly patients are initially started on lower doses (such as 0.5–2.0 mg of IV haloperidol) and increased as necessary.

6. **Atypical antipsychotics have been successful in the treatment of delirium and agitation in elderly and critically ill patients.** Again, the doses must be titrated slowly to minimize adverse side effects. Patients are maintained on the optimal dose until the symptoms resolve.

VI. Psychosis

A. Overview

Criteria for the diagnosis of psychosis include one or more of the following: delusions, hallucinations, disorganized speech, or disorganized or catatonic behavior. Delusions often involve several themes: stolen items or infidelity, not recognizing familiar items, and being afraid of being alone or of being abandoned. Hallucinations may relate to sensory losses or involve visual, auditory, and rarely tactile modalities. Frequent misconceptions include misperceiving objects, not recognizing oneself, or perceiving designs or objects as real.

While psychosis is most commonly associated with schizophrenia and delusional disorders, **in the elderly delirium and psychosis are more commonly associated with dementia.**

Side effects associated with medications complicate the treatment of psychosis. **Drugs that possess anticholinergic, orthostatic, sedative, and extrapyramidal symptoms are relatively con-**

traindicated. The elderly are more susceptible to tardive dyskinesia than are other populations. Conventional antipsychotic medications have more adverse side effects; higher-potency agents are more useful than are the lower-potency ones. Atypical antipsychotics are most useful in this population because of their sedative properties and their lack of extrapyramidal symptoms when used in lower doses. These atypical antipsychotics have more beneficial side effects, such as sedation, anxiolysis, and reduction of aggression in dementia. Dose equivalents of the atypical antipsychotics (using 100 mg/d of chlorpromazine as the standard) are as follows: 2 mg/d for risperidone, 5 mg/d for olanzapine, 75 mg/d for quetiapine, 60 mg/d for ziprasidone, and 7.5 mg/d for aripiprazole. The caveat "start low and titrate up slowly" remains the key principle. In certain instances when agitation is the primary symptom but psychosis is absent, other medications, such as selective serotonin reuptake inhibitors (to reduce anger) or other antidepressants (that may sedate and be calming) can help.

VII. Substance Abuse and Withdrawal

A. Overview

Alcoholism, especially in the elderly, often goes unreported or overlooked. A lifelong pattern of daily drinking, even small amounts, is problematic and withdrawal can occur even after use of smaller amounts chronically in the elderly. The prevalence of alcoholism in this population is about 10–20%. As with the general population, the risk of suicide in the older alcoholic is staggering; it is second only to major depression.

1. **Older alcoholics refuse treatment because of denial of the problem and perceived negative stigma.**

2. Alcohol withdrawal is characterized by two or more of the following symptoms: autonomic hyperactivity; tremor; insomnia; nausea or vomiting; transient visual, tactile, or auditory hallucinations or illusions; psychomotor agitation; anxiety; or tonic-clonic seizures.

3. With aging the volume of distribution is reduced; this results in an increased concentration after any amount of alcohol is consumed.

4. Comorbid illness confounds an accurate diagnosis of both alcoholism and its medical presentations.

5. Treatment of withdrawal in the elderly must be aggressive and be closely monitored. Shorter-acting benzodiazepines are the medications of choice; one should begin with low doses and increase them slowly in order to avoid oversedation. Some older

patients require larger doses and longer-acting benzodiazepines (especially when a history of seizures or delirium tremens [DTs] is present). Chronic alcoholics with a history of DTs or seizures should be treated with benzodiazepines with long-acting metabolites in an effort to provide a slow taper and to reduce the risk of seizures. Most importantly, aggressive treatment of symptoms limits the possibility of complications due to withdrawal or development of delirium tremens.

VIII. Anxiety

A.   Overview

Anxiety disorders have not been as widely studied in the context of depression and dementia. **The strongest risk factor for anxiety in the elderly is the patient's loss of control.** Vulnerability and stress contribute to worse symptoms of anxiety. All of these risk factors are common to elderly hospitalized patients.

Many antidepressants have indications for treatment of anxiety and are effective. Trazodone and mirtazapine are used more frequently due to their sedating properties. However, benzodiazepines remain the standard for rapid treatment for inpatients and outpatients. Benzodiazepines should be used cautiously, as some older patients may have a paradoxical reaction, become oversedated, or fall.

IX.   Families and Caregivers

A.   Overview

Dementia causes a high burden of suffering for patients, for their families, and for society. Patients are forced to become more dependent and to lose their independence in basic self-care, which can complicate comorbid conditions. Family members or caregivers can develop anxiety, depression, and become isolated due to the increased time spent caring for a patient. While caring for the patient it is important to watch out for caregivers of the patient.

X. Elder Abuse

A.   Overview

Each year thousands of elderly are abused, neglected, and exploited (by spouses, family members, and caregivers). Many of the elderly are frail and vulnerable and depend on those who abuse to assist them. These issues result in noncompliance with medications or medical care. All fifty states have toll-free hotlines to report concerns anonymously. Adult protective services (APS) agencies will then investigate the reports and determine if abuse or neglect exists. However, elders can refuse the assistance unless they lack the capacity to makes decisions independently. Types of abuse are physical, sexual, psychological, and financial, and involve exploitation and neglect. The group at greatest risk is those over the age of 80 years; they are certainly the most frail. **In 90% of cases, the person responsible for the abuse is a family member.** The warning signs are subtle and a patient may not be willing to cooperate or to agree to go forward with the investigation. Family members or caregivers may be overwhelmed, depressed, or physically unable to continue to care for the patient, and the APS can guide them to appropriate services.

Suggested Readings

Blow FC, Barry KL: Older patients with at risk and problem drinking patterns: New developments and brief interventions. *J Geriatr Psychiatry Neurol* 2000;13:134–140.

Brodaty H, Green A, Koschera A: Meta-analysis of psychosocial interventions for caregivers of people with dementia. *J Am Geriatr Soc* 2003;51:657–664.

Bruce ML, Ten Have TR, Reynolds CF, et al: Reducing suicidal ideation and depressive symptoms in depressed older primary care patients. *JAMA* 2004;291:1081–1091.

Cremens MC, Goldstein LE, Gottlieb GL: Geriatric psychiatry. In Stern TA, Herman JB (eds): *Psychiatry Update and Board Preparation,* 2nd edition. New York: McGraw-Hill, 2004.

Cremens MC, Gottlieb GL: Acute confusional state: Delirium, encephalopathy. In Sirven JI, Malamut BL (eds): *Clinical Neurology of the Older Adult.* Philadelphia: Lippincott Williams & Wilkins, 2002.

Cremens MC, Jenike MA: Management of Alzheimer's disease and related disorders. In Goroll AH, Mulley AG (eds): *Primary Care Medicine,* 4th edition. Philadelphia: Lippincott Williams & Wilkins, 2000.

Cremens MC, Langan ML: Approach to the geriatric patient. In Stern TA, Herman JB, Slavin PL (eds): *The MGH Guide to Primary Care Psychiatry,* 2nd edition. New York: McGraw-Hill, 2004.

Cremens MC, Okereke OI: Alzheimer's disease and dementia. In Carlson KJ, Eisenstat SA (eds): *Primary Care of Women,* 2nd edition. St. Louis: Mosby, 2002.

Cremens MC: Polypharmacy in the elderly. In Ghaemi SN (ed): *Polypharmacy in Psychiatry.* New York: Marcel Dekker, 2002.

Cummings JL, Mega SM: *Neuropsychiatry and Behavioral Neuroscience.* New York: Oxford University Press, 2003.

Cummings JL: Use of cholinesterase inhibitors in clinical practice: Evidence-based recommendations. *Am J Geriatr Psychaitry* 2003;11:131–145.

Feldman H, Gauthier S, Hecker J, et al: Efficacy of donepezil on maintenance of activities of daily living in patients with moderate to severe Alzheimer's disease and the effect of caregiver burden. *Am J Geriatr Soc* 2003;51:737–744.

Folstein MF, Folstein SE, McHugh PR: Mini-mental state: a practical method for grading the cognitive state of patients for the clinician. *J Psychiatr Res* 1975; 12:189–198.

Geldmacher DS, Whitehouse PJ: Evaluation of dementia. *N Engl J Med* 1996;335: 330–336.

Krauthammer C, Klerman GL: Secondary mania. *Arch Gen Psychiatry* 1978;35: 133–1339.

Lipowski ZJ: Delirium in the elderly patient. *N Engl J Med* 1989;320:578–582.

Lyketsos CG, Sheppard JE, Rabins PV: Dementia in elderly persons in a general hospital. *Am J Psychiatry* 2000;157:704–707.

Lyketsos CG, Sheppard JM, Steele CD, et al: Randomized, placebo-controlled, double-blind clinical trial of sertraline in the treatment of depression complicating Alzheimer's disease: initial results from the Depression in Alzheimer's Disease study. *Am J Psychiatry* 2000;157:1686–1689.

Lyketsos CG, Steele C, Galick E, et al: Physical aggression in dementia patients and its relationship to depression. *Am J Psychiatry* 1999;156:66–71.

Petersen RC, Stevens JC, Ganguli M, et al: Practice parameter: Early detection of dementia: Mild cognitive impairment (an evidence-based review): Report of the Quality Standards Subcommittee of the American Academy of Neurology. *Neurology* 2001;56:1133–1142.

Reisberg B, Doody R, Stoffler A, et al: Memantine in moderate to severe Alzheimer's disease. *N Engl J Med* 2003;348:1333–1341.

Sadavoy J, Jarvik LF, Grossberg GT, Meyers BS (eds): *Comprehensive Textbook of Geriatric Psychiatry,* 3rd edition. New York: W.W. Norton and Co., 2004.

Saravay SM, Kaplowitz M, Kurek J, et al: How do delirium and dementia increase length of stay of elderly general medical inpatients? *Psychosomatics* 2004;45: 235–242.

Stern TA: Continuous infusion of haloperidol in agitated, critically ill patients. *Crit Care Med* 1994;22:378–379.

Stern TA, Fricchione GL, Cassem NH, et al (eds): *Massachusetts General Hospital Handbook of General Psychiatry,* 5th edition. Philadelphia: Mosby, 2004.

Vermeer SE, Prins ND, den Heijer T, et al: Silent brain infarcts and the risk of dementia and cognitive decline. *N Engl J Med* 2003;348:1215–1222.

Waern M, Rubenowitz E, Runeson B, et al: Burden of illness and suicide in elderly people: case-control study. *BMJ* 2002;324:1355.

Wengel SP, Burke WJ, Roccaforte WH: Donepezil for postoperative delirium associated with Alzheimer's disease. *J Am Geriatr Soc* 1999;47:379–380.

Chapter 26

An Approach To Psychopharmacological Treatment

MICHAEL HIRSCH, MD
ROBERT J. BIRNBAUM, MD, PHD

I. Overview

The field of psychopharmacology has grown dramatically over the past two decades; for several years, psychopharmacological agents (e.g., antidepressants, antipsychotics, and anxiolytics) have been among the top-selling classes of prescription drugs in the United States. With an abundance of medical information available on the Internet, as well as a substantial amount of direct-to-consumer advertising of pharmaceutical products, the public has been exposed to much information about psychotropics. **Physicians who prescribe psychotropic medications must understand the psychopharmacological properties of a wide variety of agents, and appreciate the conceptions and expectations of their patients regarding medication treatment.**

II. Evaluation

The process of taking a thorough psychiatric history is described elsewhere in this book (see Chapter 3). However, some elements of the psychiatric history have particular significance when one considers the initiation of psychopharmacological treatment, and they warrant further scrutiny.

A. **Chief Complaint**
1. **Explore the patient's agenda.** Some patients come to an appointment with an interest in starting a particular medication. They may have heard of a medication through advertisements or from a family member who has had a successful medication response. Alternatively, some patients hope to be told that they do not need medication, and become anxious if use of a psychopharmacologic agent is suggested. Questions such as, "When you were coming to today's appointment, did you have any hopes or concerns about what I would recommend to you?" can help elicit underlying wishes or fears about psychopharmacologic treatment.

Address for correspondence: Dr. Michael Hirsch, Beth Israel Deaconess Medical Center, Rabb 2, 330 Brookline Ave., Boston, MA 02215, email: mhirsch@bidmc.harvard.edu.

2. **Elucidate the patient's symptoms with an eye towards targets of treatment.** For example, if a patient describes symptoms of depression that include insomnia and loss of appetite, treatment with mirtazapine rather than bupropion may be considered; a description of depression marked by fatigue and hyperphagia could lead to the opposite choice.

B. **Past Psychiatric History**
   1. **Obtain a detailed medication history,** including names of prior medications and their doses, the length of treatment, side effects, and which if any medications were used in combination. A lack of response to a medication used at a subtherapeutic dose or for an inadequate length of time does not constitute a failed trial.
   2. **Ask carefully about a history of mood cycling** if a patient is presenting with symptoms of depression (because it is suggestive of a bipolar disorder). This is important to discern, as antidepressant monotherapy can precipitate manic episodes in bipolar patients. Discrete episodes of racing thoughts, irritability, agitation, rapid speech, hypersexuality, or a decreased need for sleep are suggestive of bipolar disorder and deserve further scrutiny.

C. **Substance Use**
   1. Be aware that abuse of alcohol or other drugs may interfere with the efficacy of psychopharmacological agents. Although active use of alcohol and other drugs does not always preclude medication treatment, **a patient who abuses alcohol or drugs should, in most cases, be actively engaged in some form of substance abuse treatment before psychopharmacological treatments are prescribed.**
   2. **Try to avoid prescribing benzodiazepines, stimulants, and other medications with addictive potential to patients with a history of substance abuse** or dependence (if other treatment options are available).
   3. **Advise your patients to limit their use of alcohol** to two or fewer drinks two to three times a week, as even moderate amounts of alcohol can lower mood.
   4. **Ask about caffeine consumption.** Patients who are particularly sensitive to caffeine may also be sensitive to the activating effects of stimulants and some antidepressants.
   5. **Consider the effects of heavy cigarette smoking on some psychotropic medications** (e.g., olanzapine and clozapine), as it may reduce their blood levels.

D. **Medical History**
1. **Obtain a full medical history, noting conditions that may influence the decision to prescribe particular psychotropic medications.** For example, a history of seizures is a contraindication to prescribing bupropion, which can lower the seizure threshold. A pre-existing cardiac conduction delay may preclude the safe use of tricyclic antidepressants (TCAs). Patients with risk factors for diabetes may be at particular risk for developing abnormalities in glucose regulation when taking atypical antipsychotics.
2. **Obtain a full list of current medications** (including over-the-counter medications, supplements, and herbal treatments) and drug allergies. Be alert to potential interactions with psychotropic medications, particularly to those that may cause QTc prolongation, orthostatic hypotension, a serotonin syndrome, or an increased risk of seizures.

III. Prescribing Psychotropic Medications

A. **General Principles**
When prescribing a psychotropic medication to a patient:
1. **Review the patient's goals and expectations of treatment.** Unrealistic expectations (e.g., "this medication will make my marriage better") may lead to disappointment and to poor adherence to treatment.
2. **Review the expected time course to efficacy.** Commonly a delay occurs before medications take effect. A patient who believes that the medication should work within the first week may discontinue the drug prematurely when rapid improvement is not forthcoming.
3. **Review the short- and long-term side-effect profile.**
4. **Encourage the patient to contact you with concerns.**
5. **Start with low doses,** but increase them to therapeutic doses; avoid underdosing.
6. **Determine the frequency of follow-up visits.**

B. **Monitoring Psychotropic Medication**
1. **Track changes in target symptoms.**
2. **Evaluate for emergent side effects.**
3. **Look for common causes of medication noncompliance:** side effects, stigma, the cost of treatment, and unrealistic treatment expectations.
4. **Obtain blood levels or laboratory tests when indicated.**

IV.   Antidepressants

A.   **Selective Serotonin Reuptake Inhibitors (SSRIs)**

The SSRIs are frequently used as first-line treatments for depression. Their popularity is due in large part to several shared characteristics:

- In addition to treating core symptoms of depression, they can have significant antianxiety and antiobsessive properties.
- They have relatively little affinity for histaminic, α-adrenergic, and cholinergic receptors, and therefore tend to have milder side effects than TCAs and monoamine oxidase inhibitors (MAOIs).
- They are relatively safe in overdose.
- They tend not to have effects on cardiac function or blood pressure.

In addition, SSRIs also share the following characteristics:

- In the brain, the SSRIs block the action of the presynaptic serotonin reuptake pump, thereby increasing the amount of serotonin available in the synapse and increasing postsynaptic serotonin receptor occupancy. It is proposed that the delay in clinical response to SSRIs is due to a gradual downregulation or decrease in some postsynaptic serotonin receptors in response to the increased amount of synaptic serotonin available; this may lead to changes in cellular protein production and to subsequent effects on neuronal protection and development.
- All SSRIs are hepatically metabolized.
- They are frequently associated with sexual side effects (including decreased libido, erectile dysfunction, ejaculatory delay, and anorgasmia) that may persist throughout the course of treatment.
- SSRIs are also associated with gastrointestinal upset, dizziness, headache, nervousness, insomnia, fatigue, and excessive sweating. These side effects frequently appear upon starting the medication, and frequently resolve during the first 2 weeks of treatment.
- Less common SSRI-induced side effects include dry mouth, constipation, bruxism, and short-term memory reduction.
- Rarely, SSRIs cause motor restlessness (akathisia), prolonged bleeding time, and hyponatremia.
- If combined with other medications that potentiate serotonin neurotransmission, they can occasionally produce dangerously high levels of brain serotonin. This "serotonin syndrome" is characterized by agitation, hyperthermia, diaphoresis, tachycardia, and neuromuscular disturbances (including rigidity).

The SSRIs appear to be equally efficacious in relieving depressive symptoms. Despite their similarities, the SSRIs are not equivalent with regard to side-effect profiles, pharmacokinetic properties, and interactions with other medications. These differences can help guide the choice of an SSRI that is appropriate for a particular patient. Some of the unique characteristics of each SSRI are listed below:

1. **Fluoxetine (Prozac®)**
   a. Fluoxetine has a half-life that is significantly longer than that of other SSRIs. Its active metabolite has a half-life of 7–15 days.
   b. **It is a potent inhibitor of the liver cytochrome (CYP) P450 enzyme 2D6;** its active metabolite, norfluoxetine, is also a mild inhibitor of P450 3A/34. Drugs metabolized by CYP 2D6 must be used cautiously when coadministered with fluoxetine, as drug levels may rise precipitously.
   c. Fluoxetine is commonly activating in the initial stages of treatment, and patients may report feeling jittery or restless.

2. **Sertraline (Zoloft®)**
   a. Sertraline is a very **mild inhibitor of the P450 2D6 isoenzyme.**
   b. It is better absorbed when taken with food.
   c. It may be more likely than other SSRIs to cause gastrointestinal upset (e.g., nausea and diarrhea) initially.
   d. Sertraline is commonly activating in the initial stages of treatment, and patients may report feeling jittery or restless.

3. **Paroxetine (Paxil®)**
   a. It is **a potent inhibitor of the P450 isoenzyme 2D6.** Drugs metabolized by CYP 2D6 must be used cautiously when coadministered with paroxetine.
   b. Paroxetine tends to be mildly sedating.
   c. It may have a higher likelihood of causing sexual dysfunction than other SSRIs.
   d. Paroxetine may be more likely to cause weight gain than other SSRIs.
   e. It has more anticholinergic effects than other SSRIs.
   f. Relative to other SSRIs, paroxetine appears to have a higher likelihood of causing "discontinuation symptoms" (including dizziness, dysphoria, and flu-like symptoms) upon abrupt cessation.

4. **Fluvoxamine (Luvox®)**
   a. This agent is commonly used as an antidepressant in Europe, **but its sole FDA indication in the U.S. is for treatment of obsessive-compulsive disorder (OCD). However, it is not necessarily more effective at treating OCD than other SSRIs.**

    b.   Fluvoxamine is **an inhibitor of the P450 isoenzymes 1A2 and 3A4.** Drugs metabolized by 1A2 and 3A4 must be used cautiously when coadministered with fluvoxamine.

    c.   It is typically given in twice-daily dosing.

5. **Citalopram (Celexa®)**

    a.   This agent **does not appear to have significant interactions with P450 isoenzymes.**

    b.   It tends to be neither particularly activating nor sedating.

6. **Escitalopram (Lexapro®)**

    a.   Escitalopram is a single-isomer formulation of citalopram.

    b.   Like citalopram, escitalopram **does not appear to have significant interactions with P450 isoenzymes.**

    c.   It is touted as having a fast onset and few side effects, but as yet there are no convincing data showing superior efficacy or tolerability relative to other SSRIs.

B.   **Serotonin-Norepinephrine Reuptake Inhibitors (SNRIs)**

SNRIs (sometimes referred to as "dual-action" antidepressants) block neuronal reuptake of both serotonin and norepinephrine, leading to increased synaptic availability of these neurotransmitters. As such, they have similarities to the TCAs in their effects on neurotransmitter systems. However, in contrast to the TCAs, they do not interact with histaminic, muscarinic, or adrenergic receptors; therefore, they tend to have a more benign side-effect profile.

1. **Venlafaxine (Effexor®)**

    a.   **At doses of 150 mg daily and below, venlafaxine has primarily serotonergic effects. At higher doses, it has both serotonergic and noradrenergic effects.**

    b.   Venlafaxine has a side-effect profile similar to that of SSRIs (i.e., it is associated with gastrointestinal upset, dizziness, headache, nervousness, insomnia, fatigue, and excessive sweating). It may be more likely than SSRIs to cause nausea and diaphoresis.

    c.   **It may cause increases in blood pressure, particularly at higher doses;** blood pressure should be monitored, particularly at doses of 225 mg daily and above.

    d.   **Venlafaxine is metabolized by the P450 2D6 isoenzyme system;** medications that inhibit this enzyme will increase the blood level of venlafaxine.

    e.   Sudden discontinuation of venlafaxine is associated with dizziness, dysphoria, and flu-like symptoms.

C. **Atypical Antidepressants**
1. **Bupropion (Wellbutrin®)**
    a. Bupropion appears to work via increasing activity of dopamine and norepinephrine in the brain, although its mechanism of action is not well characterized. It has few if any serotonergic effects.
    b. **It structurally resembles amphetamine, and can be mildly stimulating.**
    c. It does not typically have anxiolytic properties.
    d. **Bupropion tends not to cause either sexual side effects or weight gain.**
    e. It may cause side effects that include anxiety, irritability, insomnia, and headache.
    f. **Bupropion may lower the seizure threshold, particularly at high doses, and it is contraindicated in patients with seizure disorders or active eating disorders** because of the risk of seizures.
    g. **Bupropion is a potent inhibitor of the P450 isoenzyme 2D6;** drugs metabolized by CYP 2D6 must be used cautiously when coadministered with bupropion.
2. **Nefazodone (Serzone®)**
    a. Nefazodone has serotonin reuptake–blocking properties, but it is also a direct antagonist of serotonin 5-HT$_2$ receptors.
    b. It may cause a variety of side effects (e.g., dry mouth, constipation, nausea, sedation, and dizziness), but it is unlikely to cause sexual side effects or to disrupt sleep.
    c. **Nefazodone is a potent inhibitor of the P450 isoenzyme 3A4;** therefore, it can interact with other drugs metabolized by that enzyme.
    d. It has been **associated with hepatic failure** (at a rate of 1 case per 250–300,000 patient-years of treatment) and should not be used in patients with pre-existing liver disease.
        i. **Nefazodone should be discontinued if patients develop signs or symptoms of liver failure,** such as jaundice, anorexia, gastrointestinal complaints, or malaise.
        ii. Unfortunately, regular monitoring of liver function tests will not necessarily indicate impending liver toxicity.

3. **Mirtazapine (Remeron®)**
   a. Mirtazapine blocks pre- and postsynaptic α_2-receptors, increases noradrenergic and serotonergic neurotransmission, and blocks 5-HT$_2$ and 5-HT$_3$ serotonin receptors.
   b. **It is strongly antihistaminic and may cause a variety of side effects (e.g., sedation, weight gain, and dry mouth).**
      i. Sedation may be more pronounced at lower doses, possibly due to increased noradrenergic activity at higher dosing.
      ii. It has anti-nausea properties.
      iii. Mirtazapine may be particularly useful for depressed patients with poor appetite and insomnia.
   c. Mirtazapine does not appear to have significant interactions with P 450 isoenzymes.
   d. In premarketing trials, mirtazapine was associated with agranulocytosis in 2 out of 2796 patients. One additional patient developed neutropenia. There are no current recommendations to monitor blood cell counts in patients on mirtazapine.

D. **Tricyclic Antidepressants (TCAs)**
   TCAs have been used for decades. Because of their side-effect profile, TCAs are less commonly used as first-line antidepressants than are SSRIs or other newer antidepressants. **Most concerning is the toxicity of the TCAs in overdose. TCAs can be fatal in doses as little as five times the therapeutic dose.** The toxicity is usually due to prolongation of the QT interval, which leads to arrhythmias. **Overdose of cyclic antidepressants can also cause anticholinergic toxicity and seizures.** Because of this risk, it is preferable to avoid use of TCAs in patients who appear to be at high risk of intentional overdose.

   TCAs interact with a wide variety of brain receptors; this provides for the basis of both their antidepressant efficacy and their side-effect profile. Blockade of cholinergic muscarinic receptors can cause dry mouth, constipation, urinary retention, and blurred vision. **Blockade of α-adrenergic receptors can cause hypotension and reflex tachycardia. Blockade of histamine receptors can cause sedation and weight gain.** Other shared side effects of TCAs include a potential slowing of cardiac conduction (through their quinidine-like antiarrhythmic effects) and sexual side effects. Because of their cardiac effects, it is prudent to obtain an electrocardiogram (ECG) prior to starting a TCA, particularly in patients over the age of 50 years. Patients with a history of heart disease should be screened by a cardiologist prior to taking TCAs. TCAs are relatively contraindicated in patients with prostatic hypertrophy or narrow-angle glaucoma.

Starting and maintenance doses of TCAs are listed in Table 26-1. Highly sedating TCAs and those with potent anticholinergic effects are rarely used as primary antidepressants. Two of the secondary amine TCAs with more tolerable side effect profiles are characterized below:

1. **Desipramine (Norpramin®)**
   a. Desipramine is primarily an inhibitor of norepinephrine reuptake; it has negligible effects on serotonin reuptake inhibition.
   b. It has less of an interaction with histaminic, muscarinic, and α-adrenergic receptors than most TCAs, and therefore it tends to have fewer anticholinergic side effects and is less sedating.
   c. Desipramine commonly causes orthostatic hypotension.
   d. Patients tend to have a more robust antidepressant response if desipramine blood levels are >125 ng/mL.

2. **Nortriptyline (Pamelor®)**
   a. Nortriptyline has significantly more effects on norepinephrine reuptake inhibition than it does on serotonin reuptake inhibition.
   b. **It is less sedating and has fewer sedative and anticholinergic side effects than most TCAs,** although it has slightly more than does desipramine.
   c. **Nortriptyline has very little effect on orthostatic hypotension.**
   d. It appears to have a therapeutic "window" of efficacy; it is often most effective at blood levels of 50–150 ng/mL and less effective at blood levels <50 ng/mL or >150 ng/mL.

E.   **Monoamine Oxidase Inhibitors (MAOIs)**
Although MAOIs are effective antidepressants, they are infrequently prescribed due to their side-effect profile and their propensity for dangerous drug-drug and drug-food interactions. MAOIs irreversibly block monoamine oxidase, the enzyme responsible for the break down of neurotransmitters (e.g., serotonin, norepinephrine, and dopamine). This property is thought to be largely responsible for the MAOIs' antidepressant effects. **Blockade of MAO in the gut is responsible for the potential to cause lethal hypertensive reactions when MAOIs are combined with sympathomimetic medications, or foods containing tyramine. Combining MAOIs with serotonergic agents such as SSRIs can produce a dangerous serotonin overload or "serotonin syndrome," characterized by**

Table 26-1. Antidepressants and Their Dosing Schedules

Generic Name	Brand Name	Tablets	Initial Dose	Maintenance Dose
SSRIs				
Citalopram	Celexa	10, 20, 40 mg	10–20 mg/d	20–60 mg/d
Escitalopram	Lexapro	10, 20 mg	10 mg/d	10–20 mg/d
Fluoxetine	Prozac/Prozac Weekly	10, 20, or 90 mg	10–20 mg/d	20–60 mg qd or 90–180 mg weekly
Fluvoxamine	Luvox	25, 50, 100 mg	50–100 mg qd	100–250 mg qd
Paroxetine	Paxil/Paxil CR	10, 20, 30, 40, 12.5, and 25 mg	10–20 mg/d or 12.5–25 mg CR	
Sertraline	Zoloft	50, 100 mg	50 mg/d	25–60 mg/d
				50–200 mg/d
SNRIs				
Venlafaxine	Effexor/	25, 37.5, 50, 75, 100 mg	37.5 mg bid	75–150 mg bid
	Effexor XR	37.5,75,150 mg	75 mg XR qd	150–300 qd XR
TCAs				
Amitriptyline	Elavil or Endep	10, 25, 50, 75, 100, 150 mg	25 mg qhs	150–300 mg qhs
Clomipramine	Anafranil	25, 50, 75 mg	25 mg qhs	150–200 mg qhs
[1]Desipramine	Norpramin	10, 25, 50, 75, 100, 150 mg	25–50 mg qhs or qam	150–300 mg qhs or in divided doses
Doxepin	Adapin	10, 25, 50, 75, 100, 150 mg	25–50 mg qhs	150–300 mg qhs

Imipramine[1]	Tofranil	10, 25, 50, 75, 100, 150 mg	25 mg qhs	150–300 mg qhs or in divided doses
Nortriptyline[1]	Pamelor	10, 25, 50, 75 mg	10–25 mg qhs	50–150 mg qhs
Protriptyline	Vivactil	5, 10 mg	10 mg qam	30–60 mg qam
Trimipramine	Surmontil	25, 50, 100 mg	25 mg qhs	150–250 mg qhs
Tetracyclic antidepressant:				
Maprotiline	Ludiomil	25, 50, 75 mg	50 mg qhs	150–200 mg qhs or in divided doses
Others				
Bupropion	Wellbutrin/Wellbutrin XL	75, 100, 150, or 300 mg	150 mg XL qd or 75–100 mg bid	150–300 mg XL qd or 150 mg tid
Mirtazapine	Remeron/Remeron Sol Tab	15, 30, and 45 mg	15 mg qhs	30–45 mg qhs
Nefazodone	Serzone	50, 100, 150, 200, 250 mg	100 mg bid	150–300 mg bid
Trazodone	Desyrel	50, 100, 150, 300 mg	50–100 mg qhs	200–600 mg/d

[1]Plasma levels: desipramine >125 ng/mL; imipramine + desipramine >225 ng/mL; nortriptyline 50–150 ng/mL.
SNRI, serotonin-norepinephrine reuptake inhibitor; SNRI, selective serotonin reuptake inhibitor; TCA, tricyclic antidepressant.
Adapted from Arana and Rosenbaum, 2000.

myoclonus, fever, delirium, and sometimes death. To avoid these drug and food interactions, patients on MAOIs must keep to careful diets and avoid many kinds of medications (see Table 26-2). Patients must also wait 2 weeks after stopping an MAOI before starting a new antidepressant or reintroducing foods with tyramine into their diet. It is also recommended to wait 2 weeks after discontinuing

---

Table 26-2. Drugs and Foods Contraindicated during Therapeutic Use of Monoamine Oxidase Inhibitors

Foods

Absolutely restricted:
Aged cheeses
Aged and cured meats
Improperly stored or spoiled meats, fish, or poultry
Banana peel; broad bean pods
Marmite
Sauerkraut
Soy sauce and other soy condiments
Draft beer

Consume in moderation:
Red or white wine (no more than two 4-ounce glasses per day)
Bottled or canned beer, including nonalcoholic (no more than two 12-ounce servings per day)

Medications
α-Antagonists
β-Blockers
Dextromethorphan
Epinephrine
Norepinephrine
Phenylephrine
Pseudoephedrine
Isoproterenol
Methoxamine
Guanethidine
Meperidine
Reserpine
Selective serotonin reuptake inhibitors

Adapted from Arana and Rosenbaum, 2000.

most antidepressants (and 5 weeks after discontinuing fluoxetine [because of its extended half-life]) prior to starting an MAOI.

MAOIs have potent hypotensive effects, and up to 50% of patients experience dizziness. Other side effects include sexual dysfunction, dry mouth, gastrointestinal upset, urinary hesitancy, and headache.

Despite their side-effect profile, MAOIs can be particularly useful agents for the treatment of "atypical" depression (e.g., when depression is accompanied by hyperphagia, hypersomnia, leaden paralysis, and rejection sensitivity), and are frequently effective in treatment-resistant depressed patients. Two MAOIs available in the U.S. for treatment of depression, and their individual properties, are outlined below:

1. **Tranylcypromine (Parnate®)**
   a. Tranylcypromine has a chemical structure similar to that of amphetamine and it has some stimulant properties.
   b. It may cause transient increases in blood pressure after dosing, lasting 3–4 hours.
   c. **It is more likely than phenelzine to cause activation and insomnia, but less likely than phenelzine to cause weight gain.**
   d. Tranylcypromine is predominantly an irreversible inhibitor of MAO_A, but it also irreversibly inhibits MAO_B to a degree; it also appears to block reuptake of serotonin and catecholamines.

2. **Phenelzine (Nardil®)**
   a. Phenelzine is less activating than is tranylcypromine, and may cause less insomnia than tranylcypromine.
   b. It is more likely than is tranylcypromine to cause weight gain, sedation, and sexual dysfunction.
   c. Rarely, it can cause hepatotoxicity.

V. Anxiolytics

A. Antidepressants

Antidepressants are commonly used as treatments for anxiety. SSRIs, SNRIs, TCAs, and MAOIs are each effective in the treatment of panic disorder, generalized anxiety disorder, and posttraumatic stress disorder (PTSD). SSRIs and MAOIs have also been effective as treatments for social phobia and obsessive-compulsive disorder (OCD). Mirtazapine and nefazodone appear to have anxiolytic properties, but they have been less studied for this indication. When antidepressants are used to treat anxiety disorders, they are typically started at one-half the usual antidepressant starting dose, and slowly titrated upwards until a therapeutic effect is achieved.

B.   Benzodiazepines

Benzodiazepines are a class of medications that increase the affinity of the γ-aminobutyric acid (GABA) receptor for its endogenous ligand, GABA. They are all relatively rapidly acting, and they are potent reducers of anxiety. Differences among benzodiazepines lie mainly in their particular pharmacokinetic and pharmacodynamic properties, and include differences in their potency and duration of action. Characteristics of commonly used benzodiazepines are listed in Table 26-3. Clinicians can use these properties to choose a benzodiazepine with the desired clinical effect for a particular patient. High-potency agents (particularly clonazepam and alprazolam) are used to treat panic disorder, as they can reach sufficient GABA receptor occupancy without inducing oversedation. Agents with a rapid onset can be used on an "as needed" basis. Agents with a long duration of action reduce the need for frequent daily dosing, and prevent interdose rebound anxiety.

Several properties are common to all benzodiazepines:

- They are effective in treatment of symptoms of generalized anxiety and insomnia.
- They are not particularly effective in reducing obsessive or compulsive symptoms.
- **They cause dose-related sedation.** These sedative properties can be useful in treating insomnia, but they can cause fatigue, slow reaction time, or cognitive slowing after daytime use. The sedative properties tend to diminish with chronic use, but patients starting a benzodiazepine should be cautioned not to drive until they have adjusted to the drug's sedating effects. Elderly patients are particularly sensitive to these effects, and may require lower doses. Chronic use in elderly patients should be avoided when possible.
- Tolerance and physical dependence to benzodiazepines can develop, particularly when prescribed for extended periods. **Abrupt drug discontinuation after chronic use can produce withdrawal symptoms** (including anxiety, tachycardia, blood pressure increases, tremor, and sometimes seizures).
- **Patients with a history of substance abuse are at particular risk for abusing benzodiazepines.** In this population, use of benzodiazepines should be avoided when there are nonaddictive alternatives. Risk of abuse can be diminished by carefully monitoring refills and by encouraging attendance at regular follow-up appointments. The majority of patients without a history of substance abuse do not abuse benzodiazepines, and they are able to use these medications safely.

Table 26-3. Comparisons of Available Benzodiazepines

Generic (Trade) Names	Oral Dosage Equivalency (mg)	Onset After Oral Dose	Half-life (Single Dose)	Half-life (Multiple Dosing)
Alprazolam (Xanax)	0.5	Intermediate	Intermediate	Intermediate
Chlordiazepoxide (Librium)	10.0	Intermediate	Slow	Slow
Clonazepam (Klonopin)	0.25	Intermediate	Intermediate	Slow
Clorazepate (Tranxene)	7.5	Rapid	Rapid	Slow
Diazepam (Valium)	5.0	Rapid	Rapid	Slow
Estazolam (ProSom)	2.0	Intermediate	Intermediate	Intermediate
Flurazepam (Dalmane)	30.0	Rapid-intermediate	Rapid	Slow
Lorazepam (Ativan)	1.0	Intermediate	Intermediate	Intermediate
Midazolam (Versed)	—	Intermediate	Rapid	Rapid
Oxazepam (Serax)	15.0	Intermediate-slow	Intermediate	Intermediate
Quazepam (Doral)	15.0	Rapid-intermediate	Intermediate	Slow
Temazepam (Restoril)	30.0	Intermediate	Rapid	Intermediate
Triazolam (Halcion)	0.25	Intermediate	Rapid	Rapid

Adapted from Arana and Rosenbaum, 2000.

1. **Clonazepam (Klonopin®)**
    a. **Clonazepam is a long-acting agent;** it can usually provide lasting anxiolysis with twice-daily dosing.
    b. It is frequently used in the treatment of panic disorder.
    c. Clonazepam may be more sedating during initial treatment than other high-potency benzodiazepines.
2. **Alprazolam (Xanax®)**
    a. **Alprazolam is a short-acting agent;** it may need to be prescribed four times daily to prevent inter-dose rebound anxiety. (Exception: the extended-release formulation can be given once daily).
    b. It is most frequently used to treat panic disorder.
    c. Due to its rapid onset and short duration of action it has a high potential for abuse.
    d. Alprazolam may be less sedating than other benzodiazepines.
3. **Lorazepam (Ativan®)**
    a. **Lorazepam has an intermediate onset and duration of action.**
    b. It is used in patients with liver disease because it lacks extensive hepatic metabolism (i.e., it requires only glucouronidation and not oxidative metabolism).

C. **Buspirone (Buspar®)**
    1. Buspirone is an azopyrine anxiolytic with serotonin $5\text{-}HT_{1A}$-receptor partial agonist properties.
    2. While it can be effective in treating symptoms of generalized anxiety disorder (GAD), it is not a primary treatment for panic disorder, OCD, or PTSD.
    3. In contrast to benzodiazepines, **buspirone has no abuse potential and does not lead to tolerance or dependence.**
    4. Side effects may include headache, flushing, and gastrointestinal upset.
    5. Initial dosing is 5 mg three times daily, and maintenance dosing is 20–30 mg daily in three divided doses. Some patients may need dose increases up to a total daily dose of 60 mg to reach full effect. **Buspirone must be taken daily, and it may take 4–6 weeks to reach maximal effect.** Patients who have previously been treated with benzodiazepines often have poor anxiolytic responses to buspirone.

D. Other Anxiolytics

There are several other medications that have not been rigorously studied for the treatment of anxiety, but they have been effectively used in clinical practice. These include:

1. **Gabapentin (Neurontin®)**
    a. Gabapentin is an anticonvulsant with apparent anxiolytic properties.
    b. It is typically given in doses of 300–900 mg three times daily.
    c. Side effects include dizziness and sedation.

2. **Beta-Blockers**
    a. β-Blockers, such as propranolol 10–40 mg daily, can be used to reduce somatic manifestations of anxiety. They may be given 1 or 2 hours before a performance in patients with social anxiety disorder to prevent tremor and tachycardia.
    b. They do not tend to directly alleviate the emotional experience of anxiety.
    c. Side effects may include hypotension and dysphoria.
    d. β-Blockers are contraindicated in patients with reactive airways disease.

3. **Antihistamines**
    Antihistamines, such as hydroxyzine 50–100 mg twice a day, have calming properties and can be effective in treating mild anxiety. Side effects include dry mouth and sedation.

VI. Mood Stabilizers

Mood stabilizers are an eclectic group of medications used in the treatment of bipolar disorder. They vary widely in their side-effect profiles and in their efficacy in treating particular stages and forms of bipolar disorder. The traditional mainstays of treatment (lithium, valproate, and carbamazepine) tend to be effective for acute mania and for maintenance phases, and somewhat less effective for treatment of acute bipolar depression. Lamotrigine has shown clinical efficacy in bipolar depression as well as in maintenance treatment, but appears less effective for treatment of acute mania. Several other anticonvulsants have shown promise as mood stabilizers, and are commonly used as "add on" or augmenting agents along with the traditional agents. Some atypical antipsychotics, including olanzapine, risperidone, and quetiapine, are effective in the treatment of acute mania. Olanzapine is also effective in bipolar maintenance treatment. Since it is unlikely that one medication will treat all phases of bipolar disorder, most patients with the illness need combination treatment to maintain mood stability. Monitoring and dosing recommendations are summarized in Tables 26-4 through 26-7.

Table 26-4. Lithium Therapy

Before beginning lithium:
Take a medical history
Perform a physical examination
Order blood urea nitrogen, creatinine T_4, T_3 resin uptake, and thyroid-stimulating hormone (TSH)
Obtain an electrocardiogram (ECG) with rhythm strip (recommended if the patient is over age 50 or has history of cardiac disease)
Draw a complete blood cell count (optional)
Check a β-hCG (pregnancy test), if appropriate

Initial dosing:
Usually 300 mg tid
Lower doses are used in the elderly or in those with renal disease (150–300 bid)

Blood levels:
Draw blood approximately 12 hours after the last oral dose
Check at the start of therapy; it takes 5 days to adjust to a dose
Check less frequently as levels stabilize
For stable long-term patients, check levels every 3–6 months
Draw immediately if toxicity suspected

Follow-up monitoring (stable patients):
Check a creatinine and TSH every 6 months
For patients over the age of 40 or with cardiac disease, obtain follow-up ECGs as indicated

β-hCG human chorionic gonadotropin.
Adapted from Arana and Rosenbaum, 2000.

A.   **Lithium**
1. Approved for use in the U.S. in 1970, lithium is the most well-studied of the mood stabilizers.
2. It may be particularly effective for the treatment of patients with euphoric mania, and less effective for patients with rapid cycling, mixed states, or comorbid substance abuse.
3. **Side effects of lithium include tremor, sedation, cognitive dulling, gastrointestinal upset, weight gain, polyuria, acne, psoriasis, and benign leukocytosis.** With chronic use, lithium may cause hypothyroidism, and rarely nephrotic syndrome.

Table 26-5. Valproic Acid and Carbamazepine Therapy

Valproic acid

Before beginning VPA:
   Take a medical history; do not administer if there is a history of liver disease
   Perform a physical examination
   Draw LFTs and CBC with platelets
   Obtain a β-hCG (pregnancy test), if appropriate

Initial dosing:
   Give a test dose of 250 mg with a meal
   Gradually increase the dose to 250 mg tid
   Increase the dose as tolerated to effective dosage (usually 1000
   to 1800 mg/d)

Note: VPA may also be administered by a rapid oral strategy, using 20–30 mg of VPA per kg body weight.

Monitoring:
   Optimal blood levels are likely in the range of 50–120 ng/mL
   Check levels weekly until the patient is stable
   Many clinicians also obtain LFTs and a CBC at the same time
   In stable patients check blood levels, LFTs, and a CBC every 6 months
   Check levels, LFTs, and ammonia level promptly if there is a new onset of nausea, anorexia, or fatigue

Carbamazepine

Before beginning CBZ: Check a CBC and LFTs

Initial dosing:
   Usually 200 mg bid
   Increase the dosage up to 200 mg weekly until an effective dose is reached (usually 800–1200 mg/d)

Monitoring:
   During the first 2 months, check a CBC and LFTs every 2 weeks
   If no laboratory abnormalities appear and no symptoms of bone marrow suppression or hepatitis occur, obtain counts and LFTs every 3 months
   Check the CBC immediately if the patient reports fever, sore throat, pallor, unaccustomed weakness, bruising, or bleeding
   Stop the drug if the white blood cell count drops below 3000/mL or the neutrophil count drops below 1500/mL, or in the case of a threefold increase in LFTs

Blood levels: Check blood levels weekly until a level of 4–12 μg/mL is reached, then check levels every 3 months

Note: In practice, clinicians typically consider less frequent blood monitoring acceptable if the patient has had no adverse effects in the first few months of dosing.

β-hCG human chorionic gonadotropin; CBC, complete blood cell count; LFT, liver function test.
Adapted from Arana and Rosenbaum, 2000.

Table 26-6. Pharmacokinetic Interactions with Lithium

Interactions that Increase Lithium Levels	Interactions that Decrease Lithium Levels
Diuretics	Osmotic diuretics
Acetazolamide	Theophylline, aminophylline
Thiazides	
Ethacrynic acid	
Spironolactone	
Triamterene	
Nonsteroidal anti-inflammatory	
agents	
Antibiotics	
Metronidazole	
Tetracyclines	
Angiotensin-converting enzyme	
inhibitors	

Adapted from Arana and Rosenbaum, 2000.

4. **Lithium is almost entirely excreted by the kidney.** Elderly patients may require lower doses due to changes in renal excretion.

5. **Lithium can cause benign ECG changes, including T-wave flattening or inversion.** It has also been reported rarely to cause arrhythmias, particularly in patients with pre-existing cardiac disease. Patients over the age of 50, or those with a history of cardiac disease, should have a baseline ECG prior to starting lithium treatment, and a follow-up ECG as clinically indicated.

6. It has a narrow therapeutic index. Blood level monitoring is required to guide treatment and to prevent toxicity. **Blood levels are drawn at 12 hours after the last dose,** and at a minimum of 5 days after the last dose change. The maintenance therapeutic range is 0.6–1.0 mEq/L, but levels of 1.0–1.2 mEq/L may be needed for treatment of acute mania.

7. **Signs of lithium toxicity can be seen with blood levels above 1.5 mEq/L.** Symptoms include gastrointestinal disturbance, ataxia, dysarthria, coarse tremor, and confusion. **Severe toxicity can cause delirium, seizures, coma, and possibly death.** Lithium levels of 3.0 mEq/L and above are considered a medical emergency, and may require dialysis.

Table 26-7. Other Medications Used to Treat Bipolar Disorder

Anticonvulsants

Lamotrigine (Lamictal)[1]

Initiating lamotrigine in adult bipolar patients:

Not taking enzyme-inducing drugs[2] or valproate:

Weeks 1 & 2: 25 mg/d; weeks 3 & 4: 50 mg/d; week 5: 100 mg/d; week 6: target dose 200 mg/d

Taking valproate:

Weeks 1 & 2: 25 mg/every other day; weeks 3 & 4: 25 mg/d; week 5: 50 mg/d; week 6: target dose 100 mg/d

Taking enzyme-inducing drugs[2] and not taking valproate:

Weeks 1 & 2: 50 mg/d; weeks 3 & 4: 100 mg/d in divided doses; week 5: 200 mg/d in divided doses; week 6: 300 mg/d in divided doses; week 7: target dose (up to 400 mg/d in divided doses)

Topiramate[3] (Topamax): Dose forms: 25, 100, 200 mg tablets

Starting dose: 12.5–25 mg qd or bid

Increase total daily dose 12.5–25 mg weekly

Final dose is typically 100–200 mg/d (range, 50–400 mg)

Oxcarbazepine[3] (Trileptal): Dose forms: 150, 300, 600 mg tablets

Starting dose: 150 mg bid; increase in 150-mg bid increments (max total increase of 600 mg/wk)

Typical range: 600–2400 mg qd

Atypical antipsychotics

Olanzapine (Zyprexa): Dose forms: 2.5, 5, 7.5, 10, 15, 20 mg tablets

Starting dose to treat acute mania: 10–15 mg/d

Typical dose for bipolar maintenance: 10–20 mg/d (range, 5–30 mg/d)

Risperidone[4] (Risperdal): Dose forms: 0.25, 0.5, 1, 2, 3, 4 mg tablets

Starting dose to treat acute mania: 2–3 mg/d (can be given once daily)

Dose may be adjusted to efficacy in the range of 1–6 mg/d

Quetiapine[4] (Seroquel): Dose forms: 25, 100, 200, 300 tablets

Starting dose to treat acute mania: 50 mg bid

Increase dose by 50 mg bid each day until effective (typical range: 200–400 mg bid)

[1]Not indicated for treatment of acute mania.
[2]If valproate or enzyme-inducing drugs (e.g., carbamazepine) are subsequently added, the dose of lamotrigine may need to be adjusted.
[3]Off-label use; not currently FDA indicated for treatment of bipolar disorder.
[4]FDA indicated for treatment of acute mania (not bipolar maintenance).

8. Dehydration can lead to increased renal reabsorption of lithium, and therefore increased blood levels with possible toxicity. Several medications can affect the blood level of lithium (see Table 26-6).

B. **Valproate (Depakote®)**
    1. **Valproate is an anticonvulsant that can be particularly effective for patients with rapid cycling, mixed states, or comorbid substance abuse.**
    2. Its side effects include sedation, weight gain, gastrointestinal upset, hair loss, tremor, and rarely hepatic failure or thrombocytopenia. Liver function tests and platelets should be monitored regularly. Hair loss from valproate may respond to selenium 50–100 µg plus zinc 50–100 mg daily.
    3. Blood level monitoring can help guide treatment. Although not well characterized, **levels between 50 and 120 µg/mL appear to be associated with maximal efficacy.** Levels above 120 µg/mL are associated with more frequent side effects, but without improved efficacy. Levels are drawn at 12 hours after the last dose, and a minimum of 4 days after the last dose change.
    4. **Valproate is teratogenic; it is associated with fetal neural tube defects.**

C. **Carbamazepine (Tegretol®)**
    1. Support for carbamazepine's efficacy as a mood stabilizer is not as strong as that for lithium and valproate, though it has been used successfully in clinical practice for many years.
    2. It can be an effective treatment for neuropathic pain.
    3. Carmabazepine induces and is metabolized by the CYP 450 isoenzyme 3A4, thereby inducing its own metabolism and potentially interacting with many other medications (see Table 26-5).
    4. Side effects of carbamazepine include sedation, dizziness, ataxia, blurred vision, diplopia, gastrointestinal upset, weight gain, and benign leukocytopenia. Rarely it can cause severe rash, hyponatremia, hepatitis, cardiac conduction delay, agranulocytosis, aplastic anemia, or thrombocytopenia.
    5. Blood monitoring of carbamazepine is necessary to guide dosing and to monitor for hematologic changes (see Table 26-5). The maintenance therapeutic range is 4–12 µg/mL, drawn at 12 hours after the last dose, and a minimum of 5 days after last dose change. Use with clozapine is contraindicated due to an increased risk of bone marrow suppression.

6. **Carbamazepine is teratogenic; it is associated with neural tube defects in the fetus.**

D. Lamotrigine (Lamictal®)

1. Lamotrigine was approved by the FDA in 2003 for maintenance treatment of adults with Bipolar I Disorder.

2. Studies and clinical use suggest that it is more efficacious in treating bipolar depression than it is in preventing or treating mania. In fact, there have been several reports of lamotrigine inducing mania. Lamotrigine may have particular efficacy in treating patients with mixed states or rapid cycling.

3. It typically has fewer side effects than other mood stabilizers, with the exception of its potential to cause a serious rash during initial treatment.

   a. **A mild rash may occur in up to 10% of patients,** with a medically serious rash (Stevens-Johnson syndrome) occurring in approximately 1 in 10,000 patients (a figure that is slightly higher in pediatric patients).

   b. Rash appears to be associated with the rate of increase of lamotrigine doses; it requires slow initial titration (see Table 26-7).

   c. **The majority of rashes occur within the first several weeks of treatment.**

   d. The majority of these rashes are benign and self-limiting, and clinicians may choose to continue the medication with close monitoring, or to discontinue treatment and rechallenge with slower titration once the rash clears.

   e. However, the medication should be immediately discontinued if the rash worsens.

   f. Particularly worrisome rash symptoms are mucosal involvement and fever. Patients who develop these symptoms should immediately discontinue lamotrigine. If lamotrigine is restarted after the rash clears, it should be done very slowly and with close monitoring.

4. Other side effects of lamotrigine include insomnia, sedation (rare), nausea, ataxia, or headache.

5. **Blood monitoring of lamotrigine is not required.**

   a. Coadministration with valproate can lead to a doubling of lamotrigine blood level. When lamotrigine is used in patients taking valproate, it should be prescribed at one-half the usual dosage (see Table 26-7).

E.   Topiramate (Topamax®)

1.   **Topiramate** has shown promise as a mood stabilizer when added to conventional treatments.

2.   Its utility is often limited by side effects (e.g., cognitive slowing, dizziness, paresthesias, and somnolence); rarely it has been associated with decreased sweating and hyperthermia (particularly in children) and with acute myopia and secondary angle-closure glaucoma.

   a.   Patients should be advised to seek immediate medical attention if they experience blurred vision or periorbital pain.

   b.   It has also been associated with an increased rate of kidney stones, possibly due to its properties as a carbonic anhydrase inhibitor.

   c.   It is frequently associated with weight loss.

3.   The effect of topiramate on oral contraceptives is not well characterized. The possibility of decreased contraceptive efficacy should be considered.

4.   Topiramate can cause hyperchloremic, non–anion gap metabolic acidosis (decreased serum bicarbonate). Symptoms may include fatigue and anorexia, or more severe sequelae such as cardiac arrhythmias or stupor. Chronic metabolic acidosis can cause osteoporosis, increased risk of kidney stones, and in children, decreased growth rate. Measurement of baseline and periodic serum bicarbonate during topiramate treatment is recommended. If a patient develops metabolic acidosis while taking topiramate, the medication should be tapered down and discontinued if there are other treatment options. The manufacturer recommends considering alkali treatment for patients who need to continue topiramate treatment after developing metabolic acidosis.

F.   Oxcarbazepine (Trileptal®)

1.   Oxcarbazepine is a chemical analogue of carbamazepine. Although it has been used in clinical practice with promising results, it has not been well studied in the treatment of bipolar disorder.

2.   It appears to be less likely to cause blood dyscrasias and hepatotoxicity than carbamazepine, and induces the CYP 450 3A4 isoenzyme less than carbamazepine.

3.   It can cause hyponatremia in up to 3% of patients. Other side effects may include headache, fatigue, dizziness, and edema.

4.   In contrast to carbamazepine, blood monitoring is not required with oxcarbazepine.

G.   New Anticonvulsants
Several new anticonvulsant medications have been used as "add-on" treatments for bipolar disorder; preliminary positive results have been received for gabitril, zonisamide, and levetiracetam. Other agents that have been tried with mixed results include benzodiazepines, calcium channel blockers, acetazolamide, thyroxine, clonidine, and omega-3 fatty acids.

VII.   Typical and Atypical Antipsychotics

Antipsychotic medications, also known as neuroleptics, are the mainstay of treatment for schizophrenia and other psychotic disorders. **The antipsychotics' blockade of dopamine D_2 receptors in the brain is thought to account for their antipsychotic properties,** as well as for several of their burdensome side effects. **The first-generation antipsychotics (also called conventional neuroleptics), frequently cause motor or extrapyramidal side effects (EPS), due to their potent antagonism of dopamine D_2 receptors in the striatum. They are also associated with tardive dyskinesia (TD),** a progressive, often permanent side effect characterized by uncontrollable writhing movements. **Second-generation antipsychotics (also called atypical antipsychotics) have a significantly lower incidence of EPS and TD,** and have largely supplanted the conventional neuroleptics as first-line antipsychotics. In addition to blocking D_2 receptors, the atypical properties also block serotonin $5\text{-}HT_{2A}$ receptors; this property is thought to mitigate some of the side effects related to dopamine blockade. While the atypical antipsychotics have fewer motor side effects than conventional antipsychotics, and may be more effective in treating the negative symptoms and cognitive impairment of schizophrenia, they can cause metabolic changes (such as abnormalities in glucose regulation). Other properties of conventional and atypical antipsychotics are described below:

A.   Typical Antipsychotics
Conventional or typical antipsychotics can be divided into two categories, high-potency and low-potency. The **low-potency agents,** although they are as effective as high-potency agents, **tend to cause more hypotension, sedation, and anticholinergic effects. High-potency agents tend to have more extrapyramidal effects.** Properties and recommended dosing of conventional antipsychotics are listed in Table 26-8. In addition to causing hypotension, sedation, and anticholinergic symptoms, side effects of conventional antipsychotics include:
1.   **Extrapyramidal side effects.** More common with high-potency agents, these motor system effects include akathisia, acute dystonia, and drug-induced Parkinsonism.

Table 26-8. Typical and Atypical Antipsychotic Drugs

Generic Name	Trade Name	Equiv. Dose	Sedative Effect	HT Effect	ACh Effect	EP Effects	Wt. Gain	Prolonged QTc	Elevated Prolactin
Typical antipsychotics									
Chlorpromazine	Thorazine	100	+++	+++	++	+	++/+++	++	+++
Thioridazine	Mellaril	100	+++	+++	+++	+	+++/++	++	+++
Molindone	Moban	10	+/-	+/-	+/-	+	+/-	+++	NA
Perphenazine	Trilafon	8	+/-	+/-	+/-	++++	+	+++	NA
Trifluoperazine	Stelazine	5	+/-	+/-	+/-	+++/++	+/-	+/-	+++
Thiothixene	Navane	5	+/-	+/-	+/-	+++/++	+/-	+/-	+++
Fluphenazine	Prolixin	2	+/-	+/-	+/-	+++	+++/++	+/-	+++
Haloperidol	Haldol	2	+/-	+/-	+/-	+++	+++/++	+/-	+++
Atypical antipsychotics									
Risperidone	Risperdal	NA	++	++	+/-	+	++	+/-	+++
Olanzapine	Zyprexa	NA	++	+/-	+++	+/-	+++	+/-	+/-
Quetiapine	Seroquel	NA	+++	+++	+/-	+/-	++	+/-	+/-
Ziprasidone	Geodon	NA	+	+++	+/-	+	+/-	++	+/-
Aripiprazole	Abilify	NA	+	+/-	+/-	+	+/-	+/-	+/-
Clozapine	Clozaril	NA	+++	+++	+++	+/-	+++	+/-	+++

ACh, anticholinergic; EP, extrapyramidal; Equiv., equivalent; HT, hypertensive; QTc, QTc interval (ECG); Wt., weight.
Adapted from Powell A, Heckers S, Bierer M: The patient with hallucinations and delusions. In Stern TA, Herman JB, Slavin PL (eds):*Massachusetts General Hospital Guide to Primary Care Psychiatry,* 2nd edition. New York: McGraw-Hill, 2004.

a. *Akathisia* is characterized by an intense sensation of motor restlessness. Patients can appear anxious or agitated, with a constant need to pace or to move their legs. Medications that can sometimes relieve these symptoms include β-blockers (such as propranolol 10–30 mg three times daily), benzodiazepines (such as lorazepam 1 mg three times daily), or anticholinergic agents (such as benztropine 1–2 mg twice daily [*Note:* In patients taking low-potency antipsychotics, the addition of an anticholinergic agent can exacerbate anticholinergic side effects]).

b. *Acute dystonia* is characterized by muscle spasms and cramping, usually in the neck, face, tongue, or back. These symptoms typically occur during the first week of treatment. **Dystonia can usually be quickly reversed by administering benztropine 2 mg IM or IV, or diphenhydramine 50 mg IM or IV.** If there is no effect after 20 minutes, repeating the injection may bring relief. If there is no effect after two injections, a benzodiazepine (such as lorazepam 1 mg IM or IV) should be given. Once the dystonia is reversed, if the antipsychotic is to be continued, it should be prescribed along with an anticholinergic medication (such as benztropine 1–2 mg twice daily for at least 2 weeks). To minimize the risk of dystonia when using a high-potency neuroleptic, clinicians often prescribe benztropine prophylactically, starting the anticholinergic at 1–2 mg twice daily when starting the antipsychotic.

c. *Drug-induced parkinsonism* includes symptoms of tremor, a masked facial appearance, bradykinesia, and cogwheel rigidity. Antiparkinsonian medications (e.g., anticholinergics, such as benztropine 1–2 mg twice daily, or dopamine agonists, such as amantadine 100 mg twice daily) may reduce these symptoms.

2. **Tardive dyskinesia (TD) is a progressive and often permanent syndrome of abnormal motor movements** affecting up to 20% of patients during long-term use of conventional neuroleptics. Symptoms include involuntary repetitive writhing movements of the facial muscles, tongue, trunk, or extremities. Risk of TD increases with age. There are no clearly effective treatments for TD, and stopping the offending medication may temporarily actually worsen the symptoms. Switching to an atypical antipsychotic, particularly to clozapine, can sometimes reduce symptoms of TD.

3. **Neuroleptic malignant syndrome (NMS) is a potentially fatal, idiosyncratic reaction to antipsychotic medications.**

Symptoms include lead-pipe rigidity, fever, delirium, and autonomic instability. Laboratory findings frequently include an elevated creatine phosphokinase (CPK) due to muscle breakdown, and elevated white blood cell count. Risk factors include dehydration, hyperthermia, and possibly concurrent medical illness. Treatment involves stopping the antipsychotic medication and providing supportive care. In some cases, the muscle relaxant dantrolene is given (at 1–3 mg/kg per day) to decrease rigidity. The dopamine agonist bromocriptine has been tried (at doses of 2.5–10 mg three times daily) to reduce symptoms of NMS, but results have been equivocal. Patients who develop NMS on a high-potency neuroleptic should not be rechallenged with a high-potency agent if other options are available.

4. **Hyperprolactinemia** can result from tuberoinfundibular D_2 blockade. Resulting symptoms can include galactorrhea, amenorrhea, and sexual side effects.

5. **Weight gain** can be caused by all conventional antipsychotics with the exception of molindone.

6. **Skin photosensitivity** can result from use of low-potency agents.

7. **A heightened risk for arrhythmias** is associated with the use of pimozide, thioridazine, and mesoridazone (which can slow cardiac conduction and increase the QTc interval).

8. **A pigmentary retinopathy** is associated with thioridazine; therefore, its use is contraindicated in doses above 800 mg/d.

B. **Atypical Antipsychotics**
Atypical antipsychotics are typically used as first-line treatments because they are less likely than conventional neuroleptics to cause EPS or TD. They are also less likely to cause the full constellation of symptoms of NMS, although they have occasionally been associated with causing a partial syndrome or "atypical NMS" (e.g., hyperthermia and autonomic changes *without* rigidity or increased CPK). They may also be more effective at treating the negative symptoms and cognitive deficits of schizophrenia, but studies have shown equivocal results. Atypical antipsychotics have been associated with abnormalities in glucose regulation; however, the majority of reported cases have occurred with olanzapine and clozapine.

Dosing recommendations and side-effect comparisons of atypical antipsychotics are listed in Tables 26-8 and 26-9. Atypical antipsychotics, particularly quetiapine, olanzapine, and risperidone, are frequently prescribed in low doses for "as needed" treatment of anxiety or agitation. In these cases, it is possible that the effects of the medication are mainly due to sedative, not antipsychotic, properties. Given the high cost and potential side effects of atypical antipsychotics, it is prudent in these instances to consider whether an alternative agent with calming properties (e.g., a benzodiazepine) may be preferable.

Olanzapine has received FDA approval for monotherapy treatment of acute mania and for bipolar maintenance treatment. Risperidone and quetiapine are both FDA-indicated for monotherapy treatment of acute mania (see Table 26-7). These agents are also frequently used as add-on medications to existing mood stabilizers. Clozapine has shown mood-stabilizing properties in clinical practice, including those with treatment-resistant disorders. Mood-stabilizing effects of ziprasidone and aripiprazole are less well characterized.

1.   **Clozapine (Clozaril®)**
      a.   The oldest atypical antipsychotic, clozapine, may also be the most effective, with particular utility in treatment-resistant schizophrenia.

Table 26-9. Atypical Antipsychotic Dosing

Drug	Initial Dose	Titration	Typical Maintenance	Range
Risperidone	0.5–1 mg bid	Increase by 1–2 mg daily	2–6 mg qd	1–12 mg qd
Olanzapine	5–10 mg qd	Increase by 5–10 mg daily	10–15 mg qd	10–40 mg qd
Quetiapine	25 mg bid	Increase to 200 mg bid by day 4	400–600 mg qd	300–800 mg
Ziprasidone	40 mg bid (w/food)	Increase by 20 mg bid q 1–2 days	60–80 mg bid	40–80 mg bid
Aripiprazole	10–15 mg qd	—	10–15 mg qd	10–30 mg qd
Clozapine	12.5–25 mg qd	Increase by 25 mg every 1–2 days	300–400 mg qd	200–900 mg qd

   b. **Approximately 1% of patients develop potentially lethal agranulocytosis.** Weekly blood monitoring of the white blood cell (WBC) count is required during the first 6 months of treatment, and then every 2 weeks thereafter. Monitoring parameters are outlined in Table 26-10.
   c. **Common side effects include sedation, weight gain, hypersalivation, and anticholinergic symptoms.** In addi-

---

Table 26-10. Clozapine and White Blood Cell (WBC) Count Monitoring

To initiate treatment, the WBC count must be greater than 3500 mm^3.

Monitor the WBC count weekly. If no abnormalities arise, monitoring every other week may be reduced after 6 months of treatment.

If the WBC count drops below 3500 mm^3,
***OR** if it has dropped by 3000 or more from baseline within 3 weeks,*
***AND** the differential reveals a WBC count between 3000 and 3500/mm^3 and an absolute neutrophil count (ANC) above 1500/mm^3:*

Perform twice-weekly WBC counts and differential counts until the WBC returns to 3500.

If the total WBC count falls below 3000/mm^3 or the ANC falls below 1500/mm^3:

Stop clozapine treatment
Perform *daily WBC count and differential*
Monitor for flulike symptoms or other symptoms suggestive of infection.

Clozapine treatment may be resumed if no symptoms of infection develop, and if the total WBC count returns to levels above 3000/mm^3 and the ANC returns to levels above 1500/mm^3. Twice-weekly WBC counts and differential counts should continue until total WBC counts return to levels above 3500/mm^3.

If the total WBC count falls below 2000/mm^3 or the ANC falls below 1000/mm^3:

Consider bone marrow aspiration to ascertain the granulopoietic status.
If granulopoiesis is deficient, protective isolation and observation may be indicated to prevent infection.
Perform a *daily WBC count and differential*.
These patients should not be rechallenged with clozapine.

tion, it may lower the seizure threshold, particularly at high doses.

    d. **The blood level may be increased by drugs (including SSRIs) that inhibit the CYP 450 isoenzymes. Blood levels may be reduced by heavy cigarette smoking.**

2. **Risperidone (Risperdal®)**

    a. **Risperidone may cause more EPS than other atypical agents, particularly at higher doses.**

    b. It commonly increases the prolactin level, due to its high affinity for D_2 receptors.

    c. It is frequently associated with orthostatic hypotension.

    d. Risperidone is devoid of anticholinergic side effects.

    e. It is available in a long-acting injectable formulation.

    f. Risperidone has antimanic properties.

3. **Olanzapine (Zyprexa®)**

    a. **Olanzapine frequently causes weight gain.** Other side effects include sedation and dizziness.

    b. As with clozapine, there are many reports of olanzapine-associated abnormalities of glucose metabolism, including new-onset diabetes and spontaneous ketoacidosis, even in patients without pre-existing risk factors.

    c. Olanzapine may be associated with increases in serum triglycerides.

    d. It has antimanic and mood-stabilizing properties.

4. **Quetiapine (Seroquel®)**

    a. Quetiapine has a very low likelihood of causing EPS or increased prolactin levels.

    b. **It commonly causes sedation and orthostasis,** particularly during initial treatment. Other side effects include weight gain, dry mouth, and headache.

    c. Quetiapine is usually given in twice-daily dosing, but it can be given once daily to enhance compliance.

    d. It has antimanic properties.

5. **Ziprasidone (Geodon®)**

    a. Ziprasidone has properties of serotonin and norepinephrine reuptake inhibition, and is a 5-HT_{1A} partial agonist in addition to a D_2 and 5-HT_{2A} antagonist.

    b. It is associated with more QTc prolongation than other atypical antipsychotics (it prolongs QTc by a mean of 20.6 milliseconds). The QTc prolongation does not appear to be dose related. Ziprasidone should not be prescribed with other medications that prolong the QTc interval, and it should be avoided in patients with risk factors for torsades de pointes (e.g., pre-existing arrhythmia or prolonged QTc, hypokalemia, or hypomagnesemia). As of this writing, there have been no reported cases of torsades de pointes caused by ziprasidone.

   c.   Ziprasidone is less likely to cause weight gain than other atypicals.

   d.   It is typically nonsedating. In fact, for some patients it may be activating.

   e.   Side effects of ziprasidone include nausea, dizziness, and headache.

   f.   It is commonly given in twice-daily dosing; an IM formulation is available.

6. **Aripiprazole (Abilify®)**

   a.   Aripiprazole has a unique mechanism of action. It is a D_2 partial agonist in addition to being an antagonist at 5-HT_{2A} receptors.

   b.   It has a low propensity to cause weight gain.

   c.   It is typically nonsedating; it may be activating for some patients.

   d.   Common side effects include nausea, anxiety, and insomnia.

VIII.   Stimulants

Stimulants are sympathomimetic amines that act by increasing brain availability of dopamine and norepinephrine. This property is responsible for their effects on increasing focus and concentration; they are commonly used for the treatment of Attention-Deficit/Hyperactivity Disorder (ADHD). Although all of the stimulants appear to be equally efficacious in treating symptoms of ADHD, individual patients may respond preferentially to one stimulant or another. The most commonly used stimulants are methylphenidate and amphetamine compounds.

Dosing recommendations and pharmacokinetic properties of stimulants are listed in Table 26-11. Shared properties of stimulants are listed below.

- In patients with ADHD, stimulants can reduce inattentiveness, distractibility, impulsivity, and motor overactivity.
- Stimulants have also been used in the treatment of narcolepsy, the augmentation of antidepressants, the potentiation of narcotic analgesics, and the treatment of apathy and fatigue in the medically ill.
- Side effects include insomnia, decreased appetite, weight loss, dysphoria, and headache. Stimulants occasionally cause increases in blood pressure and heart rate, and worsen tics in patients with tic disorders. Concerns about growth retardation have been raised about stimulant use in children. High doses of stimulants can cause emotional lability, paranoia, and rarely florid psychosis.

Table 26-11. Medications Used in Attention-Deficit/Hyperactivity Disorder

Generic (Trade) Names	Daily Dose	Daily Dosage Schedule	Common Adverse Effects
Stimulants			
Methylphenidate			
(Ritalin)	0.3–2.0 mg/kg	bid–qid	Insomnia; decreased appetite/weight loss;
(Focalin)	0.6–1.0 mg/kg	bid–qid	possible reduction in growth velocity with
(Metadate CD)	0.3–2.0 mg/kg	qd	chronic use; stomach aches; headaches;
(Concerta)	18–54 mg	qd	dysphoria
(Ritalin LA)	0.3–2.0 mg/kg	qd	
Amphetamine			
(Dexedrine)	0.3–1.5 mg/kg	bid	Headaches; dysphoria
Dextroamphetamine			
(Adderall)	0.3–1.5 mg/kg	tid	Rebound phenomena (short-acting preparations)
Mixed amphetamine salts			
(Adderall XR)	0.3–1.5 mg/kg	qd	Same as other stimulants; abnormal liver function tests
Magnesium pemoline			
(Cylert)	0.5–3.0 mg/kg	qd	Nausea; headache; stomach upset
Noradrenergic agents			
Atomoxetine			
(Straterra)	40–100 mg daily	qd or bid	Headaches; stomach aches

Adapted from: Wilens TE, Biederman J, Spencer TJ: The patient with attention-deficit hyperactivity disorder. In Stern TA, Herman JB, Slavin PL (eds): *Massachusetts General Hospital Guide to Primary Care Psychiatry,* 2nd edition. New York: McGraw-Hill, 2004.

(*Note:* Pemoline has been associated with cases of hepatotoxicity, and it is not typically used as a first-line treatment.)
- Short-acting forms of stimulants typically require multiple daily dosing. Even with long-acting forms, some patients experience a waning of an effect in the afternoon and require the addition of a short-acting form to bolster its effect.
- The use of stimulants is limited by their restricted schedule II status, by their abuse potential, and by their ability to cause tolerance and psychological dependence. Although most patients receiving stimulants use them responsibly, there has been a surge in popularity of stimulants as drugs of abuse; stimulants in tablet form are sometimes crushed and inhaled intranasally or injected to produce effects that are similar to those of cocaine. Long-acting formulations (particularly those in capsule form, e.g., Concerta) may be less prone to this type of abuse.

A. **Atomoxetine (Straterra®)**
  1. Atomoxetine is not a stimulant, but it is indicated for treatment of ADHD.
  2. It appears to work through selectively inhibiting reuptake of norepinephrine.
  3. It is not a controlled medication, and it does not appear to be associated with abuse or dependence.
  4. There may be a delay of several weeks before maximal clinical effect is seen with atomoxetine.
  5. Side effects of atomoxetine include somnolence, nausea, stomach ache, and insomnia; blood pressure may increase slightly.
  6. Atomoxetine is metabolized by the CYP 450 isoenzyme 2D6. Medications that inhibit 2D6 (e.g., paroxetine, fluoxetine, and bupropion) will increase the blood level of atomoxetine.
  7. Although studies have suggested that atomoxetine is equally efficacious with once- or twice-daily doses, in clinical practice most patients seem to require the twice-daily dosing regimen.

IX. Natural Treatments

The use of medicinal herbs and over-the-counter supplements has risen dramatically in recent years. Factors driving this surge in popularity include dissatisfaction with traditional medicine, an increase in nonphysician practitioners who recommend these treatments, and easy availability, as these treatments are obtained without a prescription. Problems with natural remedies include limited data on efficacy and a lack of FDA regulation (that results in inconsistencies in potency and quality among brands). Several herbs and supplements have psychotropic properties. These agents are described below:

A. St. John's Wort

1. St. John's wort (SJW) is used as a treatment for mild to moderate depression.
2. Data on its efficacy is equivocal. Although several small placebo-controlled trials suggested moderate efficacy, a larger controlled study did not show SJW as being more effective than placebo.
3. **The principal psychoactive components of SJW are thought to be hypericin and hyperforin.**
4. The mechanism of action of SJW is unclear. The crude plant extract mildly inhibits MAO_A and MAO_B in vitro, but is not thought to have these effects in vivo at usual dosing. In vivo, SJW also appears to interact with a variety of other receptors, including adenosine, inositol triphosphate (IP_3), and GABA. Although it is sometimes described as inhibiting the uptake of serotonin, norepinephrine, and dopamine, this has not been clearly demonstrated. Given the lack of consensus about its mechanism of action, it is prudent not to combine SJW with other antidepressants. There have been reports of serotonin syndrome when SJW was combined with SSRIs.
5. Side effects, although usually mild, include dry mouth, dizziness, and phototoxicity.
6. SJW is an inducer of the CYP 450 isoenzyme 3A4 and it may reduce the blood levels and efficacy of several medications (including oral contraceptives, cyclosporine, warfarin, and some protease inhibitors).
7. The usual dosing is 300–600 mg three times daily.

B. S-Adenosyl Methionine (SAMe)

1. Although data are limited, several small studies suggest that SAMe has antidepressant effects at doses up to 1600 mg daily.
2. SAMe is thought to work by donating methyl groups in reactions that promote synthesis of serotonin, norepinephrine, and dopamine, neurotransmitters associated with mood regulation.
3. Deficiency of vitamin B_{12} and folate prevent SAMe from exerting its mood-elevating effects.
4. SAMe is deactivated by prolonged exposure to sunlight.
5. Evaluation of many manufactured brands of SAMe has shown frequent variation between purported and actual potency.
6. SAMe is generally well tolerated. Side effects include nervousness, insomnia, dry mouth, and nausea.

7.   Drug interactions have yet to be reported with SAMe.
8.   The typical dosing of SAMe is 400–1600 mg daily. Its cost can be prohibitive, as SAMe can cost up to $1.50 per 200-mg tablet.

C.   **Omega-3 Fatty Acids**
1.   Initial studies suggested that high-dose omega-3 fatty acids (up to 9 g daily) were effective in bipolar disorder (i.e., they prevented recurrence of mania and depression). Recent studies, however, have not clearly replicated this finding. Several case reports have shown mixed results in treating unipolar depression.
2.   **Active components of omega-3 fatty acids are thought to be eicosapentaenoic acid (EPA) and docosahexaenoic acid (DHA).** Research has suggested that EPA is the more active of the two, and some clinicians recommend preparations with high EPA:DHA ratios.
3.   The mechanism of action of omega-3 fatty acids is unknown, but it may involve regulation of signal transduction inside cells.
4.   Although omega-3 fatty acids are generally well tolerated, side effects can include stomach upset and a fishy aftertaste from some commercial brands of fish oil capsules.
5.   There are no known drug interactions.
6.   Although initial studies were conducted with doses as high as 9–10 g daily, recent studies suggest that doses of 1–2 g daily may be sufficient.

D.   **Kava (*Piper methysticum*)**
1.   Kava is a root that has been used in Polynesian tribal rituals for hundreds of years.
2.   **Kava has mild anxiolytic properties;** its active components, kavapyrones, bind to GABA receptors and exert mild muscle relaxant properties. Kava may also inhibit uptake of norepinephrine, although the clinical relevance of this property is unclear.
3.   Several cases of hepatotoxicity have been associated with kava use; because of this, kava has been removed from the market in several countries.
4.   Other side effects include stomach upset, headache, and dizziness. Chronic use has been associated with a yellowing of the skin, visual problems, and ataxia.
5.   Drug interactions have yet to be reported.
6.   The typical dosing is 60–300 mg daily.
7.   Given its association with hepatotoxicity, it is prudent to avoid

taking kava until there is a better understanding of its safety profile.

E. Valerian

1. Derived from the root *Valeriana officinalis*, valerian has been
    shown in small studies to have mild sedative properties. It is
    commonly used as a mild sleep aid.
2. Valerian's mechanism of action is unclear, but it may decrease
    GABA breakdown, causing decreased sleep latency and an im-
    proved sleep quality.
3. Valerian's side effects are uncommon, but there have been rare
    reports of blurred vision, stomach upset, and headache.
4. It has a notably pungent, unpleasant odor, but as yet no known
    drug interactions.
5. Recommended doses are 300–600 mg 1–2 hours prior to bed-
    time.

F. Ginkgo Biloba

1. Derived from the leaf and seed of the ginkgo biloba tree, it has
    been purported to have cognitive-enhancing properties. Studies
    have suggested that ginkgo may promote modest cognitive
    improvements in severely demented patients, but it may pro-
    duce little or no benefit to those with moderate or no dementia.
2. Ginkgo has also been reported to alleviate antidepressant-
    induced sexual dysfunction. However, a recent double-blind
    study failed to show efficacy.
3. The mechanism of action of ginkgo is unknown, but it may pos-
    sess antioxidant properties.
4. Side effects tend to be mild, but may include anxiety, GI upset,
    and headache.
5. Ginkgo has also been shown to have anticoagulant properties,
    and it has been rarely associated with cerebral hemorrhage in
    elderly patients. Although it may potentiate effects of anticoag-
    ulants, no other known drug interactions have been reported.
6. The typical dosing is 60–120 mg twice daily.

G. Inositol

1. Inositol is a precursor in brain second messenger systems.
2. Small controlled studies and case reports have suggested that
    inositol reduces symptoms of OCD, trichotillomania, depres-
    sion, bulimia, and panic disorder.
3. Side effects of inositol include GI upset and flatulence, and
    rarely dizziness, sedation, headache, or insomnia.
4. No known drug interactions have been reported with inositol.

5. Manufactured in powdered form, inositol is used in doses as high as 12–18 g daily to achieve clinical effect.

X.   Drug-Drug Interactions

Drug-drug interactions are a common occurrence in medical practice, particularly with the increasing number of patients on multiple medications. While some interactions involving psychotropic medications are idiosyncratic, many are predictable and result from known pharmacodynamic and pharmacokinetic properties of the drugs.

A.   **Pharmacodynamic Interactions**
Pharmacodynamic interactions are interactions involving known pharmacological properties of medications. Examples include over-sedation or respiratory depression if benzodiazepines are combined with barbiturates, or cardiac conduction delay caused by combining medications (such as cisapride and thioridazine) that prolong the QTc interval.

B.   **Pharmacokinetic Interactions**
Pharmacokinetic interactions are interactions involving effects on drug absorption, distribution, or metabolism. Examples include decreased absorption of a benzodiazepine when taken with a stomach H_2-blocking medication, such as famotidine, or an increased distribution of lithium (and increased lithium blood level) caused by coadministration with a nonsteroidal anti-inflammatory drug (NSAID). Metabolic induction or inhibition of hepatic enzymes is a frequent cause of pharmacokinetic drug interactions. An increased understanding of the effects of medications on CYP 450 isoenzymes has helped to define and to predict potential drug interactions.

Interaction profiles of specific psychotropic medications are described in the sections above devoted to each medication class.

Common substrates, inhibitors, and inducers of CYP 450 isoenzymes are listed in Table 26-12.

XI.   Side Effects

Side effects are a leading cause of poor compliance with psychotropic medications. Prescribers should have a good understanding of common side-effect profiles of psychotropic medications and of the strategies used to minimize or alleviate them. A full review of psychotropic medication side effects is beyond the scope of this chapter, but some of the commonly encountered side effects and suggestions for their management are described below.

Table 26-12: Common Substrates, Inhibitors, and Inducers of Cytochrome P450 Enzymes

Substrates

2D6

Alfentanil	NSAIDs
Angiotensin inhibitors	Omeprazole
	Paroxetine
Calcium channel blockers	Phenothiazines
	Phenytoin
Celecoxib	Piroxicam
Codeine	Propafenone
Dextromethorphan	Propranolol
Diazepam	Risperidone
Diclofenac	Rosiglitazone
Encainide	Secondary TCAs
Flecainide	S-Warfarin
Glipizide	Tertiary TCAs
Glyburide	Timolol
Hydrocodone	Tolbutamide
Mephenytoin	Tramadol
Metoprolol	Venlafaxine
Naproxen	

3A4

Alprazolam	Oral contraceptives
Buspirone	Propafenone
Caffeine	Quinidine
Carbamazepine	Ritonavir
Diazepam	Saquinavir
Lidocaine	Sildenafil
Loratadine	Steroids
Lovastatin	Tamoxifen
Macrolide antibiotics	Tertiary TCAs
Methadone	Triazolam
Midazolam	Vinblastine
Nefazodone	Zaleplon
	Zolpidem

1A2

Acetaminophen	Phenacetin
Aminophylline	Phenothiazines
Caffeine	Tacrine
Clozapine	Tertiary TCAs
Haloperidol	Theophylline
Olanzapine	

Inhibitors

3A4	2D6
Cimetidine	Bupropion
Clarithromycin	Cimetidine
Diltiazem	Clomipramine
Erythromycin	Fluoxetine
Fluoxetine	Paroxetine
Fluvoxamine	Ritonavir
Grapefruit juice	
Indinavir	
Itraconazole	
Ketoconazole	
Nefazodone	
Nelfinavir	
Ritonavir	
Saquinavir	
Verapamil	

Inducers
3A4

Carbamazepine
Phenobarbital
Phenytoin
Rifabutin
Rifampin
St. John's wort

NSAID, nonsteroidal anti-inflammatory drug; TCA, tricyclic antidepressant.
Adapted from: Alpert JE: Drug-drug interactions: The interface between psychotropics and other agents. In Stern TA, Herman JB, Slavin PL (eds):*Massachusetts General Hospital Guide to Primary Care Psychiatry*, 2nd edition. New York: McGraw-Hill, 2004.

A.   **Antidepressant-Induced Sexual Side Effects**
Antidepressants, primarily SSRIs, SNRIs, TCAs, and MAOIs are frequently associated with sexual side effects (including decreased libido, erectile dysfunction, ejaculatory delay, and anorgasmia). The incidence of sexual side effects from SSRIs is higher than initially predicted, and side effects may affect 50% or more of patients on these agents.

1.   **Management**

a.   For patients on antidepressant doses higher than typical maintenance doses, a decrease in dose may be a reasonable first step. As there is a risk of diminishing antidepressant efficacy when lowering the dose, this strategy must be instituted carefully and evaluated on an individual basis.

b.   For men with antidepressant-associated erectile dysfunction, a trial of a phosphodiesterase inhibitor, such as sildenafil 50–100 mg, may be tried (if there are no cardiac contraindications). Other phosphodiesterase inhibitors, such as vardenafil or tadalafil, may also be effective, although clinical experience with these agents in treating antidepressant-induced erectile dysfunction is rather limited. While there were initial suggestions that sildenafil could be helpful in treating antidepressant-associated sexual dysfunction in women, this was not shown to be effective in a recent study.

c.   For women and men who do not benefit from sildenafil, switching to an antidepressant with minimal sexual side effects (e.g., bupropion or mirtazapine) can be considered. This should also be evaluated on an individual basis, as changing antidepressants may not be clinically indicated for some patients.

d.   Patients who experience sexual side effects on a SSRI may benefit from adding bupropion, starting at 100–150 mg daily and increasing to 300 mg daily if needed. This strategy is not well characterized in patients on SNRIs, and should generally be approached carefully in patients on TCAs and MAOIs due to potential for serious drug interactions.

e.   Other strategies with anecdotal support include the use of adjunctive methylphenidate or dextroamphetamine (5–10 mg three times a day), or adjunctive buspirone (5–20 mg three times a day).

f.   Other agents with limited anecdotal support include amantadine (100 mg twice or three times a day), cyproheptadine (2–12 mg 1 hour before sexual activity), and yohimbine

(5.4 mg three times a day). These medications are seldom used, however, as they frequently cause side effects.

B.   **Psychotropic-Induced Weight Gain**
Many psychotropic medications are associated with substantial weight gain; these include conventional antipsychotics, clozapine, olanzapine, quetiapine, risperidone, lithium, valproate, mirtazapine, paroxetine, TCAs, and MAOIs. As obesity is associated with significant morbidity, efforts should be made to avoid this problem. In some cases, choosing a medication with less propensity for weight gain is an appropriate option. In others, trying to minimize the amount of weight gain is the best strategy.
1.   **Management.** Diet and exercise tend to be the most reliable methods of minimizing psychotropic-induced weight gain. Although this is not feasible for all patients, those who are able to exercise regularly and to maintain a healthy diet may be able to prevent substantial weight gain. Consultation with a nutritionist can help patients establish a diet and monitor progress.
2.   Medications have been used in attempts to minimize psychotropic-induced weight gain, usually with equivocal results. Some success has been reported in minimizing weight gain associated with olanzapine and valproate by coprescribing H_2-blockers such as nizatidine (300 mg twice daily). Topiramate may prevent weight gain in doses of 100–300 mg daily. Amantadine (100 mg two or three times daily) has been reported in small studies to reduce weight gain in patients on olanzapine.
3.   Patients on atypical antipsychotics should also have periodic monitoring of plasma lipids, as well as periodic evaluation of other markers of metabolic abnormalities (Table 26-13).

C.   **Atypical Antipsychotics and Diabetes**
Atypical antipsychotics have been associated with an increased risk of developing abnormalities of glucose metabolism (including hyperglycemia, new-onset diabetes, and spontaneous ketoacidosis). These have occurred regardless of psychotropic-induced weight gain. Because this phenomenon is not yet well understood, **the FDA has required each maker of atypical antipsychotics to add information about potential glucose abnormalities to product literature.** The majority of reports of glucose abnormalities, however, have been linked to treatment with olanzapine and clozapine.
1.   **Recommendations**
a.   **Patients taking atypical antipsychotics should be monitored for signs and symptoms of hyperglycemia,** such as

Table 26-13. Suggested Metabolic Monitoring for Patients on Atypical Antipsychotics

Parameter	Baseline	4 Weeks	8 Weeks	12 Weeks	Quarterly	Annually	Every 5 Years
Personal/family history	X					X	
Weight (BMI)	X	X	X	X	X		
Waist circumference	X					X	
Blood pressure	X			X		X	
Fasting plasma glucose	X			X		X	
Fasting lipid profile	X			X			X

BMI, body mass index.
Adapted from American Diabetes Association et al, 2004.

fatigue, thirst, polyuria, weight loss, and blurred vision. Patients at particular risk for developing glucose abnormalities include those with risk factors for diabetes (e.g., family history, obesity, age >45, hypertension, hypertriglyceridemia, and a sedentary lifestyle).

b. Recent consensus guidelines recommend regular monitoring of metabolic parameters in patients on atypical antipsychotics (see Table 26-13).

c. Some clinicians will avoid using olanzapine or clozapine in patients with pre-existing diabetes if other options are available. In some countries, olanzapine has been labeled as contraindicated in patients with diabetes.

Suggested Readings

American Diabetes Association; American Psychiatric Association; American Association of Clinical Endocrinologists; North American Association for the Study of Obesity: Consensus development conference on antipsychotic drugs and obesity and diabetes. *Diabetes Care* 2004;27:596–601.

American Psychiatric Association practice guidelines for the treatment of patients with bipolar disorder (revision). *Am J Psychiatry* 2002;159(4 Suppl):1–50.

Arana GW, Rosenbaum JF: *Handbook of Psychiatric Drug Therapy,* 4th edition. Baltimore: Lippincott Williams & Wilkins, 2000.

Fava M, Judge R, Hoog SL, et al: Fluoxetine versus sertraline and paroxetine in major depressive disorder: changes in weight with long-term treatment. *J Clin Psychiatry* 2000;61:863–867.

Fava M: The role of the serotonergic and noradrenergic neurotransmitter systems in the treatment of psychological and physical symptoms of depression. *J Clin Psychiatry* 2003;64(Suppl 13):26–29.

Ghaemi SN, Berv DA, Klugman J, et al: Oxcarbazepine treatment of bipolar disorder. *J Clin Psychiatry* 2003;64:943–945.

Gitlin M: Sexual dysfunction with psychotropic drugs. *Expert Opin Pharmacother* 2003;4:2259–2269.

Hirsch M, Birnbaum RJ: Pharmacology and use of antidepressants. Up-to-date CD-ROM Textbook and Online, version 12.1:2004.

Hirsch M, Birnbaum RJ: Sexual dysfunction associated with selective serotonin reuptake inhibitor (SSRI) antidepressants. Up-to-date CD-ROM Textbook and Online, version 12.1:2004.

Hirsch M: What are the uses and dangers of kava? *Harv Ment Health Lett* 2000;17:8.

Kane JM: Pharmacologic treatment of schizophrenia. *Biol Psychiatry* 1999;46:1396–1408.

Kasper S: Issues in the treatment of bipolar disorder. *Eur Neuropsychopharmacol* 2003;13(Suppl 2):S37–S42.

Ketter TA, Manji HK, Post RM: Potential mechanisms of action of lamotrigine in the treatment of bipolar disorders. *J Clin Psychopharmacol* 2003;23:484–495.

Ketter TA, Wang PW, Becker OV, et al: The diverse roles of anticonvulsants in bipolar disorders. *Ann Clin Psychiatry* 2003;15:95–108.

LaRoche SM, Helmers SL: The new antiepileptic drugs: scientific review. *JAMA* 2004;291:605–614.

Masand PS: Tolerability and adherence issues in antidepressant therapy. *Clin Ther* 2003;25:2289–2304.

Newcomer JW, Haupt DW, Fucetola R, et al: Abnormalities in glucose regulation during antipsychotic treatment of schizophrenia. *Arch Gen Psychiatry* 2002;59: 337–345.

Reid IC, Stewart CA: How antidepressants work: new perspectives on the pathophysiology of depressive disorder. *Br J Psychiatry* 2001;178:299–303.

Sachs GS: Decision tree for the treatment of bipolar disorder. *J Clin Psychiatry* 2003;64(Suppl 8):35–40.

Sachs GS, Printz DJ, Kahn DA, et al: The Expert Consensus Guideline Series: Medication Treatment of Bipolar Disorder 2000. *Postgrad Med Spec* 2000;No. 1–104.

Stahl SM, Grady MM: Differences in mechanism of action between current and future antidepressants. *J Clin Psychiatry* 2003;64(Suppl 13):13–17.

Stern TA, Herman JB, Slavin PL (eds): *Massachusetts General Hospital Guide to Primary Care Psychiatry,* 2nd edition. New York: McGraw-Hill, 2004.

Strakowski SM, DelBello MP, Adler CM: Comparative efficacy and tolerability of drug treatments for bipolar disorder. *CNS Drugs* 2001;15:701–718.

Chapter 27

An Approach to Forensic Issues

REBECCA W. BRENDEL, MD, JD

I. Overview

Legal issues arise frequently in psychiatric practice, and are often a source of concern and anxiety for psychiatrists. Careful assessment and thoughtful treatment, combined with a basic understanding of relevant legal contexts, are crucial skill sets that psychiatrists can apply to assure competent care of patients and practice in accordance with prevailing law. This chapter provides a practical approach to critical issues in forensic psychiatry.

II. Suicide

A. **Epidemiology**
Suicide is the **eleventh leading cause of death** in the United States, accounting for approximately 29,000 deaths each year.
1. The ratio of suicide attempts to completed suicides is between 10 and 25 to 1. More females than males attempt suicide, but males are more likely to succeed.
2. In general, the **risk of suicide increases with age,** with the exception of individuals 15–24 years of age, for whom suicide is the third leading cause of death.
3. Caucasians and Native Americans have the highest suicide rates in the U.S.
4. Personal factors associated with higher suicide rates include being divorced or widowed, unemployed, or in financial difficulty and living alone.

B. **Evaluation**
Evaluation and treatment of the suicidal patient are important skills for psychiatrists since approximately 90% of completed suicides occur in individuals with at least one psychiatric diagnosis and approximately two-thirds of individuals who commit suicide have seen a psychiatric or nonpsychiatric physician in the month prior to making an attempt. Like any other psychiatric assessment, the evaluation of the suicidal patient **includes performing a complete men-**

Address for correspondence: Dr. Rebecca W. Brendel, Massachusetts General Hospital, Fruit Street, Warren Building Room 605, Boston, MA 02114, email: RBrendel@Partners.org.

tal status examination and screening for the presence of major psychiatric illness. However, the evaluation also requires critical attention to specific historical elements to form a careful risk assessment. Suicidal individuals are often hesitant to share their suicidal thoughts; therefore, a suicide risk assessment must occur in every patient, not just patients voicing suicidal ideas.

1. The central elements of a suicide evaluation include:
   a. Assessment of the extent of suicidal ideas;
   b. Determination of the presence of a suicide plan, including access to means, potential lethality, and likelihood of rescue;
   c. Identification of precipitants to suicidality;
   d. Inquiry about past suicide attempts (since 50% of suicides occur in patients who have a history of prior attempts);
   e. Assessment of social supports; and,
   f. Assessment of additional risk factors.
2. **Risk factors** may include those detailed in the epidemiology section above (male, age >60, white or Native American, widowed or divorced, living alone, unemployment, financial difficulties, and recent loss) as well as psychiatric risk factors. **Psychiatric risk factors** include presence of a mood disorder, substance abuse, anxiety, psychosis, personality disorder, impulsivity and risk-taking behavior, and family history of suicide.

C. **Management and Treatment**
If a patient has attempted suicide, **the first priority in caring for the patient is medical evaluation and stabilization.**

1. Throughout the medical and psychiatric assessment, the safety of the patient and of staff must be ensured. Patients may make additional suicide attempts in emergency rooms and hospitals. **The least restrictive means to ensure patient safety should be employed,** ranging from frequent or one-to-one supervision and medication to use of physical restraints.
2. The mainstay of suicide assessment lies in clinical judgment, and **careful documentation** of a complete evaluation and the thought process leading to decisions is critical.
3. Acutely suicidal patients will generally require hospitalization in a locked facility. For less suicidal patients, other arrangements involving social, family, treatment, and community supports may be adequate and preferable in protecting the patient's safety.
4. Treatment for underlying psychiatric illness may include con-

tainment and psychosocial, pharmacologic, and somatic therapies.

5. Prior to discharge, it is critical that psychiatrists and patients together achieve the following interventions:
    a. Removal of potential means for suicide;
    b. Exploration of the precipitants for suicidal ideas and behavior and identification of alternative coping strategies;
    c. Treatment of the underlying psychiatric illness and/or substance abuse;
    d. Establishment of, or increase in, outpatient supports and arrangement of close follow-up; and
    e. Development of a plan to address future suicidal thoughts.

III. Boundary Issues

A. **Overview**

Boundaries in psychiatric treatment are essential to the therapeutic relationship; they also serve to provide rules, to guide expectations, and to foster trust. Boundaries are a result of the fiduciary nature of the doctor-patient relationship (i.e., the physician's legal and ethical obligation to act in the patient's best interest). **Boundary crossings and boundary violations** may occur, the former referring to small but potentially important disruptions and the latter involving more obvious transgressions. Determination of whether a boundary crossing or violation has occurred depends both on the action and the setting in which it happens. For example, interactions between a doctor and patient outside of appointments may be viewed differently in rural and urban areas.

B. **Sexual Contact between Doctors and Patients**

However, certain behaviors, such as **sexual contact between doctors and patients, are uniformly considered unethical.**

1. Ethics guidelines of the American Medical Association and the American Psychiatric Association proscribe sexual contact between physicians and patients.
2. The APA guideline refers both to current and former patients.
3. Medical boards in all 50 states view sexual contact and other physician exploitation of patients as grounds for discipline, and some states have gone further by criminalizing this behavior by physicians.

C.   **Business and Social Dealings with Patients**
      While sex in the treatment relationship is perhaps the most egregious
      boundary violation, other boundary issues include business and
      social dealings with patients.
      1.   Anything that can detract from the physician's objectivity and
            attention to the patient's condition and best interest presents the
            potential for harm to the patient and could render the psychia-
            trist legally responsible.
      2.   It is therefore critical to obtain consultation and supervision in
            situations in which a potential boundary crossing or violation
            has or could occur.

IV.   Informed Consent

A.   **A Process, Not a Form**
      Informed consent is the process by which a physician obtains the
      patient's permission to provide treatment.
      1.   This permission may be obtained from the patient or from a sub-
            stitute decision-maker, so long as the person making the deci-
            sion does so
            a.   **Competently** (has the mental capacity or ability to make
                  the decision) and
            b.   **Voluntarily,** based on adequate information.
      2.   Informed consent is both **an ethical and a legal concept.**
            a.   As an ethical concept, it functions to respect the patient's
                  autonomy and right to self-determination.
            b.   As a legal concept, it is a fundamental of the standard of
                  medical and psychiatric care and **failure to obtain
                  informed consent is grounds for a medical malpractice
                  lawsuit.**
      3.   However, several narrow **exceptions to the informed consent
            requirement exist.**
            a.   **Emergencies** are the first exception. Where failure to pro-
                  vide treatment would lead to serious and imminent deterio-
                  ration, treatment may be initiated without consent, but when
                  time permits, consent must be obtained for continuing treat-
                  ment.
            b.   **Other exceptions include waivers,** in which the patient
                  may defer to someone else's judgment, **and therapeutic
                  privilege,** which allows deferral of obtaining consent if the
                  consent process would pose a serious risk of harm or dete-
                  rioration of the patient's condition.
                  i.   However, therapeutic privilege may not be used as an
                        exception on the grounds that an attempt to obtain in-
                        formed consent would lead to treatment refusal.

B. **Standards**

Various standards exist regarding the amount and nature of information that must be provided in order to obtain informed consent for treatment.

1. In general, **five elements must be met to ensure that enough information is given for the patient** to be able to make an informed decision regarding treatment. These five parameters are:

   a. The nature of the condition and the proposed treatment;

   b. The nature and probability of risks associated with the treatment, including small but frequently-occurring risks, and large but infrequently-occurring risks;

   c. The inability to predict results;

   d. The irreversibility of the treatment, if applicable; and

   e. Available alternative treatments.

2. Each of these elements should be documented in the appropriate institutional consent documents.

V. Capacity and Competency

A. **Overview**

As discussed in the previous section, medical and psychiatric decision-making requires that a patient possesses the physical and mental abilities to meaningfully participate in the decision-making. **Capacity** is a clinical term referring to a patient's ability to make decisions whereas **competency** is the analogous legal determination, made by a judge, with specific legal consequences. How much capacity a patient must have to make a decision depends on the **risk:benefit ratio of the proposed treatment.** For example, where the proposed intervention is low risk and high benefit, a lesser degree of capacity would be required than for a higher risk, less potentially beneficial result.

B. **Specific or Global Capacity**

Capacity and competency can either be global—referring to all adult responsibilities, or specific—referring to a single area or decision, such as a treatment decision.

1. All adults are presumed competent, but a capacity evaluation is clinically indicated any time there is a question about a patient's ability to make decisions.

2. Clinical determinations of capacity by psychiatrists most frequently involve specific capacity determinations for acceptance or refusal of a proposed treatment or intervention.

3. A patient's capacity to make treatment decisions is evaluated with a four-step analysis. All four parts of the capacity test must

be met in order to make a finding of capacity. The four-step analysis is:

   a. Does the patient express a consistent preference?

   b. Does the patient have a factual understanding of the information provided?

   c. Is the patient able to appreciate the consequences of accepting and rejecting treatment?

   d. Can the patient rationally manipulate the information and come to a logical decision?

4. If any one or more of these four criteria is not met, the patient lacks capacity to make the decision and a substitute decision-maker should be asked to give consent, unless the proposed treatment is emergent (see above, under Informed Consent).

C. **The Health Care Proxy, Durable Power of Attorney, and Advance Directive**

A finding of incapacity triggers the applicability of a health care proxy, durable power of attorney for health care decisions, or another type of advance directive designating a substitute decision-maker.

1. In situations in which no prior designation of a substitute decision-maker was made by the patient, a substitute decision-maker may be designated by state law where applicable (the general practice is initially to approach the next of kin), or court proceedings may be held to appoint a guardian. Alternate decision-makers make decisions based on what the patient would have wanted or substituted judgment.

2. A finding of incapacity may trigger legal proceedings to determine competency and the need for a **court-appointed guardian.**

3. As opposed to a clinical determination of incapacity, a legal determination of incompetence takes away rights from the patient in areas in which the patient is felt to lack decisional ability. Depending on the state where the guardian is appointed, the **guardian makes decisions based on either the best interests of the individual, substituted judgment, or a combination of the two.**

VI. Civil Commitment

A. Overview

Civil commitment is the process by which an individual is admitted to a psychiatric facility. Civil commitment may be voluntary, where a competent patient voluntarily consents to admission, or involuntary, where a person is hospitalized against his or her will. Like other treatments in psychiatry, voluntary civil commitment occurs via the process of informed consent. In many states, laws limit the ability of voluntarily civilly committed patients to leave the hospital at will; instead, admissions are frequently referred to as *conditional voluntary admissions* which allow for a brief period of prolonged hospitalization after a patient desires to leave to allow staff to perform an evaluation and safety assessment prior to the patient's departure.

B. **Dangerousness to Self or Others**
Involuntary civil commitment impinges on patient autonomy and is permitted only when the patient is a danger to him- or herself or others.
1. Different states have different procedures and legal requirements for involuntary civil commitment, although all states require a finding of dangerousness to self or others due to mental illness.
2. In addition, an initial commitment period authorized by one or more psychiatrists without court intervention is generally permitted. It is important for psychiatrists to familiarize themselves with applicable law in every jurisdiction in which they practice.
3. Because involuntary civil commitment is considered a deprivation of constitutionally protected rights, all state laws must guarantee adequate procedural protections, such as court hearings, to avoid arbitrary and prolonged involuntary hospitalization.

C. **Improper Commitment**
Improper commitment **may result in lawsuits for deprivation of civil rights, false imprisonment, and negligence (malpractice).** However, psychiatrists should not hesitate to invoke civil commitment if a patient poses a risk of danger to self or others.
1. If a psychiatrist releases a patient he or she knows poses a danger to self or others due to mental illness and the patient causes harm to self and/or others, the psychiatrist could be held responsible for malpractice.
2. In some jurisdictions, psychiatrists may have **an obligation to warn a third party of potential harm** by a patient when the patient has made threats toward an identifiable victim (see below, under confidentiality). It is important for psychiatrists to be aware of these laws, often referred to as **Tarasoff obligations** after a landmark California case establishing this duty, in their jurisdictions.

D. Fiduciary Duty

Overall, the guiding principle in clinical determinations of involuntary civil commitment is no different than that in good clinical practice—the psychiatrist's fiduciary duty to the patient. A psychiatrist acting in the patient's best interest, under applicable law, who carefully documents examination findings and the basis for a clinical judgment of need for involuntary commitment will be in a good position against challenges to the legitimacy of a civil commitment.

VII. Confidentiality

A. Overview

Psychiatrists are ethically, customarily, and legally bound to keep patient information private unless the patient gives consent for release of the information to a third party. The confidential nature of the doctor-patient relationship is considered a fundamental foundation allowing for the trusting disclosure of patient information to facilitate treatment. However, the ideal of confidentiality often conflicts with other societal goals, leading to exceptions to the general rule of confidentiality. One example is mandated reporting of abuse and neglect (see below) and reporting of cases of certain infectious diseases. Different states have varying reporting obligations for physicians regarding danger to third parties and other issues, and it is critical for psychiatrists to familiarize themselves with the law in every jurisdiction in which they practice.

B. HIPAA

In 2003, the Health Insurance Portability and Accountability Act of 1996 (HIPAA) went into effect, potentially altering the traditional notion of confidentiality and the consent requirement for disclosure of private medical and psychiatric information.

1. Under HIPAA, provisions for administrative simplification, once a patient in a certain practice is given a **privacy notice,** consent is not required for information release for treatment, payment, and health care operations.

2. One important **exception to this non-requirement for consent is for substance abuse records,** which are protected under separate federal law and for which consent is always required prior to release.

     a. HIPAA is explicitly a "floor" of patient protection, and state and local laws that provide a higher degree of protection for patient health information and/or allow patients greater access to their own medical records supersede the HIPAA provisions. It is therefore critical for psychiatrists to familiarize themselves with prevailing law in jurisdictions in which they practice.

3. **HIPAA also grants patients broad rights of access to their medical records,** including psychiatric records, with only one small exception for psychotherapy notes.

    a. It is critical to appreciate that the **definition of psychotherapy notes under HIPAA** is extremely narrow and is available only if these notes are

        i. Kept separate from the remainder of the psychiatric and medical chart,

        ii. Contain only information related to a confidential therapy session, and

        iii. Do not contain information more properly kept in the general chart, such as diagnosis, prognosis, medication, lab results, session start and end times, and other such information.

    b. It is important for psychiatrists to think carefully about documentation, as patients and other entities (such as insurance companies) have increased access to health information in the age of HIPAA.

    c. Psychiatrists should be familiar with institutional HIPAA officers and other resources available to assist with management of information under this new law.

VIII. Domestic Violence

A.   **Overview**

Domestic violence is intentionally violent or controlling behavior by a current or previous intimate partner of the victim. The purpose of the domestic violence is to control or assert power over the victim. Domestic violence is repetitive, escalates over time, and poses unique challenges for intervention since victims who leave their abusers are at a greater risk of being murdered by the perpetrator than are victims who stay. Examples of such behaviors include physical injury (actual or threatened), sexual assault, psychological or emotional torment, economic control, and social isolation.

B.   **Epidemiology**

1. Each year, 3 to 4 million women are victims of domestic violence in the United States.

2. Women are six times more likely than are men to be victims of domestic violence; 90% of abusive relationships involve male perpetrators and female victims.

3. Less is known about same-sex couples, but their rate of domestic violence appears to be similar to that of heterosexual couples. Although domestic violence spans all cultures and all segments of society, women with the following characteristics are at greater risk:
    a. Single, separated, or divorced
    b. Recent application for a restraining order
    c. Age between 17 and 28
    d. Poverty
    e. Alcohol or substance abuse in self or partner
    f. Pregnancy and history of abuse
    g. Jealous or possessive partner
4. The risk of perpetrating violence is greater in men who are young, poorly educated, and of low income with antisocial personality disorder and/or depression.

B.   Evaluation
Victims and perpetrators represent all segments of the population. Many victims will not volunteer information regarding abuse, so screening should be a routine part of every psychiatric and medical evaluation. **All evaluations should be carefully and thoughtfully documented,** as they may become important legal evidence.
1. One question, "Have you been hit, kicked, punched, or otherwise hurt by someone within the past year?" will identify more than 70% of women in violent relationships.
2. If a patient reports past or current abuse regarding first episode, worst episode, and last episode, further history should be obtained.
3. The victim's perception of current risk should be taken seriously and given credence.
4. A safety assessment should be performed in all cases and must include evaluation of:
    a. The presence of guns or other weapons
    b. Escalating frequency or severity of beatings and/or threats
    c. New violence outside the relationship by the perpetrator
5. A complete mental status examination and psychiatric assessment should be completed in all evaluations. Particular attention should be given to evaluation of homicidal and suicidal thoughts and the presence of a psychiatric disorder, as victims of domestic violence may suffer from a broad spectrum of psychiatric disorders (including adjustment disorder, depression with or without psychotic features, anxiety disorders, dissociative disorders, eating disorders, substance abuse, and mental disorders due to acute or repeated head trauma).

6. Trauma may also exacerbate pre-existing psychiatric disorders. Patients must be asked questions about abuse in private settings and partners, friends, and family members should not be used as interpreters. Conducting a domestic violence assessment in the presence of an abusive partner both lessens the chance of a truthful response and puts the victim at increased risk for future violence. Victims may be hesitant to be truthful about abuse due to the effects of chronic abuse (such as shame, fear, and concerns that they won't be believed).

7. Victims from vulnerable groups such as illegal aliens, substance users, and the mentally and cognitively impaired are often more difficult to evaluate due to fear of retaliation or lack of ability to communicate about the violence.

8. A complete medical history, physical examination, and neurologic screening should also be performed by a trained physician. The medical history may offer information about previously unsuspected abuse in the form of previous treatment for non–motor vehicle traumas or unusual injuries, and frequent emergency room visits.

9. It is also critical to determine whether children in the household have seen or been victims of violence, as **physicians in all 50 states are legally obligated to report suspected or known child abuse or neglect.**

C. **Management and Treatment**
Treatment begins with detection.
1. Physicians should not measure their success by whether the victim leaves the perpetrator. Instead, physicians should listen to the patient, take the patient seriously, document the evaluation carefully, and assert four critical elements to the patient:
   a. Violence is criminal.
   b. The victim does not deserve to be hurt.
   c. The victim is not at fault and is not responsible.
   d. The abuser is unequivocally responsible for the abusive behavior. Primary psychiatric disorders should be treated and a safety plan should be developed with the patient.
2. A safety plan includes an assessment of social and financial supports, coping strategies, level of functioning, outcome of previous attempts to leave and identification of safe destinations, timing, and access to phone and transportation.
3. In summary, the acronym "RADAR" is often used to highlight the key elements of domestic violence screening:
   a. **R**emember to ask routinely.
   b. **A**sk directly about violence.

    c.   Document information carefully.

    d.   Assess the patient's safety.

    e.   Review options with the patient and know referral options.

IX.   Abuse and Neglect

A.   **Epidemiology**

Although the number of reported cases of child and elder abuse and neglect in the United States is increasing, the majority of cases go unreported to protective agencies. While **abuse is generally referred to an act of "commission"** of physical or emotional abuse, **neglect is an act of "omission"** or failure of parents or other responsible parties to fulfill obligations to the vulnerable child or elder in their care. In the elderly, self-neglect may also occur. Abuse and neglect may be physical and/or emotional and occur in all sectors of society.

1.   Child abuse and neglect affect more than 1 million children in the U.S. each year, although the exact prevalence and incidence are unknown due to several factors, including reporting bias, cultural consideration, and location of health care delivery.

2.   Younger children are at greater risk of fatality from child abuse, and the majority of deaths occur in children under the age of 1.

3.   Mothers are more often the perpetrators of abuse in prepubertal children, whereas fathers are more likely to abuse adolescents.

4.   Elder abuse and neglect may occur in any setting, domestic or institutional.

    a.   A 2003 study estimated that 1 to 2 million Americans age 65 or older have been subjected to abuse or neglect by a caretaker; however, research in this area is limited.

    b.   Elder mistreatment and self-neglect correlate with shortened survival.

B.   **Evaluation**

Psychiatrists and other physicians are mandated reporters of abuse and neglect in all 50 states. Practitioners should familiarize themselves with requirements in their jurisdictions and the procedures for initiating reports to protective agencies of abuse and neglect.

1.   Because psychiatrists have an affirmative legal obligation to report abuse and neglect, all allegations by potential victims should be taken seriously and evaluated by an experienced clinician with expertise and training in abuse and neglect assessment.

2. In the elderly, hospitals may be the only source of assistance for an elder at risk, and physicians should therefore be alert to the possibility of medical symptoms arising from abuse and neglect.

3. In child abuse, both psychological and physical sequelae of abuse may be present.
   a. Psychopathological findings include impulsivity and hyperactivity, depression, conduct disorder, learning difficulties, and substance abuse.
   b. Self-mutilation and suicide attempts may also occur.
   c. A thorough physical exam should be performed by a pediatrician for physical signs of abuse, which may include:
      i. Bruises and welts that leave the pattern of the inflicting instrument
      ii. Burns via immersion, an object, a cigarette, or a rope
      iii. Fractures, often multiple or spiral, of different ages
      iv. Bruising of the abdominal wall or bruising, perforation, and/or rupture of abdominal viscera
      v. CNS injuries including hematomas and hemorrhage (subarachnoid and/or retinal)

5. In child neglect, physical evidence of:
   a. Malnutrition (including pica)
   b. Poor hygiene
   c. Failure to thrive
   d. Developmental delay
   e. Lack of appropriate medical and dental care for illness or age (such as immunizations)
   f. Clothing incongruent with weather conditions

6. Psychopathology of neglected children is less well studied than in abuse, but often includes insecure attachments, low-self esteem, and poor frustration tolerance.

7. Children who witness domestic violence are also considered to be victims of neglect.

C.   Management and Treatment

The first critical step is to ensure safety of the victim or suspected victim. **Ensuring the safety of the vulnerable individual may require hospitalization for continued evaluation or other emergency interventions by protection agencies** to ensure no further abuse or neglect is perpetrated.

1. As described above, all suspected abuse and neglect must be reported to the appropriate protection agency, regardless of concerns about breach of confidentiality.

2. In the elderly, additional services may be required in a current setting, or a change in living situation may be needed.

3. In children, treatment requires a collaborative approach with both the parents and the child(ren).
   a. Assessment and treatment of psychopathology in both the child and the parent is critical.
   b. A multimodal approach targeting the etiology of abuse and neglect is essential for effective outcomes.
   c. Treatment may include family, individual, and couples therapy, psychopharmacologic management, and/or substance abuse treatment.
   d. Preventive measures including targeting of high-risk groups for early intervention and parent education are also used to decrease the incidence and prevalence of child abuse and neglect.

Suggested Readings

Beck BJ: Domestic violence. In Stern TA, Herman JB (eds): *Massachusetts General Hospital Psychiatry Update and Board Preparation,* 2nd edition. New York: McGraw-Hill, 2004:533–537.

Gutheil TG, Appelbaum PA: *Clinical Handbook of Psychiatry and the Law,* 3rd edition. Baltimore: Lippincott Williams & Wilkins, 2000.

Kazim A, Brendel RW: Abuse and neglect. In Stern TA, Herman JB (eds): *Massachusetts General Hospital Psychiatry Update and Board Preparation,* 2nd edition. New York: McGraw-Hill, 2004:539–544.

Perlis RH, Stern TA: Suicide. In Stern TA, Herman JB (eds): *Massachusetts General Hospital Psychiatry Update and Board Preparation,* 2nd edition. New York: McGraw-Hill, 2004:405–409.

Schouten R, Brendel RW: Legal aspects of consultation. In Stern TA, Fricchione GL, Cassem NH, et al (eds): *The Massachusetts General Hospital Handbook of General Hospital Psychiatry,* 5th edition. Philadelphia: Mosby/Elsevier, 2004: 349–364.

Schouten R: Psychiatry and the law I: informed consent, competency, treatment refusal, and civil commitment. In Stern TA, Herman JB (eds): *Massachusetts General Hospital Psychiatry Update and Board Preparation,* 2nd edition. New York: McGraw-Hill, 2004:411–415.

Schouten R: Psychiatry and the law III: malpractice and boundary violations. In Stern TA, Herman JB (eds): *Massachusetts General Hospital Psychiatry Update and Board Preparation,* 2nd edition. New York: McGraw-Hill, 2004:503–506.

Chapter 28

An Approach to Psychotherapy

DAVID H. BRENDEL, MD, PHD

I. Overview

Psychotherapy is a treatment modality that depends on talking to effect psychological and behavioral change. In the last few decades there has been an explosion in the number of available psychotherapeutic interventions. Most of these schools of psychotherapy can be broadly classified within the categories enumerated below. Some psychotherapies are short-term (ranging from one to several sessions) and some are long-term (lasting months to years) and open-ended. Psychotherapy may occur one-on-one (individual psychotherapy) or in larger cohorts (couples, families, and groups). This chapter describes several commonly practiced forms of psychotherapy:

A. **Individual Psychotherapy**
    1. Psychodynamic psychotherapy
        a. Classical Freudian
        b. Ego psychology
        c. Object relations theory
        d. Self psychology
        e. Relational approaches
        f. Brief psychodynamic approaches
    2. Cognitive-behavioral therapy (CBT)
    3. Interpersonal therapy (IPT)
    4. Dialectical behavior therapy (DBT)
    5. Psychotherapy with psychopharmacologic management

B. **Group Psychotherapy**

C. **Couples Therapy**

D. **Family Therapy**

Address for correspondence: Dr. David H. Brendel, McLean Hospital, 115 Mill St., North Belknap, Belmont MA, 02478, email: dbrendel@ partners.org.

II. Individual Psychotherapy

Psychotherapy most commonly occurs in a one-to-one relationship: patient and clinician. All forms of individual psychotherapy depend on the establishment of a **therapeutic alliance** (or working alliance) that can be characterized as a respectful, trusting, and collaborative partnership that aims for beneficial changes in the patient's life. In all forms of individual psychotherapy, the clinician is ethically obligated to maintain appropriate **professional boundaries,** thereby avoiding exploitation of the patient (emotionally, sexually, financially, or otherwise).

A.   **Psychodynamic Psychotherapy**

   Psychodynamic psychotherapy is a term that encompasses multiple forms of treatment that are usually of a long-term nature. It is rooted in the theoretical suppositions that the mind is **complex,** operates by **conscious and unconscious processes,** seeks and creates **meaning,** and interacts with other people and things **(objects)** in the outside world. Several distinct psychodynamic theories and technical approaches exist, which may be applied in relatively pure form, but often are combined to fashion an individually tailored approach (psychiatrist **Robert Abernethy** has written on **integrative psychotherapy,** which aims to synthesize the various psychodynamic approaches described below). Common psychodynamic approaches can be broadly classified as follows:

   1. **The classical Freudian approach**
       a. This approach is based on the work of **Sigmund Freud,** who believed that human experience and behavior are determined by **unconscious** dynamics. According to this model the mind is always in **conflict** with itself.
       b. **Sexuality** (Eros, libido) and **aggression** are basic **drives,** and **repression** is the process by which unacceptable drives are blocked from reaching consciousness.
       c. Freud created a **topographical model** of the mind that involves the unconscious, the preconscious, and the conscious mind.
       d   As an individual ages, he or she passes through several **developmental stages** (e.g., oral, anal, phallic, latency, and genital). Psychopathology may be caused by **fixations** (i.e., arrested development) at any of these stages.
       e. The **Oedipal complex** is a nodal moment in psychological development. During this phase the child desires the opposite-sex parent but experiences the same-sex parent as an obstacle to that desire and also fears retaliation from the same-sex parent (e.g., **castration anxiety**). The Oedipal

complex is resolved by renouncing the desire for the oppo-site-sex parent and forming identification with the same-sex parent. Parental values and rules are **introjected** as the Oedipal complex resolves ("the superego is heir to the Oedipal complex").

f   A **repetition compulsion** involves the unconscious repetition of painful or traumatic early childhood experiences.

g.   **Transference** is the process by which the compulsion to repeat important early experience is introduced into the relationship with the therapist.

h.   **Countertransference** is the therapist's emotional reaction to the patient; Freud believed that it distracted from the treatment and needed to be factored out.

i.   Unconscious meaning can be found in **dreams** and **para-praxes,** such as "Freudian slips" (the psychopathology of everyday life); symptoms often carry multiple unconscious meanings (i.e., **overdetermination**).

j.   **Free association** is the patient's spontaneous and undirected expression of thoughts and feelings with the intention of elucidating unconscious dynamics.

k.   Cure occurs via **interpretation** of these unconscious dynamics.

l.   **Resistance** is the term used to describe the patient's avoidance of or refusal to accept the therapist's interpretations.

2.   **Ego psychology**

a.   Rooted in Freud's **structural model** of the mind (with Id, Ego, and Superego), the focus of ego psychology is on the ego's **adaptation** to the demands of the id (basic drives), the superego (moral conscience), and reality.

b.   According to **Anna Freud,** the ego uses various **defense mechanisms** (e.g., displacement, reaction formation, isolation of affect, somatization, humor, altruism, and sublimation) to fend off anxiety and to negotiate the needs of the id, the superego, and reality.

c.   **Charles Brenner** believed that the ego seeks **compromise formations** that synthesize the demands of the id, the superego, and reality.

d.   **Heinz Hartmann** held that the ego also deals with a **conflict-free sphere** in which it adapts to ordinary challenges of everyday life.

e.   In ego psychology, **transference** is a displacement of feelings about important figures (e.g., parents) onto the therapist, while **countertransference** is a distraction from an analysis of the patient's ego.

    f.   **Resistance** may be an adaptive defense mechanism that protects the patient against painful, anxiety-ridden thoughts and feelings.

3. **Object relations theory**

    a.   According to the object relations theory, the basic drive is toward an interpersonal relationship with another person (in this jargon, an "object"). Sexuality and aggression remain important drives, but they can only emerge in the context of a relationship (i.e., there is no infant without the mother).

    b.   Through the process of **introjection,** the infant internalizes the parent. **Internal objects** structure the developing person's mind. The nature and quality of internal objects determine the individual's psychological health or pathology (e.g., critical and overly-punishing parents may be introjected and cause intense self-criticism and depression). Since internal objects have **plasticity,** the psychotherapist may be experienced as a new object (e.g., a supportive and empathic relationship with the therapist may lead to a diminution of the patient's self-criticism and self-hatred).

    c.   According to **Melanie Klein,** the infant's earliest experience of the object occurs via **splitting** (the **paranoid-schizoid position**). Splitting remains a primitive defense in adult patients with borderline personality disorder, who tend to see others as all good or all bad. The focus here is on **pre-Oedipal** developmental stages.

    d.   Good parenting helps the child to experience the world and other people in shades of gray rather than as purely black or white (the **depressive position**).

    e.   **D.W. Winnicott** believed that the **"good-enough mother"** helps the child toward the depressive position by satisfying most needs, but at times delaying gratification or unintentionally causing frustration. The "good-enough therapist" functions as a similar kind of object for some patients in psychotherapy. According to **D.W. Winnicott,** the child uses **transitional objects** to represent the good object (i.e., the parent) when the object is not present. The patient in therapy may use symbols or other reminders of the therapist (such as a memento from the office) as transitional objects as well.

    f.   **Projection** and **projective identification** are seen as primitive defense mechanisms. With **projection** the patient cannot tolerate some uncomfortable affect or desire and instead attributes it to the therapist. With **projective identification** the patient projects conflicts or anxieties onto the therapist and evokes these very same feelings in the therapist; the patient and therapist affectively resonate with one another. The therapist's job is to contain rather than enact these projective identifications.

4. **Self psychology**

   a. According to self psychology, psychological struggles are often rooted in a defective sense of self caused by early childhood deprivation or neglect, and not by conflicts. As a consequence, the focus in self psychology is on learning how interpersonal relationships promote **self-cohesion** and maintain **self-esteem.**

   b. **Heinz Kohut** put forth the concept of the **self-object** as a means to support, soothe, validate, or admire another person. Under good circumstances, parents serve as important self-objects for the developing child. In emotionally deprived environments, the child lacks such a self-object and may fail to develop a robust sense of self.

   c. Failure to develop a healthy sense of self may lead to **narcissism** as a defense against inner emptiness, despair, and low self-esteem.

   d. The psychotherapist can function as a self-object who helps to build or to restore the patient's healthy sense of self.

   e. When a patient suffers from a lack of positive self-regard, he or she turns to the therapist for meaning and lives in the reflected glory of the therapist; this process leads to an **idealizing transference.** Kohut believed that the idealizing transference generally should be promoted rather than interpreted.

   f. When the therapist is in a state of **affective attunement** with the patient, he or she reflects, admires, validates, and empathizes with the patient's experience; this is called a **mirroring transference.**

   g. Contemporary researchers of infant behavior as well as psychoanalysts who advocate for **attachment theory** (such as Daniel Stern and Peter Fonagy) also have developed notions that affective attunement on the part of parents and therapists is critical for healthy development. According to attachment theorists, healthy attachment allows the individual to **mentalize** (i.e., to reflect on the experiences of other people), which is considered essential for psychological and social well-being.

5. **Relational approaches**

   a. Relational approaches are rooted in the work of **Harry Stack Sullivan** (associated with the interpersonal school of psychotherapy). However, the term "relational" was first used in this context by **Jay Greenberg** and **Stephen Mitchell** in 1983. The development of a relational theory reflected **postmodern** shifts in culture, politics, and intellectual life in the second half of the twentieth century.

b. According to this approach, the therapist is a **participant-observer** in the therapy, rather than an objective, scientific observer of the patient's behavior and inner dynamics. The therapist is not an authority figure with privileged access to psychodynamic truth; clinical interpretations, formulations, and treatment decisions are **co-constructed** by the patient and the therapist, who work collaboratively.

c. In this type of therapy the therapist is more focused on the nature of present relationships (the **here and now**) rather than on past relationships (the **there and then**). Examination of the nature of the here-and-now relationship with the therapist may be paramount in the treatment.

d. Contrary to classical theory, the therapist's subjectivity and emotional response to the patient (countertransference) cannot be excluded from clinical considerations and treatment decisions. There is no emotionally neutral position from which the therapist can understand and interpret.

e. Awareness of **countertransference** is a critical part of the therapy. The therapist's subjective experience of the patient may be used to generate hypotheses about important dimensions of the patient's mental functioning and interpersonal relationships.

f. The therapist may make therapeutic use of descriptions of his or her own reactions to the patient (i.e., **self-disclosure**); this must be done judiciously and always with the patient's best interest in mind.

6. **Brief psychodynamic approaches**

a. Whereas most psychodynamic approaches entail long-term therapy that aims to help the patient achieve fundamental intrapsychic and interpersonal change, some psychodynamic approaches aim to effect these changes rapidly by providing the patient with a short-term, high-impact therapeutic experience. These techniques are controversial and not widely accepted by most psychodynamic psychotherapists or by psychoanalysts, who believe that basic characterological transformation requires long-term therapy in which various cognitive and affective themes are explored repeatedly.

    b. Some brief psychodynamic approaches are associated with the work of the individual therapists who developed and promoted them.

        i. **Peter Sifneos** developed a brief anxiety-provoking psychotherapy that explores unconscious Oedipal themes.

        ii. **David Malan** developed a brief therapy that focuses on triangles of conflict (wish, threat, and defense) and on triangles of insight (past relationships, contemporary relationships, and the relationship with the therapist).

        iii. **Habib Davanloo** developed a brief, intensive dynamic therapy that focuses on breaking through defenses to reveal unconscious processes and conflicts.

        iv. **Lester Luborsky** developed a brief, manualized psychotherapy that focuses on the **"core conflictual relationship theme" (CCRT) method,** in which the therapist aims to understand the patient's needs and wishes as phase-appropriate developmental needs.

B.   **Cognitive-Behavioral Therapy (CBT)**

    1. CBT is a highly effective form of individual psychotherapy that is rooted in the theory that thoughts, feelings, and behaviors are intimately related and can affect one another in profound ways. It differs from psychodynamic psychotherapy insofar as it primarily regards conscious thoughts and beliefs, rather than unconscious processes, as pathogenic. Nonetheless, psychodynamic therapy and CBT are not mutually exclusive. CBT techniques can often be effectively incorporated into primarily psychodynamic treatment; an appreciation of psychodynamic theory can often help the CBT therapist to work more effectively.

    2. CBT theorists, such as **Aaron Beck,** postulate that psychopathology often results from **distorted cognitions** that have an unhealthy impact on emotion and behavior. Moreover, CBT postulates the existence of cognitive **schemas,** which are fundamental patterns by which individuals organize and interpret their experiences.

    3. CBT identifies several pathogenic types of cognition.

        a. **Automatic thoughts:** spontaneous, dysfunctional patterns of thinking and misinterpreting situations and interactions with others.

        b. **Negative core beliefs:** maladaptive and pathogenic beliefs that are rooted in previous life experiences that underlie dysfunctional automatic thoughts.

    c. **Errors in logic:** illogical and unfounded patterns of reasoning that are maladaptive and pathogenic. Examples of such errors in logic are:
        i. **Black-and-white thinking:** the patient tends to interpret life experiences as all good or all bad rather than as nuanced, complex, and ambiguous.
        ii. **Overgeneralization:** the patient makes unfounded, arbitrary inferences from specific feelings or thoughts that are painful and maladaptive.
        iii. **Catastrophic thinking:** the patient automatically worries that everything in his or her life will fall apart in the absence of objective evidence for such worry.
        iv. **Personalization:** the patient incorrectly believes that he or she is the target of other people's anger, hostility, or other negative emotions.

4. CBT is **evidence-based;** there is a growing empirical literature that demonstrates its efficacy for a wide range of psychiatric illnesses, including mood disorders, anxiety disorders, and eating disorders.

5. CBT is based on the principle that cognitive techniques can change a person's maladaptive core beliefs, automatic thoughts, and errors in logic. It can thereby help to effect lasting improvements in cognition, mood, and behavior. In CBT, the therapist and patient collaborate to identify the goals of therapy and the **agenda** for each session. Whereas most sessions in psychodynamic therapy are open-ended, CBT sessions are highly **structured.**
    a. Elements of the agenda of a CBT session may include:
        i. Review of symptoms and significant events since the previous session
        ii. Review of what was helpful or unhelpful from the previous session
        iii. Review of homework assignments from the previous session
        iv. Discussion of the nature of ongoing and/or new problems
        v. Development of new homework tasks
        vi. Review of what seemed helpful or unhelpful in the current session.
    b. During the course of a CBT session, one of the main tasks of the therapist is to **coach** the patient in cognitive and behavioral techniques that identify and then challenge distorted, pathogenic cognitions.

    i.   **Eliciting automatic thoughts:** as the patient and therapist identify a series of negative thoughts, certain patterns and schemas emerge.

    ii. **Testing automatic thoughts:** when maladaptive cognitive patterns or schemas are identified, the patient can perform a "pro versus con" analysis, which allows him or her to assess the effects of these patterns. Therapist and patient then work together to generate alternative, healthier core beliefs by focused discussions or specific techniques, such as **brainstorming, guided discovery, and imagery.**

    iii. Behavioral techniques that may complement these cognitive techniques include **role play, scheduling activities, self-reliance training, diversion techniques, and graded task assignment.** The patient tests these alternative cognitive-behavioral approaches outside the therapy session and makes adjustments as needed. Ongoing practice inside and outside CBT sessions helps to deepen and solidify positive transformations in cognition, behavior, and affect.

    iv. CBT is generally **time-limited.** The outcome of a successful CBT treatment is that the **patient increasingly develops the skills to serve as his or her own therapist.**

C.   **Interpersonal Therapy (IPT)**

    1. First described, performed, and empirically researched by **Gerald Klerman and Myrna Weissman,** IPT is a brief, focused form of individual psychotherapy.

    2. IPT is rooted in part in **Adolf Meyer's theory of psychobiology,** which views the patient's interpersonal world and struggles to react adaptively to psychosocial stressors as central to psychiatric illness. IPT is also rooted in part in **attachment theory,** which emphasizes the importance of interpersonal relations to mental health.

    3. IPT addresses current psychological difficulties and relationship issues in the **"here and now."** It presumes that major depression always occurs in a social matrix. IPT has been used primarily in the treatment of major depression and there is growing empirical evidence for its efficacy.

    4. From the outset of IPT, four common interpersonal issues are reviewed with the patient in order to determine the optimal focus of therapy.

        a.   **Grief:** pathological grief is thought to result from a failure to mourn the loss of a person; in IPT the therapist helps the patient to mourn the loss and begin to establish alternative relationships and interests.

        b.   **Role transitions:** the patient experiences difficulties coping with a change of role; in IPT the therapist helps him or her develop greater flexibility and competence with regard to the new life role.

        c.   **Role disputes:** the patient experiences nonreciprocal expectations in an important relationship; in IPT the therapist helps the patient to communicate more effectively about the dispute and to reassess interpersonal expectations with which he or she is grappling.

        d.   **Interpersonal deficits:** the patient lacks healthy, vital, and supportive interpersonal relationships; in IPT the therapist helps the patient strategize, in order to reduce his or her social isolation.

5.   There are several different **IPT techniques:**

        a.   **Exploratory interviewing**

        b.   **Encouragement of expression of suppressed affect**

        c.   **Clarification and analysis of content of the patient's communications**

        d.   **Observation of the nature of the therapeutic relationship to elucidate the nature of other relationships** (similar to analysis of the transference in psychodynamic therapy).

        e.   **Role play and behavior change**

6.   IPT is time-limited. It commonly occurs over **12–16 weekly sessions** in which the patient and the therapist maintain a practical and active focus on problems that they have identified at the outset of treatment.

D.   **Dialectical Behavior Therapy (DBT)**

1.   **Marsha Linehan** originally described DBT and later studied its efficacy empirically in clinical trials.

2.   DBT is a **manual-based** therapy designed specifically for patients with **borderline personality disorder;** it usually lasts for several months or longer.

3.   DBT aims to promote **affective regulation** in borderline patients and to reduce the frequency of self-injurious behavior, suicide attempts, and inpatient psychiatric hospitalizations.

4.   DBT is largely psychoeducational; it focuses on promoting numerous skills:

        a.   **Mindfulness**

      b.   **Distress tolerance**

      c.   **Affective stability**

      d.   **Interpersonal effectiveness**

  5. The **dialectic** in DBT is an attempt to synthesize the following two opposing exigencies:

      a.   **The wish to stay the same:** the therapist must respect and validate the patient's emotional distress and suffering.

      b.   **The need to change:** the therapist must help the patient to improve coping skills and to develop safer, more adaptive ways to manage distressing affect.

E.   **Psychotherapy with Psychopharmacological Management**

  1. For decades many psychoanalysts and psychodynamic therapists thought that medications might prevent individual patients from confronting their emotions in treatment; this attitude has largely given way to the belief that good medication management can help a patient to manage the exploration of painful thoughts and feelings in psychotherapy. However, contemporary thinking purports that the previously described individual psychotherapies can be combined with psychopharmacological interventions. A growing body of empirical evidence reveals that combining individual psychotherapy with medication treatment is more efficacious in the treatment of several psychiatric conditions (including anxiety and depressive disorders) than use of either modality alone.

  2. When the psychotherapist is also a physician-psychiatrist trained as a psychopharmacologist, **combined treatment** is a viable option. If the psychotherapist does not prescribe psychotropic medication, then split treatment is necessary. In **split treatment,** the patient attends individual psychotherapy sessions with a nonprescribing therapist and meets separately with a psychopharmacologist for medication management. Close communication and collaboration between the prescriber and the therapist is critical to ensure the safety and efficacy of split treatment.

III. Group Psychotherapy

Group psychotherapy provides patients with the opportunity to receive emotional support and to learn more about themselves along with other individuals who have similar problems (with a therapist who leads and facilitates the group interaction).

A.   **Goals and Success of Therapy**

The success of a therapy group depends on the therapist's defining the goals and purpose of the group and on facilitating the development of a safe, empathic, and respectful environment for the members of the group. Group therapy may be beneficial insofar as it generates interpersonal situations that **reduce isolation and shame, evoke powerful feelings, expand a person's emotional and behavioral repertoire, provide support, and furnish a safe place for empathic confrontation.** Some of the main goals of group therapy are to:

1. Stabilize a crisis and provide support to help a patient return to his or her usual day-to-day functioning and responsibilities.
2. Support patients with common problems, such as chronic medical illnesses, chronic psychiatric illnesses, and acute psychological challenges (e.g., grief and mourning).
3. Provide relief and to enhance adaptive strategies for targeted symptoms, such as social anxiety and symptoms associated with eating disorders.
4. Promote lasting character change by allowing patients to work through maladaptive patterns of thinking about and interacting with other people.

B.   **Structure of the Therapy**

The leader establishes secure boundaries for the group by establishing a therapeutic framework, which comprises a regular meeting time and place as well as guidelines (such as the need to arrive on time, stay throughout the session, and make regular payments of the fee) for the group's functioning. Confidentiality of material shared in sessions is also critical to maintain the safety and integrity of the group. The therapist is legally bound to maintain patient privacy and confidentiality. Each member of the group should also make a commitment to respect confidentiality of other members; reminders of that commitment should be provided periodically.

C.   **Theoretical Factors**

There are numerous potentially therapeutic factors in group therapy.

1. **Acceptance:** feeling respected by others can be therapeutic in itself.
2. **Altruism:** helping others can enhance self-esteem and a sense of self-efficacy.
3. **Creation of a corrective experience:** the group allows individuals to work through important family dynamics, such as sibling rivalry.

4. **Insight:** the group promotes development of cognitive and emotional awareness of one's inner life.
5. **Inspiration:** individuals in the group may be instilled with hope by the statements and achievements of other group members.
6. **Interpretation:** by pointing out meanings of a patient's utterances or actions, the group leader promotes psychological understanding.
7. **Mentalization:** patients learn to put themselves into the shoes of other people who are suffering or grappling with similar experiences. According to contemporary attachment theorists, this process is critical for psychological well-being.
8. **Modeling:** patients come to see each other as role models and can thereby expand emotional and behavioral repertoires, including those in the realm of social mores.
9. **Reality testing:** the group helps its members to assess their own feelings and reactions in less distorted and more adaptive ways.
10. **Ventilation:** disclosure of powerful thoughts and feelings can help to reduce shame and guilt.

D. **Forms of Group Psychotherapy**
1. **Supportive group therapy**
   a. This type of group focuses on symptom management and on coping with everyday challenges.
   b. A positive transference to the therapist and to the group is encouraged to improve the functioning of patients.
   c. The therapist helps the patients to reinforce adaptive defenses and he or she gives patients advice and support.
   d. Patient interaction and support outside the group may be helpful.
2. **Cognitive-behavioral group therapy**
   a. This type of group focuses on cognitive distortions and on automatic thoughts insofar as they cause depression, anxiety, and/or other symptoms.
   b. A positive transference to the therapist and to the group as a whole is encouraged, rather than interpreted.
   c. The therapist helps the patients to challenge cognitive distortions and automatic thoughts.
   d. Patient interaction and support outside the group may be helpful.
3. **Psychodynamic group therapy**
   a. This type of group focuses on identifying unconscious factors that affect relationships among group members and that may relate to childhood dynamics of individual members.

        b.   Both positive and negative transference to the therapist and to the group as a whole are encouraged, interpreted, and worked through.

        c.   The therapist promotes elaboration of transference, challenges maladaptive defenses, and analyzes unconscious processes in the group.

        d.   Patient interaction outside the group is discouraged because it could interfere with development of transference reactions within the group itself.

        e.   Group members should function at similar levels of ego development but may have dissimilar symptoms or problems in other regards.

    4. Combined individual and group psychotherapies

        a.   Group therapy may be effectively combined with various forms of individual psychotherapy.

        b.   Patients in combined therapy may be treated by the same therapist or by two different therapists.

        c.   If the patient is being treated by the same therapist for individual and group treatment, the patient and therapist should have an agreement as to what material the therapist may or may not take from the individual sessions and introduce into the group sessions.

        d.   If the patient is being treated by one therapist for individual therapy and another therapist for group treatment, the two clinicians usually should maintain regular contact to share observations and to prevent splitting.

IV.   Couples Therapy

This form of psychotherapy is comprised of two individuals who are involved in an intimate relationship and a couples therapist who aims to help them understand and work through difficulties in that relationship. Couples therapy can be helpful in a wide variety of contexts, including (but not limited to) situations of interpersonal discord, sexual infidelity, divorce/child custody, or serious illness in one or both members of the couple. Many clinicians conduct couples therapy and some specialize in it. It is a complex undertaking insofar as **it requires the therapist to pay careful attention to numerous intrapsychic and interpersonal dynamics in what are often highly charged situations.** The couples therapist also must be diplomatic in the general approach to the couple and to the use of language, so that both members of the couple trust the therapist and feel that their points of view are recognized and incorporated into the treatment. Some of the particular challenges that characterize couples therapy include:

A. **Strategic Decisions**

1. The couples therapist must attend both to the psychology of each member of the couple and to the pattern of interactions between them.

2. The couples therapist must recognize and work with projective identification, the process by which an individual member of the couple disavows intolerable affects and evokes those very same affects in the other member of the couple. For example, a man who cannot tolerate his own hostility and aggression may act in maladaptively passive ways that evoke anger in his partner and that cause great distress for both members of the couple. When projective identification is a core dynamic in the couple, the couples therapist must carefully point it out to both partners and help each partner to reown his or her projections.

3. The couples therapist also must strive to understand the nature of each partner's important early life relationships, because those relationships can shape and/or distort expectations in the contemporary relationship with the partner.

4. When one partner has a distorted set of ideas or expectations about the other partner, the couples therapist must help the patient to disentangle his view of this relationship from that of important early relationships, which may have been unsatisfying, neglectful, or abusive.

5. During the initial evaluation stage of couples therapy, some therapists prefer to meet with both members of the couple and also with each individual partner separately.

6. The couples therapist may find that couples treatment is contraindicated because of lack of motivation on the part of one member of the couple or because of a general lack of safety in the relationship (e.g., situations marked by domestic violence).

7. If couples therapy is deemed appropriate after a thorough evaluation, there are numerous theoretical approaches available.

   a. **Psychodynamic:** this model focuses on working through projective identifications and on clarifying distorted assumptions based on previous relationships.

   b. **Communication skills training:** this model focuses on enhancing each partner's capacity to listen and to speak to the other in a respectful, empathic, and effective manner.

   c. **Experiential model:** this model utilizes role playing and other techniques.

   d. **Narrative approach:** this model focuses on the elaboration of a new language for the interpersonal difficulty that might empower the couple to find new approaches to working it through.

V.   Family Therapy

This form of psychotherapy includes members of a family system working along with a family therapist who aims to help them better understand and work through family problems. It is similar to couples therapy in some respects. Like couples therapy, family therapy can be helpful in a wide variety of contexts, including (but not limited to) situations of marital discord, divorce, and behavioral problems or mental illness in one or more family members. It too is a complex undertaking insofar as **it requires the family therapist to pay careful attention to intrapsychic and interpersonal dynamics in highly charged situations.** The family therapist also must be diplomatic in the use of language, so that all members of the family trust the therapist and feel that their points of view are recognized and incorporated into the treatment. The family therapist must attend both to the psychology of each member of the family (and there may be several) and to the pattern of interactions among them. A sampling of approaches to family therapy include:

A.   **Psychodynamic**

Family functioning is understood by using such concepts as repetition compulsion, projective identification, affective attunement, and attachment. The family therapist helps the members of the family to recognize and work through the emotional (and often unconscious) processes that structure their interactions.

B.   **Symbolic-Experiential**

Family functioning is conceptualized by patterns of interaction observed in the "here-and-now" of therapy sessions, and change in the family system is facilitated by active attempts to change those patterns in the consulting room.

C.   **Structural**

Family functioning is understood in terms of structured patterns of interaction that are maladaptive and susceptible to therapeutic change by way of provocative interventions in the session and assignments outside the sessions.

D.   **Narrative**

Family functioning is conceptualized in terms of fixed attitudes and beliefs that restrict interactions among members of the family; the therapist helps the family to co-construct a new, more flexible set of narrative themes that free the members of the family for healthier and more gratifying interaction.

Suggested Reading

Abernethy III RS, Schlozman SC: An overview of the psychotherapies. In Stern TA, Herman JB (eds): *Massachusetts General Hospital Psychiatry Update and Board Preparation,* 2nd edition. New York: McGraw-Hill, 2004:425–428.

Alonso A: Group psychotherapy. In Stern TA, Herman JB (eds): *Massachusetts General Hospital Psychiatry Update and Board Preparation,* 2nd edition. New York: McGraw-Hill, 2004:449–456.

Blais MA, Groves JE: Planned brief psychotherapy: an overview. In Stern TA, Herman JB (eds): *Massachusetts General Hospital Psychiatry Update and Board Preparation,* 2nd edition. New York: McGraw-Hill, 2004:429–433.

Fishel AK: Couples therapy. In Stern TA, Herman JB (eds): *Massachusetts General Hospital Psychiatry Update and Board Preparation,* 2nd edition. New York: McGraw-Hill, 2004:435–439.

Gabbard GO: *Psychodynamic Psychiatry in Clinical Practice: The DSM-IV Edition.* Washington: American Psychiatric Press, 1994.

Matthews J, Rayburn NR, Otto MW: Cognitive-behavioral therapy. In Stern TA, Herman JB (eds): *Massachusetts General Hospital Psychiatry Update and Board Preparation,* 2nd edition. New York: McGraw-Hill, 2004:457–465.

Mitchell SA, Black MJ: *Freud and Beyond: A History of Modern Psychoanalytic Thought.* New York: Basic Books, 1995.

Slovik LS, Griffith JL: Family therapy. In Stern TA, Herman JB (eds): *Massachusetts General Hospital Psychiatry Update and Board Preparation,* 2nd edition. New York: McGraw-Hill, 2004:441–448.

Chapter 29

Clinical Utility of Genetic Information in Psychiatric Practice

CHRISTINE T. FINN, MD

I. Overview

A. **Evidence of a Genetic Basis for Psychiatric Illness**
Results of family, twin, and adoption studies have provided strong evidence for the now well-established genetic basis of psychiatric illness; knowledge of recurrence risks (i.e., the probability that the same disease will occur in a first-degree relative of a patient) for relatives of individuals affected with psychiatric disorders is currently the most useful factor for predicting risk of development of psychiatric illness. In addition, recent reports have highlighted potential susceptibility genes that may play a role in the etiology of major psychiatric illnesses such as schizophrenia and bipolar disorder. **Despite these advances, it is difficult to translate research findings into the current clinical care of psychiatric patients. Alzheimer disease remains the only major mental illness for which specific causal genes have been established and for which genetic testing is currently available on a clinical basis** (see Chapter 11 for further discussion of Alzheimer disease genetics). In the absence of specific measurable genes, or the ability to offer genetic testing, the question arises as to whether the current state of knowledge of the genetics of psychiatric disorders warrants clinical application.

B. **Clinical Application of Genetic Knowledge**
A patient's right to know what knowledge currently exists is tempered by the limitations of what can be known. **At this time, clinical application of genetic knowledge of psychiatric illness relies on the use of recurrence risks generated from the results of family studies.** Because the risks are derived from specific patterns of illness in families ascertained for research studies, they likely do not reflect the risks in individual families; real risks may be far higher or lower based on the underlying genetic etiology in each family. The likely multifactorial inheritance, and unknown environmental

---

Address for correspondence: Dr. Christine T. Finn, 77 Avenue Louis Pasteur, Suite 250, Boston, MA 02115-6195, email: cfinn@partners.org.

influences make it difficult to arrive at accurate risk estimations when counseling patients. Empiric risks are likely most helpful in families with relatively few affected family members, and less so for multiply-affected families or those with comorbid psychiatric illnesses.

C.   **Recurrence Risks**
Despite these limitations, empiric risk estimates for psychiatric disorders are currently being employed in various clinical settings. While psychiatrists may feel quite comfortable reviewing a family history of psychiatric illness, discussion of risk estimates may be an area of relative inexperience. Several references exist that can aid a clinician in estimating recurrence risks and providing genetic counseling based on the degree of relatedness to affected family members. At all times, **consultation with, and referral to, genetics professionals are appropriate for further discussion of risk and genetic topics.** When discussing recurrence risks with patients or their family members, it is necessary to highlight the limitations of the information. A complete discussion of how risks are generated, the spectrum of diagnosis assessed in the supporting family studies, and the difference between empiric and individual risks is essential. Often, it is most helpful to provide a range of risk, accompanied by the above caveats. Table 29-1 summarizes estimated recurrence risks to first-degree relatives and heritabilities (i.e., the proportion of the

Table 29-1. Estimated Recurrence Risk and Heritability for Major Psychiatric Disorders

Disorder	Recurrence Risk for First-Degree Relatives (%)	Heritability (%)
Schizophrenia	5–16	70–86
Bipolar disorder	4–18	33–80
Major depression	5–25	21–45
Autism	2–9	>90
ADHD	15–40	75–98
Alcoholism	5–27	47–75
Panic disorder	8–17	35–46

ADHD, attention-deficit/hyperactivity disorder.

population variance in a disorder due to genetic factors) for major psychiatric illnesses.

II. Genetic and Metabolic Illnesses with Psychiatric Symptoms

A. Overview

While the majority of psychiatric patients do not have either a well-defined genetic syndrome or an inborn error of metabolism, an awareness of these disorders is important for the diagnostic assessment of patients in clinical practice. Many genetic and metabolic syndromes may present with psychiatric and behavioral findings as their earliest or most disabling symptoms; in some cases (e.g., hyperphagia with Prader-Willi syndrome) these symptoms may be the most useful for making the diagnosis. Patients may fulfill full DSM-IV criteria for psychiatric illness, or may have more general behavioral symptoms. **Due to the prominence of psychiatric symptoms in some disorders, psychiatrists may be among the first clinicians to see these patients** and it is important for them to recognize these disorders and to refer patients for appropriate diagnostic work-ups. **Making the diagnosis of a genetic syndrome or an inborn error of metabolism** (i.e., identifying and treating associated medical conditions, maximizing opportunities for treatment directed at a primary pathological process, and providing overall prognostic information) **has important implications for patients. Making accurate diagnoses also allows for identification of other family members** who may be at risk for the disorder.

B. Diagnostic Assessments

Currently, patients presenting with psychiatric symptoms undergo a diagnostic assessment directed towards uncovering underlying organic processes that may contribute to illness. In select patients, expansion of this assessment is warranted to uncover a genetic syndrome or disorder of metabolism. Table 29-2 outlines supplemental areas of investigation to explore during a comprehensive diagnostic assessment of psychiatric patients when considering a diagnosis of a genetic or metabolic syndrome.

1. **Assessment for genetic syndromes**
   a. Genetic syndromes are disorders with a characteristic set of features that share a common genetic etiology.
   b. In addition to psychiatric and behavioral symptoms, features may include associated medical problems, cognitive deficits, congenital anomalies, and physical findings.

Table 29-2. Expanded Diagnostic Assessment for Genetic Syndromes and Metabolic Disease

Prenatal history

Were there any pregnancy complications, and if so, what was the timing of complications (e.g., diabetes, infection, fevers, systemic illness)?

Was there maternal hypertension, eclampsia, toxemia, or HELLP (*h*emolysis, *e*levated *l*iver enzymes, *l*ow *p*latelets) syndrome?

Were there toxic exposures (e.g., medications, illicit substances, alcohol, radiation, chemicals)?

Were there any abnormalities on ultrasound?

Were there any indications for amniocentesis/chorionic villus sampling (CVS)? What were the results of amniocentesis/CVS?

Birth/perinatal history

What was the mode of delivery (vaginal vs. cesarean section, natural vs. induced vs. emergent)?

Were there complications with birth or in the early perinatal period?

Was a neonatal intensive care unit or prolonged hospital stay required in infancy? Did the baby go home with the mother on time?

Were there issues with feeding or growth?

Developmental history

What was the timing of major verbal and motor milestones?

Was there a history of developmental regression?

Was there a history of speech, occupational, or physical therapy?

Was there a decline in school performance?

Was there a history of special education services or the need for academic supports?

Multiorgan review of systems

Was there a history of decompensation with illness?

Was there a dietary history of food intolerances, or unusual food preferences?

Were there episodic neurologic symptoms?

Were there problems with linear growth or weight gain?

Psychiatric review of systems

Were there nonspecific behavioral problems (e.g., tantrums, violent outbursts, or hyperactivity)?

Were there any self-injurious behaviors?

Were there difficulties with sleep?

Family history

What was the ethnicity/race of the parents?

Was there a history of consanguinity?

What were the patterns of illness in family members?

Was there a history of infertility or miscarriages?

Was there a history of sudden infant death syndrome or infant/child deaths?

Did any family members have surgeries in childhood?

Is there anyone in the family with special needs?

Physical examination

Is there any asymmetry of features?

Are there dysmorphic features?

Are there congenital anomalies?

Are there signs of neurological dysfunction?

   c. **Diagnostic clues that indicate the presence of a genetic syndrome in a patient with psychiatric and behavioral symptoms may be uncovered through careful review of the medical and family histories and physical examination findings.**

   d. **An increased suspicion for genetic syndromes is appropriately raised when psychiatric symptoms are accompanied by birth defects** (e.g., congenital heart disease, cleft palate, or renal agenesis) or dysmorphic facial features.

   e. Findings on the physical examination are supplemented by results of imaging studies, if clinical findings indicate the possibility of an underlying abnormality (e.g., an echocardiogram to investigate structural cardiac defects if a murmur is appreciated).

   f. Inquiring about medical issues during pregnancy or in the perinatal and early childhood periods can uncover surgical correction of congenital anomalies.

   g. A detailed review of the developmental history that focuses on the timing of early milestones (e.g., motor and verbal skills) may suggest the presence of developmental delays or mental retardation.

   h. Additional support for underlying genetic syndromes may be gathered from review of a family history in which specific questions about recurrent miscarriages, stillborn children or early infant deaths; and a family history of mental retardation, seizures, congenital anomalies, or other illness that seem to "run in the family" can indicate areas for further investigation. Furthermore, the pattern of illness (e.g., autosomal dominant or X-linked recessive) in families may also point toward an underlying genetic syndrome.

2. **Assessment for inborn errors of metabolism**
   Inborn errors of metabolism are a class of genetic disorders that result in disrupted enzyme production, regulation, or function. Disease states may result from a build-up of pathway by-products, production of alternate substances that cause toxicity, or the absence of essential pathway end products.

   a. Testing for metabolic illnesses begins at birth through state-mandated newborn screening programs, but the number of diseases tested for varies greatly from state to state; even the states with the most comprehensive panels do not test for all, or even most illnesses.

   b. Comprehensive testing, when available, has been relatively recently introduced, making it unlikely that adults or older

children would have benefited from these screening programs at birth. Information about what each state offers as
a newborn screen, and when tests were incorporated into
the panel, can be obtained from the department of public
health.

c. Many metabolic illnesses lack specific physical findings;
careful history-taking is often the key to making a diagnosis of an inborn error of metabolism. Additional information
to gather during the psychiatric evaluation includes a review of dietary history (e.g., avoided foods or unusual food
preferences, food intolerances, or frequent colic or reflux),
questions regarding a history of medical or psychiatric
decompensation with minor illness, or transient neurological symptoms (e.g., ataxia, lethargy, or delirium).

d. Abnormalities in neurodevelopment or cognition, especially of a history of developmental regression or cognitive decline, may also indicate the possibility of metabolic disease.

e. Because many metabolic illnesses are inherited in an autosomal recessive manner, inquiries regarding family history
of illness should also include questions about ethnicity and
consanguinity.

f. Although the specific diagnosis of a metabolic illness often
requires specialized testing, abnormalities on routine laboratory studies may be the first indication of metabolic disease. Even more important, laboratory studies may be
abnormal only during periods of acute metabolic decompensation. Laboratory tests that aid in diagnostic assessment of patients with suspected metabolic illnesses are listed in Tables 29-3 and 29-4.

C. **Treatment Implications**
1. **Overview**
    a. **Optimism regarding the use of genotypic information to
    predict patient response to medications, or the potential
    for adverse events, remains high.** Several studies have
    shown promising results in their preliminary investigation
    of the role of various polymorphisms in genes thought to be
    important in the metabolism of psychiatric medications.
    b. Genetic testing is currently commercially available to deter-
    mine whether patients have high, medium, or low activity
    of some cytochrome P450 enzymes, based on underlying
    genotypes. However, the clinical utility of this testing for
    psychiatric patients has not yet been conclusively estab-
    lished.

Table 29-3. Helpful Laboratory Studies for Evaluating Metabolic Disease

Laboratory Abnormality	Associated Disorders
Acidosis; abnormal anion gap	Associated with many metabolic disorders, use blood gas results and electrolyte panel to determine
Elevated transaminases, other liver dysfunction	Storage disorders with deposition of abnormal substances in liver
Hyperammonemia (NH_3)	Primary elevation in urea cycle disorders; secondary elevation in organic acidemias, disorders of fatty acid oxidation
Elevated lactate	Disorders of energy metabolism
Elevated pyruvate	Disorders of energy metabolism
Abnormal pattern of plasma or cerebrospinal fluid amino acids	Amino acid disorders (e.g., urea cycle defects, homocystinuria)
Abnormal pattern of urine organic acids	Organic acidemias, fatty acid oxidation disorders
Abnormal pattern on acylcarnitine profile	Disorders of fatty acid oxidation, organic acidemias
Elevation of very long chain fatty acids	Peroxisomal disorders
Elevation of urine mucopolysaccharides or urine oligosaccharides	Lysosomal storage disorders

2. **Treatment**

   a. Treatment of psychiatric and behavioral findings in genetic and metabolic syndromes is currently accomplished through a symptom-based approach. The medical literature provides guidance based on case reports and reviews of psychopharmacological and behavioral interventions that have been found to be useful in a variety of disorders. However, large, prospective studies of treatment outcomes are lacking for the majority of genetic and metabolic disorders.

Table 29-4. Sampling of Genetic and Metabolic Illnesses with Psychiatric Symptoms

Disorder	Etiology	Selected Psychiatric and Behavioral Findings	Diagnostic Clues	Diagnostic Testing
Genetic syndromes				
Velocardiofacial syndrome	Microdeletion at chromosome 22q11	Schizophrenia, mood disorders, ADHD, autism, ODD, anxiety	Cleft palate, CHD, immune problems, low calcium levels, characteristic appearance; learning disabilities (nonverbal learning disorders)	FISH testing for microdeletion
Smith Magenis syndrome	Microdeletion at chromosome 17p11.2	ADHD, tantrums, impulsivity self-injurious behaviors (onychotillomania, polyembolokoilamania, skin picking)	Prominent sleep disturbances, abnormal lipid profiles, characteristic facial appearance, "self hug" when happy; IQ range borderline intelligence–moderate MR	FISH testing for microdeletion
Williams syndrome	Microdeletion at 7q11.23	Autism, ADHD, depression, anxiety, circumscribed interests or obsessions, may be somatically focused, socially disinhibited and overly friendly	CHD (supravalvular aortic or pulmonic stenosis), short stature, microcephaly, "elfin" facial appearance; IQ range mild–severe MR	FISH testing for microdeletion

Prader-Willi syndrome	Most due to deletion at chromosome 15q11-q13	Hyperphagia, obsessional thoughts, compulsions, repetitive behaviors, mood disorders, anxiety, psychosis, ADHD, autism, skin picking, and temper tantrums	Obesity, short stature, small hands and feet, small external genitalia, fair skin and hair coloring, characteristic facial appearance; decreased IQ and specific learning problems, although areas of strength (visual spatial)	FISH testing for microdeletion methylation status of affected region; testing for uniparental disomy
Turner syndrome	45,X (absence of one X chromosome)	ADHD, depression, anxiety, and problems with social skills	Females, with physical characteristics of short stature, webbed neck, and a flat, broad chest, failure to achieve secondary sexual development, infertile; IQ usually normal, some learning disabilities	Karyotype analysis of chromosomes
Klinefelter syndrome	47,XXY	ADHD, immaturity, and depression	Males, typically tall, may have small penis and testes, gynecomastia, low testosterone and associated physical findings; IQ usually normal, some learning disabilities	Karyotype analysis of chromosomes

(continued)

Table 29-4. Sampling of Genetic and Metabolic Illnesses (continued)

Disorder	Etiology	Selected Psychiatric and Behavioral Findings	Diagnostic Clues	Diagnostic Testing
Genetic syndromes (cont'd)				
Huntington disease	Mutataion in HD gene on 4p16	*Early:* changes in personality, depression, or apathy; *later:* dementia , mood lability, psychosis	Dysarthria, clumsiness, chorea; characteristic atrophy of the caudate and putamen may be apparent on MRI or CT of the brain	Molecular detection of increased number of CAG repeats in the *HD* gene
Tuberous sclerosis	Mutations in *TSC1* (on 9q23) or *TSC2* (16p13.3) genes	ADHD, PDD	Seizures, skin findings (ash leaf spots, shagreen patches, angiofibromas), dental pits, tumors in multiple organ systems (CNS tubers, retinal hamartomas, cardiac rhabdomyomas, and renal angiomyolipomas)	Most often made on a clinical basis, but mutation analysis of the *TSC1* and *TSC2* genes is available
Fragile X syndrome	Dysfunction of *FMR1* gene at Xq27.3	Full syndrome: autistic features, ADHD, ODD, mood disorders, and avoidant personality disorder and traits	Males: large testes, connective tissue disease (loose joints), low muscle tone, and characteristic facial appearance (large head with prominent forehead and jaw, long face with large ears); mental retardation in the moderate to severe range; carrier females with full mutation may be symptomatic	Molecular detection of increased number of trinucleotide repeats in the FMR1 gene

Rett syndrome	Mutations in MECP2 gene at Xq28	PDD	Initially normal with progressive loss of developmental skills associated with acquired microcephaly, loss of purposeful hand movements, gait abnormalities, seizures, and bruxism	Mutation testing for MECP2 gene

Inborn errors of metabolism

Acute intermittent porphyria	Mutations in the HMBS gene on 11q23.3	Episodic delirium, psychosis, depression, anxiety, histrionic personality	Acute "neurovisceral attacks" (recurrent abdominal pain, vomiting, generalized body pain, weakness; psychiatric medications that upregulate the CYP450 system may exacerbate symptoms)	Identification of by-products of heme synthesis in the urine, or measurement of PBG deaminase levels in the blood
Homocystinuria	Mutations in the CBS gene on 21q22.3	Depression, OCD, personality disorders	"Marfanoid" body habitus, connective tissue disease, (pectus excavatum, lens dislocation, scoliosis, high-arched palate), restricted joint mobility, thrombotic events	Newborn screening programs, amino acid analysis; mutation testing available

(continued)

Table 29-4. Sampling of Genetic and Metabolic Illnesses (continued)

Disorder	Etiology	Selected Psychiatric and Behavioral Findings	Diagnostic Clues	Diagnostic Testing
Inborn errors of metabolism (cont'd)				
Wilson disease	Mutations in the *ATP7B* gene, on 13q14-21	Personality changes, mood lability (including pseudobulbar palsy), cognitive decline	Signs and symptoms of liver dysfunction with abnormal liver function tests, tremor, dysarthria, muscular rigidity, parkinsonism, dyskinesia, dystonia, chorea, Kayser-Fleischer rings, copper deposits may be seen on brain MRI, or in the liver via a liver biopsy	Measurement of reduced bound copper and ceruloplasmin in the serum and increased copper excretion in the urine
Metachromatic leukodystrophy	Mutations in the *ARSA* gene on 22q13.31	Late onset forms: decline in cognition, personality changes, psychosis	Ataxia and walking difficulties, dysarthria, dysphagia, and pyramidal signs, vision loss, brain MRI may show periventricular changes with progression to white matter atrophy due to loss of myelin	Elevated urine sulfatides, and decreased levels of aryl sulfatase-A in blood

		Psychosis, dementia	Ataxia, coordination problems and dysarthria; vertical supranuclear palsy is the hallmark of the disorder; seizures and hepatosplenomegaly may be present	Pathologic findings in the skin or in the bone marrow, abnormal cholesterol esterification in fibroblasts, and molecular analysis of the *NPC1* gene
Niemann-Pick disease, type C	Mutations in the *NPC1* gene on 18q11-q12			
Tay-Sachs (late onset)	Mutations in the *HEXA* gene on 15q23-q24	Psychosis, mood lability, catatonia, and cognitive decline	Ataxia, coordination problems, dysarthria, dystonia, spasticity, and seizures; macular cherry-red spots, the hallmark of the early-onset form, are not present in the later-onset form	Decreased enzyme levels in the blood, or mutation analysis of *HEXA* gene
X-linked adrenoleuko-dystrophy	Mutations in the *ABCD1* gene on Xq28	*Childhood onset:* ADHD-like symptoms are an early sign, with progressive cognitive decline; *adult onset:* mania and psychosis	In males: early difficulty with gait, handwriting, or speech; progressive loss of motor skills, vision, and hearing; elevation of ACTH; and other findings associated with adrenal dysfunction; female carriers may also be symptomatic	Elevated levels of VLCFA in the blood and mutation analysis of *ABCD1* gene

(continued)

Table 29-4. Sampling of Genetic and Metabolic Illnesses (continued)

Disorder	Etiology	Selected Psychiatric and Behavioral Findings	Diagnostic Clues	Diagnostic Testing
Inborn errors of metabolism (cont'd)				
Mitochondrial disease	Various	Depression, delirium, psychosis, dementia	Multiple medical problems, often affecting different organ systems, especially those with high energy demands (i.e., brain and cardiac and skeletal muscle)	Varies depending on etiology, mutation testing available for some disorders, functional analysis of electron transport chain on muscle biopsy tissue, pathological changes on muscle tissue, characteristic MRI/MRS pattern

Teratogen exposure

| Fetal alcohol syndrome (FAS) | In utero alcohol exposure | ADHD, depression, mood lability, anxiety, aggression, and oppositional-defiant behaviors | Pre- and postnatal growth deficiency, characteristic facial appearance (small head, flattened mid-face, epicanthal folds, flat philtrum with a thin upper lip, small jaw); learning disabilities and cognitive limitations are common, MRI studies have documented structural abnormalities of the brain, with absence or small size of the corpus callosum being reported in FAS patients | Clinical diagnosis, no confirmatory testing available |

ACTH, adrenocorticotropic hormone; ADHD, attention-deficit/hyperactivity disorder; CHD, coronary heart disease; CNS, central nervous system; FISH, fluorescence in situ hybridization; IQ, intelligence quotient; ODD, oppositional defiant disorder; PBG, porphobilinogen; MR, mental retardation; MRI, magnetic resonance imaging; MRS, magnetic resonance spectroscopy; VLCFA, very long chain fatty acid.

b. Psychiatrists who care for patients with genetic and metabolic disorders should work closely with other members of a multidisciplinary team to provide comprehensive management of the diverse symptoms that are seen in these conditions.

Suggested Readings

Gene Clinics web site http://www.Geneclinics.org

Online Mendelian Inheritance in Man (OMIM) web site http://www.ncbi.nlm.nih.gov/omim/

POSSUM web site and software http://www.possum.net.au/

Bassett AS, Chow EW: 22q11 deletion syndrome: a genetic subtype of schizophrenia. *Biol Psychiatry* 1999;46:882–891.

Estrov Y, Scaglia F, Bodamer OA: Psychiatric symptoms of inherited metabolic disease. *J Inherit Metab Dis* 2000;23:2–6.

Faraone SV, Tsuang MT, Tsuang BW: *Genetics of Mental Disorders.* New York: Guilford Press, 1999.

Golomb M: Psychiatric symptoms in metabolic and other genetic disorders: is our "organic" workup complete? *Harv Rev Psychiatry* 2002;10:242–248.

Jones KL, Smith DW: *Smith's Recognizable Patterns of Human Malformation,* 5th edition. Philadelphia: Saunders, 1997.

Korf BR: *Human Genetics: A Problem-Based Approach,* 2nd edition. Malden, MA: Blackwell Science, 2000.

Lyon G, Adams RD, Kolodny EH: *Neurology of Hereditary Metabolic Diseases of Children,* 2nd edition. New York: McGraw-Hill, Health Professions Division, 1996.

NIMH Genetics Workgroup. Report of the NIMH Genetics Workgroup: Summary of Research. *Biol Psychiatry* 1999;45:573–602.

Moldavsky M, Lev D, Lerman-Sagie T: Behavioral phenotypes of genetic syndromes: a reference guide for psychiatrists. *J Am Acad Child Adolesc Psychiatry* 2001;40:749–761.

Moldin SO: *Psychiatric Genetic Counseling.* In Guze SB (ed): *Washington University Adult Psychiatry.* St. Louis: Mosby, 1997.

Scriver CR: *The Metabolic & Molecular Bases of Inherited Disease,* 8th edition. New York: McGraw-Hill, 2001.

Chapter 30

The Importance of Culture

DAVID C. HENDERSON, MD
DANA DIEM NGUYEN, PHD
CATHERINE VUKY, PHD

I.　Introduction

Ethnicity, race, gender, and culture have a tremendous impact on the diagnosis, treatment, and outcome for many individuals. In theory, psychiatric training prepares physicians to diagnose patients correctly and to treat people from all over the world empathetically. While treating a patient from a different culture, care must be taken when making observations or applying stereotypes. A clinician must be aware at all times of his or her own feelings, biases, and stereotypes. It is important to consider a patient's culture and how it may impact the presentation of illness, health-seeking behaviors, and treatment approaches and responses.

A.　**Culture**
Culture involves a pattern of customs, beliefs, and behaviors that are acquired socially and transmitted from one generation to another. It provides the tools by which people of a given society adapt to their physical environment, to their social environment, and to one another.
1.　The **physical aspects of culture** include art, literature, architecture, tools, machines, food, and clothing.
2.　The **ideological aspects of culture** include the beliefs and values of the people that must be observed indirectly, usually through the behavior of people. Religion, philosophy, psychology, literature, and the meanings that people give to symbols are all part of the ideological aspect of culture.

II.　The Impact of Culture on Psychiatric Diagnosis

A.　**Misdiagnosis**
In the United States, race and ethnicity have a significant impact on psychiatric diagnosis and on treatment. Moreover, treatment ap-

---

Address for correspondence: Dr. David C. Henderson, Freedom Trail Clinic, 25 Staniford Street, Boston, MA 02114, email: dchenderson@partners.org.

proaches and responses, as well as prognosis, are often different for disparate diagnoses.

1. **Several studies have confirmed the misdiagnosis of schizophrenia in blacks, Hispanics, and the Amish in the United States; those who are misdiagnosed are often found to have either bipolar disorder or psychotic disorder.**

2. **African-American patients also are more likely to receive higher doses of antipsychotic agents,** to have higher rates of involuntary psychiatric hospitalizations, and to have significantly higher rates of seclusion-restraints applied to them while in psychiatric hospitals.

3. **Biases in psychiatric treatment must be acknowledged.**

4. **Certain groups may seek medical or psychiatric attention later in the course of their illness and present with a more severe illness and worse prognosis.**

5. While there is a tremendous overlap of symptoms (e.g., aggression, agitation, anxiety, mood swings, psychotic thinking, anger, and impulsivity) between schizophrenia, bipolar disorder, major depression, posttraumatic stress disorder (PTSD), and intermittent explosive disorder, the diagnosis depends heavily on the interpretation of symptoms by clinicians.

B. **Differences in the Presentation of Illness**
Cultural differences allow psychiatric illnesses to present in a variety of ways.

1. Depression may be easily missed by a primary care physician (PCP) when a patient presents with a host of symptoms including headaches, dizziness, back pain, weakness, or fatigue.

2. **A nonpsychotic patient may admit to hearing voices of his or her ancestors (a feature which is culturally appropriate in certain cultural groups).**

3. In many traditional, non-Western societies, spirits of the deceased are regarded as capable of interacting with and possessing those who are still alive.

4. **Performing a cross-cultural evaluation of the meanings of bizarre delusions, hallucinations, and psychotic-like symptoms remains a clinical challenge.** An adequate understanding of a patient's sociocultural and religious background is required to determine whether symptoms are bizarre enough to yield a diagnosis of schizophrenia.

C. **The Impact of Acculturation and Immigration**
Literature on the contribution of acculturative stress to the emergence of mental disorders is abundant. **Acculturative stress may**

lead to symptoms of depression, to "culture shock," and even to symptoms reminiscent of PTSD. Recent immigrants or refugees often arrive in the United States with a host of difficulties and psychosocial problems. Physicians should ask about and make an effort to understand the circumstances surrounding immigration (e.g., were they a political prisoner, a victim of trauma and torture, or separated from family members).

III. DSM-IV Cultural Formulations

The *Diagnostic and Statistical Manual, Fourth Edition* (DSM-IV), Appendix I, provides an outline for cultural formulations. The DSM-IV emphasizes that a clinician must take into account an individual's ethnic and cultural context during the evaluation of each of the DSM-IV axes.

A. **Cultural Formulation**
   Cultural formulation contains the following components:
   1. **Cultural identity**. Ethnic or cultural references and the degree individuals are involved with their cultures of origin and their host cultures are important. It is crucial to listen for clues and to ask specific questions concerning a patient's cultural identity. Attention to language abilities and preference must also be addressed.
   2. **Cultural explanations.** How individuals understand their distress or their need for support is often communicated through symptoms (e.g., nerves, possessing spirits, somatic complaints, or misfortune); therefore, the meaning and severity of the illness must be placed in the context of one's culture, family, and community. This "explanatory model" may be helpful when developing an interpretation, a diagnosis, and a treatment plan.
   3. **Psychosocial function.** Cultural factors have a significant impact on the psychosocial environment and on functioning. Cultural interpretations of social stress, support, and one's level of disability and function must be addressed. It is the physician's responsibility to determine the level of disability, and to help the patient and his or her family adjust to role changes. The physician must also play a role in determining when patients can return to work, and to their roles as members of their families and their communities.
   4. **The relationship between the clinician and the patient.** Cultural aspects of the relationship between the individual and the clinician are also noteworthy. Moreover, cultural differences and their impact on the treatment should not be ignored. Language difficulties, difficulty eliciting symptoms or understand-

ing their cultural significance, negotiating the appropriate relationship, and determining whether a behavior is normal or pathological are common obstacles to care.

IV.   The Interview

A.   **Working with Interpreters**

Communication problems are common even between English-speaking physicians and patients from a similar socioeconomic background. As a consequence, it is not difficult to imagine the range of challenges and obstacles that a physician faces when working with those whose English language skills are poor or when a patient's culture is unfamiliar to the doctor. **Misunderstanding or a lack of comprehension about a patient's physical or psychiatric complaints may lead to misdiagnosis and result in an unnecessary or inappropriate treatment.** Patients, in turn, may feel frustrated, discouraged, or dissatisfied with their health care and fail to comply with treatment or will terminate their visits altogether. Fortunately, interpreters can help bridge the communication gap between doctors and non–English-speaking patients.

1.   Difficulties encountered working with interpreters:
     a.   Clinicians may feel that they have less control in their work because their direct contact with the patients is decreased by the presence of the interpreters.
     b.   A clinician may feel uncertain about his or her role when working with interpreters who are more active and involved in the treatment process.
     c.   A clinician may have transference issues toward the interpreter.
     d.   Conflicts may arise when clinicians and interpreters hold opposing views on the patient's diagnosis and treatment plan.
     e.   A clinician may feel frustrated when he or she cannot verify what is being said to the patient.
     f.   A clinician may feel left out if the patient appears to have more of a connection with the interpreter.
     g.   An interpreter may find it difficult to work with a clinician of a different gender.
     h.   An interpreter may feel uncomfortable when asked to translate certain issues, such as a sexual history or childhood abuse.
2.   Recommendations when working with interpreters:
     a.   When a clinician works with an interpreter, it is crucial to know the qualifications of the interpreter.

      i.   Does the interpreter have any prior experience working with psychiatrists and psychologists?

      ii.   How much does he or she know about mental illness and mental health services? What is his or her personal view about mental illness?

      iii. An interpreter who comes from a culture in which mental illness is highly stigmatized may bring certain biases or beliefs into the therapeutic process.

b. Clinicians should avoid using family members, friends, or clerical staff as interpreters.

      i.   A patient may not be able to disclose certain information in front of a spouse or child. At the same time, it may be too difficult or distressing for a young child to have to hear certain details about his or her parent.

      ii.   In addition, family members have been known to omit or to alter information they feel is too embarrassing or inappropriate to reveal to the clinician.

c. Literal translations from one language to another can be inaccurate and inappropriate.

      i.   For example, "feeling blue," when translated word for word into Vietnamese, does not make any sense to the patients because it literally translates to *"cam giac xanh"* which means "feeling color blue."

      ii.   Certain words or concepts, such as depression and mental health, may not exist in every patient's country of origin.

      iii. Interpreters may have to explain or to describe the concept of depression to the patient; this requires much more time than is suspected by clinicians.

d. Clinicians must be patient; keep in mind that it may take 10 minutes to translate one word. In addition, certain issues may be culturally inappropriate to ask or say to a patient. Many women from an Asian or Hispanic background feel uncomfortable if asked directly about sensitive topics, such as sexual abuse or family discord.

e. The clinician should meet with the interpreter briefly before each session to discuss expectations or to clarify any issues or points that the clinician would like to address during the session.

f. Be sure to introduce the interpreter to the patient at the start of the session if they have not met. Reaffirm issues of confidentiality. As most ethnic communities are close-knit, a patient may fear that the interpreters will divulge their private information to those in the community.

g. Clinicians should face and speak directly to the patients instead of to the interpreters. While patients and clinicians may not be able to communicate through language, they can communicate and connect through eye contact, gestures of acknowledgment, and other nonverbal behaviors.

h. It is helpful for the interpreter if a clinician can speak slowly and avoid using long and complicated sentences.

i. Stay away from technical or psychological terminology; such terms often do not translate well. Pause often to allow the interpreter to translate.

j. Just as clinicians and interpreters should not engage in lengthy discussions in front of the patients, clinicians should interrupt when a patient and an interpreter are talking too long.

k. At the end of each session, encourage the interpreter to share impressions about the session; they can often provide important observations and feedback.

l. Ask interpreters to clarify any issues or points that were not clear during the session.

V.   Culture-Bound Syndromes

A.   **Definition**

A culture-bound syndrome is a collection of signs and symptoms restricted to a limited number of cultures by reason of certain psychosocial features. Culture-bound syndromes are usually restricted to a specific setting and have a special relationship to that setting. However, with significant population migration, it is possible to see culture-bound syndromes in host countries. Culture-bound syndromes are classified on the basis of a common etiology (e.g., magic, evil spells, or angry ancestors), so clinical pictures vary (Table 30-1).

B.   **Projection**

Projection is a common ego defense mechanism in many non-Western cultures. Guilt and shame are often projected into cultural beliefs and ceremonies.

1. **Guilt and shame** are often attributed to other individuals, to groups, or to objects, and they may involve acting out, blaming others, and needing to punish others.

2. **Projection** is also seen in magic and supernatural perspectives of existence. This leads to projective ceremonies, and may lead to illness when the ceremonies are not performed.

Table 30-1. Culture-Bound Syndromes

Culture-Bound Syndrome	Population	Signs & Symptoms
Sleep paralysis (amafufanyane)	Zulu population of southern Africa	Abdominal pains, paralysis, blindness, hysterical seizures, shouting, sobbing, and amnesia
Sudden mass assault (amok/benz)	Malaysia, Indonesia, Laos, Philippines, Polynesia (called cafard or cathard); Papua New Guinea, Puerto Rico (called mal de pelea); and among the Navajo (itch'aa)	Sudden, unprovoked outburst of rage, causing the person to run madly and attack or kill people; person is often amnesic
Ataque de nervios	Latin-American and Latin-Mediterranean groups	Uncontrollable shouting, attacks of crying, trembling, sense of heat in the chest that migrates to the head, and verbal/physical aggression
Boufée delirante	West Africa and Haiti	Sudden outbursts of agitated and aggressive behaviors, confusion, and psychomotor agitation; may be accompanied by auditory or visual hallucinations
Genital retraction (koro)	China and Malaysia	Intense anxiety about the retraction of one's genitals, leading to the attachment of devices to prevent such retraction
Startle-matching (Latah)	Malaysia and Indonesia	Characterized by echo phenomena (echolalia and echopraxis) where a sudden stimulus triggers compulsion to imitate any action or words and a person has no voluntary control

(continued)

Table 30-1. Culture-Bound Syndromes (continued)

Culture-Bound Syndrome	Population	Signs & Symptoms
Running (piblokto)	Eskimos	Attacks last 1–2 hours, during which the patient screams and tears off clothing, throws himself in snow, or runs wildly about on the ice; echo phenomena, hysterical seizures, and amnesia are common; broodiness and mutism may precede an attack
Falling-out or blacking-out	Southern United States and Caribbean groups	Involves a sudden collapse, sometimes preceded by dizziness; afflicted individuals have their eyes open, yet they cannot see; they hear and understand what is going on around them yet cannot respond
Fright illness (hexing, voodoo, and ghost illness)	Africa, Brazil, and native West Indians in Haiti	The dominant symptom is a delusion that one is doomed to die because of a voodoo spell; it produces a variety of somatic symptoms, often with the belief that one is possessed
Ghost sickness	Kiowa Apache Indians	The afflicted individuals feel that the ghost of a dead person is torturing them; symptoms include bad dreams, hallucinations, confusion, fear, anxiety, dizziness, weakness, and loss of consciousness

Table 30-1. Culture-Bound Syndromes (continued)

Culture-Bound Syndrome	Population	Signs & Symptoms
Mal de ojo ("evil eye")	Mediterranean cultures and elsewhere	A term meaning "evil eye"; children are at highest risk; symptoms include crying without a reason, sleeping fitfully, vomiting, and having diarrhea
Qi-gong psychotic reaction	Chinese	An acute, brief episode of dissociative, paranoid, or other psychotic or nonpsychotic symptoms
Taijin kyofusho	Japanese	A phobia that refers to an individual's intense fear that his or her body parts or functions (appearance, odor, movement, facial expressions) displease, embarrass, or are offensive to others
Neuroasthenia or Shenjing shuairo	Chinese	Physical and mental fatigue, dizziness, headaches, pains, poor concentration, sleep difficulties, and memory loss; individuals may also experience nausea, vomiting, diarrhea, sexual dysfunction, irritability, and agitation
Susto (meaning fright or soul loss)	Latinos in the United States, Mexico, Central America, and South America	A frightening event that causes the soul to leave the body; symptoms include changes in appetite and sleep, sadness, a lack of interest or motivation, headache, pain, and diarrhea

C.   **Cultural Psychoses**

Cultural psychoses are difficult to define. In cultural syndromes, hallucinations may be viewed as normal variants. Delusions and thought disorder must be re-evaluated within a particular cultural setting. A culture may interpret abnormal behavior as relating to some kind of voodoo or anger, and may regard the symptoms as normal even though symptoms are consistent with schizophrenia.

VI. Ethnicity and Psychopharmacology

There are numerous factors that impact on the metabolism of psychotropic medications. Understanding how nonbiological and biological factors, including ethnicity, impact on psychopharmacology and psychobiology is necessary to ensure that quality care is provided for ethnic minorities.

A.   **Nonbiological Issues Affecting Psychopharmacology**

1. **Cultural beliefs.** Culturally shaped beliefs play a major role in determining whether an explanation and treatment plan will make sense to a patient (see explanatory models) (e.g., Hispanics or Asians often expect rapid relief with treatment, and are cautious about potential side effects induced by Western medicine). Concerns about addictive and toxic effects of medications often arise. As some Asian populations are often prescribed multiple herbal substances, they typically feel polypharmacy is more effective.

2. **Traditional and/or alternative methods.** Every patient must be asked about the use of herbal medicines, which has increased dramatically in the United States in the past few years. The potential for drug-herbal medicine interactions exists and should be carefully considered. Many herbal medicines have not been well studied; they may induce side effects or interactions with other medications. A number of potential problems with herbal medicines are listed in Table 30-2.

3. **Patient compliance.** Compliance may be affected by incorrect dosing, by medication side effects, and by polypharmacy. Other factors include a poor therapeutic alliance and a lack of community support, money, or transportation, as well as substance abuse or concerns about the addictiveness of a medication.

    a. Beliefs held by a patient regarding illness and treatment should be explored.

    b. Communication difficulties and divergence between a patient and his treaters ("explanatory model") play an important role in a patient from an ethnic minority, and such a patient is significantly more likely to drop out of treatment.

Table 30-2. Side Effects and Drug Interactions of Selected Herbal Medicines

The Japanese herbs, *Swertia japonica* and Kamikihi-To, and Cuban *Datura candida*	Have anticholinergic properties that may interact with tricyclic antidepressants (TCAs), low-potency neuroleptics, cloza-pine, and olanzapine
South American holly, *Ilex guayusa*	Has a high caffeine content
Nigerian root extract of *Schumanniophyton problematicum* (which is used to treat psychosis)	Has a sedative effect and may interact with neuroleptics and benzodiazepines
The Chinese herbs, *Fructose schizandrae, Corydalis bungeana, Kopsia officinalis, Clausena lansium,* muscone, ginseng, and glycyrrhiza	Increase the metabolism of many psychotropics by stimulation of cytochrome P450 (CYP450) enzymes
Oleanolic acid in *Swertia mileensis* and *Ligustrum lucidum*	Inhibits CYP450 enzymes
An herbal weight-loss supplement containing *Ephedra sinica* (ma-huang), which is the main plant source of ephedrine	Reported to cause mania, psychosis, and cardiovascular-related death
Catharanthus roseum (periwinkle); *Cinnamomum camphora; Corynanthe yohimbi* (yohimbe); *Datura stramonium* (thorn apple); *Eschscholtzia californica* (Californian poppy); *Humulus lupulus* (common hop); *Hydrangea paniculata* (hydrangea); *Lobelia inflata* (lobelia); *Mandragora officinarum* (mandrake); *Myristica officinatrum* (mandrake); *Myristica fragrans* (nutmeg); *Passiflora incarnata* (passion flower); *Piper methysticum* (kava, kava-kava); *Psilocybe semilanceta* (liberty cap, magic mushrooms)	May cause hallucinations

(continued)

Table 30-2. Side Effects and Drug Interactions of Selected Herbal Medicines (continued)

Swertia japonica; Kamikihi-to; Datura metel; *Atropine belladonna* (deadly nightshade); *Hyoscyamus* (black henbane); *Datura stramomium;* Naoyanghua (flos *Rhododendri mollis*); Gan di huang (*Rehmannia glutinosa*); Hong hus (*Carthamus tinctorius*); *Datura candida;* Yangjinhua contains atropine and scopolamine; Ginseng sometimes adulterated w/*Mandragora officinarum* (scopolamine), *Rauwolfia serpentia* (reserpine) and cola	Have anticholinergic properties and may interact with psychotropic agents with similar side effects
Aconitum naellus (aconite, monkshood, wolfsbane); *Chelidonium majus* (celandine); *Conium maculatum* (hemlock); *Humulus lupulus* (common hop); *Lactuca virosa* (wild lettuce); *Papaver somniferum* (opium poppy); *Passiflora incarnata* (passion flower); *Scopolia carniolica* (scopolia); *Scutellaria laterfolia* (skullcap); Tropane alkaloid-containing plants; *Atropa belladonna* (deadly nightshade); *Datura stramonium* (jimson weed, thorn apple); *Valeriana officinalis* (valerian)	Have sedative properties and may interact with benzodiazepine and antipsychotic agents
Glycyrrhiza glabra (licorice root or extracts)	Has mineralocorticoid effects which result in sodium and water retention and can cause edema and hypertension; use caution with monamine oxidase inhibitors

4. **Social support systems.** The way a family interacts and functions has a significant impact on psychiatric treatment. Hispanics have a greater number of interactions with relatives and may become more demoralized when interactions in treatment do not occur. Hispanics and Asians typically have a "closed network," which consists of family members, kin, and intimate friends.

5. **Language issues.** The use of well-trained interpreters and a patient's understanding of treatment recommendations significantly impact compliance.

6. **Other factors** also affect psychopharmacology. Misdiagnosis of a psychiatric condition, a placebo response, mistrust of the health care system, attention-seeking at a later stage of illness, and cultural beliefs and expectation all may affect drug response and compliance. Often clinicians do not take the time to explain the reason for the use of medications and the drug's anticipated side effects.

B. **Biological Aspects of Psychopharmacology**

1. Pharmacokinetics of medications deal with metabolism, blood levels, absorption, distribution, and excretion. However, other pharmacokinetic variables (e.g., conjugation, plasma protein-binding, and oxidation by the cytochrome 450 [CYP450] isoenzymes) exist. The activity of liver enzymes is controlled genetically, although environmental factors can alter activity. Understanding how pharmacokinetics and environmental factors relate to different populations will help to predict side effects, blood levels, and potential drug-drug interactions.

   a. **Pharmacokinetics** may be influenced by a number of factors (e.g., genetics, age, gender, total body weight, environment, diet, toxins, drug use and alcohol, and other disease states).

   b. **Environmental factors** include use of medications, drugs, herbal medicines, steroids, caffeine, alcohol, constituents of tobacco, and dietary factors, as well as sex hormones.

2. CYP450 2D6 metabolizes many antidepressants, including the tricyclic and heterocyclic antidepressants, and the selective serotonin reuptake inhibitors (SSRIs).

   a. CYP450 2D6 also plays a role in metabolizing antipsychotics, including clozapine, haloperidol, perphenazine, risperidone, thioridazine, and sertindole.

   b. The incidence of poor metabolizers of CYP450 2D6 ranges from 3–10%: in Caucasians the incidence of poor metabolizers is 0.5–2.4%, in Asians it is 4.5%, and in Hispanics and African-Americans it is 1.9%.

   c. Recently a genetic variation of the extensive metabolizer gene that decreases activity of the CYP450 2D6 enzymes ("slow metabolizers") was discovered. This group appears to have enzyme activity levels that are intermediate between poor and extensive metabolizers (Table 30-3).

Table 30-3. CYP450 Metabolism Status for Different Populations

Enzyme and Status	African-Americans	Caucasians	Asians	Latinos/Hispanics
2D6				
Poor metabolizers	0–18%	3–8%	0.5–2.4%	1–4.5%
Slow metabolizers	33%	0%	37%	0–34.3%
2C9				
Poor metabolizers	18–22%	3%	18–22%	
2C19				
Poor metabolizers	3.6–18.5%	3–6%	12–23%	4–4.8%

     i. Approximately 18% of Mexican-Americans, and 33% of Asians and African-Americans have this gene variation. This may explain ethnic differences in the pharmacokinetics of neuroleptics and antidepressants.

3. The CYP450 2C9 isoenzyme is involved in the metabolism of ibuprofen, naproxen, phenytoin, warfarin, and tolbutamide. Approximately 18–22% of Asians and African-Americans are poor metabolizers of these drugs.

4. CYP450 2C19 is involved in the metabolism of diazepam, clomipramine, imipramine, and propranolol; it is inhibited by fluoxetine and sertraline. The rates of poor metabolizers of this enzyme are approximately 3–6% in Caucasians, 4–18% in African-Americans, and 18–23% in Asians.

C. **Clinical Significance**

Some observations can be made concerning the use of psychotropics in different ethnic groups; significant interindividual variations are common.

1. **Asians tend to require lower doses of tricyclic antidepressants (TCAs), while African-Americans may respond faster to TCAs and at lower doses,** but with a greater risk of neurotoxicity.

2. **Hispanics may respond to lower doses of TCAs and yet experience greater side effects;** results of studies have been mixed.

3. **Asians experience extrapyramidal symptoms (EPS) at a greater rate** than African-Americans, Hispanics, and Caucasians.

4. **Asians appear to respond to clozapine at lower doses** and to have greater side effects at the lower doses.

5. **Asians appear to be more sensitive to benzodiazepines,** than Caucasians.

6. **Asians respond to lower levels of lithium** (0.4–0.8 mEq/L), while **African-Americans appear to have a greater risk of neurotoxicity** (likely related to a slower lithium-sodium pathway and connected to higher rates of hypertension).

VII. Techniques to Minimize Cultural Clashes, Misdiagnosis, and Adverse Events

A. **Be respectful to all patients and address them formally (i.e., Mr./Ms./Mrs.…).**

B. **Anticipate that the patient may have frustrations from prior experiences in the health care system.**

C. **Acknowledge the need to spend more time with a patient from a different culture.** The relationship will be more complex and it will take longer to develop trust and alliance.

D. If a diagnosis is unclear or impacted by ethnicity or culture, **consider a structured diagnostic interview** (such as the SCID-DSM-IV), to reduce the possibility of misdiagnosis.

E. **Educate a patient** about mental illness to reduce stigmas and **the length of treatment.**

F. Expect a longer session when using an interpreter; certain languages or words take longer to translate from English; be patient.

G. Assure the patient about **confidentiality,** and be mindful of shame, fear, or paranoia from their past traumatic experiences.

H. **Pay attention to communication:** There is no one best method of moving things along; nonverbal, expressive styles, and knowledge of meaning of words are important.

I. **Make use of consultants who have cultural knowledge.**

J. **Ask about herbal medicines and alternative treatments.**

K. **Learn how to start psychotropic medications.**

1. Choose medication with a safer side-effect profile for an individual patient.

2. Start at a lower dose and titrate the medication slowly (as tolerated).

3. Inform patients about side effects and when they should expect to respond to medications.

4. If a patient is unable to tolerate a medication at a low dose, consider **switching to an agent that is metabolized through a different enzyme system.**

Suggested Readings

American Psychiatric Association: *Diagnostic and Statistical Manual of Mental Disorders, Fourth Edition*. Washington, DC: American Psychiatric Association, 1994.

Bhugra D, Bhui K: Transcultural psychiatry: do problems persist in the second generation? *Hosp Med* 1998;59:126–129.

Harper G: Cultural influences on diagnosis. *Child Adolesc Psychiatr Clin North Am* 2001;10:711–728.

Herrera JM, Lawson WB, Sramek JJ: *Cross Cultural Psychiatry*. New York: Wiley, 1999.

Lin KM, Poland R, Nakasaki G: *Psychopharmacology and Psychobiology of Ethnicity*. Washington, DC: American Psychiatric Press, 1993.

Lin KM: Psychopharmacology in cross-cultural psychiatry. *Mt Sinai J Med* 1996;63:283.

Mezzich JE, Kleinman A, Fabrega H, Parron DL: *Culture and Psychiatric Diagnosis*. Washington, DC: American Psychiatric Press, 1996.

Mollica RF, Lavelle J: Southeast Asian refugees. In Comas-Diaz L GE (ed): *Clinical Guidelines in Cross-Cultural Mental Health*. New York: Wiley, 1988:262–304.

Rayburn TM, Stonecypher JF: Diagnostic differences related to age and race of involuntarily committed psychiatric patients. *Psychol Rep* 1996;79:881–882.

United States Public Health Service. Office of the Surgeon General. Mental health: culture, race and ethnicity: a supplement to mental health: a report of the surgeon general. Washington, DC: U.S. Public Health Service, 2001.

Tribe RRH, ed: *Working with Interpreters in Mental Health*. New York: Brunner-Routledge, 2003.

Chapter 31

An Approach to Collaborative Care

B.J. BECK, MSN, MD

I.   Overview

A.   **Driving Forces for Collaborative Care**

Evolution of the health care system necessitates novel approaches to the comprehensive treatment of patients in the primary care setting. Rising costs, limited resources, improved technology, and new medications have propelled the development of collaborative models of care.

1. **An attempt to contain medical costs** has shifted psychiatric consultation of medically ill patients from inpatient facilities to the ambulatory setting. Briefer inpatient psychiatric stays have also placed more seriously ill psychiatric patients in the community before they have been stabilized.

2. **Changes in health care reimbursement,** from direct fee-for-service to third party (prepaid, managed, and capitated) plans, have unveiled the noteworthy expense of high utilizers of medical care who suffer from untreated or poorly managed psychiatric problems.

3. **Primary care providers (PCPs)** have become gatekeepers to specialty care. Incentives exist for PCPs to initiate care for certain common psychiatric disorders (e.g., depression or anxiety). However, such systems of care may also deter PCPs from making such diagnoses or from recognizing psychiatric symptoms.

4. **The allocation of limited resources requires a shift to population-based care** from the patient-based model that better suits the sensitivities of our individualistic culture. This shift is evident in the federal mandate for community health centers (i.e., to adopt chronic disease management programs [including one for depression] that standardize evidence-based, quality care and decrease health disparities across the population). This change has illuminated the tremendous fiscal and societal cost of psychiatric disability, which decreases work productivity and raises medical care utilization, work absenteeism, unemployment, subjective disability, and mortality.

Address for correspondence: Dr. B.J. Beck, Massachusetts General Hospital, WACC 812, Boston, MA 02114, Email: bbeck@partners.org.

B.   **Epidemiology**

1.   **Psychiatric problems in the general population are prevalent.** The Epidemiologic Catchment Area (ECA) **study of the early 1980s found that 7% of community residents sought care in a 6-month period.** Roughly 75% of community respondents with full-criteria mental disorders sought care in the general medical (i.e., not mental health) setting, frequently from their PCP. **The more recent (1990–1992) National Co-morbidity Survey (NCS) suggested that the lifetime prevalence of one or more psychiatric disorders in U.S. adults is about 50%; the 1-year prevalence for at least one disorder was 30%,** while alcohol dependence and major depression were the most common disorders.

   The **2001–2002 replication of the NCS (NCS-R),** was a rigorous study that incorporated measures of severity, clinical significance, overall disability, and role impairment; it found that the risk of major depression was relatively low until early adolescence, then it began to rise in a linear fashion, with the slope of that line becoming **increasingly steep with each successive birth cohort since World War II. The lifetime prevalence of significant depression is 16.2%, and the 12-month prevalence is 6.6%.** More than half **(55.1%)** of depressed community respondents **currently receive their care in the mental health sector,** and most **(90%) who receive care in any medical setting receive psychotropic medications** (a practice probably due to a combination of educational efforts and safer, more tolerable medications). Still, almost half (42.7%) of patients with depression fail to receive treatment, and only **about one in five (<21.6%) receive** what recent, evidence-based guidelines (APA and AHRQ [Agency for Healthcare Research and Quality]) would consider **minimally adequate treatment.**

2.   **Psychiatric problems in primary care patients are also prevalent** (i.e., detected in **25–35% by structured diagnostic interviews**). More than three-fourths of the problems discovered are depressive syndromes; anxiety disorders account for most of the rest.

3.   **Recognition of psychiatric problems in primary care may be improving,** with recent studies suggesting that **PCPs recognize their more severely depressed** patients. Nonetheless, the primary care recognition of psychiatric morbidity remains a complicated issue because:

   a.   One-third or more of these patients present with **subsyndromal symptoms** (i.e., they do not reach full DSM-IV criteria for a diagnosable mental disorder).

    b.   Primary care patients may present **earlier in the course** of illness, and

    c.   Primary care patients often present with **physical (not mental) complaints.**

4. **Outcomes in primary care** have not clearly established the clinical significance of the PCPs' failure to diagnose less severe psychiatric pathology. Much **subsyndromal primary care angst and distress** resolves spontaneously, as evidenced by studies that indicate that less severely depressed primary care patients have relatively good outcomes, even with brief, substandard medication trials. PCPs encounter a great deal of patient distress that is improved by supportive listening and by encouragement. (The early presentation of psychiatric symptoms also suggests the possible diagnosis of an adjustment disorder that resolves with the resolution of the initial event or the expressed concern, and placebo effect of a few days of medication, from the PCP.)

C.   **Barriers to Treatment**

The collusion of the PCP, the patient, and systems factors, prevent the requisite patient-provider communication ("Don't ask/Don't tell").

1. **PCP factors ("Don't ask")** include **time and productivity pressures, personal defenses, fear that patients will leave their practice** if asked about mental health issues, **skepticism that treatment will help,** and **insecurity about what to do** (i.e., how and whether to treat or refer). **Time** is a persistent provider and systems factor that has been somewhat ameliorated by the advent of **more easily initiated, safer medications,** such as the selective serotonin reuptake inhibitors (SSRIs).

2. **Patient factors ("Don't tell")** include persistent **stigma,** shame, and embarrassment (about what patients often perceive as a **personal weakness**). **Patients may not know** that they have a treatable mental disorder. **Moreover, diagnostic complexity** is compounded in the medical care setting:

    a.   **Medical disorders may simulate psychiatric disorders;**

    b.   **Psychiatric disorders may lead to physical symptoms;**

    c.   **Psychiatric and medical disorders may coexist.**

3. **Systems factors include the ever-changing health care finance and reimbursement** landscape: managed care, carveouts, provider risk, capitation, fee-for-service, free care, coding nuances, differential formularies, and prior authorization. The rate of flux, confusion, and **administrative time creep** easily overpower the impulse to explore and to treat something that might resolve spontaneously. The necessity to **increase pro-**

ductivity (*and* documentation) has tended to shorten the "routine visit" to less than 15 minutes. **Mental health carve-outs** have either eliminated, or greatly complicated, the possibility of reimbursing PCPs for treatment of mental disorders. **Prepaid plans,** such as health maintenance organizations (HMOs), significantly decrease incentives to offer anything "extra." **Access and quality of care have become bigger issues** than the development of clinically effective therapies. **Soaring pharmacy costs** have led to **restrictive (possibly short-sighted) formularies** that further limit access to existing, tolerable, and effective treatments.

II.   The Goals of Collaboration

A.   Improve Access

1. **Patients are more comfortable and familiar with the less-stigmatizing primary care setting;** even a separate mental health floor or wing in the primary care facility is less acceptable to many patients.
2. **Collaboration decreases the PCP's reticence** to identify mental disorders.
3. **PCPs are more willing to initiate appropriate treatment** when familiar and trusted psychiatric consultation is readily available.

B.   Improve Treatment

1. In the past, PCPs (without the benefit of a collaborating psychiatric consultant) **often prescribed insufficient doses of older medications** (e.g., amitriptyline, 25 mg, for major depression). Now PCPs are more likely to use newer medications (e.g., SSRIs), **but still in minimal amounts and without appropriate follow-up. Benzodiazepines continue to be more frequently prescribed by PCPs than any other class of psychotropic medication,** even for major depression.
2. Psychiatric collaboration **improves the choice, the dose, and the management of psychotropic medications in the general medical setting.**

C.   Improve Outcomes

1. PCP-psychiatrist collaboration **improves the clinical and functional outcome of more seriously depressed, primary care patients.**
2. **Cost-offset is difficult to demonstrate** because of the **hidden social costs of psychiatric disability** (e.g., unemployment and

lost productivity). However, in some studies, adequate management of mental health problems is associated with reduced total medical care costs.

3. Appropriate psychiatric treatment is **cost-effective,** especially when one considers the funds spent addressing the often nonresponsive somatic manifestations of patients who consume large amounts of medical care (without psychiatric care).

D. **Improve Communication**
  1. **Provider-consultant communication is integral** to the relationship.
  2. **The provider-consultant relationship must be explained to the patient.**
  3. **Written communication is enhanced by verbal communication.**
  4. **Communication is two-way:**
     a. PCPs provide pertinent information and state the clinical question;
     b. Psychiatrists relate the findings, the diagnosis, and the recommendations.

III. Collaborative Roles, Relationships and Expectations

While the **PCP** is the provider **responsible for the patient's overall care,** the **psychiatrist** is often a **consultant** to the PCP, and **sometimes a co-treater.**

A. **Referrals**
  1. **When the PCP makes a referral, the patient should be told what to expect.**
  2. The psychiatrist should restate that expectation **during the initial contact.** The PCP-psychiatrist relationship is **worth restating if the patient is seen again,** or repeatedly, by the psychiatrist, to **avoid a sense of abandonment** by the PCP (when the patient is referred to the psychiatrist), or by the psychiatrist (when the patient is returned to the PCP for ongoing psychiatric management).

B. **Collaboration**
  1. **Collaboration does not breach patient confidentiality because the patient understands that the PCP and the psychiatrist are now within the circle of care.** Still, patients may ask that certain details not be placed in their general medical record. If there is no

direct impact on medical care (e.g., history of childhood incest), the patient's wish should be respected. A more general phrase can relay the significance (e.g., "The patient experienced a childhood trauma.").

2. Information that does impact medical treatment (e.g., current or past drug addiction) or safety (e.g., suicidal or homicidal intent) cannot be ethically withheld from the PCP and the patient should be informed of this.

C.   **Psychiatric Records**
1. **Psychiatric or mental health notes in the general medical record should be color-coded, or otherwise flagged,** so that they can be removed when records are copied for a general medical release of information.
2. Most states require a specific release for mental health or substance abuse treatment records.
3. The advent of the electronic medical record has further challenged psychiatric confidentiality.

IV.   Models of Collaboration

A.   **Outpatient Collaboration**
Outpatient consultation implies collaboration because the **PCP refers** or presents the patient to the psychiatrist **for expert opinion or recommendations.** The setting or system determines whether there is a shared medical record or separate records (with shared, pertinent information), and whether patients are seen in the psychiatric or primary care setting.

1. **Some private psychiatrists** have established, primary care referral sources, but they **generally do not develop truly collaborative relationships** (i.e., with ongoing communication and shared records).
2. **Specialty psychiatric clinics** (e.g., an eating disorders clinic) provide **expert, multidisciplinary care for complex medical patients** who have **well-defined, recognized, psychiatric diagnoses;** they are most often located in teaching hospitals or tertiary care centers. Such clinics tend to keep separate records, to see patients in the psychiatric clinic, and to establish a system for consistent, clinically relevant communication with the PCP. **Stigma may thwart patient adherence with such a referral.**
3. **Consultation psychiatrists** most often provide **one-time evaluations** in the primary care clinic. The **written consultation** should be placed in the primary care record, and ideally, **followed-up by verbal communication,** in person, or by phone or

voice mail. Such consultants generally do not initiate treatment, but instead give practical recommendations. The primary care setting and PCP sanction enhance patient acceptance and decrease stigma. This model also **promotes opportunities for ongoing informal education** between the PCP and the consultant.

4. **Psychiatric teleconsultation** is provided by **full-time, experienced consultation psychiatrists available for immediate telephonic consultation to PCPs** (but not to patients). The teleconsultant provides general **psychiatric information, pharmacological or behavioral recommendations, or triage and referral functions.** Database maintenance, timely referrals, and follow-up letters to the PCPs are accomplished with computer support. (Currently there is **no direct third-party reimbursement** for teleconsultation; this limits the practicality of this service. In the most remote regions, teleconsultation may exist as the sole access to specialty opinion.)

B. **Collaboration and Shared Care**

These strategies are promoted by the psychiatrist's membership in the primary care clinic medical staff. The psychiatrist may (1) **consult** as a member of the medical team, (2) **evaluate and treat patients** in parallel with the PCP, (3) **alternate visits with the PCP** while treatment is initiated, or (4) **evaluate, stabilize, and return the patient to the PCP with recommendations** for continued care. The consistency of an on-staff (on-site) psychiatrist facilitates PCP-consultant communication, formal and informal education, and real-time curbside consultation. This is also an **excellent training venue for both psychiatric and primary care residents.** Patients appreciate receiving care in the familiar primary care setting and frequently feel less stigmatized.

1. **Consultation reports** reside in the regular medical record. The **psychiatrist capitalizes on the PCP's extensive, longitudinal knowledge of the patient** to promote more timely treatment. The **consistent consultant-PCP relationship** provides the opportunity to **develop efficient conventions,** such as **having the consultant initiate treatment, seeing patients during their primary care visit** with the PCP, or **offering clinically relevant suggestions during case conferences.** The psychiatric consultant is available for **curbside consultation** or for discussions of more complex patients.

2. **Psychiatric care providers,** (and psychiatric clinics) often maintain separate mental health charts. Communication between providers with separate records requires a more assertive approach.

    a. If there is an **identifiable mental health unit** within the primary care clinic, this invokes the same **stigma** as when the clinics are truly separate.

    b. **The psychiatric capacity of primary care clinics** that offer these services **is often inadequate to meet the needs** of the total patient population. Because most patients would like to be treated in this setting, access to care may be unacceptably delayed unless uniform criteria are established to triage patients for either in-house care or for outside referral. **Such criteria might include diagnosis, available community resources, language requirements, or payment source.**

        i. Not all insurance plans with **mental health carve-outs** will cover psychiatric and medical care in the same setting.

        ii. **Capitated** plans favor treating the patient in-house.

        iii. **Indemnity plans** may offer a patient more options for outside referrals.

3. In **collaborative management,** a strategy developed as a research protocol; **patient visits during the initiation of treatment** (the first 4–6 weeks) **in the primary care setting alternate between the psychiatrist and the PCP.** The PCP is responsible for the patient's ongoing medication management.

    a. **Underlying assumptions of collaborative management include:**

        i. **PCPs can initiate appropriate treatment** for depression.

        ii. **PCPs can manage the care of a patient who has been stabilized** with antidepressant medications.

        iii. **Collaboration begins with PCP education.**

        iv. **PCPs can better care for a more seriously depressed patient with the collaboration of in-house psychiatric consultation.**

    b. **PCPs receive prior training** and participate in regular teaching conferences.

    c. **A patient is referred by the PCP,** usually after an initial, ineffective medication trial.

    d. **Psychoeducation of a patient** is an integral part of the treatment.

    e. This type of intensive program of care has been **cost-effective for more severely depressed primary care patients.**

    f. This model has been adapted to other primary care/mental health problems.

4. The **primary care–driven model** is a practical approach to assist PCPs in the provision of quality psychiatric care for their own primary care patients with limited psychiatric resources. **It incorporates elements of consultation, teleconsultation, and collaborative management.** Its goal is to optimize the treatment of appropriate primary care patients in the primary care setting. **Uniform triage criteria are used. The first consideration is whether the patient is appropriate for management by a PCP.** Photocopies or secure electronic transmissions of all psychiatric notes and evaluations are sent to the PCP and placed in the regular (or electronic) medical record. The clinic provides **psychiatric training for both psychiatric and primary care residents.**

    a. Underlying **assumptions of the primary care–driven model include:**

        i.   **Collaboration begins with education of PCPs *and* psychiatrists.**

        ii. **A patient's psychiatric needs should be met in the primary care setting when they are consistent with good care.**

        iii. **PCPs can manage the care of a patient who has been stabilized on psychiatric medications.**

        iv. **PCPs can initiate appropriate treatment for some psychiatric disorders.**

        v.   **With the collaboration of in-house psychiatric consultation, PCPs can better care for the psychiatric needs of more patients.**

        vi. **Some patients and some disorders are unlikely to be stable enough for management by PCPs.**

        vii. **Responsibility for total care requires communication between the PCP and any other involved care provider or consultant.**

    b. **A request for consultation or for referral comes from the PCP in writing, or its electronic equivalent.** It includes the clinical question or problem to be addressed and a summary of any medication trials initiated by the PCP. **PCPs are also encouraged to call or to stop by the psychiatrist's office located within the primary care clinical area,** for more general information about diagnoses, medications, or psychiatric or behavioral management.

    c. **Mental health services include:**

        i.   **Formal evaluation, stabilization over several visits, return of the patient to the PCP's care with recom-**

mendations (e.g., how to follow the patient, how long to continue, and when to re-refer).

   ii. **Informal consultation without the patient present** (i.e., "curbside consultation").

   iii. **Brief consultation with the patient and the PCP during the patient's appointment with the PCP.**

   iv. **Behavioral treatment planning for difficult-to-manage patients.**

   v. **Re-evaluation of patients previously seen when there is a change** (e.g., recurrence of symptoms, a new problem, medication side effects, or a change in the patient's medical condition or medications that affect psychiatric symptoms or other medications).

   vi. **Facilitation of referral to an outside psychiatrist and/or therapist.**

   vii. **Focused, short-term, goal-oriented, individual or group therapy with masters-level clinicians** located within the primary care clinical areas they serve.

   viii. **Collaborative care management for patients with complicated medical, mental health, and/or addictions problems** who utilize services in multiple settings. (Care management is ideal, but not reimbursed.)

  d. **Patients not recommended for PCP management** include those with inherently unstable conditions, those with complicated medication regimens, or those who require close monitoring, such as patients with:

   i. **Bipolar disorder**

   ii. **Psychotic disorders**

   iii. **Suicidal ideation**

   iv. **Severe personality disorders**

   v. **Primary substance abuse**

  e. **The psychiatrist helps the PCP recognize which patients need ongoing specialty care, and assists with the appropriate referral.**

  f. **Collaborative care management** improves the care of patients with complex medical, psychiatric, and addiction problems, who often require **treatment at several community agencies.**

   i. With signed releases, the **care manager serves as a liaison between the PCP and all other care providers.**

   ii. The care manager involves the patient and all treaters in the development of a **comprehensive treatment plan**

    within a network of services, and tracks the patient throughout this plan.

    iii. As **a member of the discharge planning team,** the care manager facilitates the patient's return to the appropriate network of services after hospitalization (e.g., to a detoxification program or other site for residential/institutional care).

C.   **Choice of Model**

    The choice of model depends on factors such as **patient population, payor mix, and community resources, as well as the location, type, and size of the practice.**

    1. **Educational or socioeconomic status:** higher-status patients may be more able, willing, and capable of securing outside services and be less stigmatized. **Culture: mental health care may be culturally unacceptable or shameful,** and only accessible through the "invisible" system of the primary care setting.

    2. **Fixed-funding (capitation)** patients most clearly benefit from the cost-offset and effectiveness of in-house, **collaborative models and teleconsultation.**

    3. **The primary care–driven model requires adequate community resources** to care for patients who are inappropriate for primary care management. **Parallel or shared care models** will work better in **suburban or rural areas** that lack such resources.

    4. **Practitioners in small groups or solo practitioners** may favor **consultation models,** either with a very part-time, but regularly scheduled consultant, or with access to an outside consultant or teleconsultant, as needed. **Large practices and training facilities frequently offer a full range of in-house consultative and collaborative services,** including formal education, case conferences, curbside consultation, and collaborative care management.

V. Summary

Market forces may have driven the collaboration movement, but the benefits (increased access, quality, and coordination of care) surpass the fiscal goals. Considerations in determining the appropriate model include patient, practice, community, and payor factors. Education (of PCPs, psychiatrists, other clinical staff, and patients) is key to the success of these programs. The rapid rate of change in the health care system requires unprecedented flexibility and foresight for psychiatrists and other medical providers to continually adapt their models of care to maintain quality, efficacy, and viability.

Suggested Readings

Beck BJ: Collaborative care: psychiatry and primary care. In Stern TA, Fricchione GL, Cassem NH, Jellinek MS, Rosenbaum JF (eds): *The Massachusetts General Hospital Handbook of General Hospital Psychiatry,* 5th ed. Philadelphia: Mosby, 2004:763–772.

Coyne JC, Schwenk TL, Fechner-Bates S: Nondetection of depression by primary care physicians reconsidered. *Gen Hosp Psychiatry* 1995;17:3–12.

Kates N, Craven MA, Crustolo A, et al: Sharing care: the psychiatrist in the family physician's office. *Can J Psychiatry* 1997;42:960–965.

Katon WJ, Roy-Byrne P, Russo J, Cowley D: Cost-effectiveness and cost offset of a collaborative care intervention for primary care patients with panic disorder. *Arch Gen Psychiatry* 2002;59:1098–1104.

Katon W, Von Korff M, Lin E, et al: Population-based care of depression: effective disease management strategies to decrease prevalence. *Gen Hosp Psychiatry* 1997;19:169–178.

Katon W, Von Korff M, Lin E, et al: Stepped collaborative care for primary care patients with persistent symptoms of depression. *Arch Gen Psychiatry* 1999;56: 1109–1115.

Olfson M, Marcus SC, Druss B, et al: National trends in the outpatient treatment of depression. *JAMA* 2002;287:203–209.

Oxman TE, Dietrich AJ, Williams JW, Kroenke K: A three-component model for reengineering systems for the treatment of depression in primary care. *Psychosomatics* 2003;43:441–450.

Pirl WF, Beck BJ, Safren SA, Kim H: A descriptive study of psychiatric consultations in a community primary care center. Primary Care Companion. *J Clin Psychiatry* 2001;3:190–194.

Robinson P: Integrated treatment of depression in primary care. *Strategic Medicine* 1997;1:22–29.

Simon GE, Walker EA: The primary care clinic. In Wise MG, Rundell JR (eds): *Textbook of Consultation-Liaison Psychiatry: Psychiatry in the Medically Ill,* 2nd ed. Washington, DC: American Psychiatric Publishing, 2002:917–925.

Stewart WF, Ricci JA, Chee E, et al: Cost of lost productive work time among U.S. workers with depression. *JAMA* 2003;289:3135–3144.

Vergouwen AC, Abraham B, Katon W, et al: Improving adherence to antidepressants: a systematic review of interventions. *J Clin Psychiatry* 2003;64:1415–1420.

Worth JL, Stern TA: Benefits of an outpatient teleconsultation unit: Results of a 1-year pilot. Primary Care Companion. *J Clin Psychiatry 2003;*5:80–84.

Chapter 32

An Approach to Managed Care

ROBERT M. STERN, MD

I.   Overview

This chapter will address the forces that shape current practices of inpatient and outpatient behavioral health/mental health services, and suggest approaches for coping with the most common yet unavoidable dilemmas encountered when providing psychiatric and substance care in a managed care environment.

II.   Background

"Population-based" health care delivery systems have a proud history. Prior to the turn of the century, workers and their families employed by the coal mining, lumber, and railroad industries received health services funded by their employers, or by prepaid fees (Tufts Managed Care Institute, 1998). It was not until the 1970s, however, following the promulgation of the Nixon Administration's new health care strategy, that HMOs transformed the health care market. Through the issuance of grants and loan guarantees, the number of HMOs grew from 30 HMOs in 1970 to 1,700 by 1976, enrolling 40 million people and 90% of the population by 1980 (Tufts Managed Care Institute, 1998).

Managed care of the 1970s and 1980s was created to solve far different societal problems than those of 100 years ago. The costs for medical care were skyrocketing. The percentage of the gross domestic product expended on medical care had risen from 8.0% in 1975 to 10.2% by 1982. American medicine became increasingly technical, keeping pace with the rest of the society. Expectations for what modern medicine might accomplish grew, and the failure to reach these lofty goals became less acceptable. A posture of "defensive medicine" intensified, as doctors feared legal retaliation for errors of omission. Additional costs for possibly unnecessary tests and procedures contributed to the already spiraling excesses of fee-for-service medicine, where physicians' livelihoods were linked to the number and type of medical procedures performed. Affiliated medical industries (e.g., pharmaceutical and medical devices) were similarly financially rewarded. The time was ripe for change. Managed care offered the promise to better align incentives by rewarding primary care physicians (PCPs) for organizing care for the "whole

Address for correspondence: Dr. Robert M. Stern, Emerson Hospital, Department of Psychiatry, Concord, MA, email: rstern@emersonhosp.org.

person," and referring to specialists only when necessary. Attention to prevention of illness, "best practices," and "practice guidelines" added to the promise of less expensive, yet improved care, guided by a long-range vision for society's overall health status.

Managed behavioral care developed in the 1980s with the recognition that patients with psychiatric and substance abuse problems had unique needs. Its purpose was also to minimize the financial liability for the HMO that facilitated care for patients with psychiatric and substance abuse issues. As of 1997, 90% of privately insured patients' mental health and substance abuse treatment was subject to some form of utilization management (Koike et al, 2000), and by 2000, 68% of those with health insurance had their mental health benefits managed by "mental health and substance abuse carve-outs" (Garnick et al, 2001).

III.　The Managed Care Industry

Managed care and its subset, managed behavioral health care, are industries in transition, constantly adjusting and adapting to the competitive forces exerted on them by multiple active players in the health care market. Among these interested parties are subscribers, providers, purchasers (corporations that provide health care for their employees) and their larger purchasing co-operatives, private for-profit behavioral health companies, regulators (including the federal government), and to a lesser extent, advocacy groups, as well as patients with psychiatric and substance problems and their families. Managed behavioral health is thus an American product, guided by innovation and opportunity and fine-tuned by a complex system of checks and balances that interact in a systematic fashion to define the "mental health benefit."

Unfortunately, the needs of mental health and substance abuse patients often remain at the bottom of the priority list (Sabin et al, 2001), mirroring the societal stigma that continues to isolate these patients from mainstream medicine. As a result, significant barriers to adequate access to mental health and substance abuse care characterize modern medicine (Iglehart, 2004). Moreover, providers of mental health and substance abuse services are often confronted with unique barriers and hurdles to overcome in order to provide needed care.

Figures 32-1 and 32-2 illustrate the complex nexus of competing forces that shape the delivery of mental health and substance abuse services. These forces exist in a dynamic equilibrium with one another. Power and clout (as well as profitability) in the marketplace are always shifting. The system is structured by contractual relationships among purchasers, insurance companies, managed care companies, managed behavioral health care companies, hospitals, and individual providers (Figure 32-1); it is impacted by the advocacy efforts of consumer groups, professional societies, trade organizations,

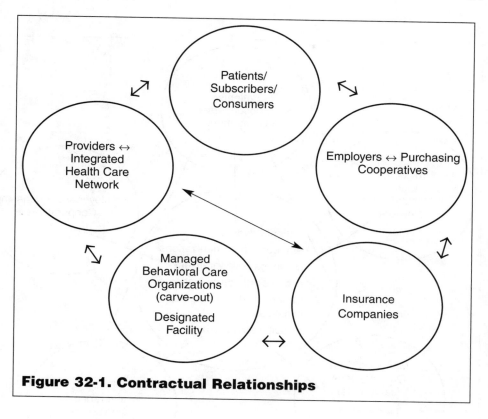

Figure 32-1. Contractual Relationships

and governmental regulatory initiatives (Figure 32-2). Legal remedies shape market factors, perceptions, and expectations, and modify business strategies (Bloche and Studdert, 2004). Thus, our current system of delivery of mental health and substance abuse treatment, like it or not, accurately reflects our cultural choices. This is a familiar political dynamic, pitting affordability on one hand, against the availability of necessary services on the other.

Economic imperatives exert a similar impact on defining "usual and customary services." For example, although there was little science to support the effectiveness of brief psychiatric hospitalization, the average length of stay has declined from more than 30 days to less than 15 days (Summergrad et al, 1995). Efforts to limit outpatient care have accentuated a false dichotomy between "mind and brain," using this dichotomy to separate psychiatric patients into the mentally ill and the "worried well" (Ford, 1998). With new "parity legislation," the former are now eligible for "extended outpatient benefits," while the latter are subject to stringent annual limits for outpatient care.

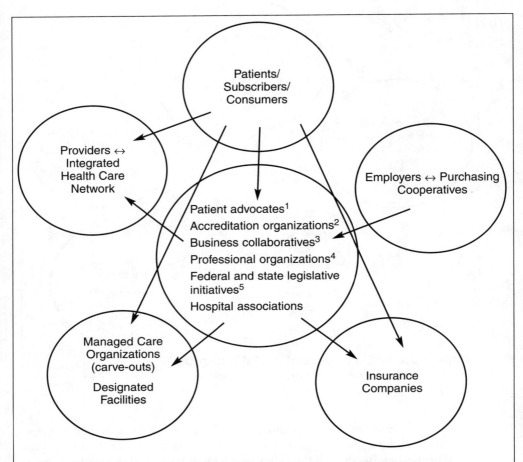

Figure 32-2. Advocacy and Noncontractual Influences

[1]National Alliance for the Mentally Ill (NAMI), National Mental Health Association (NMHA) Mental Health Advocacy Center, National Alliance for Research in Schizophrenia and Depression (NARSAD), Depression and Bipolar Support Alliance (DBSA).
[2]National Committee on Quality Assurance (NCQA), Joint Commission on Accreditation of Healthcare Organizations (JCAHO).
[3]Quality initiatives sponsored by business. Many are large purchasers of insurance for their employees (Leapfrog Group is one example).
[4]American Psychiatric Association (APA), National Association of Social Workers (NASW), American Psychological Association (APA). State psychiatric associations and their lobbying groups.
[5]Patient protection committees.

IV. Managing Costs: Management Techniques

A. Precertification, Concurrent Review, and Case Management

Managed behavioral health organizations (MBHOs) have been effective in reducing both utilization and expenditures of psychiatric and substance abuse services (Summergrad et al, 1995; Koike et al, 2000; Marci et al, 2004; Iglehart, 2004). On a case-by-case basis, approval for admission and continued care are reviewed frequently. Interestingly, in one study, as few as 0.8% of requests were denied, and only 1.3% were authorized at a lower level of care, suggesting that over time, providers have learned what to expect when requesting additional services, their expectations "shaped" by the review process. Both the "sentinel" effect, of simply being watched and judged, coupled with understandable efforts to avoid additional (and intrusive) time-consuming paperwork and telephone calls have discouraged providers from requesting additional care (Koike et al, 2000). Fears of "provider profiling" further deter some clinicians, because being perceived as an "outlier" among their peers might impact future referrals or continued inclusion in the provider network.

Outpatient service utilization has been historically reined in through "benefit design," limiting reimbursed services to either a fixed annual dollar limit or a predetermined number of covered visits. Parity legislation, initiated at the federal level during the Clinton Administration, and later state initiatives, have eliminated some of these benefit limitations.

Eligibility for parity benefits varies greatly from state to state. In some states, eligibility is limited to patients with narrowly defined "biologically-based" diagnoses (e.g., schizophrenia, schizoaffective disorder, major depressive disorder, bipolar disorder, paranoia and other psychotic disorders, obsessive-compulsive disorder, panic disorder, delirium, and dementia), while other states include all DSM-IV diagnoses (including substance abuse). Some states mandate parity for all health plans, while others restrict parity to large group insurance plans.

For the majority of states, "non-biological" conditions continue to be subject to annual visit limits, with frequent reviews for psychotherapy to ensure that treatment meets the plan's criteria for "medical necessity."

B. Medical Necessity

"Medical necessity," the criteria the insurance industry employs to evaluate the need for initial or continued mental health or substance abuse service, has emerged as the key concept for reducing mental health and substance abuse expenditures. It is a potent double-edged sword used to prioritize the expenditure of scarce resources and to maximize financial gain for the insurance company. Criteria for medical necessity are broadly defined and ambiguous; they leave considerable discretion to the insurance company (National Mental Health Information Center, 2002).

Medical necessity for inpatient care is reserved for psychiatric crises that place the patient's life in jeopardy and require 24-hour-a-day supervision by hospital staff. Active treatment must take place, and treatment is expected to produce clinical improvement. Services capable of being provided in a less restrictive setting are uncovered. Substantial costs are thus shifted to psychiatric facilities for conditions beyond their control (including the care of adolescents or demented elders stuck in hospitals while awaiting placement in nursing homes or unavailable halfway houses).

The above criteria were challenged in Iowa when medical necessity criteria imported from the private sector were applied to patients being served in the public sector. A negotiated settlement expanded medical necessity criteria to include the impact of environmental factors that "inhibit or hamper the effectiveness of treatment unless they are addressed." Criteria for "psychosocial necessity" ensured payment for "unique circumstances such as the unavailability of transportation, lack of natural supports, or a place to live" (Sabin and Daniels, 1994).

V.   Managing Conflict

Conflict and its resultant stress are inevitable when caring for patients in a managed care environment. Denials of payment for services rendered based on the insurance company's medical necessity criteria can be experienced as an indictment of the clinician's skills, or experienced as an accusation that "medically unnecessary" treatment was being requested, further impugning the intentions of the clinician. Encountering rigid and narrow criteria for continued treatment that appears to place the profits of the insurance company above the needs of the patient is enraging. If poorly channeled, frustration and anger adversely affect treatment and erode a clinician's enthusiasm for his or her work. It is not uncommon for tempers to flare between similarly trained clinicians when they face off on opposite sides of the clinical divide. Several essential principles for providing care in a managed care environment have emerged:

A.   Health Care Delivery
The delivery of health care remains the responsibility of the provider and his or her health care facility. Decisions governing admission to a psychiatric or substance abuse facility, the length of stay (LOS),

and plans regarding treatment and discharge remain the responsibility of the provider.

B.   What Is Covered
The insurance company, by contrast, is responsible for deciding what services they will pay for and how much they will pay.

C.   Patient Interests
Medically, legally, and ethically, the needs of the patient must override all other imperatives. Pressures engendered from patients, families, hospital administrators, and insurance companies are occasionally unavoidable.

D.   Conflict Resolution
Mechanisms for conflict resolution are established by contractual agreements among providers, the hospital, and insurance companies.

E.   Appeals
Active pursuit of appeals will result in the overturning of most denials if the clinical rationale for continued care is well documented.

F.   Professionalism
Behaving in a professional manner encourages mutual respect that is essential for developing a working relationship with reviewers.
        Comprehensive clinical notes that follow a template and are consistent with Medicare guidelines will help clinicians organize their thoughts and address the rationale for ensuring that the patient will receive the appropriate level of care. Notes referring to the current mental status, the problems being addressed, changes in medication or treatment plan, and a discussion of the risks of premature discharge, including thoughts, intentions, and plans for suicide, are most helpful. Adequate documentation will also ensure appropriate payment for services rendered (Stern et al, 2004).

VI.   Managing Expectations

Satisfaction with treatment is highly correlated with meeting expectations. Adding to the difficulties of coping with a mental health crisis, overcoming the frustrations generated when seeking treatment in the current mental health system can be a daunting task for patients. Many patients who are naive to mental health care are unaware that a different company than their primary health insurance manages their mental health benefit or that their hospital choices are limited. Moreover, even those patients with prior inpatient care learn that what once was "standard treatment" in many cases no longer exists. Even specialty units for a patient with an eating disorder or for the treatment of the aftermath of psychological trauma or sexual abuse have adjusted to the changing reimbursement realities by developing partial hospitalization programs and adjunctive residential care. Some patients expect that the cost of treatment will match their limits or that discharge from the facility is indicative of successful treatment. Instead, treatment should be considered sucessful when patients feel better. Families, who shoulder the burden of care for disabled adolescents, persistently mentally ill relatives, or demented parents or spouses, may long for respite, which is rarely available.

An educational process that acknowledges this changing reality is essential to maximally building trust (Whittemore, E, personal communication). Eliminating the element of surprise is essential. Alliance building must now include an articulated commitment to shepherd the patient and his or her family through the health care maze (i.e., from the admitting process to the establishment of a clinically and financially workable after-care plan).

VII. Managing Risk

Treating psychiatric inpatients and hospital-prone outpatients exposes clinicians to medicolegal risks. Psychiatrists working in fast-paced, brief-stay inpatient units are acutely aware of these risks, as most patients admitted for inpatient care are at risk of being a danger to themselves or others. With "stabilization" as the primary focus of the inpatient stay, patients are often discharged in better condition, but not well. Patients suffering severe mental illness and those with severe character pathology are especially challenging, as their baseline functioning may be unstable. Moreover, errors in judgment are inevitable, and unexpected bad outcomes are not uncommon.

Until recently, physicians bore the lion's share of liability exposure. Managed care organizations (MCOs) benefited from overly broad interpretations of the Employment Retirement Income Security Act (ERISA), protecting them from financial damages in malpractice suits (Bursztajn, 1999). Paralleling cost-shifting for treatment, medicolegal responsibility cascades down the food chain, with insurers off-loading their medicolegal responsibility to a "carve-out" company or "a designated facility" in capitated arrangements. By contract, each accepts responsibility for managing care and their attendant costs. Recent litigation has attempted to challenge these protections by holding the managed care company accountable when the denial of medically necessary care has contributed to a bad outcome.

Risk management for the practicing clinician working in the managed care environment relies on being knowledgeable about the details of the contractual relationships with the managed care company. The best protection is afforded when it is clear that the clinician is assessing the safety and risk for the patient. Thorough clinical documentation, as outlined in the discussion for managing conflict, includes a discussion of risks and benefits of continued hospitalization or discharge. When payment for treatment is denied, discussions with the insurance company should also be documented. When in doubt, or when conflict is anticipated, a second opinion by a psychiatrist who has interviewed the patient is recommended.

VIII. Managing Quality

Managed care organizations delegate responsibility for quality initiatives to the managed behavioral health organization (MBHO). Managed behavioral care organizations, through their quality assurance committees, conduct patient satisfaction surveys, track behavioral health performance indicators, distribute practice guidelines, and to a lesser extent conduct clinical outcome assessments (National Mental Health Information Center, 2002). Guidelines for documentation, medication administration, and management can be formulated and monitored. Adherence to quality initiatives is fostered by the sizable contracting clout of the MBHO, although treatment guidelines distributed to providers "may be ineffective in changing clinicians' practice." (Azocar et al, 2001).

The performance of managed care organizations, in turn, is measured and reported on by the National Committee on Quality Assurance (NCQA) employing Healthplan Data and Information Set (HEDIS) indicators. The NCQA, like the Joint Committee on Accreditation of Healthcare Organizations (JCAHO) is a voluntary, nonprofit organization funded by foundations and corporate sponsors.

Drawing conclusions from current indicators for evaluating treatment requires extrapolation from available data, as clinical outcome data have yet to be systematically employed. For example, the adequacy of hospitalization is evaluated by the rate of rapid rehospitalization, while discharge planning is evaluated by examining follow-up visits within 7 or 30 days following discharge. Treatment for patients with schizophrenia is evaluated by monitoring the number of medication visits per year. Indicators for the treatment of depression examine the frequency of follow-up medication management visits, and how many patients are on their medication after 12 weeks. Access to care is assessed by reviewing changing utilization patterns by diagnosis. A representative child mental health indicator is "having one family visit for children undergoing mental health treatment" (Kaplan, 1999).

IX. Unintended Consequences

As participants in this sea change, problems are encountered daily and conclusions are elusive. Reactions to economic imperatives, however, have reshaped mental health and substance abuse treatment. Dramatically shortened hospital stays have led to the closing of many psychiatric units, and tightening criteria for continued psychotherapy has led to the shrinking or closing of many outpatient services (Applebaum, 2003). Differential reimbursement for "biologically-based" diagnoses may be leading to an overdiagnosis of severe psychopathology and an increasing reliance on medications as a first-line response to psychological distress. Psychotherapy is increasingly left to the province of non-MDs, leaving diagnosis and medication management to the psychiatrist. This in turn has had an adverse effect on the training of future psychiatrists, further exaggerating a false dichotomy between mind and brain. Treatment approaches that emphasize short-term, behaviorally-oriented outcomes are currently in vogue. The cumulative effect of many of these changes has been an increasing dissatisfaction with the profession that has led many psychiatrists to withdraw from managed care panels.

X.   Conclusion

The American Psychiatric Association proclaims that "effective care is the most economical care." In the real world, however, meeting only minimal standards for staffing and quality is all too common. Many psychiatric inpatient and outpatient facilities operate on shoestring budgets and struggle to remain financially viable. Relatively inadequate reimbursement for facilities and providers is the rule.

As shown in Figures 32-1 and 32-2, the "system of care," maintains the current status quo. Change comes slowly if at all. In an environment of scarcity, without major policy and financing changes, psychiatric and substance abuse treatment services will remain in crisis. Efforts of the media and advocacy groups that enable legislative and legal challenges, combined with the leadership of national figures through their visibility, passion, and commitment, may play a powerful role in redirecting critical resources necessary to improve care for patients with mental health and substance abuse problems.

References

Applebaum PS: The "quiet" crisis in mental health services. *Health Aff (Milwood)* 2003;22:110–116.

Azocar FA, Cuffel, BD, Goldman W, McCulloch J: Best practices: Guidelines for the treatment of major depression in a managed health care network. *Psychiatr Serv* 2001;52:1014–1016.

Bloche MG, Studdert DM: A quiet revolution: Law as an agent of health system change. *Health Aff* 2004;23:29–42.

Bursztajn HJ: Treatment for managed care pain. *Harv Med Alumni Bull* 1999; Autumn:9.

Ford WE: Economic Grand Rounds: Medical necessity: Its impact in managed mental health care. *Psychiatr Serv* 1998;49:183–184.

Garnick D, Horgan CM, Hodgkin D, et al: Risk transfer and accountability in managed care organizations' carve-out contracts. *Psychiatr Serv* 2001;52:1502–1509.

Kaplan A: AMBHA releases new performance measures. *Psychiatr Times* 1999; XVI(1):1999.

Koike A, Klap R, Unutzer J: Utilization management in a large managed behavioral health organization. *Psychiatr Serv* 2000;51:621–626.

Iglehart JK: The mental health maze and the call for transformation. *N Engl J Med* 2004;350:507–514.

Marci C, Gottlieb G, Jellinek MS, Summergrad P: Managed care and psychiatry. In Stern TA, Herman JB, (eds): *Psychiatry Update and Board Preparation,* 2nd ed. New York: McGraw-Hill, 2004:569–572.

National Mental Health Information Center. Medical Necessity in Private Health Plans, 2002. http://www.mentalhealth.sabhsa.gov/publications/allpubs/sma03-3797/content08.asp.

Sabin J, Daniels N: Determining "medical necessity" in mental health practice. *Hastings Cent Rep* 1994;214:5–13.

Sabin JE, O'Brien MF, Daniels N: Managed care: Strengthening the consumer voice in managed care: II. Moving NCQA standards from rights to empowerment. *Psychiatr Serv* 2001;52:1303–1305.

Stern RM, Alessandrini V, Stern TA: Billing documentation and cost-effectiveness of consultation. In Stern TA, Fricchione GL, Cassem NH, et al. (eds): *Massachusetts General Hospital Handbook of General Hospital Psychiatry,* 5th ed. Philadelphia: Mosby, 2004.

Summergrad P, Herman JB, Weilburg JB, Jellinek MS: Wagons Ho: Forward on the managed care trail. *Gen Hosp Psychiatr* 1995;17:251–259.

Tufts Managed Care Institute, 1998.

Chapter 33

Dealing with the Rigors of Psychiatric Practice

ANNA C. MURIEL, MD, MPH
EDWARD MESSNER, MD

I. Overview

A. Introduction

Psychiatric practice provides a breadth of clinical experiences that can be deeply satisfying (like helping to lift a patient out of the depths of depression) and stimulating; however, it carries with it the risks of any challenging and potentially all-consuming vocation. Sometimes the very ideals of hard work and service to others that led us into medicine and psychiatry can also lead to extreme stress and dysfunction. **This chapter focuses on how being mindful of the pitfalls of practice can allow psychiatrists to avoid burnout and to continue to lead gratifying and productive careers.**

B. Burnout

The concept of **burnout** was developed to describe a psychological syndrome that develops in response to chronic interpersonal stressors on the job, especially in the health and human services professions. Many physicians feel elements of this syndrome at one time or another, during training or when there are particular time-limited stressors during personal or professional transitions. However, when these feelings persist over time, or co-occur with intensity, physicians are at risk for the inability to work, disrupted personal lives, and problems with depression, substance abuse, and suicide. **The three dimensions of this response include:**

1. The individual component of **exhaustion and depletion;**
2. The interpersonal component of **cynicism or depersonalization; and**
3. The self-evaluative component of a sense of **reduced efficacy or accomplishment** (Maslach et al, 2001).

C. Prevalence

Approximately 15% of physicians are unable to fulfill their personal or professional responsibilities due to impairment from

Address for correspondence: Dr. Anna C. Muriel, Massachusetts General Hospital, WACC 725, 15 Parkman Street, Boston, MA 02114, email: amuriel @partners.org.

psychiatric illness or substance abuse at some point during their careers (Boisaubin and Levine, 2001). Rates of depression among physicians are comparable to those for the general American population (12% lifetime prevalence for men and 20% for women), and suicide, especially among women, is a disproportionately high cause of physician mortality (Center et al, 2003).

II. Antecedents of Stress and Burnout

A. **Workload**
Younger, **less experienced clinicians are at higher risk for burnout** and distress early in their careers, when their expectations and competencies are often least consistent with one another. **The challenges of long work hours, sleep deprivation, limited control, and little time and energy for personal pursuits also contribute to strain and to demoralization.** Practice environments can be less than ideal, with inadequate staffing and excessive administrative responsibilities related to billing and reimbursement.

B. **Clinical Challenges**
The intense interpersonal nature of psychiatric practice can be particularly grueling.
1. **Exposure to suffering and trauma**
   The work of psychiatry involves bearing witness to and responding to some of the most disturbing aspects of human experience. Listening to the suffering of our patients and being vicariously exposed to psychic and physical trauma can lead to antipathy and cynicism that interferes with good clinical care and satisfaction associated with one's work.
2. **Role conflict/role ambiguity**
   Psychiatrists often need to maintain an empathic stance and yet set limits for patient safety. We may have to address conflicting agendas (e.g., of the patient, the family, the institution, insurers, and society at large). Unlike many of our medical colleagues, we must become comfortable with the inherent subjectivity of much of our clinical work and bear uncertainty and ambivalence in our patients and in ourselves.
3. **Transference and countertransference**
   The strong feelings that patients bring to the treatment relationship (based on their prior experiences) can be difficult to manage; they can generate equally intense positive or negative feelings in the psychiatrist. The treatment of patients with porous boundaries and unmodulated needs can be particularly challenging to the therapist's own psychological defenses.

4. **Feelings of helplessness**

The chronic nature of many mental illnesses, and the complex psychosocial situations that patients reveal to us, can leave physicians feeling inadequate and hopeless about the ability to effect meaningful change or to relieve the patients' suffering. The suicide of a patient can be particularly devastating, as it induces feelings of failure and guilt.

C. **Lack of Social Support**

Close colleagues and coworkers frequently help to maintain perspective while practicing psychiatry. These professional relationships provide opportunities for mutual support and stimulation that enhance job satisfaction. The absence of trusted peers with whom to share everyday challenges, and for junior clinicians the absence of helpful supervisors and mentors, create a sense of isolation and burden that make clinical practice especially stressful. These risks are elevated in psychiatrists who conduct full-time private practice.

D. **Imbalance between Professional and Personal Life**

A meaningful personal life with close relationships and recreational activities can mediate some of the stressors of psychiatric practice. When work occupies too much of one's time and energy, there is little capacity for repletion, and clinicians become especially vulnerable to exhaustion. In addition, overinvolvement with work can disrupt family relationships and create further distress that may develop into an inability to find respite from clinical practice. Women may be particularly vulnerable to the conflict between work and home lives, feeling that neither is receiving enough of one's energy.

III. Signs and Symptoms of Personal Stress

Psychiatrists need to be vigilant for the early signs of stress and burnout in themselves; these can develop into depression or anxiety syndromes that can impact their own health, and the health of their families and patients.

A. **Physical Features**

Fatigue, changes in sleep or appetite, headaches, gastrointestinal symptoms, and frequent infections are common with burnout.

B. **Emotional Features**

Feelings of being overwhelmed, anhedonia, apathy, and irritability develop.

C.   **Cognitive Features**
Having difficulty with concentration, memory, and organizational ability arise.

D.   **Behavioral Features**
Having difficulty interacting with others, working longer but being less efficient at work, and taking uncharacteristic risks or abusing substances are common features. Getting multiple suggestions from relatives, friends, or coworkers can be helpful.

IV.   Ways to Enhance Coping

As much as psychiatrists may want to feel invulnerable to emotional strain and dysfunction, they are susceptible to stress and overwork that can impair the capacity to care for patients and to live satisfying lives. Good coping strategies allow us to be flexible, to take breaks, and to remain even-tempered when faced with the challenges of practice.

A.   **Take an Inventory of Your Past Responses to Stress**
Understanding one's usual pattern of response to stress helps one to anticipate and to prevent maladaptive coping. Clinicians can use their skills in history-taking to review their own ways of dealing with stressful experiences or transitions. Some are helpful (e.g., advance preparation and talking with others); some are not (e.g., procrastination, being socially isolated, and using illicit substances).

B.   **Take an Inventory of Coping Strategies that Have Worked**
Undoubtedly, individuals develop particular affective, behavioral, and cognitive skills that help to manage challenges. Some use exercise to release tension and to re-energize. Others find quiet reflection, writing, reading, or a conversation with a friend restorative. Hobbies, creative pursuits, or home improvement projects also provide a respite from work. For some, a good cry helps to restore equilibrium. Borrowing coping methods from the experience of others can expand one's own repertoire. Keeping a list of possible outlets in mind is useful when energy stores are low and we may have trouble accessing appropriate distractions or restorative activities.

C.   **Make Regular Efforts to Process Clinical Experiences**
None of us can contain all of the narratives and affects we are faced with in daily practice. One should seek appropriate opportunities to process and to discharge clinical experiences (e.g., by discussing issues with colleagues, yet maintaining confidentiality), or by using quiet reflection to consider what has occurred during the day. Humor

can relieve tension and facilitate recognition of common experiences. Peer-supervision groups and professional societies offer structured environments for venting and receiving feedback that can transform disturbing experiences into growth-promoting lessons.

D. Maintain Healthy Behaviors

Good sleep hygiene, healthful eating habits, and regular exercise can go a long way towards enhancing resiliency. Taking care of one's appearance can provide a sense of well-being or much needed pampering. Promptly attending to routine health checks and minor illnesses can prevent physical problems that will only exacerbate stress.

E. Use Mental Rehearsal and Directed Fantasies

Keeping in mind that imagined experiences are distinct from actions, one can mentally rehearse difficult situations, and anticipate one's responses and various courses of events. A dreaded discussion with a controlling superior can be made less daunting by imagining a full range of behaviors (e.g., from calmly explaining the reasons for requesting a change in duties, to physically ousting him from his chair and telling him off). Directed fantasies can provide expression of intense aggressive feelings and relieve tension (e.g., that caused by a patient whose behavior makes one want to throttle him or her). The more outrageous the fantasy, the more it can bring release of pent-up feelings and be kept distinct from actual behavior (Messner, 1993).

F. Communicate Openly with Loved Ones about Anticipated Unavailability

Anticipating times of additional workload and unavailability to family and friends can prevent misunderstandings and bitterness when one is not able to spend time with them. While it will not erase the burden of extra work, communicating the experience of these challenges can allow one to build intimacy and a sense of weathering the difficulties together.

G. Learn Relaxation Techniques, Self-Hypnosis, or Mindfulness Exercises

Relaxation techniques (in the form of self-directed progressive relaxation, listening to audiotapes, sitting or active meditation, or yoga) can help with stress reduction, and can restore peace of mind. They may also be good alternatives to medication for sleep difficulties and they may relieve physical tension.

V.   Seeking Additional Help

Significant barriers exist to psychiatrists seeking care from other mental health professionals; 35% of physicians do not have a regular source of health care (Center et al, 2003). In addition, physicians perceive additional barriers such as lack of time, lack of confidentiality, stigma (Jamison, 1998), cost, and fear of discrimination in medical licensing, obtaining hospital privileges, and obtaining insurance coverage (Center et al, 2003). Psychiatrists, in particular, may feel that they should be able to address their own emotional difficulties independently; therefore they struggle with seeking professional consultation. As we know well from our clinical work, mental health is not usually a matter of will. **Even the most self-directed individuals can benefit from objective observation and support.** Psychiatrists who seek mental health care can become informed about state and federal protections of confidentiality, as well as local physician health programs that offer treatment, monitoring, and advocacy specifically for impaired physicians. Although, it is prudent to get support to assist with any significant distress or occupational burnout, certain problems require consultation for the safety of the clinician, their significant others, and their patients.

A.   **Reasons for Psychiatric Consultation**
1.   Neurovegetative signs of **depression: SIGECAPS** (sleep [insomnia or hypersomnia], interest [anhedonia], guilt, energy [loss], concentration [lack], appetite [loss or increase], psychomotor [retardation or agitation], and suicide [suicidal ideation])
2.   **Thoughts and fantasies of suicide** or plans for self-harm
3.   Presence of **anxiety** that interferes with professional or social activities
4.   **Substance use** that interferes with work or family responsibilities
5.   Recurrent **explosive anger**
6.   **Symptoms of an eating disorder**

B.   **Psychotherapy**
Individual psychodynamic or cognitive-behavioral psychotherapy can be meaningful ways to address stress, burnout, and more pervasive emotional difficulties. Psychiatrist-patients who undergo psychotherapy often find that it not only provides relief from distress, but it can also be a growth-enhancing personal and professional process.

C.   **Psychopharmacology**
Sometimes psychiatrists are reluctant to take medication, as they consider it a sign of weakness. However, pharmacological consultation may be a necessary component of treating biologically-based

disorders. Self-treatment is never appropriate and can lead to further complications and dangerous oversights.

D. Group Therapy
Groups that address particular diagnoses or interpersonal difficulties can provide support, perspective, and a venue for working out relational issues. Groups specifically designed for mental health clinicians typically respond to and actively address concerns about stigma or loss of confidentiality.

E. Couples' and Family Therapy
When partnerships or family relationships are significant stressors or are significantly disrupted by a physician's personal or professional difficulties, couples' or family therapy can be useful to restore effective communication and shift dynamics to allow for renewed intimacy and mutual support.

VI. Conclusion

Even the most competent and accomplished physicians are vulnerable. Our very devotion to and high standards for our work can lead physicians to stress, occupational burnout, and disabling emotional difficulties (Lee and Messner, 2000). Being mindful of our limitations and attending to our own needs and responses to the rigors of practice can prevent professional impairment. Having good coping strategies and seeking additional help (as necessary) can provide opportunities for personal enrichment and for increased effectiveness in the practice of psychiatry.

References

Boisaubin EV, Levine RE: Identifying and assisting the impaired physician. *Am J Med Sci* 2001;322:31–36.

Center C, Davis M, Detre T, et al: Confronting depression and suicide in physicians: a consensus statement. *JAMA* 2003;289:3161–3166.

Jamison KR: Stigma of manic depression: a psychologist's experience. *Lancet* 1998; 352:1053.

Lee B, Messner E: Coping with the rigors of psychiatric practice. In *Massachusetts General Hospital Psychiatry Update and Board Preparation.* New York: McGraw-Hill, 2000:573–577.

Maslach C, Schaufeli WB, Leiter MP: Job burnout. *Annu Rev Psychol* 2001;52: 397–422.

Messner E: *Resilience Enhancement for the Resident Physician.* Durant, OK: EMIS, 1993.

Chapter 34

Supplemental References and Internet Sites

BRIAN P. BRENNAN, MD

I.   Selected References

American Psychiatric Association: *Diagnostic and Statistical Manual of Mental Disorders, Fourth Edition, Text Revision* (DSM-IV-TR). Washington, DC: American Psychiatric Press, 1995.

Cremens MC, Calabrese LV, Shuster JL, Stern TA: The Massachusetts General Hospital annotated bibliography for residents training in consultation-liaison psychiatry. *Psychosomatics* 1995;36:217–235.

Stern TA, Herman JB, Slavin PL (eds): *Massachusetts General Hospital Guide to Primary Care Psychiatry, Second Edition.* New York: McGraw-Hill, 2004.

Stern TA, Fricchione GL, Cassem NH, et al (eds): *Massachusetts General Hospital Handbook of General Hospital Psychiatry, Fifth Edition.* Philadelphia: Mosby, 2004.

Stern TA, Herman JB (eds): *Massachusetts General Hospital Psychiatry Update and Board Preparation, Second Edition.* New York: McGraw-Hill, 2004.

World Health Organization: *International Statistical Classification of Diseases and Related Health Problems, Tenth Revision,* Clinical Modification (ICD-10-CM). Geneva: World Health Organization, 2003.

II.   Mental Health Associations and Foundations

Academy of Psychosomatic Medicine (APM): www.apm.org
Association for Ambulatory Behavioral Healthcare (AABH): www.aabh.org
American Academy of Child and Adolescent Psychiatry (AACAP): www.aacap.org
American Association for Geriatric Psychiatry (AAGP): www.aagpgpa.org
American Association for Marriage and Family Therapy (AAMFT): www.aamft.org
American Association of Suicidality (AAS): www.suicidology.org
American Foundation for Suicide Prevention (AFSP): www.afsp.org
American Medical Association (AMA): www.ama-assn.org
American Mental Health Counselors Association (AMHCA): www.amhca.org
American Psychiatric Association (APA): www.psych.org
American Psychological Association (APA): www.apa.org
American Psychosomatic Society (APS): www.psychosomatic.org
Anxiety Disorders Association of America (ADAA): www.adaa.org
Association for the Advancement of Behavior Therapy (AABT): www.aabt.org

Address for correspondence: Dr. Brian P. Brennan, McLean Hospital, Admissions Building, 1st Floor, 115 Mill Street, Belmont, MA 02478, email: bbrennan@partners.org.

Association of Medicine and Psychiatry (AMP): www.amedpsych.com
Child and Adolescent Bipolar Foundation (CABF): www.bpkids.org
Children and Adults with Attention Deficit/Hyperactivity Disorder (CHADD): www.chadd.org
Child Welfare League of America (CWLA): www.cwla.org
Depression and Bipolar Support Alliance (DBSA): www.dbsalliance.org
Depression and Related Affective Disorders Association (DRADA): www.drada.org
National Alliance for Research on Schizophrenia and Depression (NARSAD): www.narsad.org
National Alliance for the Mentally Ill (NAMI): www.nami.org
National Eating Disorders Association (NEDA): www.nationaleatingdisorders.org
National Foundation for Depressive Illness (NAFDI): www.depression.org
National Mental Health Association (NMHA): www.nmha.org
Obsessive-Compulsive Foundation: www.ocfoundation.org
SAMHSA's National Mental Health Information Center: www.mentalhealth.org
Suicide Prevention Advocacy Network USA (SPAN): www.spanusa.org
The Stanley Medical Research Institute: www.stanleyresearch.org

III. Federal Agencies and Related Links

Centers for Disease Control and Prevention (CDC): www.cdc.gov
National Institute on Aging (NIA): www.nia.nih.gov
National Institute on Alcohol Abuse and Alcoholism (NIAAA): www.niaaa.nih.gov
National Institute of Child Health and Human Development (NICHD): www.nichd.nih.gov
National Institute on Drug Abuse (NIDA): www.nida.nih.gov
National Institute of Mental Health (NIMH): www.nimh.nih.gov
Substance Abuse and Mental Health Services (SAMHSA): www.samhsa.gov
World Health Organization (WHO): www.who.int/en

IV. Pharmaceutical Company Patient Assistance Programs

AstraZeneca Drug Assistance: www.astrazeneca-us.com/content/drugassistance
Helping Patients.org: www.helpingpatients.org
Lilly Answers: www.lillyanswers.com
Pfizer for Living Share Card: www.pfizerhelpfulanswers.com
The Medicine Program: www.themedicineprogram.com

Index

•I•